UNDERSTANDING WHAT ONE READS

ANNUA NUNTIA LOVANIENSIA
XLVI

Jan Lambrecht

Understanding What One Reads
New Testament Essays

Edited by
Veronica Koperski

PEETERS
LEUVEN – PARIS – DUDLEY, MA
2003

Library of Congress Cataloging-in-Publication Data

Lambrecht, Jan
    Understanding what one reads : New Testament essays / Jan Lambrecht ; edited by
    Veronica Koperski.
        p. cm. -- (Annua nuntia Lovaniensia ; 46)
    Includes bibliographical references and indexes.
    ISBN 90429-1302-9 (alk. paper)
        1. Bible. N.T.--Criticism, interpretation, etc. I. Koperski, Veronica. II. Title. III. Series.

BS2361.3.L36 2003
225.6--dc21

                                                                          2003043878

The cover illustration of the deacon Philip instructing the eunuch, referred to in
Acts 8,30-35, is used with permission of The Department of Religious Education of
the Greek Orthodox Archdiocese of America, on whose website it appears.

© Uitgeverij Peeters, Bondgenotenlaan 153, B-3000 Leuven (Belgium)
ISBN 90-429-1302-9
D/2003/0602/57

Contents

Mark and Matthew

Mark and Q

Luke

Preface

Veronica Koperski

The title of this work is taken from chapter 8 of the Book of Acts which tells the story of Philip who, at an angel's direction, encounters an official of the Ethiopian court reading the prophet Isaiah. Philip asks, "Do you understand what you are reading?" In reply, the official asks for guidance. Professor Jan Lambrecht has long followed the model of Philip in helping non-specialists, as well as students of the bible, understand what they were reading in the sacred text. However he has also directed attention toward his own better understanding in dialogue with fellow biblical scholars. In the course of his long and distinguished scholarly career, Professor Lambrecht has been a prolific writer from both an academic and a pastoral perspective. In addition to publications that originally appeared in Dutch, German, English, and French, a number of his writings have been translated and/or reworked from one of these languages into another, as well as into Spanish, Italian, Portuguese, Polish, and Chinese.

The topics of these writings have been similarly wide-ranging. Professor Lambrecht's early interest in the gospel of Mark expanded into a focus on the Synoptic gospels, resulting in a number of articles and several books. Among others, *Terwijl Hij tot ons sprak. Parabels van Jezus*, originally published in Dutch in 1976, appeared in English in India in 1978 and in the U.S.A. in 1981, in French in 1980, and in Italian in 1982, while *Maar Ik zeg u. De programmatische rede van Jezus (Mt. 5–7; Lc. 6,20-49)*, published in Dutch in 1983, appeared in German in 1984, in English in 1985, in French in 1986, and in Spanish in 1994. Both of these works, as well as a number of articles and homiletic writings, are indicative of Professor Lambrecht's ability to present the work of scholars to a wider audience.

Numerous shorter studies on the Pauline corpus, as well as his commentary on Second Corinthians in the Sacra Pagina series, reflect Professor Lambrecht's teaching duties at the K.U. Leuven for many years as well as his scholarly interests. In 1979 he revisited an interest in apocalyptic, reflected in his dissertation, when he chaired the Colloquium Biblicum Lovaniense, the topic of which was the Book of Revelation and Apocalyptic in the New Testament. At that time he edited the conference proceedings and contributed two articles. He has returned to that topic at times, most recently while teaching at the Pontifical Biblical Institute in Rome after his retirement from K.U. Leuven.

Since 1994, attempts have been in process to collect as many as possible of Professor Lambrecht's shorter writings into volumes that would be more accessible. In 1994, many of his writings on Paul appeared in *Pauline Studies* (BETL, 115) and, together with some from his former student, Reimund Bieringer, in *Studies on 2 Corinthians* (BETL, 112). In 2001, upon completion of his teaching at the Biblicum, he was honored with a volume of *Collected Studies* (AnBib, 147) representing his then more recent works. This volume, as its full title indicates, consists for the most part of studies on Pauline literature and the Book of Revelation, but it also includes a short article on Christian freedom in 1 Peter.

However, Professor Lambrecht has not stopped writing. In 2002, a collection of his articles in Dutch, some that had appeared previously and some new, was published as *De kracht van het geloof* ("The Power of Belief"). In addition, there remain some of his works that have not yet been brought into a collection, and, it would seem, important articles in the recent Dutch collection are not available to a wider audience. Having edited Professor Lambrecht's work in English for some fifteen years, and having become aware of the appreciation of his students and the scholarly community at large for his work, as evidenced in their response to the *Festschriften* Reimund Bieringer and I have edited in 1992 and in 2002, I believed it worthwhile to make at least one more attempt to bring together some writings from the past eleven years.

The present volume contains twenty-two articles and is reflective of Professor Lambrecht's academic and pastoral interests over his entire career, although the studies have all been written or published relatively recently. Some of the writing is less technical because of the audience for which it was intended. Three studies are previously unpublished (nos. 3, 15, and 21). Twelve of the contributions appear in English for the first time, including nine from *De kracht van het geloof*. The first four sections (Mark and Matthew, Mark and Q, Luke, and Acts) demonstrate Professor Lambrecht's continued interest in the Synoptic gospels and Acts. The second section (nos. 2-6) particularly focuses on the question of whether Mark knew and used Q, a topic of research dealt with in a number of his older studies (cf. note 109 of no. 2). No. 3 gives a synthetical presentation of three previous publications. More than ten years ago, when he was working on the first article of this volume, Professor Lambrecht expressed to me that his intention in raising this issue was, of course, not to challenge the Two-Source Hypothesis or dispute Markan priority, but simply to call attention to the fact that Q is after all a hypothetical document (even though we now have a critical edition of it), and some caution should be exercised in making sweeping claims about the content of Q as well as the assumption that its existence was unknown to Mark.

With the exception of the final article, which is indicative of his interest in the Book of Revelation, the remaining writings appropriately disclose Professor Lambrecht's continued research in Paul. Having debated various points of interpretation with Professor Lambrecht already as his student and further over the years, I have always been impressed by his willingness to consider another point of view, to rethink an old argument, sometimes to change his mind, but always to be cautious in paying attention to the biblical text. The articles on "Knowledge and Love" in 1 Corinthians 8 (no. 15) and "The Identity of Christ Jesus" in Philippians 2,5-11 (no. 21) have been the subject of lively discussion between us as we worked on this manuscript. On the one hand, he has written much on the Corinthian correspondence, while I have intensely pursued the topic of knowledge and love, both in 1 Corinthians and elsewhere. On the other hand he has not written much on Philippians, while I have focused strongly on that letter. In the course of our discussion we have not come to agreement on all the details, but we have moved much closer to understanding and respecting each other's positions.

Within this volume, there will be some writings that will challenge scholars to rethink some positions and others addressed to a more general audience. Though many of these articles have been published previously, most contain minor revisions and updating of bibliographical references. The type has been completely reset for uniformity. Deepest appreciation is due to the publisher, Peeters, as well as to the series editor, Leo Kenis, for accepting the book into the Annua Nuntia Lovaniensia series, as well as for his careful editing, suggestions, and copy work. As volume editor, I would like to express my appreciation to my graduate assistants George Aboutanos, for typing the scripture index, and José Deida, for proofreading both the author and the scripture indices. This work is offered in the hope that the dialogue will continue and be fruitful in bringing forth "new and old" out of the treasure of the biblical writings.

20 April, 2003
Feast of the Resurrection

Acknowledgements

The following essays originally appeared in:

1. Dutch original in *De kracht van het geloof. Bijdragen over het Nieuwe Testament,* ACCO – Vlaamse Bijbelstichting, Leuven, 2002, 29-41.
2. *New Testament Studies* 38 (1992) 357-384. Copyright: Cambridge University Press, Cambridge.
3. Unpublished.
4. *Journal for the Study of the New Testament* 85 (2002) 117-125. Copyright: Sheffield Academic Press, London.
5. C. NIEMAND (ed.), *Forschungen zum Neuen Testament und seiner Umwelt. FS Albert Fuchs* (Linzer philosophisch-theologische Beiträge, 7), Frankfurt am Main, Peter Lang, 2002, 223-234.
6. R. A. PIPER (ed.), *The Gospel Behind the Gospels. Current Studies on Q,* Leiden – New York – Köln, E. J. Brill, 1995, 73-96.
7. Dutch original in *De kracht van het geloof,* 87-96.
8. *Vaiharai. A Theological Quarterly* (FS J. Raja) 4 (1999) 113-127. Copyright: Theological Publications, St. Paul's Seminary, Tiruchirapalli (India).
9. Dutch original in *VBS-Informatie* 32 (2001) 73-78; also in *De kracht van het geloof,* 113-117.
10. FS D. L. Dungan (2003).
11. Dutch original in *De kracht van het geloof,* 119-131.
12. Dutch original in *Collationes* 32 (2002) 199-206; also in *De kracht van het geloof,* 139-147.
13. Dutch original in *De kracht van het geloof,* 149-169.
14. *Ephemerides theologicae Lovanienses* 78 (2002) 156-160. Copyright: Peeters, Leuven.
15. Unpublished.
16. Dutch original in *VBS-Informatie* 33 (2002) 32-39; also in *De kracht van het geloof,* 163-169.
17. Dutch original in *De kracht van het geloof,* 171-179.
18. Dutch original in *De kracht van het geloof,* 181-195.
19. T. J. BURKE & J. K. ELLIOTT (ed.), *Paul and the Corinthians. Studies on a Community in Conflict. FS M. Thrall* (SupplNT, 109), Leiden – Boston, Brill, 2003, 259-206.
20. *Biblica* 82 (2001) 305-324. Copyright: Editrice Pontificio Istituto Biblico, Rome.
21. Unpublished.
22. A. DENAUX (ed.), *New Testament Textual Criticism and Exegesis. FS J. Delobel* (BETL, 161), Leuven, Leuven University Press – Peeters, 2002, 331-347.

Thanks are hereby expressed to the editors and publishers who kindly granted us permission to reprint these studies.

Abbreviations

AB	Anchor Bible
AnBib	Analecta biblica
Baker	Baker Exegetical Commentary on the New Testament
Bauer-Aland	W. BAUER, K. ALAND, V. REICHMANN, *Griechisch-deutsches Wörterbuch zu den Schriften des Neuen Testaments und der frühchristlichen Literatur*, 6th ed., Berlin, 1988 (English: *A Greek-English Lexicon of the New Testament and Other Early Christian Literature*, 3rd ed., Chicago, IL, 2000)
BBB	Bonner biblische Beiträge
BBET	Beiträge zur biblischen Exegese und Theologie
BETL	Bibliotheca Ephemeridum theologicarum Lovaniensium
BEvTh	Beiträge zur evangelischen Theologie
Bib	*Biblica*
BibIntSer	Biblical Interpretation Series
Bijdr	*Bijdragen*
BNTC	Black's New Testament Commentaries
BR	*Biblical Research*
BSt	Biblische Studien
BZ	*Biblische Zeitschrift*
BZNW	Beihefte zur ZNW
CBET	Contributions to Biblical Exegesis & Theology
ConBNT	Coniectanea Biblica. New Testament Series
CBQ	*Catholic Biblical Quarterly*
EB	Études bibliques
EDNT	H. BALZ & G. SCHNEIDER (eds.), *Exegetical Dictionary of the New Testament*, vol. 3, Grand Rapids, MI, 1993
EKK	Evangelisch-katholischer Kommentar zum Neuen Testament
EstBibl	*Estudios bíblicos*
ETL	*Ephemerides theologicae Lovanienses*
EvTh	*Evangelische Theologie*
EWNT	*Exegetisches Wörterbuch zum Neuen Testament*
ExpT	*Expository Times*
FRLANT	Forschungen zur Religion und Literatur des Alten und Neuen Testaments
FrThSt	Frankfurter theologische Studien
FS	Festschrift
FzB	Forschung zur Bibel
GNS	Good News Studies

GNT³   *Greek New Testament*, 3rd edition
HNT   Handbuch zum Neuen Testament
HTKNT   Herders Theologischer Kommentar zum Neuen Testament
HTR   *Harvard Theological Review*
Huck-Greeven   A. HUCK, *Synopse der drei ersten Evangelien mit Beigabe der*
   Synopsis   *johanneischen Parallelstelllen. Synopsis of the First Three Gospels*
               with the Addition of the Johannine Parallels, new ed. by
               H. GREEVEN, 13th ed., Tübingen, 1981
ICC   International Critical Commentary
JBL   *Journal of Biblical Literature*
JSNT   *Journal for the Study of the New Testament*
JSNT SS   JSNT Supplement Series
JTS   *Journal of Theological Studies*
LD   Lectio divina
Liddell-Scott H. G. LIDDELL & R. SCOTT, *A Greek-English Lexicon*
LTPM   Louvain Theological & Pastoral Monographs
LXX   Septuagint
Meyer   Kritisch-exegetischer Kommentar über das Neue Testament
N²⁶   *(Nestle-Aland) Novum Testamentum Graece*, 26th edition
N²⁷   *(Nestle-Aland) Novum Testamentum Graece*, 27th edition
NICNT   New International Commentary on the New Testament
NIGTC   New International Greek Text Commentary
NRSV   New Revised Standard Version
NT   *Novum Testamentum*
NTA   Neutestamentliche Abhandlungen
NTOA   Novum Testamentum et orbis antiquus
NTS   *New Testament Studies*
ÖkTKNT   Ökumenischer Tasenchenbuch-Kommentar zum N.T.
ÖstBiblSt   Österreicher biblische Studien
PL   Patres latini
QD   Quaestiones disputatae
RAC   *Reallexikon für Antike und Christentum. Sachwörterbuch zur*
               Auseinandersetzung des Christentums mit der antiken Welt
RB   *Revue biblique*
RHPR   *Revue d'histoire et de philosophie religieuses*
RivBibl   *Rivista biblica*
RNT   Regensburger Neues Testament
RSV   Revised Standard Version
SBB   Stuttgarter biblische Beiträge
SBL.SBS   Society of Biblical Literature. Sources for Biblical Studies
SBL.SP   Society of Biblical Literature. Seminar Papers
SBS   Stuttgarter Bibelstudien
SN.S   Studia neotestamentica subsidia

SNTS	Studiorum Novi Testamenti Societas
SNTSMS	Society for New Testament Studies. Monograph Series
SNTU	*Studien zum Neuen Testament und seiner Umwelt*
SP	Sacra Pagina
StAntChr	Studies in Antiquity and Christianity
StNTAux	Studiorum Novi Testamenti auxilia
StudBibl	Studia biblica
SupplNT	Supplements to *Novum Testamentum*
SupplRivBib	Supplementi alla *Rivista Biblica*
TBNT	Theologische Bücherei. Neues Testament
THNT	Theologischer Handkommentar zum Neuen Testament
TrTZ	*Trierer theologische Zeitschrift*
TS	*Theological Studies*
TvT	*Tijdschrift voor Theologie*
TZ	*Theologische Zeitschrift*
WBC	Word Biblical Commentary
WMANT	Wissenschaftliche Monographien zum Alten und Neuen Testament
WUNT	Wissenschaftliche Untersuchungen zum Neuen Testament
ZNW	*Zeitschrift für die neutestamentliche Wissenschaft*

I

The Rich Man
(Mark 10,17-31 and Matthew 19,16-21)

The preacher or teacher who deals with the pericope of the rich man encounters an unevenness in the Markan text. Jesus requires the observance of the Torah commandments and seems to thus suggest that this suffices to inherit eternal life. Yet, immediately after this, he says to the man who has kept all these commandments since his youth that he lacks one thing. This one thing is to follow Jesus after having sold what he owns. One asks: are the commandments not sufficient after all? Moreover, the homilist or catechist may remember that in Matthew's gospel Jesus reacts to the man's question "what do I still lack?" with the introductory clause "if you wish to be perfect". Especially in view of the Matthean version of the rich man narrative, other difficulties arise: Is perfection more than the keeping of the commandments? Are there two kinds of Christians, the majority of believers who comply with what is strictly prescribed and keep the commandments, and a smaller group who by observing the "evangelical counsels" (poverty, chastity, obedience) follow Jesus truly and so try to reach perfection? Many modern Christians will refuse to agree with a positive answer to these questions. Yet how then must the passage be interpreted?

This paper will contain three brief sections. First we will examine the line of thought in the Markan text; then a few details of the pre-history of this text will be brought forward; the third section will address the question how Mt 19,16-22 is to be understood and how the Matthean term "perfect" can be explained. So, I begin with Mark, then attention will be devoted to the pre-Markan tradition and Jesus, while at the end I go to Matthew but will consider only the first part of his version. A few reflections will conclude this paper.

The Line of Thought in Mark 10,17-31

In the gospel of Mark the pericope of the rich man is found immediately before the third prediction of the passion (10,32-34). In 10,17 Mark writes (literally): "As he went out into the way" (καὶ ἐκπορευομένου αὐτοῦ εἰς ὁδόν). The readers remember that in 10,10 Jesus was still "in the house". The phrase εἰς ὁδόν does not yet possess the pregnancy of the later ἐν τῇ ὁδῷ: "And they were on the road, going up to Jerusalem. Jesus was walking ahead of them..." (10,32). The unity of 10,17-31 is formed by the chain of thoughts; it is confirmed by the repetition of the expression "eternal life" in verse 30 (cf. v. 17: what must I do to inherit "eternal life?")

The passage contains three parts which each have a distinct situation of dialogue: verses 17-22 (the dialogue with the rich man); verses 23-27 (the dialogue with the disciples); verses 28-31 (the dialogue with Peter). The parts also differ contentwise. In the first part there is the concrete case of a rich person who does not accept the invitation of Jesus to follow him; in the second part one is confronted with the general saying about riches: they make it very difficult to enter the kingdom of God; in the third part Jesus indicates the reward for those who have left everything.

The Rich Man (vv. 17-22)

In this paper no attention can be given to the "dogmatic" problem of Jesus' reaction in v. 18: "Why do you call me good? No one is good but God alone". According to Mark Jesus takes the question of the man "What must I do?" seriously. His straightforward answer is: Keep the commandments and you will inherit eternal life. There equally is no reason to doubt the honesty of the man who claimed to have done all this since he was a boy. Hence it would be wrong to use verse 22 (in which the man's attachment to his possessions appears) and suppose that the spontaneous reaction in verse 20 is hypocritical.

In verses 17-20 Jesus "teaches" the man how eternal life can be reached. Yet in verses 21-22 the teaching dialogue changes into a call. Jesus looks at the man and loves him; then Jesus expresses the invitation to a radical change. Selling what one has and giving it to the poor are preliminary conditions for the final summons: follow me. One must not overemphasize "and you will have treasure in heaven", since this clause is little more than a passing remark (perhaps a metaphorical description of the inheritance of eternal life). Leaving all things is the condition *sine qua non* for following Jesus. As the man hears it sadness overmasters him; he goes away grieving for, as Mark notes, the man "had many possessions". Verses 21 and 22 soberly but clearly depict the emotions of both Jesus and the rich man.

Most likely one should assume that verses 21-22 do not overrule what is indicated in verses 17-19. The following of Jesus does not replace the keeping of the commandments to inherit eternal life. What Jesus first said remains valid. Verses 21-22 cause a sudden change of situation, a transposition to a different level. Mark does not say in all clarity whether the imperatives of verse 21 contain a real obligation or a free invitation. Nor does he indicate what the consequences of the man's refusal will be. It seems erroneous to suppose that, because of his refusal, this man can no longer inherit eternal life. Or are these prudent remarks perhaps contradicted by the content of the second part of the pericope?

The Disciples (vv. 23-27)

After the departure of the rich man Jesus addresses his disciples saying: "How hard it will be for those who have wealth to enter the kingdom of God!" (v. 23). The disciples are perplexed. In verses 23-24a three items may strike the readers: Jesus deals with "those who have wealth" in general; riches appear to be a great obstacle; instead of "to inherit eternal life" Mark now writes: "to enter the kingdom of God", yet the two expressions point to the same reality.

In verses 24b-26 the saying is reiterated with even more emphasis. (1) Jesus uses the rather uncommon address: "Children". (2) Although the saying of verse 23 is repeated almost literally, one wonders why the expression "those who have wealth" is lacking here; however, from the preceding and consequent context it is evident that the same rich people are meant. (3) The illustration of the camel and the eye of a needle is added to the saying. (4) The disciples are now greatly astounded. (5) They ask one another: "Then who can be saved?" Verse 27 stresses the power of God; yet this verse seems to mitigate what precedes. What is practically impossible (and for mortals remains so) is possible for God, since for God all things are possible. Therefore, after all, rich people can be saved.

The reading of the second part immediately after the first makes one wonder whether the rich man's refusal might endanger his eternal salvation. It would seem that the answer to this spontaneous question is not a simple yes. An enlargement occurs in verses 23-27, an extrapolation from a concrete case to a statement of universal validity, a shift from one rich person to rich people in general. At the same time Mark returns from his brief call story in verses 21-22 to the theme of the doctrinal dialogue in verses 17-20. The expression "to enter the kingdom of God" (vv. 23 and 24) is the equivalent of "to inherit eternal life" (v. 17) just as the verb "to save" (v. 26) refers to the same eschatological reality. Yet all this data does not allow us to assume that the rich man who goes away not only refuses to follow Jesus but also throws away his eternal salvation. It may be better to connect the elements of verses 21-27 and construe them into a comparison. Just as his many possessions for the rich man constituted an invincible obstacle to following Jesus, so also wealth renders it hard for people to enter the kingdom of God. If God did not take care of it, their salvation would be as good as impossible. Of course, the question can be asked whether the attachment to his possessions does in fact not endanger the rich man's salvation. The answer to this new question is yes. However, in this pericope that question is not explicitly raised nor is the answer to it given.

Peter (vv. 28-31)

As far as content is concerned Peter's reaction links up with the following of Jesus. Peter says that the disciples have acted differently than the rich man: they have left everything and followed Jesus. The reply of Jesus is meant not only for Peter but for the whole group of disciples ("truly I tell you", plural). Jesus even refers to all those who act as the disciples do ("there is no one who..."). The "leaving" here has become more radical than that indicated in v. 21: not merely material possessions such as house and fields but also the giving up of human connections, the leaving of "brothers or sisters or mother or father or children" (v. 29). But Jesus holds out the prospect of a reward to the disciples. He distinguishes between "now in this age" (v. 30a) and "in the age to come" (v. 30b). The "hundredfold" which the followers of Jesus can expect, already during their life, is the new family of a sharing Christian community: houses and fields, Christian spiritual brothers and sisters, mothers and children, be it with persecutions. In the age to come, moreover, they will receive eternal life (cf. perhaps "treasure in heaven" mentioned in verse 21). A final saying is added: many who do not follow Jesus and are considered as the first in this life will ultimately be last, and "the last will be first" (v. 31).

In the third part one notices not only the shift over against the second (the return to "following") and the more radical giving up than in verse 21, but also a real tension with the first part. Through considering "eternal life" in verse 30b as the reward for leaving everything and following Jesus, the impression returns that the keeping of the commandments is not enough to inherit that eternal life (cf. vv. 17-20). Yet it cannot be true that the new brothers, sisters, mothers and children, those who "now in this age" receive the followers in their families and community, will not be saved. To be sure, these Christians have not become "followers" of Jesus in the strict sense, they have not left everything; nonetheless they are genuine disciples and keep the commandments. To avoid the tension mentioned above one should paraphrase verse 30b as follows: "and in the age to come, of course together with the other 'ordinary' disciples, eternal life".

In the lengthy pericope of the rich man one detects a going to and fro from "eternal life" (or "entering the kingdom of God") to "following Jesus":

vv. 17-20 ("to inherit eternal life" by keeping the commandments);

vv. 21-22 (not "following Jesus" because of wealth);

vv. 23-27 (for those who have wealth "entering the kingdom of God" will be almost impossible);

vv. 28-31 (the "following of Jesus" will be rewarded both in this life and in the age to come).

As indicated above the mention of eternal life in verse 30b forms an inclusion with the question of verse 17. Yet it is also the cause of the tension between the keeping of the commandments and the following of Jesus, two clearly distinguished behaviors which will each receive the same eschatological "reward". Moreover, from verses 28-31 (and the whole of Mark's gospel) it appears that there are two types of disciples, those who leave everything and follow Jesus and the other disciples who remain in their ordinary situation at home.

One problem, and a pastoral one at that, remains to be dealt with. Readers today will ask whether the evaluation of wealth and riches in this gospel passage is not negative to the extreme. However, one should take into account the Semitic style which easily speaks of impossibility where as a matter of fact only serious difficulty is meant. Moreover, Jesus' instruction is basically intended as an exhortation; exaggeration belongs to this literary genre. Further, possessions as such are not evil, only the disorderly attachment to them: we cannot serve two lords. Notwithstanding all these qualifications a fundamental correction must be admitted. In the course of history the vision of the world and its inhabitants has changed the evaluation of money and wealth. The end of the age is not so close as was thought in the early church. Material goods are needed to eliminate hunger from this world and make life on earth more human. This much needed actualizing consideration, however, should not lead to underestimating the ever present danger of enslavement to riches and a consumption mentality in this "paradise" on earth.

The Pre-History of Mark 10,17-31

In the first section of this paper a distinction between the evangelist and Jesus, between the Markan Christ and the earthly Jesus, was omitted. One could now be tempted to reason as follows. Without too much trouble the line of thought of the evangelist has been reconstructed. What Mark has written, why could Jesus not have spoken? One then regards the threefold dialogue as having taken place just as Mark presents it in his gospel. Of course, it will easily be admitted that Mark has told the narrative in his own peculiar style, but the conclusion could remain: the events are in substance historical; this is the important point. Yet three factors call into question this type of conservative interpretation.

Three Simple Considerations

First there is an a priori reflection. In between Jesus and Mark a time-span of about forty years of oral traditions (and beginning written sources) has to be postulated, inclusive of a change of region and language. One gets the impression that in verses 29-30 not Jesus but Mark depicts how Christian missionaries experience the "hundredfold" in the postpaschal churches. Moreover, Matthew later altered the pericope in a thorough manner and inserted a saying in 19,28. Why could Mark, too, not have composed in a similar way? A quick comparison with passages in the Markan gospel itself is instructive. It appears that, e.g., in chapters four, seven and thirteen the evangelist has written freely and independently: he has brought together dispersed traditions and composed them into extended discourses.

A second consideration should devote attention to the specifically Markan character of the pericope. The vocabulary is Markan, especially in the initial verse and the verses which connect the three parts, but not only there. A list may be offered of some terms and expressions which are more peculiar to Mark and thus betray his editing hand:

— v. 17: to go out (ἐκπορεύομαι), into the way (εἰς ὁδόν), to run to (προσ-τρέχω), to kneel (γονυπετέω), to question (ἐπερωτάω).
— v. 21: to look at (ἐμβλέπω).
— v. 23: to look around (περιβλέπομαι).
— v. 24: to be amazed (θαμβέομαι).
— v. 26: to be astonished (ἐκπλήσσομαι).

- v. 27: to look at (ἐμβλέπω; cf. v. 21).
- v. 28: to begin (ἄρχομαι).
- v. 29: (for the sake of me and) for the sake of the gospel: cf. 8,35 (see also 8,38); persecution: cf. 4,17.

Moreover, Mark characteristically uses clauses at the end which add motivating information; see in verse 22: "for he had many possessions", and in verse 27: "for God all things are possible". Most probably the psychologizing characteristics of the rich man, as well as of Jesus, likewise point to Mark as author: see verses 21a, 22a, 24a, 26a and 27a.

A third factor must not go unnoticed. The very tensions within the pericope suggest that one cannot reckon with the historical sequence of the parts; a later, not overly successful composition has to be assumed. In the first part wealth is an obstacle to the call of the rich man, while in the second part wealth is the obstacle to eschatological salvation. Furthermore, the rich man of the first part becomes, in the second, as it were an example for those who because of riches gravely endanger their salvation; yet in the first part it appeared that salvation solely depends on the keeping of the commandments and that the rich man can honestly say that he has kept them since he was a boy. Is the earthly Jesus responsible for this lack of logic? Most probably not. It is also strange that in verse 21 Jesus declares that one has treasure in heaven by giving up the possessions and says nothing about the hundredfold in this age as in verse 30 while in this verse the same Jesus does not mention the treasure in heaven but speaks of eternal life. In addition, why does Jesus speak of "inheriting (or receiving) eternal life" in the first and third parts, whereas in the second part, suddenly, of "entering the kingdom of God" and of "being saved"? Why does Mark employ a term which means property and real estate (κτήματα) in the first part while, in the second, a term which more generally indicates goods and money (χρήματα)? And, finally, what about the proverb about the first who will be last and the last who will be first, a logion which also occurs in Lk 13,30: is this not originally an isolated saying that Mark, not Jesus, has placed in this context?

In view of these three considerations a twofold conclusion must be drawn: most likely the pericope as a whole came into being after Easter and much of its composition has to be attributed to the evangelist Mark. The degree of probability of this double conclusion relies not on one factor in isolation, but on the converging strength of the three arguments together. Yet, to be sure, not everything in this gospel passage is redactional just as the whole of it is not traditional or authentic.

Tradition and Redaction

There is no serious reason to doubt the historicity of the encounter of the rich man with Jesus. The question about the way to eternal life, Jesus' reply pointing to the keeping of the commandments, the rich man's honest assertion and, finally, Jesus' inviting "order" to follow him which is not accepted by that man: all this most probably goes back to an encounter which really occurred and a dialogue which really took place. Regarding the second part, the traditional character of the saying about the impossibility for those who have wealth to enter the kingdom of God, as well as of the comparison with the camel and the needle's eye, should best be admitted. Some exegetes, however, are of the opinion that these words came into being after Easter, but this position remains highly uncertain. Yet even if the words are postpaschal, their content is in complete agreement with Jesus' own conviction about the dangers of riches. As to the third part, it is much less risky here on the one hand to suppose that the saying within verses 29-30 is pre-Markan and on the other to claim that this saying does not come from Jesus himself (although, again, its content is not in the least opposed to his doctrine). This prophetic statement probably has its roots in the experiences of the early church. To conclude, it seems safe to regard the three traditional kernels as having originally had separate existences.

The connection of the first part with (the tradition from) the second may have already occurred in a church which was still mainly Jewish. Through this linking the rich man becomes an example concerning the dangers of wealth. Little or no consideration is given to the fact that wealth in the first part constitutes the obstacle to following Jesus while in the second it is the eschatological salvation that is endangered. In the Palestinian Jewish Christian church much attention is given to the poor and the wealthy people are warned; one is concerned with personal salvation while the missionary initiative does not come to the fore. Such a church provides a tenable life setting for connecting the two first parts.

The three-part pericope which now exists is most likely the result of the literary work of the evangelist himself. It is Mark who has composed verse 17a and in the first part emphasized the man's initial faith in Jesus and mentions how Jesus, "looking at him, loved him". It is Mark who in verse 22 intended to indicate the man's grievance at his disappointing departure. It is most likely also Mark who created the able construction of verses 23-27: dialogue form, the pairing of the saying in verses 23b and 24c, the climax reached not only by that duplication but also by the increasing intensity in the disciples' astonishment in verses 24 and 26. Yet apparently, while writing verses 23-26, Mark realized that his Jesus risks going too far. Verse 27 constitutes an editorial weakening, a kind of anticlimax: what is humanly impossible becomes possible – through God. Furthermore, one should probably regard as Mark's composition not only the question of Peter (v. 28) and the addition of the concluding logion (v. 31) but also the attachment of the whole third part to what precedes. Thus Mark is able to direct his readers' attention again to the theme of following Jesus; he evidently does it influenced by the missionary activity of the hellenistic Gentile church. Within the double saying of verses 29-30 Mark inserts the mission-filled expression "for the sake of the gospel" (= the preaching of the gospel), as well as the sobering qualification "not without persecutions".

True, the chain of thought is somewhat uneven and tensions have been caused by the editorial connection of materials which originally were independent. But then again, on the other hand, the sequence of ideas is logically not overly disturbing.

"Perfection" in Matthew 19,16-22

Only the first part of the Matthean version will be briefly analyzed here, first the change of structure, then the alteration in content and, by way of conclusion, a search for the exact meaning of "perfect" (τέλειος) in verse 21.

The Structure

Verse 22 corresponds to verse 16a: the going away of the young man who had come to Jesus. In between these two verses is to be found the animated dialogue of the man with Jesus. The man asks his brief questions and Jesus answers them more extensively. The NRSV version of this dialogue (vv. 16b-21) runs as follows:

Teacher, what good deed must I do to have eternal life? (v. 16b)

Why do you ask me about what is good? There is only one who is good. If you wish to enter into life, keep the commandments (v. 17b).

Which ones? (v. 18a)

You shall not murder; You shall not commit adultery; You shall not steal; You shall not bear false witness; Honor your father and mother; also, You shall love your neighbor as yourself (vv. 18b-19).

I have kept all these; what do I still lack? (v. 20b)

If you wish to be perfect, go, sell your possessions, and give the money to the poor, and you will have treasure in heaven; then come, follow me (v. 21b).

The Alterations

In the Matthean gospel the rich man has become a "young" rich man; at the beginning of his adult life he is confronted with a choice. The young man does not address Jesus as "good teacher", only as "teacher". The adjective "good" appears in the question that literally reads: "What good must I do in order to have eternal life?" Jesus first reacts by pointing to the only One who is good; the answer itself, "keep the commandments", is introduced by the conditional clause "if you would enter life". Before Jesus can cite the individual commandments the man briskly asks: "which?"

In the enumeration Matthew omits "You shall not defraud", but at the end adds "You shall love your neighbor as yourself". The young man says that he has kept all these commandments; then the man himself asks: "what do I still lack?" Again Jesus introduces his answer by means of a conditional clause: "if you would be perfect"; then, as in Mark, the instructions follow in the imperative.

It cannot but strike the reader that, as elsewhere in his gospel, Matthew composes in a more compact and less psychologizing way. But what is the difference between "if you wish to enter into life" (v. 17b) and "if you wish to be perfect" (v. 21b)?

"Perfect"

What is the problem with "perfect"? In the Markan gospel the departure of the rich man is immediately followed by the sayings about riches as an obstacle to eschatological salvation; for a moment the readers must be thinking that through his refusal the man also rejects his salvation. The sequence in Matthew is the same; yet an element from the broader gospel context calls for attention. On the one hand a first reading of the parallel conditional clauses as it were suggests that perfection is more than the keeping of the commandments. On the other hand those who are familiar with the Matthean gospel already know that perfection is required from every Christian in order to enter the kingdom of heaven.

The term τέλειος ("perfect") occurs only two more times in the gospel of Matthew, namely in the same verse: "Be perfect, therefore, as your heavenly Father is perfect" (5,48). Together with 5,20 this verse frames the six antitheses of 5,21-47: "For I tell you, unless your righteousness exceeds that of the scribes and Pharisees, you will never enter the kingdom of heaven". More abundant righteousness requires a more radical keeping of the commandments and is no less than perfection. Must the program of perfection in 19,21, therefore, not be explained as a clarification of the commandments in verses 18b-19 and is this perfection not necessary for the young man's final salvation?

The reasoning in this last question supposes that the meaning of "perfect" in 19,21 is exactly the same as in 5,48. However, this is not certain. As is well known, it is the immediate context that ultimately determines the exact nuance of a term's signification. Just as was the case with Mark, one can hardly assume for Matthew that the keeping of the commandments would be inadequate to enter life. The answer to the question "what do I still lack" no longer refers to the receiving of eternal life and salvation. Jesus' new offer is situated on a different level: that of following him and, one could expand, that of the mission which is connected with this type of discipleship, i.e., the continuation of the evangelization. Otherwise than in 5,48, "perfection" in 19,21 points to following Jesus and the fulfillment of the conditions for such discipleship.

Conclusion

What are the main insights one gains through this brief analysis of the rich man pericope? Mk 10,17-31 does not provide a direct access to the earthly Jesus. The evangelist Mark has thoroughly reworked and ordered his traditions. Part of them probably came into being only after Easter (be it in line with Jesus' message). Yet the first part of the pericope (vv. 17-22) contains an authentic encounter with Jesus, as well as an authentic dialogue. It is not to be excluded that both the saying about wealth and the comparison with the camel and the needle's eye go back to Jesus. Given these basic insights three conclusions can be formulated.

First, the line of thought in Mk 10,17-31 is convoluted; one finds a going to and fro from "eternal life" to "following". The exegesis of the passage must take into account the following data. (1) Verses 21-22 do not annul Jesus' teaching of the preceding verses 17-20 since the consequent verses no longer deal with eternal life but with the following of Jesus. (2) In verse 27 Mark somewhat softens the radicality of verses 23-25. The eschatological salvation that is almost impossible for those who have wealth now is no longer excluded – thanks to God. (3) After the distinction between verses 17-20 (keeping the commandments to inherit eternal life) and verses 21-22 (following Jesus), the addition in verse 30 "and in the age to come eternal life" remains strange since verses 28-31 contentwise rather belong to verses 21-22. Therefore, to understand that clause the paraphrasing proposal can be made "and in the age to come (of course also) eternal life". (4) With regard to Mt 19,21 "perfect" must be related to the following of Jesus and the later sending, not to the more perfect keeping of the commandments nor to a more perfect Christian life.

Second, both from Mark and Matthew it appears that two types of disciples exist. The first and more numerous group remain at home, have a family and possess goods. In order to enter the kingdom of heaven their righteousness must exceed that of the scribes and Pharisees, i.e., they must keep God's commandments in a radicalized and internalized way, even unto love of the enemy. The second group of disciples hear the special call of Jesus and follow him. To do this they must leave everything: possessions, family and work. Later, after Easter, they will be sent to spread the gospel. It will be their privilege to experience the "hundredfold" in the Christian communities, already in this age. Such a call is a charism, without merit on the part of those who are called. Nowadays many hesitate, rightly it would seem, to regard this second group as better Christians, more generous or perfect.

Third, both Jesus and Mark (and Matthew) emphasize the great danger of wealth. Money easily becomes mammon; it rules over life and confines people within the boundaries of their earthly existence. According to the pericope of the rich man the danger threatens both groups of disciples. Even though today one evaluates value and disvalue of material goods in a manner much more nuanced than in the first century, it would be impossible to deny that the warning of Mk 10,17-31 retains its actuality.

Bibliographical Note

Recently more attention has been given to the passage of the rich man because of the fact that the first part of the encyclical *Veritatis splendor* offers an extensive commentary on the Matthean version. Cf., e.g., R. A. McCormick, "Some Early Reactions to 'Veritatis Splendor'", in *TS* 55 (1994) 481-506: "The first three chapters is a protracted and beautiful meditation on Christ's dialogue with the rich young man of Matt 19:16 … Thus Chapter 1 basically presents the moral life as a response to Christ's invitation. Its biblical base is a breath of fresh air" (p. 484).

Three important monographs are devoted to this pericope: S. LÉGASSE, *L'appel du riche (Marc 10,17-31 et parallèles). Contribution à l'étude des fondements scripturaires de l'état religieux* (Verbum Salutis), Paris, 1966; W. EGGER, *Nachfolge als Weg zum Leben: Chancen neuerer exegetischen Methoden dargelegt an Mk 10.17-31* (ÖstBiblSt, 1), Klosterneuburg, 1979; V. FUSCO, *Povertà e sequela. La pericope sinottica della chiamata del ricco (Mc. 10.17-31 parr.)* (StudBibl, 94), Brescia, 1991. See also the article by R. BURGGRAEVE, "Prohibition and Taste: the Bipolarity in Christian Ethics", in *Ethical Perspectives* 1 (1994) 130-144.

John the Baptist and Jesus in Mark 1,1-15:
Markan Redaction of Q?

In the most recent monograph on John the Baptist Josef Ernst first deals with the Baptist in the Markan gospel and only then, in his second chapter, with the Baptist in Q, although it is generally recognized that Q is older than Mark[1]. Moreover, in Ernst's opinion there is no contact between Mark and Q. Ernst does not even consider that Mk 1,2bc may be taken from Q (cf. Mt 11,10 = Lk 7,27)[2], nor does he see in Mk 1,7-8 a more recent, re-written text of a more original version of Q[3]. The extent of Q in John's preaching is, as in many Q studies, limited to Mt 3,7-12 = Lk 3,7-9.16b-17. In this text Mt 3,11 = Lk 3,16 is "trimmed": "I baptize you with water, but the Most Powerful One [= God] is coming. ... He will baptize you with a holy Spirit and fire". Thus neither "after me" nor the qualification of John's unworthiness is retained[4].

In his *Q Parallels* John S. Kloppenborg distinguishes in Q 3 and 4 the Coming of John the Baptist (3,2-4), John's Preaching of Repentance (3,7-14), John's Preaching of the Coming One (3,16b-17), the Baptism of Jesus (3,21-22), and the Temptations of Jesus (4,1-13). The following texts, however, are put in square brackets: 3,2-4; 3,10-14; and 3,21-22[5]. Over these texts "there has been sustained scholarly debate". In Kloppenborg's opinion none of them probably belongs to Q, John's ethical preaching in 3,10-14 almost certainly not. With regard to John's coming in 3,2-4 he

---

1. J. ERNST, *Johannes der Täufer. Interpretation – Geschichte – Wirkungsgeschichte* (BZNW, 53), Berlin, 1989, pp. 4-38 and 39-80.

2. *Ibid.*, pp. 10,12.

3. *Ibid.*, pp. 13-16. This possibility is mentioned on p. 13. But "die für diese Möglichkeit angeführten Gründe ... sind nich zwingend" (p. 13).

4. *Ibid.*, pp. 40-55. For the analysis of Mt 3,11 and Lk 3,16 see pp. 48-55. According to Ernst, for John the ἰσχυρότερος in this verse is (most probably) still God the Judge. He will baptize with the holy Spirit and fire.

5. J. S. KLOPPENBORG, *Q Parallels: Synopsis, Critical Notes & Concordance* (Foundations & Facets), Sonoma, CA, 1988, pp. xxxi and 4-21. On p. xxiv he writes: "Following the convention of the SBL Q Seminar, Q texts are designated by their *Lukan* location". We adopt this procedure in this contribution.

writes: "While one cannot be dogmatic in this case, the large amount of Markan material in this section as well as the likelihood of Lukan redaction in vv. 1-2 render it unwise to include it in Q 3"[6]. And as far as the Baptism of Jesus of 3,21-22 is concerned Kloppenborg states: "The extent of Matthew-Luke agreements is too slight to posit a Q *Vorlage* and all of the 'minor agreements' are easily explained as redactional modifications of Mark. ... The title 'Son of God' in Q 4 does not require an explanatory narrative..."[7]. Most biblical scholars agree with this negative position. We may ask: rightly so? If neither Jesus' baptism nor the Isaiah quotation pointing to the coming and the function of Baptist was mentioned in Q, can it, at least, be presumed that Mark used Q for John's preaching of repentance as well as Jesus' temptations? The majority answer to this question is likewise negative[8]. Again, we venture to wonder whether this answer is justified.

In order to presuppose dependence on Q in Mark's redaction, the mere existence of older Q parallels is, of course, not sufficient. Likewise, if it can be shown that the later Mark *may* have altered Q texts in a coherent way, this is not strict proof that this actually happened[9]. Moreover, it can be asked whether our existing texts will ever allow a firm conclusion which either defends or rejects an assumed dependence. It would, however, be not a small merit of this article if it could shake the almost *a priori* certainty of those who negate any possibility of Markan knowledge of Q as well as the, it would seem, unjustified minimization of those who limit the extent of Q.

We begin with a first reading of Mk 1,1-15: what is its structure and line of thought? Then, the analysis of Mark's redaction will be studied in two stages: can we detect and reconstruct his sources and can we retrace his compositional creativity? Finally, out of Markan structure and composition a characterization of the two main figures must be possible: how does Mark in 1,1-15 depict the forerunner John the Baptist and Jesus Christ, the Son of God?

6. KLOPPENBORG, *Q Parallels*, p. 6.

7. *Ibid.*, p. 16.

8. Cf., e.g., the position taken in J. S. KLOPPENBORG, *The Formation of Q. Trajectories in Ancient Wisdom Collections* (StAntChr, 2), Philadelphia, 1987.

9. Cf. F. NEIRYNCK, "Recent Developments in the Study of Q", in J. DELOBEL (ed.), *Logia. Les paraboles* de Jésus – *The Sayings of Jesus* (BETL, 59), Leuven, 1982: "On the level of the individual saying it is common practice to give a tentative description of Mark's redaction activity by comparing the saying in Mark with the Q version, but how do we prove Mark's dependence on Q, and not on a traditional saying or on some pre-Q collection of sayings?" (p. 45). See also D. LÜHRMANN, "The Gospel of Mark and the Sayings Collection Q", in *JBL* 108 (1989) 51-71, esp. p. 53.

Structure and Line of Thought

A first reading of Mk 1,1-15 asks from us at the very onset a number of both text-critical and exegetical decisions with regard to vv. 1-4. Within the framework of this study, however, no justification can be given for the text-critical choices: in v. 1 the inclusion of "the Son of God"; in v. 2 the reading "in Isaiah the prophet", and more importantly, in v. 4 the clause and its grammatical structure: ἐγένετο Ἰωάννης βαπτίζων ἐν τῇ ἐρήμῳ καὶ κηρύσσων[10]. As far as the exegesis is concerned, v. 1 may be considered as nothing more than an indication of the beginning of the gospel. Vv. 2-3 probably constitute the first member of a comparison ("as it is written...") to which v. 4 then provides the second member "[so] John came baptizing in the wilderness and proclaiming...")[11]. One must probably not ask where the "beginning" ends: at v. 8, or v. 11, or v. 13, or v. 15. No, v. 1 simply states: "Here, i.e., at vv. 2-4, with the coming and preaching of the Baptist, begins the gospel of Jesus Christ, the Son of God"[12]. The genitive Ἰησοῦ Χριστοῦ may be objective, not subjective, nor both together; neither does it point to Jesus as the proclaimer of the gospel (but see vv. 14-15)[13].

---

10. We may just refer to B. M. METZGER, *Textual Commentary on the Greek New Testament*, London – New York, corrected ed. 1975, p. 73. And what about Χριστοῦ in v. 1: proper name or title?

11. Otherwise recently, e.g., G. ARNOLD, "Mk 1,1 und die Eröffnungswendungen in griechischen und lateinischen Schriften", in *ZNW* 68 (1977) 123-127 (see pp. 123-124); R. A. GUELICH, "'The Beginning of the Gospel' Mark 1:1-15", in *BR* 27 (1982) 5-12, esp. pp. 6-8; M. A. TOLBERT, *Sowing the Gospel: Mark's World in Literary-Historical Perspective*, Minneapolis, 1989, pp. 239-248. It is true that elsewhere in the Bible "as it written" does not appear at the beginning of a sentence and, moreover, the absence of οὕτως (cf. Lk 11,30; 17,26; John 3,14) is strange. On the other hand there is most probably no καί before ἐγένετο at the beginning of v. 4; vv. 1 and 2-3 would form an even more peculiar unit than 2-3 and 4 do.

12. A good overview is given in J. J. A. KAHMANN, "Marc. 1,14-15 en hun plaats in het geheel van het Marcus-evangelie", in *Bijdr* 38 (1977) 84-98 (see pp. 88-90). I wonder whether the often quoted Hos 1,2a (LXX: ἀρχὴ λόγου Κυρίου πρὸς Ὡσῆε; a free rendering of the Hebrew text) is a good parallel. Further according to ARNOLD, "Eröffnungswendungen", Mk 1,1 is not an "Überschrift, Buchtitel" but an "Eröffnungswendung", an opening clause. Yet, Mark calls his writing "the gospel of...".

13. For a survey of the opinions see G. DAUTZENBERG, "Die Zeit des Evangeliums. Mk 1,1-15 und die Konzeption des Markusevangeliums", in *BZ* 21 (1977) 219-234, and 22 (1978) 76-91 (esp. pp. 219-225). Cf. also H. KOESTER, "From the Kerygma-Gospel to Written Gospels", in *NTS* 35 (1989) 361-381, esp. pp. 367-370 and 380-381; ID., *Ancient Christian Gospels. Their History and Development*, London – Philadelphia, 1990, pp. 9-14; D. DORMEYER, "Die Kompositionsmetapher 'Evangelium Jesu Christi, des Sohnes Gottes' Mk 1.1. Ihre theologische und literarische Aufgabe in der Jesus-Biographie des Markus", in *NTS* 33 (1987) 452-468: "Aufgrund der metaphorischen Komposition lassen

Vv. 2-15 contain two major sections, vv. 2-8 on John and vv. 9-15 on Jesus. In each section three small text units can be distinguished. For John: his appearance in the wilderness (vv. 2-4), his success, clothing and food (vv. 5-6), and his proclamation (vv. 7-8). For Jesus: his baptism (vv. 9-11), his temptation (vv. 12-13), and also his proclamation (vv. 14-15)[14]. The two sections are closely united. Ἦλθεν ... Ἰησοῦς of v. 9 is the fulfillment of John's announcement in v. 7: ἔρχεται ὁ ἰσχυρότερός μου ὀπίσω μου; and his being baptized in the Jordan (v. 9) reflects what happens in v. 5b (but without a confession of sins). But do vv. 2-15 (or 1-15) really constitute a unity? Two remarks are here in order.

First, by the new introduction in v. 9, καὶ ἐγένετο ἐν ἐκείναις ταῖς ἡμέραις, a break is clearly indicated. Vv. 9-13, moreover, possess their own "apocalyptic" atmosphere. There are here no longer huge crowds. After the mention of John in v. 9 even the Baptist is no longer a *dramatis persona*. What we have is the Father ("a voice ... from heaven", v. 11), the Son, the Spirit ("as a dove", v. 10), Satan and angels, apocalyptic vision and audition. The heavens are being rent for revelation and divine descent. All that happens is related to Jesus; he is the central figure. After he has come up out of the water, he remains alone without human companions. A "spiritual" world surrounds him and confronts him. Vv. 9-13 stand between the preaching of John (vv. 2-8) and that of Jesus (vv. 14-15). These verses are framed and somewhat isolated by these units; they have their own content and colour[15].

The second remark is even more important. It has often been pointed out that vv. 14-15 form, together with v. 1 or vv. 1-4, an inclusion. Several terms or concepts appear at both ends: God, John, Jesus, κηρύσσω, repentance, gospel. Moreover, several other terms are repeated within the whole section: ἐγένετο, ἔρημος, βαπτίζω, ἔρχομαι, πνεῦμα, εὐθύς. Are vv. 1-15,

---

sich die Genitive in 1.1 and 1.14 nicht mehr nach subjektivus oder objektivus bestimmen" (p. 461: see *ibid.* for bibliography). Can this thesis be defended on a grammatical basis?

14. Cf. e.g., R. PESCH, "Anfang des Evangeliums Jesu Christi. Studie zum Prolog des Markusevangeliums (Mk 1,1-15)", in G. BORNKAMM & K. RAHNER (eds.), *Die Zeit Jesu*, Freiburg – Basel – Wien, 1970, 108-144, esp. pp. 111-112; *Das Markusevangelium* (HTKNT, II), Freiburg – Basel – Wien, 1976; J. GNILKA, *Das Evangelium nach Markus* (EKK, II/1), Zürich – Neukirchen-Vluyn, 1978, p. 39; W. EGGER, *Frohbotschaft und Lehre. Die Sammelberichte des Wirkens Jesu im Markusevangelium* (FrThSt, 19), Frankfurt, 1976, pp. 55-56; GUELICH, "The Beginning", p. 7; T. SÖDING, *Glaube bei Markus. Glaube an das Evangelium, Gebetsglaube und Wunderglaube im Kontext des markinischen Basileiatheologie und Christologie* (SBB, 12), Stuttgart, 1985, pp. 135-136.

15. Cf., e.g., PESCH, *Markusevangelium*, pp. 88-89.

therefore, a single major pericope[16]? Vv. 14-15 are, it would seem, in a certain sense transitional; they also function as a new beginning. In v. 14 the clause μετὰ δὲ τὸ παραδοθῆναι τὸν Ἰωάννην ἦλθεν ὁ Ἰησοῦς explicitly separates Jesus from John. The parallelism between κηρύσσων βάπτισμα μετανοίας εἰς ἄφεσιν ἁμαρτιῶν (v. 4) and κηρύσσων τὸ εὐαγγέλιον τοῦ θεοῦ (v. 14) is very striking: the two clauses point to the outset of two careers, that of John and that of Jesus. Moreover, both figures have their own proclamation in direct discourse: compare vv. 7-8 with v. 15. Further, structural considerations regarding the first eight chapters of Mark have confirmed the thesis which sees vv. 14-15 as a really fresh start: 1,14-15 corresponds with 3,7-12 and 6,6b; each of these three "summaries" of Jesus' activity precedes a disciples-pericope (1,16-20; 3,7-12; 6,7-13) and introduces a substantial section of the first half of the Markan gospel[17]. The summary of 1,14-15, however, not only introduces 1,14–3,6a but also the whole of the gospel[18]. It is the only summary in Mark in which Jesus is quoted. The theological condensation of these two verses manifests their programmatic character. With the proclamation of God's gospel Jesus' public life begins: "The time is fulfilled, and the Kingdom of God is at hand; repent, and believe in the gospel"[19].

A Search for Q in Mark 1,1-15

It would seem that in 1,1-15 Mark was redactionally very active, not at all slavish. Can Mark's creative compositional endeavour be evaluated in

16. So many exegetes today; see, however, DAUTZENBERG, "Die Zeit des Evangeliums", pp. 229-231, who also takes vv. 1-15 as a unit but refuses the term "Prolog".

17. First proposed by E. SCHWEIZER, "Anmerkungen zur Theologie des Markus", in *Neotestamentica et Patristica. FS O. Cullmann* (SupplNT, 6), Leiden, 1962; also in SCHWEIZER, *Neotestamentica*, Zürich, 1963, pp. 93-104, and "Die theologische Leistung des Markus", in *EvTh* 24 (1964) 337-355; also in SCHWEIZER, *Beiträge zur Theologie des Neuen Testaments*, Zürich, 1970, pp. 21-42. See also the influential proposals by N. PERRIN, esp. *The New Testament. An Introduction*, New York, 1974, pp. 143-167.

18. Cf. EGGER, *Frohbotschaft und Lehre*, p. 63: "Überschrift des Evangeliums".

19. Cf. G. VAN OYEN, *De summaria in Marcus en de compositie van Mc 1,14–8,26* (StNTAux, 12), Leuven, 1987, pp. 44-52 and 129-153. Van Oyen gives an overview of the recent discussion: is 1,14-15 a conclusion of the "prologue", or a real summary statement of Jesus' preaching and appeal, or a programmatic proclamation ("Eröffnungslogion, Heroldsruf")? See pp. 152-153 for his own balanced threefold position: transitional between prologue and 1,16-3,6; closely connected with 1,16-20; and theologically relevant for the whole gospel. For a break between 1,13 and 1,14 an additional argument is provided by F. J. MATERA, "The Prologue as the Interpretative Key to Mark's Gospel", in *JSNT* 34 (1988) 3-20: "In 1.1-13 the narrator communicates privileged information about John and Jesus to the reader" (p. 5); the events of that prologue "are told solely for the reader's benefit; the characters of the story (Jesus excepted) are not aware of them" (*ibid.*); what follows is public in nature.

a concrete, scientifically responsible way? Rudolf Pesch writes: "Wie es auch somit überwiegend seine Art ist, scheint der konservative Redaktor Markus nur an den Rändern der ihm vorgegebenen Texte gearbeitet zu haben"[20]. What precisely are the "vorgegebenen Texte", Mark's source texts? The working hypothesis of this paper is that Mark knew and used Q (in its final form)[21]. To be sure, again, I do not think that the documentary situation of our gospel enables us strictly to prove either this position or its opposite. But let us bring together the data and argue about their implications; let us reconstruct in a rather generous way the possible elements of Mark's Q source; and let us then, finally, examine whether or not a better insight into Mark's composition arises from his supposed dependence on Q: would that insight then not plead in favour of the correctness of our working hypothesis?

The first verse of the gospel is no doubt created by Mark. Yet further in this study (see pp. 26-27 and p. 33) it will appear that possibly Mark wrote τὸ εὐαγγέλιον and υἱὸς θεοῦ under the influence of Q. We may commence the discussion, however, immediately with vv. 2-8 and continue, then, with vv. 9-15.

---

20. PESCH, "Anfang", p. 112. Cf. ERNST, *Johannes der Täufer*, p. 10: 'Das ingesamt konservative Verfahren der markinischen Redaktion, die dem Bewahren mehr Gewicht gibt als der Veränderung". In Mk 1,1-15 Pesch distinguishes (a) several traditions (vv. 2a.3-5; 6; 7-8; 9-11 and, perhaps already connected, vv. 12-13); (b) a pre-Markan redactor who composed the pericope vv. 2-15ab: by the insertion of v. 2bc and the addition of vv. 7-8 he strengthened the already christological interpretation of the Baptist tradition. The redactor then continued with the Jesus tradition (vv. 9-13) and, moreover, composed a concluding summary (vv. 14-15b); (c) the evangelist Mark, who received this composition, writes the opening verse 1, probably inserts τῆς Γαλιλαίας in v. 9, perhaps εὐθύς in v. 10, and adds v. 15c: καὶ πιστεύετε ἐν τῷ εὐαγγελίῳ. See "Anfang", pp. 112-115 and 136-137. For the later Pesch (*Markusevangelium*, p. 103) v. 15c is no longer Mark's redaction.

21. Cf. B. H. STREETER, "St Mark's Knowledge and Use of Q", in W. SANDAY (ed.), *Studies in the Synoptic Problem*, Oxford, 1911, 166-183. E. P. SANDERS and M. DAVIES, *Studying the Synoptic Gospels*, London, 1989, p. 82, rightly refer to the earlier publication as "a detailed and excellent study". W. SCHENK, "Der Einfluss der Logienquelle auf das Markusevangelium", in ZNW 70 (1979) 141-165, speaks of Mark's "Auseinandersetzung mit der Q-Redaktion" (p. 453). For the opposite view see, e.g., M. DEVISCH, "La relation entre l'évangile de Marc et le document Q", in M. SABBE (ed.), *L'Évangile selon Marc. Tradition et rédaction* (BETL, 34), Leuven, 1974, ²1984, 59-91; R. LAUFEN, *Die Doppelüberlieferungen der Logienquelle und des Markusevangeliums* (BBB, 54), Bonn, pp. 383-385; NEIRYNCK, "Study of Q", esp. pp. 41-53; M. SATO, *Q und Prophetie. Studien zur Gattungs- und Traditionsgeschichte der Quelle* (WUNT, II/29), Tübingen, 1988, pp. 383-385 ("unbeweisbar und unwahrscheinlich"; Sato accepts an occasional "Wechselbeziehung" between Q and pre-Markan traditions and "gegenseitige Rezeption und Überarbeitung").

John (vv. 2-8)

Verses 2-6: Appearance and Preaching

Four agreements of Matthew and Luke against Mark seem to suggest that they must have, besides Mark, a Q text for their description of John's coming. (1) Both place the coming of the Baptist ἐν τῇ ἐρήμῳ before the Isaiah quotation; (2) both omit the Malachi quotation of Mark 1,2b; (3) both connect John's coming immediately with John's preaching (Mt 3,7-10 and Lk 3,7-10) and, most strikingly, (4) both write πᾶσα ἡ περίχωρος τοῦ Ἰορδάνου (Mt 3,5 and Lk 3,3)[22]. It is true that lengthy analyses have shown, some might tend to say conclusively, that Matthean and Lukan redaction of the Markan text *can* explain, without Q, each of these so-called minor agreements taken separately[23]. Will such an explanation do for the four taken together? Hardly. Moreover, with regard to the citation in vv. 2-3, even if we do not agree with Streeter's reasoning, his opinion appears correct: "It looks as if Mark's double quotation in this passage is a conflation of the two quotations applied to John in two different contexts of Q"[24]. Finally, one must admit the likelihood that the Q preaching of John needs a kind of introduction such as the one present in our gospels[25]. We should not too easily and theoretically postulate the

22. See the brief discussion with the bibliographical references in KLOPPENBORG, *Q Parallels*, p. 6. With regard to Mk 1,6 we refer to the recent but rather confusing study of R. P. MERENDINE, "Testi anticotestamentari in *Mc* 1,2-6", in *RivBibl* 35 (1987) 3-25, esp. pp. 7-8. He opines ("è ... probabile") that v. 6 "sia stato retocatto ... da Marco" (p. 8).

23. See DEVISCH, *De geschiedenis van de Quelle-hypothese* (unpubl. S.T.D. dissertation, K.U.Leuven, 1975), pp. 402-421; H. FLEDDERMANN, "The Beginning of Q", in *SBL.SP* (1985), pp. 153-159 (he states: "Michel Devisch has shown ... that the linguistic evidence does not support a Q text behind Luke 3:3-6", p. 153). The fourth agreement is the most important; the second may suggest that Matthew and Luke, independently, thought of the same Q passage (Jesus' Eulogy) but their reaction is much easier to understand if Q possesses a pericope on John's coming with the Isaiah quotation.

24. "Mark's Knowledge and Use of Q", p. 168. Streeter grounds that statement as follows: "Seeing that in no other case does the editor of Mark himself introduce a quotation or reference to the Old Testament it is probable that this [= the Isaiah-quotation] also occurred in Q". Yet one must refer to Mk 7,6-7 where "the editor of Mark himself" introduces a quotation (of Isaiah). GUELICH, "The Beginning", pp. 8-9, thinks that the mixed quotation in 1,2-3 must be pre-Markan: "Mark's use of the OT is often much more subtle and not as direct" (p. 14, n. 36). Is this so? Why could not Mark have done this? The introductory formula is very common in the NT. For Mark see also 9,13 and 14,21, but without citation.

25. Cf. B. H. STREETER, "The Original Extent of Q", in *Studies in the Synoptic Problem*, pp. 185-206: "Since Q recorded John's preaching and the Temptation it would be very strange if no mention were made of the Baptism, which is the connecting link between the two" (p. 187); see also H. SCHÜRMANN, *Das Lukasevangelium* (HTKNT,

purity of Q as a source with sayings alone[26]. So by its convergence our careful guessing in this paragraph becomes almost an objective cogency. In our view Matthew and Luke have known two texts, Mark and Mark's source (= Q).

A reconstruction of the coming of John in Q should, it seems to me, contain at least the following elements: the coming in the wilderness, the proclamation of the baptism of repentance, the Isaiah quotation, the success and, probably, the actual baptism. Because of a possible influence of Q 7,25 on Mark (see further), we may do better to eliminate the depiction of John's clothing and food of Mk 1,6. This verse, moreover, looks like a biographical insertion and interrupts the connection between vv. 2-5 and 7-8[27]. The phrase "preaching a baptism of repentance for the forgiveness of sins" (1,4) is perhaps a Markan specification of John's activity, although the idea of repentance was probably present[28]. Not without much hesitation, we may present the following reconstructed Q text:

Q 3,2   John came in the wilderness,
    3   preaching a baptism of repentance,
    4 a   as it is written in Isaiah the prophet
      b   "The voice of one crying in the wilderness:
      c   Prepare the way of the Lord,
      d   make his paths straight"(Isa 40,3).
    6 b   All the region about the Jordan went out to him,
      c   and they were baptized by him in the river Jordan.

III/1), Freiburg – Basel – Wien, 1985, p. 143; F. BOVON, *Das Evangelium nach Lukas* (EKK, III/1), Zürich – Neukirchen-Vluyn, 1989, pp. 166 and 169-170; KOESTER, *Gospels*, p. 135: "It is reasonable to assume that Q must have introduced the appearance of John in some fashion".

26. On the "genre" of Q see now esp. KLOPPENBORG, *The Formation of Q*. Cf. also his "Tradition and Redaction in the Synoptic Sayings Source", in *CBQ* 46 (1984) 34-62, esp. pp. 57-62 ("Genre and Redaction").

27. Cf. ERNST, *Johannes der Täufer*, p. 284: "Der Evangelist Markus hat in seinen auf die Busstaufe und das Kommen des Geisttäufers ausgerichteten Verkündigungstext eine Notiz über die Kleidung und Nahrung des Täufers (Mk 1,6) eingeschoben. Der knappe Zwischensatz fällt nicht nur in stilistischer Hinsicht – Unterbrechung des Zusammenhangs von V. 4-5 und V. 7-8 –, sondern auch durch das biographische Interesse aus dem Rahmen" (not mentioned, however, on pp. 8-9).

28. Cf. H. MERKLEIN, "Die Umkehrpredigt bei Johannes dem Täufer und Jesus von Nazaret", in *BZ* 25 (1981) 29-46. For μετανοέω see the Markan usages in 1,15 and 6,12 (perhaps from Q 10,13 – see further in this study); for "forgiveness of sins" see 2,1-10 and 3,28-29. We may also refer to the reconstruction in Greek by A. POLAG, *Fragmenta Q. Textheft zur Logienquelle*, Neukirchen, 1979, ²1982, p. 28, and its translation in English by I. HAVENER, *Q: The Sayings of Jesus. With a Reconstruction of Q by A. Polag* (GNS, 19), Wilmington, DE, 1987, p. 123: without v. 6c and in v. 6b "he went onto" (from Lk 3,3).

Verses 7-8: Announcement of the Coming One

A parallel of Q 3,7-9 is not present in Mark. The words of John are easily reconstructed (with "fruit" in the singular). Only the introduction is somewhat uncertain[29]. We propose:

Q   3,7a   He said to the people that were coming to the baptism:
      b   You brood of vipers! Who warned you to flee from the wrath to come?
     8a   Bear fruit that befits repentance,
      b   and do not begin to say to yourselves, "We have Abraham as our father";
      c   for I tell you, God is able from the stones to raise up children to Abraham.
     9a   Even now the axe is laid to the root of trees;
      b   every tree therefore that does not bear good fruit is cut down
      c   and thrown into the fire.

Mt 3,11 and Lk 3,16 differ from Mk 1,7-8 in the order of the individual clauses. They possess, moreover, three striking word agreements: the μέν construction, the present tense of βαπτίζω, and the presence of καὶ πυρί[30]. We may also refer to Mt 3,12 and Lk 3,17: these nearly identical verses stand immediately after Mk 1,8 and are both introduced by the relative pronoun οὗ which already in Q must have had an antecedent[31]. Here both Matthew and Luke almost certainly used not only the Markan text but also a Q version[32]. In the reconstruction of Q 3,16 ἐν ὕδατι (otherwise Lk), ὁ δὲ ὀπίσω μου ἐρχόμενος ἰσχυρότερός μοῦ ἐστιν (otherwise Lk), λῦσαι τὸν ἱμάντα τῶν ὑποδημάτων αὐτοῦ (otherwise Mt), and

29. In our neutral proposal we try to avoid both Matthean and Lukan style. ERNST, *Johannes der Täufer*, correctly writes: "Der urspüngliche Wortlaut wird sich kaum noch rekonstruieren lassen" (p. 42). After his careful study DEVISCH, *De Quelle-hypothese*, pp. 493-497, retains only "Jesus said". He is followed by FLEDDERMANN, "The Beginning of Q", pp. 154-155.

30. See the brief discussion in KLOPPENBORG, *Q Parallels*, p. 12. He mentions also "the placing of ὑμᾶς before βαπτίζει". In our reconstruction we maintain "holy Spirit".

31. Cf. STREETER, "Mark's Knowledge and Use of Q", p. 168: this verse "has no meaning apart from the preceding verse, which therefore must have stood in Q and not have been derived ... from Mark".

32. Cf. KLOPPENBORG, *Q Parallels*, p. 12 ("most authors"); DEVISCH, *De Quelle-hypothese*, pp. 489-532; H. FLEDDERMANN, "John and the Coming One (Matt 3:11/Luk 3:16-17)", in *SBL.SP* (1984) 377-384.

33. Compare, e.g., S. SCHULZ, *Q – Die Spruchquelle der Evangelisten*, Zürich, pp. 366-368, who omits ὀπίσω μου and "holy Spirit" and prefers "whose sandals I am not worhty to carry". For a discussion on "holy Spirit and fire" see, e.g., ERNST, *Johannes der Täufer*, pp. 53-54; J. A. FITZMYER, *The Gospel according to Luke I-IX* (AB, 28), Garden City, NY, 1981, pp. 473-474: "The likelihood is that both Spirit and fire were in the original 'Q' form of the saying" (p. 473); FLEDDERMANN, "John and the Coming One", pp. 378-381 and 382.

the presence of "holy Spirit and fire" are preferable[33]. In Q the expression ὀπίσω μου probably has the local meaning "behind me".

No major difficulties arise regarding Q 3,17[34]. So we may reconstruct both Q verses as follows:

Q 3,16b I baptize you with water;
  c but he who is coming after me is mightier than I,
  d the thong of his sandals I am not worthy to untie;
  e he will baptize you with the holy Spirit and with fire.
 17a His winnowing fork is in his hand,
  b and he will clear his threshing floor
  c and gather the wheat into his granary,
  d but the chaff he will burn with unquenchable fire[35].

Conclusion

In Q we have thus postulated the presence of three small units: the Appearance of John the Baptist (3,2-6), John's Preaching of Repentance (3,7-9), and John's Announcement of the Coming One (3,16b-17). For Q John is the forerunner of Jesus or, better, the eschatological prophet-messenger of the coming judge-Son of man[36]; as it written in Isaiah, John proclaims in the wilderness; he administers a baptism of water. For Q John announces a mightier one who will baptize with the Holy Spirit and fire; that announcement is preceded by a call to repentance and by harsh accusations and threatening metaphors; the judgment is imminent. In John's expectation Jesus will (also) be the severe judge[37].

Jesus (vv. 9-15)

Verses 9-11: Baptism

It would not be surprising if Q, immediately after John's preaching, also offered a version of the baptism of Jesus. Five minor Mt-Lk agreements seem to point to the existence of a Q text of the baptism.

---

34. Cf. SCHULZ, *Die Spruchquelle*, pp. 368-369, on Luke's redactional infinitives and his postposition of αὐτοῦ in Q 3,17.

35. This is the version of the Greek text in FLEDDERMANN, "John and the Coming One", p. 380. For Q 3,16 see also LAUFEN, *Doppelüberlieferungen*, pp. 96-97.

36. Cf. P. HOFFMANN, *Studien zur Theologie der Logienquelle* (NTA, 8), Münster, 1972, ³1982, pp. 198-233.

37. Cf. recently HAVENER, *The Sayings of Jesus*, pp. 62-67, where we find a radical presentation: in Q 3 John did not yet know who Jesus was. John saw himself as a forerunner of God ("Lord" in v. 4) and announced in the "more powerful one" an apocalyptic figure. In Q 7 we are then confronted with an uncertain Baptist. Of course, for the Q redactor the Baptist is from the beginning the forerunner of Christ (see p. 87).

(1) Matthew in 3,16 and Luke in 3,21 utilize the passive of ἀνοίγω instead of σχιζομένους in Mk 1,10. (2) Matthew has πνεῦμα θεοῦ in 3,16 and Luke, in 3,22, τὸ πνεῦμα τὸ ἅγιον while Mk 1,10 has only τὸ πνεῦμα. (3) Both evangelists write in the same passage ἐπ᾽ αὐτόν while in Mk 1,10 we find εἰς αὐτόν. (4) Both mention the dove after the verb καταβαῖνω while Mark places "as a dove" before this verb. (5) After the baptism both use the name "Jesus" (see Mt 4,1 and Lk 4,1; cf. Lk 3,23)[38]. Just as with regard to the parallels of Mk 1,2-6 here again it has been demonstrated that the two evangelists *can* have independently changed the Markan text into each of their common variants[39]. But once more we must question whether we have to accept the fortuitous coincidence of all these nearly identical changes. Such a coincidence appears highly unlikely.

A strong confirmatory argument is present in the Q temptations narrative. There, in the first and second temptations (see Mt 4,3 and 6 and Lk 4,3 and 9) the devil addresses Jesus with the clause: "If you are the Son of God". The use of this title most probably refers to its presence in the baptism pericope to be postulated for Q. The devil seems to take up the title given by the voice from heaven (cf. Mk 1,11 and parallel texts)[40].

---

38. Cf. the listing in KLOPPENBORG, *Q Parallels*, p. 16 (with bibliography). BOVON, *Das Evangelium nach Lukas*, p. 166, mentions only ἀνοίγω; since in 3,22 Luke follows Mk "bleibt der Rückgriff auf Q unsicher". Cf. KOESTER, *Gospels*, p. 135: "The agreements of Matthew and Luke are very slight and do not justify the inclusion of this pericope [into Q]".

39. Cf. DEVISCH, *De Quelle-hypothese*, pp. 444-488.

40. For SCHÜRMANN, *Lukasevangelium*, p. 197, this is, together with τὸ πνεῦμα, the main argument: "eine ursprüngliche Zuordnung der Versuchungsgeschichte [= Q] zum Taufbericht", and p. 218: "Lukas fand die Berichte von Taufe und Wüstenaufenthalt schon in der Redenquelle kombiniert vor". See also I. H. MARSHALL, *The Gospel of Luke* (NIGTC), Exeter, 1978, p. 150: "The slight agreements with Mt. against Mk. are insufficient in themselves to prove use of another source … But the way in which the temptation narrative (Q) presupposes the divine sonship of Jesus makes it likely that some reference to the Baptism followed the account of John's ministry in Q so as to give a link between John and Jesus"; A. SUHL, *Die Funktion der alttestamentlichen Zitate und Anspielungen im Markusevangelium*, Gütersloh, 1965, p. 99: "nicht unmöglich, dass auch Q eine Taufgeschichte kannte"; U. LUZ, *Das Evangelium nach Matthäus*, Neukirchen-Vluyn, 1985, pp. 150-151 ("wahrscheinlich"); D. KOSCH, *Die eschatologische Tora des Menschensohnes. Untersuchungen zur Rezeption der Stellung Jesu zur Tora in Q* (NTOA, 12), Freiburg (Schw.), 1989, p. 236. Otherwise KLOPPENBORG, *Q Parallels*, p. 16: "The title 'Son of God' in Q 4 does not require an explanatory narrative any more than does the title 'Son of Man', which is by far the more common title for Q"; A. VÖGTLE, "Die sogenannte Taufperikope Mk 1,9-11. Zur Problematik der Herkunft und des ursprünglichen Sinns" (EKK Vorarbeiten, 4), Neukirchen-Vluyn – Zürich, 1972, pp. 105-139 (see pp. 109-110); J. DUPONT, *Les tentations de Jésus au désert* (SN.S, 4), Brugge, 1968, p. 94: "il faut reconnaître d'abord que la manière dont, selon cette source, le diable s'adresse à Jésus en lui disant, dans les deux premières tentations: 'Si tu es le Fils de Dieu', fait naturellement écho à la proclamation de la filiation divine de Jésus au moment du baptême", but: "Il n'en reste pas moins que l'épisode du baptême et celui des tentations nous sont rapportés sous des formes très

A similar remark can be made concerning the anaphorical mention of the Spirit: the Spirit who drives Jesus out into the desert (Q 4,1) is the same Spirit who descended on Jesus after his baptism (Q 3,22).

A reconstruction of Q 3,21-22 must, of course, take into account those minor agreements. But since both Matthew and Luke follow Mark so closely, we cannot know whether or not Q differed much from Mark. One feature must be mentioned. Athanasius Polag remarks that the Markan words of the heavenly voice are hardly a quotation of Isa 42,1: "es hat vielmehr den Anschein, dass die beigefügten Attribute den Sinn der Bezeichnung als 'Sohn' verdeutlichen sollten"[41]. According to Josef Blank the expression ἀγαπητὸς υἱός is original in Mk 12,6 and from there Mark inserted ἀγαπητός in 1,11 and 9,7[42]. Even if we hesitate to accept the originality of the term in 12,6, Mark's threefold use of ἀγαπητός in his gospel and the striking parallelism between 1,11b (σὺ εἶ ὁ υἱός μου ὁ ἀγαπητός) and 9,7c (οὗτός ἐστιν ὁ υἱός μου ὁ ἀγαπητός) suggest that the presence of ὁ ἀγαπητός is due to Markan redaction. If so, the same probably applies to the explicative continuation in v. 11c with ἐν σοὶ εὐδόκησα. Therefore we should not be surprised that in Q 4,3 and 9 the testing devil does not use ἀγαπητός, but only "Son of God". Gerhard Sellin, moreover, notes that in the first half of the Markan gospel the divine sonship of Jesus remains secret so that we may perhaps presume: "Es ist erst Markus, der die Geistesbegabung und die Erwählung zum Gottessohn zu einem nur von Jesus selbst wahrgenommenen Vorgang macht"[43]. One cannot exclude, thus, that Q had a simpler (without ἀγαπητός and ἐν σοὶ εὐδόκησα) and more public manifestation of Jesus as Son of God[44].

différentes; il n'y a pas d'unité organique entre les deux récits" (p. 95). Is this last consideration a sufficient reason to exclude the baptism's presence in Q?

41. A. POLAG, *Die Christologie der Logienquelle* (WMANT, 45), Neukirchen-Vluyn, 1977, p. 153. He assumes in the Markan tradition a strengthening of the visionary elements and reckons with the influence of the transfiguration pericope on the words of the heavenly voice.

42. Cf. J. BLANK, "Die Sending des Sohnes. Zur christologischen Bedeutung des Gleichnisses von den bösen Winzern Mk 12,1-12", in ID., *Der Jesus des Evangeliums. Entwürfe zur biblischen Christologie*, München, 1981, pp. 117-156; repr. from J. GNILKA (ed.), *Neues Testament und Kirche. FS R. Schnackenburg*, Freiburg – Basel – Wien, 1974, 11-41.

43. G. SELLIN, "Das Leben des Gottessohnes. Taufe und Verklärung Jesu als Bestandteile eines vormarkinischen Evangeliums", in *Kairos* 25 (1983) 237-253. We need not discuss here the thesis of this article. According to Sellin Mark used a pre-Markan gospel, very much similar to the so-called Johannine "Semeia-Quelle", with a "Täuferbericht" at the beginning.

44. SELLIN, "Das Leben", p. 242, continues his reasoning: since the object of εἶδεν is the rent heavens and the Spirit in v. 10 but not the voice of v. 11, and since the heavenly voice has its original function in Mk 9,2-8 (v. 7), it would seem that Mark has anticipated

Because of the amount of uncertainty we refrain from reconstructing a
hypothetical Q baptism version.

Verses 12-13: Temptation

The great majority of NT scholars accept the presence of the long
temptation narrative in Q, at least in its final stage: see Mt 4,1-11 and
Lk 4,1-13[45]. The Matthean sequence of the individual temptations is most
probably the original one. We can neglect the discussion of the few
vocabulary differences between Mt and Lk. From the Mt-Lk agreements
at the beginning (compare Mt 4,1-2 and Lk 4,1-2 with Mk 1,12-13) we
learn that the Q introduction had διάβολος, the motifs of fasting and
being hungry, and, most logically, the start of the tempting activity at the
end of the fasting period[46]. No detailed reconstruction of this Q text is
necessary.

Verses 14-15: Preaching in Galilee

Although Mark has used traditional concepts and expressions, the summary in vv. 14-15 is no doubt his own composition[47]. As is well known,
εὐαγγέλιον is a pre-Pauline missionary term. The fact, however, that we
have already detected one or two Markan contacts with Q 7,24-28 (the
Malachi quotation, Q 7,27, and, hypothetically, the notice about John's

that voice in his baptism pericope "um die Geistherabkunft zu einer *geheimen* Epiphanie
zu machen" (p. 242). In the transfiguration pericope "aber hat die Stimme eine genuine
Funktion: Es ist die aus der Sinai-Tradition stammende Stimme aus der Wolke" (*ibid.*).
Already in M. HORSTMANN, *Studien zur markinischen Christologie. Mk 8,27–9,13 als Zugang
zum Christusbild des zweiten Evangeliums* (NTA, 6), Münster, 1969, pp. 91-92: "In der ...
Einheit von Tauf- und Versuchungsgeschichte ... nimmt sich die Himmelsstimme wie
ein Fremdkörper aus, so dass man den Eindruck gewinnt, dass der Evangelist in V 11
den christologischen Gehalt dieser Perikopen zusammengefasst wissen möchte" (p. 91).
We very much hesitate, however, to remove the heavenly voice from the postulated baptism pericope in Q.

45. Cf. the enumeration of the data in KLOPPENBORG, *Q Parallels*, p. 20 ("most authors")
and his discussion on pp. 256-262, and ID., "*Nomos* and *Ethos* in Q", in J. E. GOEHRING,
C. W. HEDRICK, C. WEBSTER (eds.), *Gospel Origins & Christian Beginnings. FS J. M. Robinson* (Forum Fascicles, 1), Sonoma, 1990, 35-48, esp. p. 46: "There is now a broad consensus that the story is the latest addition in the evolution of Q". KOESTER, *Gospels*, p. 137,
maintains that the temptation story requires a common source but that "it is difficult to
prove that this source was Q". He adds: "... the entire opening section must be assigned
to the redaction of this document".

46. Cf. DUPONT, *Les tentations*, p. 82 (on Mt): "La faim de Jésus devait fournir l'occasion des tentations".

47. Cf. DAUTZENBERG, "Die Zeit des Evangeliums", pp. 225-231; EGGER, *Frohbotschaft
und Lehre*, pp. 43-64; VAN OYEN, *Summaria*, pp. 129-153. Otherwise, e.g., besides Pesch,
J. SCHLOSSER, *Le Règne de Dieu dans les dits de Jésus* (EB), Paris, 1980, pp. 91-126.

ascetic life, 7,25) suggests the possibility of a (supplementary?) Q influence on Mark's use of εὐαγγέλιον in vv. 14 and 15 (and, hence, also in v. 1): see πτωχοὶ εὐαγγελίζονται of Q 7,22 (in John's Inquiry, 7,18-23)[48].

Still more attention is merited by an expression from the Q missionary discourse. In Lk 10,9 we read ἤγγικεν ἐφ' ὑμᾶς ἡ βασιλεία τοῦ θεοῦ (cf. 10,11 and Mt 10,7)[49]. We may also refer to the phrase κηρύσσω τὴν βασιλείαν τοῦ θεοῦ in Lk 9,2 (cf. Mt 10,7). Instead of speaking vaguely of contact with a Palestinian Jesus tradition one must ask the specific question whether Mark did not compose 1,14-15 (with κηρύσσων and ἤγγικεν ἡ βασιλεία τοῦ θεοῦ under the actual influence of Q's missionary discourse[50].

And what about μετανοεῖτε in 1,15? We should certainly here mention μετάνοια in Q 3,8. If Mark, however, used Q 10,9 from the Q Mission Speech (Q 10,2-12), he must have also known the ensuing Woes on the Galilean Towns (Q 10,13-15). At the end of his own missionary discourse Mark, in 6,12, seems to have retained the verb μετανοέω present in Q 10,13[51]. So for μετανοεῖτε in Mk 1,15 one may perhaps equally refer to Q 10,13. A number of Q terms and phrases, thus, have parallels in Mk 1,14-15, but a longer, continuous Q parallel cannot, of course, be discerned.

48. For Mark's way of redaction we may perhaps refer to Rom 10 where in v. 15 Isa 52,7 is cited with the verb εὐαγγελίζομαι and where then in v. 16 Paul takes up the idea with the noun εὐαγγέλιον. Cf. DAUTZENBERG, "Die Zeit des Evangeliums", pp. 231-233 and 76-79. He states: "Obwohl das Mk-Ev literarisch jünger ist als die Paulusbriefe, ist die in ihm bezeugte Konzeption vom εὐαγγέλιον τοῦ θεοῦ traditionsgeschichtlich älter als die in den Paulusbriefen erkennbare Konzeption vom εὐαγγέλιον" (p. 79). See ID., "Der Wandel der Reich-Gottes-Verkündigung in der urchristlichen Mission", in G. DAUTZEN-BERG, H. MERKLEIN, K. MÜLLER (eds.), Zur Geschichte des Urchristentums (QD, 87), Freiburg – Basel – Wien, 1979, 11-32.

49. Cf. DAUTZENBERG, "Die Zeit des Evangeliums", pp. 231-233; W. SCHENK, "Gefangenschaft und Tod des Täufers. Erwägungen zur Chronologie und ihren Konsequenzen", in NTS 29 (1983) 453-483: Mark 1,15 is "redaktionell markinisch ... und literarisch von den entsprechenden Formulierugen der Sendungsrede in Q (Mt 10.7; Lk 10.9; vgl. 9.2) her formuliert" (p. 455). It is possible that in Q 10,9 εἰς ὑμᾶς (present in Lk 10,9, absent in Mt 10,7) is original; cf. Q 11,20: ἄρα ἔφθασεν ἐφ' ὑμᾶς. See POLAG, Christologie, p. 69, n. 212; SATO, Q und Prophetie, p. 129, n. 48. Otherwise, e.g., SCHULZ, Die Spruchquelle, p. 407.

50. If this view is correct one can no longer speak of two separate, independent traditions, Q and the "vormarkinische Tradition", as is done, e.g., in H. MERKLEIN, Jesu Botschaft von der Gottesherrschaft. Eine Skizze (SBS, 111), Stuttgart, 1983, p. 25 (cf. p. 37). Furthermore, it strikes us as strange that F. MUSSNER, "Ansage der Nähe der eschatologischen Gottesherrschaft nach Markus 1,14.15. Ein Beitrag der modernen Sprachwissenschaft zur Exegese", in J. AUER, F. MUSSNER and G. SCHWAIGER (eds.), Gottesherrschaft – Weltherrschaft. FS R. Graber, Regensburg, 1980, 33-49, in his discussion of the tradition behind the clause "the rule of God is at hand", does not even mention Q (see pp. 44-46).

51. For Mark and "repentance" see note 28 above.

Conclusion

In Q the two pericopes of the Baptism of Jesus (3,21-22) and the Temptations of Jesus (4,1-13) were probably linked together not only through historical sequence but also on the level of the narrative by the presence in Jesus of the Spirit and the title "Son of God". Heaven approves of Jesus; the Spirit is in Jesus a dynamic force; the devil tries to divert Jesus from his divine call; the angels serve the victorious Jesus. Where Israel failed, there, in the desert, Jesus, "Son of God", remained faithful.

We may conclude the search for Q parallels which could be termed "an essay in detection"[52]. For each small unit in Mk 1,2-13 there is, we think, certainty or strong (be it unequal) probability that Q possessed its own text. Even for 1,1 and 1,14-15 Q influence is not to be excluded. Moreover, not only for each of these five or six passages individually is there cumulative evidence, but, taken together, they constitute a remarkable cluster which, because of the amount of convergent data, points in the direction of dependence on Q. A responsible study of Mark should not neglect the possible existence of these earlier texts; they may have been Mark's sources. A comparison forces itself upon us.

Markan Redaction?

Our working hypothesis puts forward that Mark knew Q. Given this supposition a first characteristic must strike every reader of Mk 1,1-15. Mark has drastically shortened the Q version of John's preaching and Jesus' temptations. Why? Could a partial but self-evident and correct answer not be that Mark did not want to copy Q since it already existed and was available in his community: "Mark was written to supplement, but not to supersede Q"?[53] Yet, more can be said. What other redactional motives as regards content were at work in Mark? Even those who reject Markan knowledge of Q must make a judgment about the differences.

52. So the subtitle of the article of J. A. T. ROBINSON, "The Baptism of John. An Essay in Detection", in *NTS* 4 (1957-58) 263-281.

53. B. H. STREETER, "The Literary Evolution of the Gospels", in *Studies in the Synoptic Problem*, pp. 210-227, citation on p. 220. We may quote the full sentence: "just, then, as Q was written to supplement, but not to supersede, a living tradition, so Mark was written to supplement, but not to supersede Q, or some deposit of material very like Q" (pp. 219-220). In this study, Streeter puts forward the idea that Mark quotes Q from memory or that he had matter parallel to Q, "usually a shorter but at the same time a less original-looking form" (p. 219). Are these guesses to the point?

It is generally admitted that with the use of εὐαγγέλιον in 1,1 Mark has innovated in a double way. For the first time a written document is called "gospel" and this gospel which narrates the story of Jesus' public life, with actions and teaching, contains more than the (oral) proclamation of Jesus' death, resurrection and future parousia. In our treatment of 1,14-15 the content of that gospel will be further elucidated.

John (vv. 2-8)

Verses 2-6: Appearance and Preaching

Mark begins his presentation of John the Baptist by citing the Old Testament. John was the prophet-forerunner announced in Scripture. In v. 2bc and v. 3 Mark brings together, rather strangely under Isaiah alone, the quotation from Mal 3,1 (modified by Exod 23,20?)[54] and Isa 40,3[55]. Mark took Mal 3,1 from Jesus' Eulogy of John (Q 7,24-28, see v. 27); in the second clause he omits ἔμπροσθέν σου, probably because of its repetitious character vis-à-vis πρὸ προσώπου σου in the first clause and because of the ensuing Isaiah quotation[56]. In the Malachi quotation of Mk 1,2 God addresses Jesus: "your face", "your way" (cf. v. 11). The second person singular was already present in Q; it is "Q-Gestaltung"[57]. By the insertion of Mal 3,1 Mark identifies John from the very start with the returning prophet Elijah, for Mal 3,1 refers to 3,22-23 (LXX): "Behold, I will send you Elijah the Thesbite…"[58].

If our Q 3,2-6bc reconstruction is correct, Mark in 1,4 explains the meaning of John's activity. John preaches a baptism of repentance for the forgiveness of sins. Mark also emphasizes and broadens the success: "all the region about the Jordan" (Q) becomes "all the region of Judea

54. This is uncertain since the Exodus context is so different. In Q the text diverges to a large extent from Malachi (LXX): omission of καί and ἐγώ (not all manuscripts in the LXX), and instead of ἐπιβλέψεται the verb κατασκευάσει which is more like the Hebrew text.

55. Note the change of τοῦ θεοῦ ἡμῶν into αὐτοῦ (= Jesus Christ).

56. See PESCH, *Markusevangelium*, p. 78: "Mk 1,2c dürfte … mit Rücksicht auf die Korrespondenz zu V 3b (τὴν ὁδόν σου – τὴν ὁδὸν κυρίου) gekürzt sein".

57. SCHENK, "Einfluss", p. 159: "… die Anrede in der zweiten Person [ist] Q-Gestaltung…". According to Schenk (pp. 159-160) the introductory γέγραπται is also taken from Q 7,27 and "in der typisch markinischen Verbindung mit καθώς" repeated in 9,13 and 14,21. Mk 1,2-3 becomes thus for Mark a very weighty "Legitimationszitat". Cf. GNILKA, *Markus*, p. 44: Mal 3,1 gives Mark "die Möglichkeit, den eben genannten Gottessohn von Gott angeredet sein zu lassen. Zudem kann er mit seiner Hilfe die Beziehung des Täufers zum Propheten Elija herstellen".

58. If one assumes dependence on Q for Mk 1,2 the unlikely thesis of TOLBERT, *Sowing the Gospel*, pp. 239-248, according to which the "messenger" is in the first place Jesus himself, is even less convincing.

and all the people of Jerusalem"[59]. They are baptized and, Mark stresses, they confess their sins. We have already seen that repentance, confession and remittal of sins are important for Mark[60].

Verses 7-8: Announcement of the Coming One

The preaching of John is abbreviated and redacted in a radical way[61]. Q 3,7-9 and 17 are completely rejected by Mark; only 3,16b-e is taken up. Since for Mark John is the returned Elijah and thus the prophet-forerunner, since John preaches no more than "a baptism of repentance for the forgiveness of sins" (v. 4), every threat with judgment, every reference to punishment is out of place and, therefore, left out[62].

In 1,7-8, moreover, Mark thoroughly rewrites Q 3,16b-e. The order is changed: from a chiastic Q structure,

A   (I baptize, 16b)
B   (he mightier, 16c)
B' (I not worthy, 16d)
A' (he will baptize, 16e),

to a parallel one (first might and unworthiness, then baptism),

B   (he mightier, 7a)
B' (I not worthy, 7b)
A   (I have baptized, 8a)
A' (he will baptize, 8b)[63].

---

59. Of course, the basic text of Q remains somewhat uncertain.

60. See note 28. We may refer here, by way of example, to the study of B. VAN IERSEL, "Theology and Detailed Exegesis", in *Concilium* 10 (1971), no. 7, pp. 80-89. In his reconstruction of a pre-Markan account (not Q!) he rejects vv. 2-3 (quotation), parts of v. 4 and v. 6, which leaves us with the following text: "And it happened that John baptized a baptism of repentance for the forgiveness of sins" (p. 84). Then follow v. 5 and vv. 7-8. See also the earlier version of this study, "Aanvang van de verkondiging over Jezus Christus", in *Vox theologica* 39 (1969) 169-179.

61. This is convincingly worked out by FLEDDERMANN, "The Beginning of Q", pp. 282-284: Mark knew and used Q 3,16bcde in its final version.

62. Cf. PESCH, "Anfang", p. 119: "Vom Gerichtsprediger Johannes ist in unserer Überlieferung freilich (bezeichnenderweise) nicht die Rede" (Pesch means the pre-Markan tradition independent from Q). STREETER, "Mark's Knowledge and Use of Q", p. 168, calls Mk 1,7-8 "a mutilated fragment" from the Q passage. See also HOFFMANN, *Studien*, pp. 19-20; I. BUSE, "St. John and 'the First Synoptic Pericope'", in *NT* 3 (1959) 57-61: "Mark i.7-8 is only loosely connected with what precedes ... The whole Marcan account gives an impression of abbreviation ... Like his narrative of the temptations of Jesus Mark's story of the baptism of Jesus reads like a summary" (p. 61).

63. Cf. HOFFMANN, *Studien*, pp. 20-22: In Mk "werden nicht zwei Personen, sondern zwei Taufen aneinander gegenübergestellt" and "unter der Voraussetzung, Markus

In Mk we first have: "After me comes he who is mightier than I" (v. 7a); the attention is at once directed toward Jesus; for Mark Jesus "comes after", i.e., later than John[64]. In v. 7b Mark adds κύψας and thus emphasizes John's unworthiness[65]. Then follows the retrospective v. 8a: "I (ἐγώ) have baptized you with water" (verb in the aorist tense). Mark stresses the time break between John and Jesus; John's activity is over. V. 8b again focuses on Jesus: "but he (αὐτός) will baptize you with the holy Spirit". Mark omits "with fire": again, no longer judgment. In retaining "holy Spirit" Mark probably does not have in mind the Christian baptism which gives the Spirit. He rather points to Jesus' work: with the help of the Spirit Jesus will purify and sanctify his disciples[66].

Conclusion

Rudolf Pesch concludes his own redactional analysis as follows: "Wir sehen also in den Vv. 2-8 den Evangelisten Markus nicht am Werk..."[67]. Our findings and guesses point to the opposite view. Mark abbreviates his source text; he inserts the Malachi quotation; he depicts John's prophetic asceticism and sees him, thus, as Elijah *redivivus*. Mark explains John's baptism of preparation theologically. In his vision Jesus is not the severe judge, but the more powerful one who will baptize with the holy

kantte Q, liess sie [= Mk 1,7-8] sich sogar als Glättung und Verbesserung der verschränkten Q-Form verstehen" (p. 21); MARSHALL, *Gospel of Luke*, p. 144: "The order [in Q] ... which separates the parallel clauses about baptism is more likely to be original"; SATO, *Q und Prophetie*, p. 126. Otherwise LAUFEN, *Doppelüberlieferungen*, p. 98: "Der streng antithetische Parallelismus membrorum der Markusfassung ist das Ursprüngliche; durch die Verschränkung der beiden Logien wird diese prägnante, für Priorität bürgende Form zerstört" (discussion on pp. 97-98).

64. Cf. HOFFMANN, *Studien*, pp. 32-33 (somewhat hesistant). PESCH, *Markusevangelium*, p. 83, notices (in the pre-Markan tradition) a "temporale Umdeutung des ursprünglichen lokal, im Sinne der Nachfolge und Jüngerschaft zu verstehenden ὀπίσω μου". He points also to the ensuing "Umformung" of ἔρχομαι to ἔρχεται. According to GNILKA, *Markus*, p. 42, in this verbal change by Mark "artikuliert sich sein Historisierungstendenz"; cf. p. 47: "Vorangestelltes ἔρχεται historisiert die Aussage vom ἐρχόμενος. ... Sie wird in 9 wieder ἦλθεν Ἰησοῦς".

65. Cf. FLEDDERMANN, "John and the Coming One", p. 383: "Mark likes to use redundant participles and there is a fairly close analogy to κύψας in Mark's redundant use of ἀναστάς (1:35; 2:4; 7:24; 10:1) ...". LAUFEN, *Doppelüberlieferungen*, p. 121, notes that it corresponds with the Markan redactional tendency "die dienende Zuordnung des Täufers Jesus gegenüber zu betonen".

66. LAUFEN, *Doppelüberlieferungen*, pp. 121-122, hesitates between the eschatological "Geistbesitz der Christen" and Christian baptism. ERNST, *Johannes der Täufer*, p. 16, rightly, it would seem, is not sure that Mark "an das kirchliche Taufsakrament gedacht hat". He writes: "Wegen des Fehlens weiterer Hinweise im Evangellium halte ich es für wahrscheinlicher, dass er die allgemeine eschatologische Geistausgiessung im Auge hatte".

67. "Anfang", p. 114.

Spirit. A more radical rewriting, a more personal act of composing by an author is hardly conceivable.

Jesus (vv. 9-15)

Verses 9-11: Baptism

"It is significant that Mark does not mention the people in his portrayal of Jesus' baptism. ... From v. 8 on all that remains for John is to baptize Jesus privately; then he disappears from the stage"[68]. Is the Markan choice of the verb σχίζομαι in v. 10 inspired by Isa 63,19b? A positive answer may be too bold[69]. It has recently been brought forward that Mark has employed the verb here, and only once again in 15,38, not without purpose. In 1,10 "the Spirit descended upon Jesus, and the Father declared that Jesus is his beloved Son. Now [in 15,38] the curtain of the temple is torn from top to bottom and the centurion confesses what the reader already knows from the baptism, that Jesus was truly the Son of God"[70]. For the reader the prologue (vv. 1-13) is the hermeneutical key to Mark.

The use of the absolute τὸ πνεῦμα in v. 10 (and v. 12) is perhaps anaphorical *vis-à-vis* v. 8, or, even more likely, Mark may have wanted to indicate in this way a Spirit nuance different from that in v. 8. Εἰς αὐτόν instead of ἐπ᾽ αὐτόν is scarcely accidental: the abiding presence of Spirit in Christ is emphasized[71].

Matthew and Luke hardly differ from Mark in their Baptism of Jesus pericope; they were using Mk, and Mark used Q. It is, therefore, almost impossible to determine exactly where and how Mark might have edited his Q source. Did he "historicize" this baptism by means of the temporal and topographical introduction of v. 9a? This might be so but must remain uncertain. If our reconstruction on pp. 23-26 is correct, in v. 11

---

68. FLEDDERMANN, "John and the Coming One", p. 383.

69. Cf. PESCH, *Markusevangelium*, pp. 90-91: "kein zwingerder Hinweis auf Jes 63,19b" (p. 91). The Septuagint version has ἀνοίγω.

70. MATERA, "Prologue", p. 14. Cf. H. M. JACKSON, "The Death of Jesus in Mark and the Miracle of the Cross", in *NTS* 33 (1987) 16-37, esp pp. 21-24. S. MOTYER, "The Rending of the Veil: A Markan Pentecost?", in *NTS* 33 (1987) 155-157.

71. Cf. PESCH, "Anfang", p. 126: "Der Geist kommt zu Jesus (εἰς αὐτόν...), zu ständigem, bleibendem Besitz. Jesus wird als der eschatologische Geistträger ausgezeichnet" (but otherwise ID., *Markusevangelium*, p. 91). A. FEUILLET, "Le baptême de Jésus d'après l'Évangile selon Saint Marc (1,9-11)", in *CBQ* 21 (1959) 468-490, however, notes: "Marc emploie volontiers εἰς pour ἐπί. ... Il ne convient donc pas d'insister sur la différence avec Matthieu et Luc" (p. 477). We are not convinced with regard to a possible εἰς-ἐπί equivalence.

Mark strengthened and explained Q's "my Son": he added ἀγαπητός (cf. 9,7 and 12,6) and probably also ἐν σοὶ εὐδόκησα. In his expansion of v. 11b Mark is certainly also influenced by Isa 42,1. We may further assume that υἱός μου in v. 11 "provided" Mark, as it were, with the title υἱὸς θεοῦ in his opening verse (1,1). So "Anfang, (1,11) Mitte (9,7) und Ende (14,61f; 15,39) des Evangeliums sind durch die *Gottesaussagen* ausgezeichnet"[72]. For Mark the aorist εὐδόκησα is probably not "timeless" ("I *am* well pleased"), but refers to what Jesus did in v. 9b: the Father, one could say, congratulates the Son for his gesture and attitude; the Father took pleasure in the Son's baptism, God *has been* well pleased[73].

Verses 12-13: Temptation

Did Mark use the Q temptation narrative? The majority opinion maintains he did not[74], but our findings suggest he may have done so and, even more, if the baptism pericope was part of Q, he had before him passages already linked together[75]. He shortens the temptation narrative in the most drastic way: there is no division into a threefold temptation; there are no citations and no fasting nor hunger. Only the bare essentials are retained. Against his custom Mark utilizes the substantive εἰς

72. PESCH, *Markusevangelium*, p. 97. He continues "und zwar in planmässiger Steigerung: die Offenbarung am Jordan gilt Jesus allein, die auf dem Verklärunsberg den drei vertrauten Jüngern; nach Jesu Selbstbekenntnis vor dem Hohen Rat, nach seinem Tod spricht der heidnische Hauptmann (als Vorbild der Gläubigen) das Bekenntnis aus". Before this he had written: "unbeabsichtigt oder vom Evangelisten beabsichtigt"! Cf. also GNILKA, *Markus*, p. 60.

73. This explanation goes against the common opinion. M. ZERWICK and M. GROSVENOR, *Grammatical Analysis of the Greek New Testament*, Rome, 1981, p. 101, e.g., explain the εὐδόκησα: "if not a constative (global) aorist, the aorist probably representing Semitic perfect of a verb denoting a state, and so may = present: 'I am well pleased with, my favour rests on'".

74. See, e.g., GNILKA, *Markus*, p. 56: "Jedenfalls darf man als Vorlage nicht den Bericht der Spruchquelle ... annehmen, da dieser ganz anderen Inhaltes ist"; and the long discussion in DUPONT, *Tentations*, pp. 80-97, whose conclusion is: Mark's tradition "constitue donc simplement à nos yeux une source parallèle" (p. 94). Cf. SCHÜRMANN, *Lukasevangelium*, p. 219: "Mk hat gewiss nicht dies [= Q] gelesen, sonst hätte er wohl anders erzählt"; also PESCH, *Markuevangelium*, pp. 89 and 96, n. 49; H. MAHNKE, *Die Versuchungsgeschichte im Rahmen der synoptischen Evangelien. Ein Beitrag zur Christologie* (BBET, 9), Frankfurt a/M – Bern – Las Vegas, 1978, pp. 21-23; and, recently, E. BEST in the preface to the second edition of *The Temptation and the Passion: The Markan Soteriology* (SNTSMS, 2), Cambridge, 1990, p. xv.

75. Otherwise, e.g., MAHNKE, *Versuchungsgeschichte*, pp. 39-42 and 210, n. 65, who, however, on pp. 183-190 shows preference for the position that in a late stage both baptism and temptation were added to Q: "Die Versuchungsgeschichte setzt eine Begebenheit voraus, in der der Gottessohntitel verwendet wird" (p. 187).

τὴν ἔρημον in v. 12[76]: he may here have taken up the term used in vv. 3 and 4 *and* in Q. The ending clause of v. 13 (καὶ οἱ ἄγγελοι διηκόνουν αὐτῷ) seems to betray Mark's acquaintance with Q: although fasting is not mentioned by him, the service of the angels presupposes this[77].

For Mark the temptation lasts forty days (otherwise in Q). The Spirit "drives out" (ἐκβάλλει, active voice) Jesus[78]. The devil is called Satan[79]. Without the threefold specification of Q and its double "if you are the Son of God", Mark's ἦν ... πειραζόμενος becomes vague. In v. 13b Mark writes in a rather mysterious way: "and Jesus was with the wild beasts". Since this detail and the angels' service in v. 13c must probably be situated after the temptation[80], they may point to the peace of the Garden of Eden. If an allusion to the peace in paradise is present, Mark depicts the tempted but victorious Jesus as a new, sinless Adam[81]. How different is this from Q where an Israel typology comes to the forefront!

"An increasing number of interpreters" (so Best) claim that in vv. 12-13 Mark, otherwise than Matthew and Luke (and Q) in their respective temptation pericopes, does not speak of Jesus' temptation or attempted seduction by Satan but of a test in which Jesus was the victor[82]. We are hesitant to assume such a radical modification and think that Mark, just as Q, means temptation to sin.

---

76. In 1,35.45; 6,31.32 we have ἔρημος τόπος (see also 6,35).

77. DUPONT, *Tentations*, p. 83, writes: "En parlant du service des anges, la notice de Marc n'invitait pas à penser que Jésus eut à souffrir de la faim au désert". Is this so? If, as is often assumed, v. 13b ("and he was with the wild beasts") indicates Jesus' victory over the temptation, v. 13c ("and the angels ministered to him"), with or notwithstanding the imperfect διηκόνουν, constitutes a reaction to something connected with that temptation, more specifically, it would seem, to Jesus' fasting or hunger. This holds, I think, even if Mark now alludes to angels once minstering to Adam and Eve in the Garden as was thought in Jewish speculation.

78. BAUER-ALAND think that the verb does not always (and not in Mk 1,9) point to "violence".

79. Mark never writes διάβολος. One is rather perplexed at the statement of PESCH, *Markusevangelium*, p. 98: "Σατανᾶς begegnet im Mk-Ev nur traditionell". See the opposite and more correct view in, e.g., GNILKA, *Markus*, p. 57: "Satan – der von Markus bevorzugte Teufelsname".

80. Cf., e.g., A. FEUILLET, "L'épisode de la tentation d'après l'Évangile selon Saint Marc (1,12-13)", in *EstBibl* 19 (1960) 49-73, esp. pp. 72-73: "... la compagnie des bêtes sauvages n'est dans le second évangile que la conséquence et comme une expression équivalente de la défaite du Tentateur" (p. 73). The imperfect tenses in v. 13bc cause "a certain inherent inconsistency" (BEST, *Temptation*, p. xvii).

81. Cf. PESCH, "Anfang", pp. 13-14; *Markusevangelium*, pp. 95-96: "die plausibelste Erklärung des kurzen, dunklen Textes" (p. 95); GNILKA, *Markus*, p. 58; GUELICH, "The Beginning", p. 9. See also BEST, *Temptation*, pp. xvi-xvii.

82. For the recent discussion see BEST, *Temptation*, pp. xv-xxiii: "The Testing".

Verses 14-15: Preaching in Galilee

With v. 14 Mark continues his biographical outline. By means of the phrase "after John was delivered" Mark separates Jesus from John (μετά; cf. the aorist indicative ἐβάπτισα in v. 8), as well as points to John's end, similar to that which will befall Jesus[83]. Ἦλθεν ὁ Ἰησοῦς εἰς τὴν Γαλιλαίαν corresponds with ἦλθεν Ἰησοῦς ἀπὸ Ναζαρὲτ τῆς Γαλιλαίας (v. 9). Just as John preached (κηρύσσων) a baptism of repentance (v. 4), so Jesus preaches (κηρύσσων) the gospel of God.

The careful critical analyses[84] of vocabulary, stylistic characteristics, structure and content[85] of vv. 14-15 should convince us that Mark himself has composed this summary. Mark, of course, has used traditional motifs. Today a distinction is made between Mark's dependence on hellenistic missionary language ("Missionssprache": esp. εὐαγγέλιον, κηρύσσω, μετανοέω and πιστεύω, and their combinations) and his use of Palestinian Jesus tradition (esp. ἤγγικεν ἡ βασιλεία τοῦ θεοῦ)[86]. The

---

83. Even with the reading καί (so N[25]; in N[26] δέ) at the beginning of v. 14 there is still a break. See KAHMANN, "Marc. 1,14-15", pp. 85-86. The verb παραδίδωμι in Mk often has the nuance of persecution, imprisonment or death; cf. G. BERÉNYI, "Gal 2,20: a Pre-Pauline or a Pauline Text?", in *Bib* 65 (1984) 490-537. See (a) for John: 1,14; (b) for Jesus: 3,19; 9,31; 10,33; 14,10.11.18.21.41.42.44; (c) for the disciples: 13,9.11.12. ERNST, *Johannes der Täufer*, p. 37, writes: "Der Täufer ist in seinem gewaltsamen Lebensende der Prototyp des leidenden Menschensohnes Jesus".

84. See references in n. 47. Before his own analysis VAN OYEN, *Summaria*, pp. 120-126, briefly discusses three works on Markan style. E. J. PRYKE, *Redactional Style in the Marcan Gospel. A Study of Syntax and Vocabulary as Guides to Redaction in Mark* (SNTSMS, 33), Cambridge, 1978; D. B. PEABODY, *The Redactional Feature of the Author of Mark: A Method Focusing on Recurrent Phraseology and its Application* (Diss. Southern Method. Univ.), 1983; P. DSCHULNIGG, *Sprache, Redaktion und Intention des Markus-Evangeliums. Eigentümlichkeiten der Sprache des Markus-Evangeliums und ihre Bedeutung für die Redaktionskritik* (SBB, 11), Stuttgart, 1984, ²1986. Besides these more recent publications Van Oyen also often refers to J. C. HAWKINS, *Horae Synopticae. Contributions the the Synoptic Problem*, Oxford, 1899 and sec. ed. Grand Rapids, 1968; F. NEIRYNCK, *Duality in Mark. Contributions to the Study of the Markan Redaction* (BETL, 31), Leuven, 1972; L. GASTON, *Horae Synopticae. Word Statistics of the Synoptic Gospels* (SBS, 3), Missoula, 1973; M. FRIEDRICH, "Tabellen zu markinischen Vorzugsvokabeln", in J. SCHEIBER, *Der Kreuzigungsbericht des Markusevangeliums* (BZNW, 48), Berlin – New York, 1986, pp. 395-433: "Exkurs".

85. Cf. EGGER, *Frohbotschaft und Lehre*, p. 40: A comparison with the parallel passages in Mt and Lk "zeigt wie stark" Mk 1,14-15 "in bezug auf Inhalt und Struktur durchkomponiert ist und sich auf Wesentliches konzentriert", and also p. 45: "die einzelnen nebeneinandergestellten Aussagen beleuchten einander: dass die Zeit erfüllt ist, wird näher erklärt durch die Aussage, dass die Gottesherrschaft sich genaht hat. Die Umkehr wird genauer beschrieben als Glauben an das Evangelium". So many commentators.

86. Cf. EGGER, *Frohbotschaft und Lehre*, pp. 46-51; VAN OYEN, *Summaria*, pp. 45-49. Behind that Jesus tradition possibly lies the earthly Jesus. See also J. GNILKA, *Jesus von Nazaret. Botschaft und Geschichte* (HTKNT Supplementband, III), Freiburg – Wien – Basel, 1990, p. 154, n. 29.

weighty question that remains is precisely what Mark meant by "gospel".
He opens his writing in v. 1 with the christocentric phrase "the gospel of
Jesus Christ" (i.e., probably "about, concerning", obj. gen.): Mark refers
to the good news proclaimed by the Church and now found in his writing that follows. In v. 14 Jesus proclaims "the gospel of God" (subj. gen.?)
and in v. 15b "the gospel"[87] refers back to the theocentric expression of
v. 14 ("the gospel of God") and to its summarized content in v. 15a[88].
Can more be said?

   Given the possibility that in v. 15 Mark anticipated ἤγγικεν ἐφ᾽ ὑμᾶς
ἡ βασιλεία τοῦ θεοῦ from the Q Mission Speech 10,9, one should pay due
attention to the following differences[89]. "At first glance this [= Mk 1,15]
seems to be the same as the Q text [and its context]: the nearness of
the kingdom and the demand for repentance"[90]. In Mk, however, it is
Jesus who proclaims while in Q those sent by Jesus must proclaim this
announcement[91]. The words ἐφ᾽ ὑμᾶς are missing from Mk; this certainly makes the announcement more general and open. There is no reference to miracle (otherwise in Q 10,13-15, Woes on the Galilean Towns).
Further, the clause ἤγγικεν ἡ βασιλεία τοῦ θεοῦ in Mk 1,15 is preceded
by a salvation-historical reflection, a "prophetic exclamation"[92], i.e.,
πεπλήρωται ὁ καιρός: twice the same structure with a verb in the perfect
tense in front. The Markan Jesus, moreover, immediately indicates what
his proclamation implies on the part of the listeners[93]; he adds "repent

----

   87. In v. 15 the article is certainly anaphorical: believe in the gospel just mentioned
in 1,14.
   88. Cf., e.g., GUELICH, "The Beginning", p. 12; E. E. LEMCIO, "The Intention of the
Evangelist Mark", in *NTS* 32 (1986) 187-206: "Mark distinguishes between the gospel
which Jesus proclaimed about the inauguration of God's Rule and the Evangelist's own
kerygma that God had begun in Jesus" (p. 189).
   89. For this paragraph see LÜHRMANN, "Mark and Q", pp. 66-69, and DAUTZEN-
BERG, "Die Zeit des Evangeliums", p. 232. Dautzenberg further writes: "In theologie-
und traditionsgeschichtlicher Hinsicht, erscheint Mk 1,14f als Weiterentwicklung der in
Q erkennbaren Aufnahme und Deutung der Basileia-Verkündigung Jesu" (p. 233).
   90. LÜHRMANN, "Mark and Q", pp. 67-68.
   91. Cf. LÜHRMANN, "Mark and Q", p. 68: "So whereas in Q the nearness of the kingdom of God is the content of the disciples' preaching, who directly continue Jesus'
preaching, in Mark the nearness is bound to the gospel which they have to proclaim".
   92. Cf. KAHMANN, "Marc. 1,14-15", p. 91, who underlines that the clause "the time
is fulfilled" is a hapax legomenon in the NT. He aptly distinguishes on pp. 93-97 two
Markan uses of the absolute ὁ καιρός: the already fulfilled time in which God's kingdom
is at hand (1,15); and the future end time (13,33 and 12,2) in which the kingdom of God
will come with power (cf. 9,1). With these two time-moments, connected with one
another in tension, Mark "covers" the time-period of the Church.
   93. It would seem that this implication (the imperative) is not just reaction to what has
occurred (the perfect tenses). What is asked for is also preparation for the eschatological

and believe in the gospel" and thus replaces ἐφ᾽ ὑμᾶς (if original in Q)[94]. For Mark the coming of God's kingdom is the kernel of the gospel. In a programmatic way Mark, by means of v. 15, places proclamation and appeal at the very beginning of Jesus' public career[95].

For the composition of vv. 14-15 one must certainly not minimize Mark's use of the vocabulary and motifs of his hellenistic Christian milieu[96]. The other influence, however, that of the Palestinian Jesus tradition, has now become, we think, more concrete. In vv. 14-15 Mark used Q, especially its Mission Speech. Through that perhaps direct influence the Markan gospel about Jesus Christ is (also) God's gospel which Jesus proclaimed, saying: "The rule of God is at hand"[97].

future. *Contra*, e.g., EGGER, *Frohbotschaft und Lehre*, pp. 44-46. See MUSSNER, "Ansage" and also "Gottesherrschaft und Sendung Jesu nach Mk 1,14f. Zugleich ein Beitrag über die innere Struktur des Markusevangeliums", in *Praesentia salutis. Gesammelte Studien zu Fragen und Themen des Neuen Testamentes*, Düsseldorf, 1967, pp. 81-98.

94. See n. 49. The verb πιστεύω does not occur in Q (but see πίστις in Q 7,9 and 17,6). Whether "die auffällige Einmaligkeit der Konstruktion πιστεύειν ἐν τῷ εὐαγγελίῳ" (PESCH, *Markusevangelium*, p. 103), pleads for tradition is less than certain. In view of the phrase πίστις ἐν (see Col 1,4; Eph 1,15; 1 Tim 3,13 and 2 Tim 3,15) the expected sense "believe in the gospel" is by far the most probable. On the expression of Mark see also GNILKA, *Markus*, pp. 64-66; MERKLEIN, "Die Umkehrpredigt", p. 39; KOESTER, "Kerygma-Gospel", p. 369, n. 4, and ID., *Gospels*, p. 13, n. 2; SCHLOSSER, *Règne*, p. 105; SÖDING, *Glaube bei Markus*, pp. 133-142. Just as for the genitive in v. 1 (obj. *and* subj.; see e.g., pp.222-223 and 234-235) and for εὐαγγέλιον in v. 1 and vv. 14-15 (christological *and* theological; see, e.g., pp. 209-227), so also for πιστεύω in v. 15 Söding in his long exposition wrongly, I think, connects the two meanings of believing and trusting, "beide Komponente ..., die der Annahme des 'Kerygmas' und die des Vertrauens auf die frohe Botschaft des Evangeliums" (p. 142; cf. e.g., pp. 299-305).

95. Cf. LÜHRMANN, "Mark und Q", p. 68: "... wherever in the following chapters Mark says that Jesus preached or taught without mentioning any specific content, 1,15 is to be inserted as the message to the people of Galilee".

96. Cf. EGGER, *Frohbotschaft und Lehre*, p. 53: "Traditionsgeschichtlich liegt die Bedeutsamkeit von Mk 1,14f darin, dass hier ein kurzer literarischer Beleg dafür gegeben ist, dass Ausdrücke der Missionssprache zur Formulierung von Aussagen über den irdischen Jesus verwendet werden". MUSSNER, "Ansage", p. 48, n. 18: "Der zweifache 'Eröffnungstext' in Mk 1 (i.e., v. 1 and v. 15) bringt eine enorme Spannung in die markinische Vita Jesu, bestimmt ihre innere Struktur und stellt, was die Lösung dieser Spannung angeht, die grösste theologische Leistung des Markusevangeliums".

97. Cf. DAUTZENBERG, "Die Zeit des Evangeliums", pp. 78-79: Mk 1,14-15 "ist aus den Voraussetzungen des palästinschen Judenchristentums und der Jesustradition erklärbar und ableitbar". For a valuable reflection on the literary and theological ingredients on the Markan "gospel", see, e.g., EGGER, *Frohbotschaf und Lehre*, pp. 47-49; VAN OYEN, *Summaria*, pp. 45-46; and 136-138; and DORMEYER, "Die Kompositionsmetapher". According to Dormeyer "Gottesherrschaft" is the "Inhaltskern" of Mark's gospel, "ein zentrales Inhaltssegment, das aber für Bedeutungsanreicherung ... offenbleibt" (p. 455).

Conclusion

Pesch writes: "Der Evangelist Markus hat also ... in die Überlieferung 1,9-15 nur am Schluss (vielleicht auch εὐθύς in V. 10!) eingegriffen"[98]. Again, our results greatly differ. Mark may have taken over vv. 9-10 (not v. 11!) from Q quite literally, but as far as Jesus' temptations are concerned, his abbreviating procedure is unexpectedly radical. Did he shorten that lengthy Q description in order to come as soon as possible to the gospel message of Jesus? Perhaps, but it is difficult to be certain. At any rate, in vv. 14-15 Mark is creatively most active. "Mark 1:14-15 is a concise *summary* of the content of the preaching of Jesus, the only one in the Gospel. Its position at the beginning of Jesus' ministry affects the reader's view of the entire narrative. It invites the reader to supply the 'general content' of Mark 1:14-15 as the substance of Jesus' message, wherever Jesus is described as preaching or teaching..."[99].

Marcus interpretator

Our working hypothesis consisted of two specific assumptions: a maximal extent of Q and Mark's knowledge of Q in its last stage[100]. Neither of these two assumptions can be taken for granted. There are, however, serious arguments for accepting the presence in Q even of such pericopes as 3,2-6 (the Appearance of John) and 3,21-22 (the Baptism of Jesus). To cite Streeter once more: "Thus at the outset we are struck by the fact that the first thirteen verses of Mark, so unlike his usual picturesque diffuseness, read like a summary of a longer and fuller account..."[101]. But this up till now has been a minority position. Even fewer people, I suppose, would be willing to consider Mark's knowledge of a fully developed Q source, not to speak of a direct Q influence on Mk 1,14-15. Yet our analysis has led us, I think, to a more appropriate insight into Mark's editorial activity. His presentation of John and Jesus is decidedly later, more christologically conditioned than that of Q. Once we accept Q as

---

98. "Anfang", p. 115.

99. C. W. HEDRICK, "The Role of 'Summary Statements' in the Composition of the Gospel of Mark: A Dialog with Karl Schmidt and Norman Perrin", in *NT* 26 (1984) 289-311, quotation on p. 294.

100. Cf. SCHENK, "Einfluss", p. 161: Q contains "die einzigen bekannten vormarkinischen Quellenstücke und damit wohl den gewiesenen Ausgangspunkt und die beste Grundlage, um die markinische Redaktionsarbeit einigermassen kontrollierbar sicher zu bestimmen".

101. "Mark's Knowledge and Use of Q", pp. 168-169.

his source text, Mark's way of redacting and composing can be much better understood. But notwithstanding unmistakable dependence on Q, the evangelist manifests a remarkable independence with regard to content. Mark's far-reaching modifications of Q are guided by personal vision. How, then, does Mark in 1,1-15 depict John and Jesus?

John

For Mark John the Baptist is above all the forerunner of Jesus Christ, the Elijah who returns for his eschatological task. John is the prophet (cf. 11,32), the messenger who prepared the way for Jesus Christ. By preaching and administering a baptism of repentance for the forgiveness of sins John clears a straight path for the Lord Jesus Christ. He proclaims that after him comes one mightier than he. He states that his baptism was only with water and at the same time plainly admits that his career is over. The mightier one, Jesus from Nazareth in Galilee, although baptized by John in the Jordan, will himself baptize the people whom John addresses with the holy Spirit. In the Markan gospel, already in 1,1-15, there can be no misunderstanding about the identity and function of the Baptist.

When one compares Mark's picture of John with that of Q, the most striking feature undoubtedly is the complete absence in Mk of judgment and threat. Of course, just as in Q the Baptist in Mk also preaches repentance, but he does not use the reproachful, insulting address "vipers' brood", he does not refer to Abraham their father and to God who can make children out of these stones, he does not mention the wrath to come, the axe laid to the trees and the tree cut down and thrown on the fire, nor the winnowing shovel and the fire that can never be put out. No judgment, but forgiveness of sins. Mark's presentation of the Baptist is concentrated on the preparatory baptism of repentance and the announcement of the coming of an ἰσχυρότερος[102].

An overall vision of the Markan Baptist should, of course, consider also the other passages: 2,18-20 (on fasting), 6,14-29 (the martyr's death of John, cf. 8,28), 9,2-13 (Elijah), and 11,27-33 (on Jesus' authority)[103].

---

102. Cf., e.g., GNILKA, Markus, p. 45: "Da Markus von der Gerichtspredigt nichts berichtet, wird die Wegbereitung ganz im Sinn der Vorläuferschaft interpretiert, die auf den messianischen Kyrios ausgerichtet ist".

103. Cf., e.g., the more recent studies on John, such as W. WINK, John the Baptist (SNTSMS, 7), Cambridge, 1968; J. BECKER, Johannes der Täufer und Jesus von Nazareth (BSt, 63), Neukirchen-Vluyn, 1972; ERNST, Johannes der Täufer; more briefly, GNILKA, Jesus, pp. 79-86.

In 1,14 Mark writes "when John was arrested". The suffering and death of John, a prefiguration of that of Jesus as well as an example for Jesus' followers, cannot but complete that picture in an impressive way. "Now when Mark speaks of the sufferings of John we see how completely Mark has integrated him into the gospel of Jesus Christ. John's suffering as Elijah incognito prepares the way for the fate of Jesus, and serves as an example to the persecuted Christians..."[104].

Jesus

"Jesus Christ, Son of God" is named in the opening verse of Mark's gospel. Jesus is very much present in the section on John, vv. 2-8. Already in v. 2 he is addressed by God through Scripture: see "ahead of you" and "your way". See also "the way of the Lord" and "his paths" in v. 3; "the mightier one" in v. 7; and "he will baptize you with the holy Spirit" in v. 8.

The Spirit descends "into" him (v. 10: εἰς) and drives him out into the wilderness (v. 12). If there is an Adam typology in v. 13, it is not emphasized. In v. 11 Jesus is addressed for the second time by God, this time through a voice from heaven: "You are my beloved Son; in you [at your baptism] I have been well pleased". For Mark, in the whole of vv. 1-15 Jesus is above all the beloved, Spirit-driven Son of God. We know to what a degree the title "Son of God" controls the entire Markan gospel (see 9,7; 12,6; 14,61-62; and 15,39)[105].

The coming of Jesus into Galilee is depicted in a brief but imposing manner. John is arrested; Jesus is now alone, on his own. Jesus proclaims God's gospel. The basic content of this gospel is provided in direct discourse: "the time has arrived; God's kingdom is at hand". Jesus at once adds the appeal: "you must repent and believe in the gospel (of God)". While κηρύσσω, εὐαγγέλιον (to a certain extent), ἤγγικεν ἡ βασιλεία τοῦ θεοῦ and μετανοέω are Q language, other terminology (such as the noun καιρός and the verbs πληρόω and πιστεύω) is brought in by Mark himself. Verses 14-15 are a thoroughly Markan composition. Through this small unit Mark confronts his readers succinctly, solemnly, with Jesus'

---

104. WINK, *John the Baptist*, p. 17.
105. One thinks here, of course, of the study of P. VIELHAUER, "Erwägungen zur Christologie des Markusevangeliums", in E. DINKLER (ed.), *Zeit und Geschichte. FS R. Bultmann*, Tübingen, 1964, 155-169; reprinted in P. VIELHAUER, *Aufsätze zum Neuen Testament* (TBNT, 31), München, 1965, pp. 199-224. See also note 72 above.

gospel of God, with proclamation and appeal. Mark's "gospel about Jesus Christ, the Son of God" (v. 1) is not only Jesus Christ crucified and risen; the forerunner John the Baptist and the earthly activity of Jesus of Nazareth also belong to it: "das Evangelium umgreift eine ganze Geschichte"[106].

Conclusion

One cannot but admire Mark's startling, highly original treatment of both John and Jesus in 1,1-15. Was Mark hereby not helped, steered, and inspired by Q, however much he might have altered it? To this question, we repeat, it is not possible to provide a definitively positive, mathematically certain answer. However, a reasonable possibility, indeed a probability, of Mark's use of Q has been suggested. If Q in its final stage contained all the units postulated, then it can no longer be taken as a pure sayings source. It is on the way to becoming a story of events[107]. Q's incipient biographical nature, then, may also have influenced Mark in creating the gospel genre[108]. All this invites us all to rethink, in the new redaction-critical framework, an old, somewhat neglected question[109].

106. PESCH, "Anfang", p. 138. Cf. DAUTZENBERG, "Die Zeit des Evangeliums"; DORMEYER, "Die Kompositionsmetapher"; LEMCIO, "Intention", p. 201.

107. KLOPPENBORG, *Formation*, p. 262, states: It is a virtual consensus that Q in its final stages "was moving *toward* a narrative or biographical cast. The fusion of Q with the Marcan narrative in Matthew and Luke only continued what had already begun in the last stages of Q redaction".

108. Cf. HOFFMANN, *Studien*, p. 16, n. 8; SCHENK, "Einfluss", p. 163.

109. We have done what SCHENK, "Einfluss", p. 163, also intended to do: "Worauf es zunächst ankam, war darzulegen, dass sich eine vernachlässigte Fragestellung unter den derzeitigen Bedingungen durchaus als sinnvoll mögliche und hilfreiche Fragerichtung anbietet".

We may refer to some of our earlier studies on Markan passages: "Die Logia-Quellen von Markus 13", in *Bib* 47 (1966) 321-360; *Die Redaktion der Markus-Apokalypse. Literarische Analyse und Strukturuntersuchung* (AnBib, 28), Rome, 1967; *Marcus interpretator. Stijl en boodschap in Mc. 3,20–4,34*, Brugge, 1969; "Redaction and Theology in *Mk., IV*", in M. SABBE (ed.), *L'Évangile selon Marc. Tradition et rédaction* (BETL, 34), Leuven, 1974, ²1988, 269-308; "Jesus and the Law: An Investigation of Mk 7,1-13", in *ETL* 53 (1977) 24-82, reprinted in J. DUPONT (ed.), *Jésus aux origines de la christologie* (BETL, 40), Leuven, ²1989, 358-415 and 428-429; "Q-Influence on Mark 8,34–9,1", in J. DELOBEL (ed.), *Logia. Les paroles de Jésus – The Sayings of Jesus* (BETL, 59), Leuven, 1982, 277-303.

Additional Note

Reference should now be made to H. T. FLEDDERMANN, *Mark and Q. A Study of the Overlap Texts. With an Assessment by F. Neirynck* (BETL, 122), Leuven, 1995. Fleddermann also defends Mark's dependence on Q. See also our methodological reflections in no. 4 (pp. 62-64) and no. 5 (pp. 77-78) of this volume.

3

A Compositional Study of Mark 3,20-35

In this third study, reference may be made to the opinion of Jens Schröter in *Erinnerung an Jesu Worte*[1]: Q and Mark brought together oral traditions, not written texts; one must distinguish between *Rezeption* by Q or Mark and *Redaktion* by Matthew and Luke, between *Überlieferungskritik* of the oral traditions and *Literarkritik* of the written texts[2]. In his recent publication, *Hearing the Whole Story*, Richard A. Horsley goes even further[3]: The gospel of Mark is an oral-derived text; it is a written text for oral performance, a text meant for an oral communication environment, a mere "libretto" of the performance, the copy of a narrative that was regularly performed orally[4]. For Horsley, Mark is hardly a real author or writer.

In assuming Mark's dependence on Q, a written text, this compositional study on Mk 3,20-35[5] is intended to refute such theories as well as to defend Mark as an author who displays literary competence. It can perhaps be called a discourse analysis. Three questions will guide the analysis: Is it possible to elucidate the surface structure of Mk 3,20-35? Can a

---

1. J. SCHRÖTER, *Erinnerung an Jesu Worte. Studien zur Rezeption der Logienüberlieferung in Markus, Q und Thomas* (WMANT, 76), Neukirchen-Vluyn, 1997.

2. See the second methodological remark in "The Son of Man" on pp. 62-64 of this volume.

3. R. A. HORSLEY, *Hearing the Whole Story: The Politics of Plot in Mark's Gospel*, Louisville, 2001. Cf. the recension by I. McDONALD, "Book of the Month", in *ExpT* 113 (2002) 306-308: "This book is a 'must' for all interested in the study of Mark. Its single-minded concern for the oral nature of the culture shared by Jesus and Mark is a much-needed correction to Markan studies" (McDonald, however, also notes that the plea is "overdone").

4. Cf. HORSLEY, *Hearing the Whole Story*, passim. We may quote, e.g., p. 56: "A written text functioned as an *aide-mémoire*, a silent record of a much richer experience"; p. 59: "Mark gives virtually no indication that he is using written texts"; p. 62: "... the Gospel of Mark ... must have begun and continued in oral performance"; p. 234: "... the developers, composers, and performers of Mark's story"; p. 265, note 28: "It may be the chimera of the modern print-culture-based scholarly imagination that a single prototype of Mark ever existed".

5. The same could be done with, e.g., Mark 4,1-34 or 13,5b-37.

better insight be reached as to how the evangelist Mark is writing and composing his texts? And what is the line of thought, what is Mark's reasoning in this section of his gospel? The study will consist of three main parts.
To begin with, a first reading of Mk 3,20-35 will be offered. Then the
parallel texts in Matthew's and Luke's gospel must be considered insofar as they witness to a Q source. Finally, I shall return to the Markan
text in order to trace in detail the composition and the line of thought[6].

A First Reading of Mark 3,20-35

A Literal Translation (Revised Standard Version)

20 Then he went in a house[7]; and the crowd came together again, so
that they could not even eat. 21 And when his relatives[8] heard it, they went
out to seize him, for they said, "He is beside himself".

22 And the scribes who came down from Jerusalem said, "He has
Beelzebul, and by the prince of demons he casts out the demons".

23 And he called them to him, and said to them in parables, "How can
Satan cast out Satan? 24 If a kingdom is divided against itself, that kingdom cannot stand. 25 And if a house is divided against itself, that house
will not be able to stand. 26 And if Satan has risen up against himself and
is divided, he cannot stand but is coming to an end. 27 But no one having entered a strong man's house can plunder his goods[9], unless he first
binds the strong man; then indeed he may plunder his house. 28 Truly, I
say to you, all sins will be forgiven the sons of men, and whatever blasphemies they utter; 29 but whoever blasphemes against the Holy Spirit
never has forgiveness, but is guilty of an eternal sin" –

---

6. This study brings together the data and results of three previous publications:
(1) *Marcus interpretator. Stijl en boodschap in Mc. 3,20–4,24*, Brugge – Utrecht, 1969,
pp. 15-99; (2) "The Relatives of Jesus in Mark", *NT* 16 (1974) 241-258", republished in
D. E. ORTON (ed.), *The Composition of Mark's Gospel*. Selected Studies from *Novum Testamentum* (Brill's Readers in Biblical Studies, 3), Leiden – Boston – Köln, 1999, 85-102;
(3) *Once More Astonished: The Parables of Jesus*, New York, 1981, pp. 112-124.
    See also H. T. FLEDDERMANN, *Mark and Q. A Study of the Overlap Texts (with an
assessment by F. Neirynck)* (BETL, 122), Leuven, 1995, pp. 41-73 and 271-277.
    7. RSV translates εἰς οἶκον: he went "home". The expression in 3,20 is ambiguous.
    8. "His relatives" (or: "his family", NRSV) renders and concretizes the vague expres-
sion οἱ παρ' αὐτοῦ (literally: "those from him"). Here the meaning probably is "those close
to him"; the data in 3,31-35 point to his relatives, indeed. Yet see J. PAINTER, "When Is
a House not Home? Disciples and Family in Mark 3.13-35", in *NTS* 45 (1999) 498-513,
who claims that there exists a link between 3,20-21 and 3,13-19 and proposes the following, it would seem, far-fetched interpretation: "In 3.20-21 the twelve came out to restrain
Jesus because the crowd was charging him with madness".
    9. RSV translates v. 27a more freely and, it would seem, less correctly: "But no one
can enter a strong man's house and plunder his goods".

30 for they had said, "he has an unclean spirit".

31 And his mother and his brothers came; and standing outside they sent to him and called him. 32 And a crowd was sitting about him; and they said to him, "Your mother and your brothers are outside, asking for you". 33 And he replied, "Who are my mother and my brothers?" 34 And looking around on those who sat about him, he said, "Here are my mother and my brothers! 35 Whoever does the will of God is my brother, and sister, and mother".

Content and Surface Structure

After the appointment of the Twelve (3,13-19), a new narrative begins in Mark's gospel. Jesus enters a house and the crowd gathers around him in such great numbers that Jesus and his disciples do not even find time to eat (cf. 3,20). When his family hears this they set out to seize him, for they say: "He is beside himself" (v. 21). Subsequently the scribes also express their opinion concerning Jesus. They make grave accusations: "He has Beelzebul" (3,22b; cf. also 3,30), and: "by the prince of demons he casts out demons" (v. 22c). Then follows Jesus' self-defence (vv. 23-29). In 3,31 the relatives appear once again: his mother and brothers, i.e., obviously those who had set out in v. 21. They remain outside but send someone to call Jesus who is seated in the house with the crowd around him. Jesus answers the message sent in to him with the words: "Who are my mother and my brothers?" Thereupon he looks at the people sitting around him and says: "Here are my mother and my brothers! Whoever does the will of God is my brother and sister and mother!" (cf. 3,31-35).

The same scene is found in 3,20-21 as well as in 3,31-35. Jesus is in the house surrounded by a crowd. It is said in v. 21 that his "relatives" (literally "those from him", but in the *Koine* Greek this expression refers to persons intimately linked to someone, e.g., his friends, his family) set out, and they are said to arrive in v. 31. In the latter verse they are also explicitly identified as his mother and his brothers. In 3,21 they set out "to seize him". From this we can infer why they call him in v. 31. The statements of the scribes (v. 22) are clearly intended to parallel what the relatives are said to be thinking in v. 21, and these charges are the occasion for the lengthy insertion within the pericope about the relatives.

The whole pericope 3,20-35 is constructed according to a pattern in which the parts correspond to one another in a concentric way, like circles around a central core:

A   Jesus' busy activity and the setting out of the relatives (vv. 20-21)
B   Accusations by the scribes (v. 22)

C   Jesus' self-defense (vv. 23-29)
B'   Repetition of one of the scribes' accusation (v. 30)
A'   Presence of the relatives; Jesus' words about true kinship (vv. 31-35)[10].

In *A* the relatives themselves take the initiative (they set out); in *A'* this leads to a reaction by Jesus (his statement about true kinship). With this saying he dissociates himself from a kinship understood in a purely natural way. This does not necessarily imply an actual hostility, but there is a certain separation and distance. *A'* is a response by Jesus and also as such it forms a counterpart to *A* which concerns the attitude of the relatives. They claimed, but obviously without much understanding of the meaning of his activity, that he "was beside himself". *A* and *A'* thus correspond, and most probably they did in the conception and intention of the redactor, in content and composition and to a certain extent also as regards vocabulary. With them Mark created a framework, a narrative which functions as an inclusion[11].

Obviously the accusation repeated in *B'* is materially the same as that in v. 22b, i.e., part of *B* – an indication that Mark has purposely constructed this schema. Not only is the content identical, but the speakers are also the same. And, in both cases the verbs "say" and "have" are used. On the other hand, verse 30 is shorter (one accusation, not two) and instead of "Beelzebul" or "prince of the demons" Mark simply speaks of an "unclean spirit".

Jesus' self-defense is the central section *C*; it is embedded within two inclusive circles *A A'* (the relatives) and *B B'* (accusation of the scribes). *B* and *B'* obviously provide the occasion for the discourse of *C*. After the introductory clause (v. 23a), Jesus first speaks of Satan and, by means of

---

10. Cf. recently J. MARCUS, *Mark 1–8* (AB, 27), New York, 2000, p. 278 (with reference to V. Robbins, 1989): "The present Markan composition is chiastically structured:
    3:20-21   Jesus' relatives
    3:23-26   Charge of demonic agency
    3:27   Parable of the strong man
    3:28-30   Charge of demonic agency
    3:31-35   Jesus' relatives".
Verse 22 is missing and the framing character of v. 22 and v. 30 is not pointed out. According to B. M. F. VAN IERSEL, *Mark. A Reader-Response Commentary* (JSNT SS, 164), Sheffield, 1998, p. 118; "3,7–4,1 forms the concentrically arranged sequence": 3:7-12 (lake); 3,13-19 (mountain), 3,20-30 (house); 3,31-35 (outside); 4,1 (lake). But what about the criteria for this arrangement, solely position and place? A brief but better analysis of the structure of Mk 3,20-35 is provided by J. R. DONAHUE and D. J. HARRINGTON, *The Gospel of Mark* (SP, 2), Collegeville, MN, 2002, pp. 133-134.

11. For PAINTER, "When Is a House not Home?", p. 503, and HORSLEY, *Hearing the Whole Story*, pp. 223-225, there is no "sandwich" structure as far as 3,20-21 and 3,31-35 are concerned.

a comparison with a kingdom and a house (family), he shows that Satan cannot be "divided" (vv. 23b-26). Then follows the figurative statement about plundering the strong man's house (v. 27). The apology ends with a double saying about possible and impossible forgiveness (vv. 28-29).

Matthew, Luke, and Q

For the composition of their gospel both Matthew and Luke have used Mark and, besides material peculiar to each, also the saying source Q. But their way of composing is highly different. In 12,22-50 Matthew follows the Markan narrative and places his text in the same context as Mark. With 11,14-32 this is not the case for Luke.

Matthew 12,22-50

In 12,22-50 Matthew presents all that is contained in Mk 3,20-35, but also adds a number of other data. We may mention the most visible additions:

(a) in vv. 22-23 a blind and dumb demoniac is healed by Jesus; the people present are amazed;
(b) in v. 27 Jesus asks the scribes by whom their sons cast out demons;
(c) in v. 28 Jesus asserts that if he casts out demons by the Spirit of God, the kingdom of God has come;
(d) in v. 30 the saying about who is not with or against me is added;
(e) vv. 38-42 narrate the request by the Pharisees and scribes for a sign and the reply of Jesus;
(f) in vv. 43-45 the return of the unclean spirit is dealt with.

Since all these additions also appear in Luke's gospel their source must be Q. It may be helpful to indicate in a diagram where one can find these additions in the gospel of Luke:

v. 22	cf. Lk	11,14ab (demoniac)
v. 23a		11,14c (astonishment of the crowd)
v. 27		11,19 (your own exorcists)
v. 28		11,20 (the kingdom has come)
v. 30		11,23 (with or against me)
v. 38		11,16 (request for a sign)
vv. 39-42		11,29-32 (Jesus' answer)
vv. 43-45		11,24-26 (return of the spirit)

Luke

Comparing the narrative of Mark with that of Luke one would expect the text units of Mk 3,20-35 to appear somewhere between Lk 6,12-16 ("choosing the Twelve", cf. Mk 3,13-19) and 8,4-8 (the "sower", cf. Mk 4,1-9). These units, however, do not appear in this Lukan context (except for Mk 3,31-35 somewhat further, in 8,19-21 : "relatives; true kinship").

The Beelzebul controversy itself comes later in Lk, at the beginning of his travel narrative (11,14-26). For a more thorough discussion of Mk 3,20-35 the whole section of Lk 11,14-32 should be considered. This section consists of:

> v. 14 (dumb demon)
> v. 15 (accusation "by Beelzebul"; cf. Mk 3,22)
> v. 16 (request for a sign)
> vv. 17-26 (Jesus' self-defense, see v. 15)
>> 17-18: divided Satan (cf. Mk 3,23b-26)
>> 19: your own exorcists
>> 20: the kingdom has come
>> 21-22: parable of the stronger (cf. Mk 3,27)
>> 23: with or against me
>> 24-26: return of the spirit
> vv. 27-28 (hearing and obeying the word of God)
> vv. 29-32 (Jesus' answer, see v. 16).

For Mk 3,28-29, the saying about possible and impossible forgiveness, a parallel is offered by Lk 12,10, which is part of 12,1-12 ("encouragement of disciples").

The Q-Version

As seen above the Matthean text often agrees with that of Luke. These agreements point to Q. This source obviously had its own version of the Beelzebul controversy and the Sign of Jonah. In line with his usual procedure, Matthew conflated the Q-version with that of Mark. Luke placed the texts in his travel narrative. It is not to be excluded that Luke in some way also used Mk 3,20-35 for the composition of 11,14-32. Moreover, he has probably re-ordered and rewritten the Q-text to a certain extent. But all in all, it does seem reasonable to suppose that, as far as content goes, Lk 11,14-32 offers a rather faithful rendering of the Q-version[12].

---

12. The delicate and often uncertain reconstruction of the Greek Q text is here omitted.

What are the implications of this for the Markan text? Did Mark in 3,20-35 use a tradition or source which already differed from Q? It seems unnecessary to assume this. Consequently, it is of interest to indicate the possible Markan redactional reworking of the Q-version. The ten most important changes may be listed at once. (The Q references are taken from Luke's gospel.)

(1) Mark's version omits many elements: the exorcism (Q 11,14ab), the astonishment of the crowd (Q 11,14c), the two applications (Q 11,19-20), and the return of the unclean spirit (Q 11,24-26).

(2) Mark places the pericope concerning the request for a sign (Q 11,16.29-32) at a later point in his gospel (Mk 8,11-12).

(3) In Mk Jesus' accusers are scribes who had come from Jerusalem (cf. 3,22).

(4) Mark doubles the accusation. In Q the text must have been more or less as follows: "He casts out demons by Beelzebul, the prince of demons" (Q 11,15; cf. Mt 12,24). Mark writes first: "He has Beelzebul" (possession), and then: "by the prince of demons he casts out demons" (activity).

(5) Mark mentions Jesus' indirect way of answering ("in parables", 3,23a).

(6) Mark duplicates the comparison. In Q 11,17 the houses (buildings) are part of the kingdom comparison. The "divided" houses which fall illustrate the laying waste of the kingdom. In Mk 3,24-25 two distinct images emerge: a divided kingdom and a divided house (no longer a building but a family).

(7) Mark makes the expression "to bind the strong man" serve as the single positive, allegorical explanation of what an exorcism is. In the Q-version (cf. 11,21-22) this statement probably was but an element of a parable, a short narrative illustrating Q 11,20 and indicating the meaning of an exorcism.

(8) The expression "in parables" (Mk 3,23a) announces not only the double comparison of vv. 24-25 which is interpreted in v. 26, but also, it would seem, the symbolic language in v. 27 that is not further explained. Although the plural form in this stereotyped formula should not be emphasized, it is nevertheless striking that the following apology of Jesus does contain several "parables" or "images".

(9) In 3,28-29 Mark adds the antithetical saying concerning guilt and forgiveness. Such a saying is also found in Q (cf. Lk 12,10 and Mt 12, 31-32), but Mark has altered it considerably[13].

13. Again, no attempt is made to reconstruct the Greek Q text.

(10) Through his redactional work Mark formed a concentric, well-structured unit of text. The creative freedom which he allowed himself in so doing is amazing.

A Second Reading of Mark 3,20-35

A more detailed analysis of Mark's redactional activity of 3,20-35 is possible. First, in three distinct paragraphs, Jesus' self-defense, the scribes' accusations, and the framing pericope of the relatives will be studied. Then, by way of conclusion, the train of thought of the whole section will be traced.

The Apology (vv. 23-29)

V. 23a introduces Jesus' discourse: καὶ προσκαλεσάμενος αὐτοὺς ἐν παραβολαῖς ἔλεγεν αὐτοῖς. Within his self-defense there seems to be a concentric pattern as well:

a　　Refutation (vv. 23b-26)
b　　　Need of exorcism (plundering, v. 27)
a'　Saying on forgiveness (vv. 28-29).

V. 27 (b) is shorter and comprises only a single sentence:

ἀλλ' οὐ δύναται οὐδεὶς εἰς τὴν οἰκίαν τοῦ ἰσχυροῦ εἰσελθὼν τὰ σκεύη αὐτοῦ διαρπάσαι,
ἐὰν μὴ πρῶτον τὸν ἰσχυρὸν δήσῃ,
καὶ τότε τὴν οἰκίαν αὐτοῦ διαρπάσει.

But no one having entered a strong man's house can plunder his goods,
unless he first binds the strong man;
then he may plunder his house.

It may prove impossible to reconstruct the original Q-text behind the heavily Lukan verses of 11,21-22:

When a strong man, fully armed, guards his own palace, his goods are in peace; but when one stronger than he assails him and overcomes him, he takes away his armor in which he trusted, and divides his spoil.

In Q this parable probably had the character of a brief narrative. Mark has condensed the elements of that narrative into a solemn declaration whose metaphors must be interpreted by the reader: the strong man is possessed by Satan and the one who breaks in and plunders is Jesus, the speaker. The rather compact character of v. 27 with its varying repetition of "plunder his goods" and "plunder his house" seems to be the result of editing. Mark wanted to summarize the idea contained in the seemingly colorful Q parable which Luke, however, transmitted to us in his own wording.

Vv. 23b-26 (*a*) are finely structured. In Lk 11,17b-18b one reads:

Every kingdom divided against itself is laid waste, and house falls upon house. And if Satan also is divided against himself, how will his kingdom stand?

In Mark this becomes:

```
1      πῶς δύναται σατανᾶς σατανᾶν ἐκβάλλειν;
2      καὶ ἐὰν βασιλεία ἐφ' ἑαυτὴν μερισθῇ,
       οὐ δύναται σταθῆναι ἡ βασιλεία ἐκείνη·
2'     καὶ ἐὰν οἰκία ἐφ' ἑαυτὴν μερισθῇ,
       οὐ δυνήσεται ἡ οἰκία ἐκείνη σταθῆναι.
1'   καὶ εἰ ὁ σατανᾶς ἀνέστη ἐφ' ἑαυτὸν καὶ ἐμερίσθη,
     οὐ δύναται στῆναι
     ἀλλὰ τέλος ἔχει.
```

```
1     How can Satan cast out Satan?
2        If a kingdom is divided against itself,
         that kingdom cannot stand;
2'       And if a house is divided against itself,
         that house will not be able to stand.
1'   And if Satan has risen up against himself and is divided,
     he cannot stand,
     but is coming to and end[14].
```

To the accusation that Jesus casts out the demons with the assistance of Beelzebul, Jesus in Q at first replies indirectly with a general assertion: every kingdom divided against itself... (v. 17bc). Then comes the application to Satan's kingdom (cf. Lk 11,18ab). Mark, however, articulates that answer in a different way. Satan's kingdom is no more mentioned by him in v. 26; in vv. 24-25 "kingdom" and "house" (= household, family) are two independent metaphors, while in Q, house (= building) was only an illustrative feature of the kingdom's destruction. The two comparisons (vv. 24-25) are framed: v. 23b raises the introductory challenging question and v. 26 drives the point home. In vv. 23b-26 Mark undoubtedly expanded his source. The structure is chiastic. The sentence 2' is longer and by means of the iterative "but is coming to an end" emphasis is added.

After the logion of scattering-gathering (Lk 11,23 = Mt 12,30) Q offered the story of the seven devils (Lk 11,24-26 = Mt 12,43-45). The phrase "unclean spirit" (Lk 11,24 = Mt 12,43) in the redactional v. 30 may be

14. Taken over by S. LÉGASSE, *L'évangile de Marc* (LD Commentaires, 5), Tome I, Paris, 1997, p. 242.

evidence that Mark was acquainted with that section of Q. He omitted
that pericope, or it might be more appropriate to say that he replaced it
in vv. 28-29 by his own version of another Q text: the unforgivable sin
(cf. Lk 12,10 and see also Mt 12,32). The logion in Lk 12,10 reads:

> And every one who speaks a word against the Son of man will be forgiven;
> but he who blasphemes against the Holy Spirit will not be forgiven.

Even though the original Q text is hardly ascertainable, Mark's interpretative rewriting and expanding must have been radical. In Mark's composition the saying obtains a new context. The expression "Son of man"
is no longer mentioned and the blasphemy against the Holy Spirit is now
explicitly related to the concrete accusation of the scribes. The formal
similarity between vv. 28-29 (*a'*) and *a* (vv. 23b-26) is hardly accidental:

Ἀμὴν λέγω ὑμῖν ὅτι
1   πάντα ἀφεθήσεται τοῖς υἱοῖς τῶν ἀνθρώπων τὰ ἁμαρτήματα
2   καὶ αἱ βλασφημίαι ὅσα ἐὰν βλασφημήσωσιν·
2'   ὃς δ' ἂν βλασφημήσῃ εἰς τὸ πνεῦμα τὸ ἅγιον,
1'   οὐκ ἔχει ἄφεσιν εἰς τὸν αἰῶνα,
         ἀλλὰ ἔνοχός ἐστιν αἰωνίου ἁμαρτήματος.

Truly, I say to you
1   all sins will be forgiven the sons of men,
2   and whatever blasphemies they utter;
2'   but whoever blasphemes against the Holy Spirit
1'   never has forgiveness,
         but is guilty of an eternal sin[15].

One finds the same chiastic *1 2 2' 1'*-structure; even the emphasizing
addition in *1'* of the last clause "but is guilty of an eternal sin" is, as to
form, equal to that at the end of *1'* in *a* (vv 23b-26). The major formal
difference is the solemn introduction of the logion "truly, I say to you"
which is perfectly appropriate in the condemning saying which concludes
Jesus' apology. Vv. 28-29 do not correspond with vv. 23b-26 as to content.
The similarity comes solely from the remarkable structural composition.

The Accusations (vv. 22 and 30)

22   Καὶ οἱ γραμματεῖς οἱ ἀπὸ Ἱεροσολύμων καταβάντες ἔλεγον·
        ὅτι Βεελζεβοὺλ ἔχει
        καὶ ὅτι ἐν τῷ ἄρχοντι τῶν δαιμονίων ἐκβάλλει τὰ δαιμόνια.

---

15. Cf. LÉGASSE, *Marc*, p. 245. See R. H. GUNDRY, *Mark*, Grand Rapids, MI, 1993,
p. 176, who also assumes "a largely chiastic structure, but moreover parallels "truly I say
to you" with "rather, he is guilty of eternal sin"".

30 ὅτι ἔλεγον·
πνεῦμα ἀκάθαρτον ἔχει.

22 And the scribes who came down from Jerusalem said,
"He has Beelzebul,
and by the prince of demons he casts out demons".

30 for they had said,
"He has an unclean spirit".

To a certain extent Mark equates relatives (v. 21: they "said, 'He is beside himself'") and scribes (v. 22: they "said, 'He has Beelzebul, and by the prince of demons he casts out demons'"). Yet some data stand in the way of a simple identification of the attitudes of each group. "They said" of v. 21b, as contrasted with that of v. 22b, does not by itself imply an accusation openly expressed; it only gives the motivation of the initiative of the relatives: "they were of the opinion that...". Besides, v. 21b is separated from the accusation in v. 22b by v. 22a which introduces a new scene. Moreover, "he is beside himself (ἐξέστη)" is a statement which, after all, sounds more vague and weaker than the blasphemous charges in v. 22bc.

While in Q (cf. Lk 11,15) the people who utter the accusation are not further specified, Mark indicates that they are "scribes who came from Jerusalem" (v. 22a); "scribes" and "Jerusalem", their place of origin, will reappear in 7,1, equally an editorial verse. Mark doubles the accusation in v. 22b and c. It would seem that the first one is created by Mark; this charge is heavier and more blasphemous than the second. According to the Markan scribes, the fact that Jesus casts out demons by the prince of demons, proves that "he has Beelzebul", i.e., that Jesus is possessed. No wonder that in the redactional verse 30 the same blasphemous accusation is repeated: "for they had said, 'he has an unclean spirit'". Through vv. 22b and 30 the apology is clearly framed. The verses constitute a redactional inclusion.

True Kinship (vv. 20-21 and 31-35)

Verses 20-21

20 καὶ ἔρχεται εἰς οἶκον·
καὶ συνέρχεται πάλιν ὁ ὄχλος,
ὥστε μὴ δύνασθαι αὐτοὺς μηδὲ ἄρτον φαγεῖν.
21 καὶ ἀκούσαντες οἱ παρ' αὐτοῦ ἐξῆλθον κρατῆσαι αὐτόν·
ἔλεγον γὰρ
ὅτι ἐξέστη.

20 Then he went home;
   and the crowd came together again,
   so that they could not even eat.
21 And when his relatives heard it, they went out to seize him,
   for they said,
   "He is beside himself".

While in Q the accusation (cf. Lk 11,15) is preceded by an exorcism
(cf. 11,14), in Mk 3,22 the accusations by the scribes are quite unexpected.
No concrete event presents the occasion for such a charge. Reading
Mk 3,20-22 one has the impression that the scribes' charge (v. 22) is
placed here by way of association with the reaction of the relatives (v. 21).
The absence of a concrete exorcism is most probably a Markan omission
and the appearance of the crowd and the relatives in vv. 20-21 its substi-
tution. V. 20 is a summary of Jesus' activity, compact to the extreme.
It must be understood in the light of 3,7-12 (cf. "the crowd come together
'again'", v. 20). There the disciples had a boat ready for him "because of
the crowd, lest they should crush him" (v. 9); here "the crowd came
together again, so that they [= Jesus and the disciples] could not even eat"
(v. 20). Even more important is to remember that in the pericope of 3,7-
12 many exorcisms took place (the unclean spirits beheld Jesus and fell
down before him, v. 11). So one can conclude that in its own way 3,7-12
prepares the accusation of the scribes. The occasion is not completely
absent; it is present in those many exorcisms. Vocabulary, style (ὥστε …
δύνασθαι) and themes (gathering crowds, not being able to eat, cf. 6,31)
clearly show that v. 20 is a creation by Mark. The introductory redactional v. 20 points forward to v. 21.

In his gospel Mark often structures the narrative by means of an *a b
a'*-pattern, his famous framing technique. Here vv. 21.31-35 are interrupted
by the scribes' accusations and the self-defense of Jesus. From vv. 31-35
one can safely conclude that οἱ παρ' αὐτοῦ ("those from him") are his
relatives: mother and brothers. We have already assumed that the scribes'
accusations of v. 22bc are paralleled with the articulated opinion of the
relatives: "he is beside himself" (v. 21c). Did Mark recollect that strange
opinion from what he had heard, from a specific tradition? This is possible, although Mark himself may have drawn the relatives' view that
Jesus has become insane as a conclusion from the Q accusation "He casts
out demons by Beelzebul, the prince of demons" (cf. Lk 11,15). The Markan
character of both vocabulary and style of v. 21 cannot be denied. The participle ἀκούσαντες (no direct object, cf. 6,14.29 and 11,18) provides the
link with v. 20 effectively.

Verses 31-35

31   καὶ ἔρχεται ἡ μήτηρ αὐτοῦ καὶ οἱ ἀδελφοὶ αὐτοῦ
     καὶ ἔξω στήκοντες ἀπέστειλαν πρὸς αὐτὸν καλοῦντες αὐτόν.
32   καὶ ἐκάθητο περὶ αὐτὸν ὄχλος,
     καὶ λέγουσιν αὐτῷ·
     ἰδοὺ ἡ μήτηρ σου καὶ οἱ ἀδελφοί σου ἔξω
     ζητοῦσίν σε.
33   καὶ ἀποκριθεὶς αὐτοῖς λέγει·
     τίς ἐστιν ἡ μήτηρ μου καὶ οἱ ἀδελφοί μου;
34   καὶ περιβλεψάμενος τοὺς περὶ αὐτὸν κύκλῳ καθημένους λέγει·
     ἴδε ἡ μήτηρ μου καὶ οἱ ἀδελφοί μου.
35   ὃς γὰρ ἂν ποιήσῃ τὸ θέλημα τοῦ θεοῦ,
     οὗτος ἀδελφός μου καὶ ἀδελφὴ καὶ μήτηρ ἐστίν.

31   And his mother and his brothers came;
     and standing outside they sent to him and called him.
32   And a crowd was sitting about him;
     and they said to him,
     "Your mother and your brothers are outside,
     asking for you".
33   And he replied,
     "Who are my mother and my brothers?"
34   And looking around on those who sat about him, he said,
     "Here are my mother and my brothers!
35   Whoever does the will of God
     is my brother, and sister, and mother".

What about the place of vv. 31-35 after the Beelzebul discussion? Lk 11,27-28 may suggest that in Q the Beelzebul discussion was followed by the reaction by a woman and Jesus' saying about true blessedness:

As he said this, a woman in the crowd raised her voice and said to him, "Blessed is the womb that bore you, and the breasts that you sucked!" But he said, "Blessed rather are those who hear the word of God and keep it".

Taking this position as a hypothesis one can explain not only the sequence of vv. 31-35 after the Beelzebul discussion but also the mention of the mother (cf. Q 11,27) by Mark and the content of v. 35. This last verse could be a Markan version of a Q logion (cf. Lk 11,28). In that saying Jesus criticizes the exaltation of mere biological relationship to himself. Was this not the source, we ask, which Mark, in a very creative way, elaborated into a definition of true kinship?

Vv. 20-21 illustrate how Mark is able to create a new scene and to stress the anxiety of Jesus' relatives: they went out to seize him, for they said, "he is beside himself". V. 31 then is the Markan continuation of v. 21. V. 32 is to a great extent repetition of v. 31, but it pictures a sympathetic crowd which the redactor has already mentioned in v. 20 (however, that crowd could also have been suggested by Q, cf. Lk 11,27: a woman "in the crowd"). In Q the woman's reaction was a kind of "choral ending", an exclamation full of admiration for Jesus' apology, a blessing of the earthly mother, corrected immediately by Jesus' blessing of obediential relationship.

Owing to Markan redaction, vv. 20-21 and 31-35 have become an independent, self-contained composition, the two parts of which are separated by the Beelzebul controversy, making its progressive action more relevant. Not only Jesus' mother, but also other relatives are present and active. They fear that Jesus has gone insane. They hear that he has gone home where people are gathering again and they go out to seize him. Meanwhile a confrontation takes place between Jesus and the scribes who accuse Jesus of demonic collusion and even demonic possession. After that confrontation his mother and brothers arrive, stand outside and send for him. The crowd sits around him and passes the message on to Jesus. Jesus answers: Who are my mother and my brothers? He looks over the crowd seated around him and says: Here they are! For whoever does the will of God is my brother, and sister, and mother. The expansion to three terms (+ sisters) as well as the inversion of the sequence (brother, sister, mother) in v. 35 may well be occasioned by the fact that v. 35 functions as the solemn concluding saying.

In view of the evidence of that all-pervading redactional activity it would seem superfluous to postulate for 3,20-21 and 31-35 another source than that which must have been present in Q and of which Lk 11,27-28 probably is a fairly faithful transmission. Yet we should keep in mind that Lk 11,27-28 is possibly *not* a Q text (no indications in Mt 12,26-50!). In that case the Markan text may either be still more redactional than presumed or contain some non-Q tradition (saying and/or incident).

The Train of Thought in Mk 3,20-35

The whole pericope of 3,20-35 appears to be composed in a concentric pattern: A (vv. 20-21), B (v. 22), C (vv. 23-29), B' (v. 30) and A' (vv. 31-35). Moreover in C, the central part, an a (vv. 23b-26) b (v. 27) a' (vv. 28-29) composition has emerged, which itself is cyclic again, certainly not as to content, but strikingly with regard to the form[16].

---

16. Mark's "sandwich" technique is well known. A more elaborate concentric parallelism similar to that in 3,20-35 can be found, I think, e.g., in the parables discourse of Mark 4 and the apocalyptic discourse of Mark 13.

The factor which complicates the study of any cyclic structure is the content of a discourse or narrative in which such a structure is employed. The material of the discourse or narrative does not completely lend itself to the static schema of a central core surrounded by inclusive elements. There is a progression, a development in the line of thought or in the recounting of an event. As long as the inclusion remains completely extrinsic, e.g., restricted to a short call for attention as is the case in Mk 4 ("Listen" and "he who has ears to hear, let him listen", vv. 3 and 9), there is no problem. The included core receives full attention and is not affected by the inclusion. However when the concentric sections are complex and, moreover, serve to structure the discourse or the narrative itself, one has to keep in mind the basic law of the cyclic pattern: the central core is the most important element and deserves more attention, a fact to which the structure itself bears witness. However, in the case of a discourse or a narrative which is constructed in a concentric way, the static restful character of the structural pattern and the dynamic particularity of the discourse or narrative necessarily go together, and many times a tension arises between emphasis on the central core and movement towards the final climax. When applied to Mark 3,20-35, these considerations are helpful to follow the train of thought.

(1) There is a definite progression from A to A', from action to reaction. The initiative of the relatives in A and at the beginning of A' is seen by Jesus as a kind of challenge. With his question and answer he makes a countermove which, with its demonstrative "see" (v. 34), gives the real point of the saying about true kinship and constitutes the climax of the narrative. It is not by accident that Mark twice notes that Jesus' relatives stood *outside* (vv. 31 and 32) and likewise twice mentions that his "new" relatives are sitting *around him* in the house (vv. 32 and 34). The distinction between the two groups of people is more than a matter of mere local separation. In Mark's conception the separation is theologically qualified by Jesus' words (vv. 34b-35).

(2) The accusations of the scribes introduce the discourse and frame the central passage. Practically no progression can be observed from B to B'. V. 30 simply reiterates the charge of v. 22b. Nevertheless, it must be said that the intervening refutation parables and, above all, the judgment saying in C make it possible for Mark to call the "Beelzebul" of v. 22b an "unclean spirit" in v. 30 (cf. also the oppositional v. 29: the Holy Spirit).

(3) The center of the pericope is C. According to the logic of the cyclic structure, it is here that the main point, the basic idea, or the chief event

should be found. And, to a certain extent, this is the case in the passage. The fact that Jesus speaks, the importance of what he says, the length of the discourse, and the conciseness of the argument confirms this. In this central section in turn, *b* (v. 27) constitutes the core. After the rather abstract and logical refutation in *a* (vv. 23b-26), this verse illustrates what an exorcism means (i.e., to bind the strong man) and what is thereby intended (i.e., plundering and regaining possession of that man). Although it is in elusive parable language, we nevertheless learn something concerning the necessity of exorcism and of a kind of mysterious struggle between a strong man and a stronger one[17]. This short parable "in effect is an argument from fact since it echoes John's description of Jesus as 'the stronger one' (1:7) and his own initial activity of vanquishing evil spirits (1:21-28, 32-34, 39; 3,11, 15). Jesus has plundered the house of Satan"[18].

However the central verse, around which everything is concentrically structured in a static way, itself functions as a part of the apology which progresses towards a climax. There are noteworthy differences between *a* (vv. 23b-26) and *a'* (vv. 28-29): *a* is an indignant, but not very aggressive, outburst (cf. "how?" in v. 23b), *a'* contains threatening and condemning language; *a* uses comparisons, *a'* is purely an utterance; *a* is addressed to the scribes in order to refute them, *a'* is introduced by "truly I say to you!" – the first "Amen" saying in Mark – and must have been understood by the hearers and readers as a definitive word, directly relating to their own persons and deeds. The solemnity of this introductory formula elevates *a'* to a climax which is both the conclusion and the culmination of the discourse.

(4) *A A'* is not merely a framework vis-à-vis *B C B'*. Just as in *A A'* the relatives' point of view is censured and corrected by Jesus' statement, so also in *B C B'* the accusation of the scribes is refuted. The scribes are told what happens in an exorcism and are made aware of the sinfulness of their insinuations against Jesus. However all this is rather negative and defensive. Actually, the entire controversy begins and ends with Jesus' more positive words and deeds. He is busy with his disciples and the people. He recruits followers and summons them to fulfill God's will.

---

17. Cf. MARCUS, *Mark 1–8*, p. 279, not without exaggeration: "The centrality of the Parable of the Strong Man is no accident, since it lays bare the underlying cause of the opposition to Jesus both from his family and from the religious authorities: the ineradicable division and fierce enmity between him and the demonic forces that hold the human race in thrall and blind it to its true good".

18. DONAHUE-HARRINGTON, *Mark*, p. 134.

He lets the people sit around him and by his preaching creates a relationship which must be called a new community, a new family. While C ends with an allusion to the negative and sinful self-exclusion of the scribes, A' opens the perspective of a discipleship which is devoted and pleasing to God, which is blessed because obedient. Over against the blaspheming of the Holy Spirit stands the doing of God's will[19].

19. At the end of this study one may ask the question to what extent "orality" is still present in Mark's gospel. It would seem that "literacy" manifests itself in 3,20-35 as elsewhere. Otherwise R. A. HORSLEY (with J. DRAPER), *Whoever Hears You Hears Me: Prophets, Performance, and Tradition in Q*, Harrisburg, PA, 1990, esp. pp. 152-157 ("'Orality and Literacy' Theory: Oral Tradition vs. Written Gospel") and 157-160 ("Oral Theory and Oral-Formulaic Theory Applied to Mark"). Is the beginning of the following statement correct: "As an oral composition or an oral-derived text, Mark stand in continuity with the oral tradition of Jesus' sayings and stories" (p. 59)?

4

The Son of Man
A Note on Mark 8,38 and Q 12,8-9

In Luke 12 we read: "(8a) And I tell you, every one who acknowledges me before men, (8b) the Son of man also will acknowledge before the angels of God; (9a) but he who denies me before men (9b) will be denied before the angels of God". If in the source text, Q 12,8-9, "Son of man" is mentioned in 8b (and also in 9b), his relation to "me" in 8a and 9a can be used in clarifying Q's opinion as to the identity of the speaker of this double saying or, if the saying is authentic, the self-awareness of Jesus himself.

In 1997 the volume *Q 12:8-12* was published in the series Documenta Q[1]; in 1998 the article "Der Menschensohn in Lukas 12.8" by Paul Hoffmann appeared in the journal *New Testament Studies*[2]. In *Q 12:8-12* the section "Confessing or Denying" (Q 12,8-9) is edited by Paul Hoffmann (together with Josef E. Amon, Ulrike Brauner and Thomas Hieke). The main and extensive evaluations of the database on the presence or absence of "the Son of Man" in Q 12,8 are provided by J.M. Robinson (pp. 200-210) and P. Hoffmann (pp. 210-238); in a second contribution (pp. 238-247) Robinson discusses Hoffmann's arguments which are also present in his *NTS* article.

Before summarizing the (unconvincing, I think) position of Hoffmann, I will present first Q 12,8-9 as it is reconstructed in *Q 12:8-12*[3]:

---

1. C. HEIL (volume editor), *The Database of the International Q Project Q 12:8-12* (Documenta Q), Leuven, 1997, pp. 1-425: "Q 12:8-9".

2. P. HOFFMANN, "Der Menschensohn in Lukas 12.8", in *NTS* 44 (1998) 357-379. A first version of this article was read as a main paper at the General Meeting of the SNTS 1997 in Birmingham. Cf. already his "Jesus versus Menschensohn", in L. OBERLINNER and P. FIEDLER (eds.), *Salz der Erde – Licht der Welt. FS A. Vögtle*, Stuttgart, 1991, 165-202, reprinted in P. HOFFMANN, *Tradition und Situation. Studien zur Jesusüberlieferung in der Logienquelle und den synoptischen Evangelien* (NTA, 28), Münster, 1965, pp. 208-242.

3. HEIL (ed.), *Q 12:8-12*, p. 776. The brackets indicate uncertain reconstruction. However, I put the whole of καί in v. 8b outside of the brackets (otherwise on p. 776). See also the synoptical presentation on pp. 2-3 (Q 12,8) and pp. 288-289 (Q 12,9).

8a πᾶς ὃς [ἂν] ὁμολογήσ[ῃ] ἐν ἐμοὶ ἔμπροσθεν τῶν ἀνθρώπων,
  b καὶ [ὁ υἱὸς τοῦ ἀνθρώπου] ὁμολογήσ[ῃ] ἐν αὐτῷ ἔμπροσθεν τῶν ἀγγέλων·
9a ὃς δ ' ἂν ἀρνήσηταί με ἔμπροσθεν τῶν ἀνθρώπων,
  b ἀρνη ... ἔμπροσθεν τῶν ἀγγέλων.

One cannot but notice the lack of symmetry between v. 8b and v. 9b, the alleged uncertainty regarding the verb in v. 9b and the absence of '(the angels) of God' at the end of vv. 8b and 9b.

In this short study I ask whether a careful consideration of Mk 8,38 could not assist us in a better reconstruction of Q 12,8.

No "Son of Man" in Q 12,8-9?

According to Paul Hoffmann it is more probable (*wahrscheinlicher*) that the double Q saying of 12,8-9 did not contain the expression "the Son of man" in its b-clauses. "Son of man" is not present in the Matthean text of 10,32-33 and, according to Hoffmann, Matthew may be more original here than Luke with his "I" in 10,32b and 33b[4]. "Son of man" is equally absent in Luke 12,9b. Hoffmann is of the opinion that Luke inserted "the Son of man" in 12,8b under the influence of the Markan parallel of 8,38[5].

Hoffmann admits that for a great number of Q specialists the Markan text constitutes the *Hauptzeuge* or *Kronzeuge* for a Q text with "Son of man". Yet he claims that Mark himself may have introduced that title in 8,38. This is confirmed, according to Hoffmann, by a close look at Mk 13,26-27 as to the coming of the "Son of man" with the angels. The Markan addition of 8,38b ("when he [= the Son of man] comes in the glory of his Father with the holy angels") does not directly depend on Dan 7,13 but on the already adapted Daniel tradition in Mk 13,26. Verse 27 of this chapter explains why in 8,38b the angels, differently from Dan 7,10, must accompany the Son of man[6].

Regarding the verb of "denying" in Q 12,9b Hoffmann hesitates. At the end of his evaluation in "Q 12:8-9" he appears to opt for the deponent verb with active meaning. However, he concludes the discussion of the verb: "since in my opinion the hypothesis that the Son of man is

---

4. Cf. HOFFMANN, "Q 12:8-9", pp. 230-236; "Menschensohn", pp. 370-374.
5. For the discussion of the Lukan text, see HOFFMANN, "Q 12:8-9", pp. 215-230; "Menschensohn", pp. 359-370.
6. Cf. HOFFMANN, "Q 12:8-9", pp. 246-247; "Menschensohn", pp. 377-378.

introduced by Luke in 12.8 under the influence of Mk 8,38 is more probable, I here too prefer Matthew's text [i.e., the deponent ἀρνήσομαι]"[7].
Yet according to Hoffmann the alternative, an original passive as in Luke
12,9b, can be excluded neither in Q 12,9b nor in Q 12,8b[8].

Hoffmann furthermore pleads for Q 12,8-9 "as a relic of authentic
Jesus tradition". If the original Q saying of 12,8-9 does not contain the
expression "Son of man", the most important argument (*der gravierendste
Einwand*) against its authenticity disappears. It must, however, be stressed
that Jesus here presents himself as witness and paraclete, not as the eschatological judge as elsewhere in Q[9].

I refer to Robinson for what would appear to be the overall decisive
refutation of Hoffmann's argumentation with regard to the absence of
"Son of man"[10]. In view of his detailed argumentation, however, Robinson's conclusion is surprising: "Hoffmann's thorough and cogent advo-
cacy of the alternative that Luke inserted 'son of man' reduces the probability that 'son of man' was here in Q"[11]. On the contrary, I would
argue that Mk 8,38 not only strongly supports the presence of "Son of
man" in Q 12,8-9, but that this verse also offers a number of other data
which can be of help in deciding the original wording of the double saying in Q.

Methodological Remarks

Before indicating the assistance Mark's text may provide in the reconstruction of Q, four methodological remarks seem required.

---

7. HOFFMANN, "Q 12:8-9", pp. 408-410, quotation on p. 410. He further writes:
Luke's "Wahl der Passivkonstruktion erfolgte aus stilistischen Gründen" (*ibid.*). On p. 376
of "Menschensohn" Hoffmann acknowledges that the deponent in Mark 8,38b confirms
the active meaning of the verb in Q.

8. HOFFMANN, "Menschensohn", pp. 376-377; "Q 12:8-9", p. 238: "... die Möglich-
keit, dass auch im Nachsatz des Bekennerspruches eine dem Passiv von 12:9 analoge
Konstruktion ursprünglich verwendet war" constitutes "eine nach wie vor diskutabele
Alternative".

9. HOFFMANN, "Menschensohn", pp. 378-379. For a recent brief and prudent discussion of Q 12,8-9 (with "Son of man") and its authenticity, see J. SCHLOSSER, *Jésus de Nazareth*,
Paris, 1999, pp. 255-258.

10. See ROBINSON, "Q 12:8-9", pp. 240-247.

11. *Ibid.*, p. 247. With regard to the work of the Project Robinson adds: "Hence the
shift from the original relatively assured vote of the International Q Project to the effect
that 'son of man' was in Q should be revised downward to represent more uncertainty".

1. Hoffmann has to posit three independent hypotheses in order to remove "Son of man" from the Q saying: (1) the "I" in Mt 10,32b and 33b is original; (2) Luke inserted the "Son of man" in 12,8; (3) Mark equally introduced the "Son of man" in 8,38. Each hypothesis is defended by a number of arguments: vocabulary, style, context, concepts and christology. Each by itself may carry a degree of probability and within the individual hypothesis the cumulative force of the arguments is not without impact. But the connection of these three suppositions is problematic. This operation leads to hypothesis upon hypothesis and, at the end, to speculative and far-fetched, if not unjustified, constructions[12].

2. In his recent monograph *Erinnerung an Jesu Worte* Jens Schröter[13] repeatedly and almost viscerally defends the opinion that (the author of) Q and Mark independently brought together oral traditions, not already written compositions. One should, therefore, clearly distinguish between *Rezeption* (by Q or Mark) and *Redaktion* (of Q and Mark by Matthew and Luke) and equally between *Überlieferungskritik* (of the oral traditions) and *Literarkritik* (of the written texts). On the level of oral tradition the material (e.g., a saying) does not yet have a fixed and stable form, but is subject to variations. To use Mark in order to reconstruct Q is thus not permitted; moreover, one should not attempt to determine the original shape (*Urfassung*) of the pre-Q and pre-Markan traditions. It would seem that with these views Schröter here is representative of some Q specialists.

Yet other critical exegetes may pause and be astonished by such dogmatic statements. They will have their questions about the duration of the period of oral tradition and about the hypothesis of its unstable condition. They will also point to the language (no longer Aramaic but Greek) and equally to the advanced date of Mark's gospel (around 70). They may claim that in the so-called overlap passages of the synoptic gospels the differences between a reconstructed Q and Mark can to a great extent be explained as due to Mark, i.e., as Markan redaction of

12. Cf. the remarks by C. TUCKETT, "The Son of Man in Q", in M. DE BOER (ed.), *From Jesus to John. FS M. de Jonge* (JSNT SS, 84), Sheffield 1993, 196-215: "Hoffmann makes a powerful case. Yet his theory has to assume coincidental, but independent, redaction of the saying by Mark (cf. Mk 8.38) and Luke into a Son of Man form" (p. 209, n. 1; Tuckett discusses Hoffmann's 1991 study "Jesus versus Menschensohn").

13. J. SCHRÖTER, *Erinnerung an Jesu Worte. Studien zur Rezeption der Logienüberlieferung in Markus, Q und Thomas* (WMANT, 76), Neukirchen-Vluyn, 1997. The author does not accept written pre-Q levels. In this second remark we omit his discusion of the Gospel of Thomas.

such a reconstructed text. Why then, they will ask, postulate loose traditions that by definition are unknowable with regard to both original
vocabulary and form? It would seem that the hypothesis of one fixed tradition or one basic version behind (some of) these overlap texts is worth
considering.

3. Whether Mark is directly dependent on Q or on an oral (or possibly another written) tradition need not affect the discussion in this note.
The two versions of the negative saying-half, present in Mk 8,38 and
Q 12,9, ultimately have their origin in the same saying. Neither is the
position in this paper altered depending on whether or not this saying is
authentic and goes back to the earthly Jesus.

4. In the Markan overlap texts one possesses, I think, in addition to
Matthew and Luke a "third" witness to the texts present in Q[14]. It is
methodologically sound to use the agreements of two witnesses against
one in the reconstruction of the original Q text[15], that is, Matthew and
Luke against Mark, but also Mark and Matthew against Luke or Mark
and Luke against Matthew. It could happen, of course, that the texts that
agree are both secondary and the third one (or none) is original. If need
be, this occurrence has to be considered. Furthermore, it seems imperative first to indicate the plausible Q elements (words and constructions)
and only thereafter to attempt to determine the motives of each author
which may point to editorial changes. It is true, "first" and "thereafter"
can be separated in a methodological reflection, but in practice the two
operations for the most part go together.

Markan Assistance

What are the possibilities that Mk 8,38 provides with regard to Q 12,8-
9? We have to begin with Q 12,9 of which Mk 8,38 is the parallel.

---

14. SCHRÖTER, *Erinnerung an Jesu Worte*, p. 364, n. 276, writes: "Von der Mk-Va-
riante ist dabei zunächst abzusehen. Das immer wieder angeführte Argument, Mk 8.38
spräche für die Ursprünglichkeit der Lk-Fassung ... ist ein klarer Zirkelschluss, da die
Lk-Fassung als Q-Text bereits vorausgesetzt wird" (p. 364, n. 276). One really does not
see why in our approach the use of Mark would constitute a "Zirkelschluss", an instance
of circular reasoning. The three witnesses are evaluated in the Q reconstruction itself;
there is no decision beforehand. On Q 12,8-9, see pp. 361-366, on Mk 8,38, see pp. 389-
396.
15. Since Mark is later than Q, the more original text will be Q or a pre-Q tradition.
For clarity's sake I will here utilize Q to refer to both possibilities.

Q 12,9

It is generally accepted that Mk 8,38 is full of Markan rewriting: the verb ἐπαισχύνομαι (twice, with active meaning), the expressions "of my words" and "in this adulterous and sinful generation" and, above all the addition "when he comes in the glory of his Father with the holy angels" (v. 38c)[16].

Notwithstanding the thoroughly Markan character of this verse, seven items may prove helpful in the reconstruction of Q 12,9:

(1) the expression "Son of man" in 8,38b (not in Matthew nor in Luke, but present in the preceding positive half Lk 12,8b);

(2) the active meaning of the verb in 8,38a and 38b (also in Matthew, not in Luke);

(3) the presence of angels in 8,38c (also in Luke, not in Matthew);

(4) the presence of "his Father" which pleads for the presence in Q of a reference to God: "before the angels 'of God'" (so in Luke; Matthew has twice, in 10,32b and 33b, the "Matthean" expression "before 'my Father in the heavens'")[17];

(5) the beginning of the relative clause in 8,38a: ὅς ... ἐάν (not in Luke; Mt 10,33a generalizes: ὅστις δ᾽ ἄν, cf. Lk 12,8a: πᾶς ὅς ἄν; this gives in Q: ὅς δ᾽ ἄν)[18];

(6) the verb in Q 12,9b may have been a compound: ἀπ-αρνέομαι (so in Luke 12,9b, not in Matthew; in 8,38 Mark has a compound verb [ἐπ-αισχύνομαι] as well; in 8,34 he uses ἀπαρνέομαι: he may have seen this last verb in the denial saying and anticipated it in v. 34);

(7) the preposition ἔμπροσθεν in Q 12,9b instead of the Lukan ἐνώπιον (see Mt 10,33b and cf. Lk 12,8b = Mt 10,32b; not in Mk 8,38 where we have an accusative after ἐπαισχύνομαι; however, the preposition appears soon afterwards in Mk 9,2, perhaps under Q influence).

One cannot but be astonished by the amount of potential Markan aid in the reconstruction of Q. Of course, item (6) and, even more, item (7) are rather tenuous, yet, I think, worth mentioning[19].

---

16. Cf., e.g., J. LAMBRECHT, "Q-Influence on Mark 8,34–9,1", in J. DELOBEL (ed.), *LOGIA. Les paroles de Jésus – The Sayings of Jesus* (BETL, 59), Leuven, 1982, 277-304, esp. pp. 285-288; also H. T. FLEDDERMANN, *Mark and Q. A Study of the Overlap Texts* (BETL, 122), Leuven, 1995, pp. 145-152, esp. pp. 149 and 151.

17. Note that "of God" is omitted in Hoffmann's reconstruction in both Q verses (12,8b and 9b). Cf. also FLEDDERMANN, *Mark and Q*, pp. 146-151, esp. p. 149.

18. See also the reconstruction in HEIL (ed.), *Q 12:8-12*, which we reproduced on p. 61.

19. For the first three items, cf. LAMBRECHT, "Q-Influence", p. 288.

Q 12,8

Among exegetes there is little doubt about the fact that Mark knew but omitted the positive half of the saying that we find in Q 12,8. Mk 9,1 is perhaps partly meant as a compensation for that omission[20]. Be this as it may, Mk 8,38 can also be used, I think, in the reconstruction of Q 12,8 regarding two elements:

(1) the presence of "Son of man" in 8,38b makes its presence in the parallel clause Q 12,8b most likely (so in Luke, not in Matthew);

(2) the beginning of the relative clause in 8,38a (ὃς γὰρ ἐάν) suggests that πᾶς ὃς ἄν in Lk 12,8 is more original (Mt 10,32a has πᾶς ὅστις; cf ὅστις in 10,33a).

Mark, a Third Witness

Each of these items, for both Q 12,8 and Q 12,9, can be elaborated at great length with regard to style and content. Such a study would presumably confirm the above suggestions, but this cannot be attempted in this note. My contention is that primary attention must be given to the literary data before drawing on hypothetical motives and possible modifications. At any rate, the sheer number of items mentioned regarding Q 12,9 (and 12,8) is impressive. Here the term "cumulative" has real meaning. For the reconstruction of Q 12,8-9 Mark can justly be called, in addition to Matthew and Luke, a third witness.

Conclusions

First of all, the analysis in this brief note confirms the majority opinion: the almost certain presence of "Son of man" in both Q 12,8b and 9b. Mk 8,38 is of great assistance in reaching this conclusion. We may aptly add here a quotation from Robinson who reflects on Hoffmann's hypothesis that Mark introduced "Son of man" into 8,38:

> Since one would actually have to postulate also a pre-Markan tradition without "son of man" in order to carry through this hypothesis, this explanation becomes increasingly speculative. The converse explanation is that

---

20. LAMBRECHT, "Q-Influence", p. 289. But see, e.g., SCHRÖTER, *Erinnerung an Jesu Worte*, pp. 391-394, who does not consider the hypothesis that Mark omits the positive half of the *Doppellogion* in Q.

"son of man" was reported by Mark as it existed in the pre-Markan tradition, and that this attestation to the status in the oral tradition suggests that Luke's inclusion of "son of man" in Luke 12:8 was the oldest form of the saying, and hence probably the form used in Q[21].

Whether the pre-Markan form was itself an oral tradition or a written text, perhaps Q (or a form of pre-Q), need not be discussed in this context. One can, however, hardly avoid the impression that Mark's *Rezeption* or *Redaktion* of this saying was in fact the thorough editing of a text (!) such as is present in the reconstructed Q.

A third conclusion should be added. In all probability a reconstruction of Q 12,9 in Greek must correspond to the following English text, a legitimate conjecture, it would seem, of the negative half of the saying: "but who denies me before men, the Son of man also will deny him before the angels of God"[22].

In Greek, Q 12,9b would then read: καὶ ὁ υἱὸς τοῦ ἀνθρώπου ἀπαρνήσεται (or ἀρνήσεται) αὐτὸν ἔμπροσθεν τῶν ἀγγέλων τοῦ θεοῦ.

---

21. ROBINSON, "Q 12:8-9", p. 246.

22. Compare the English translation of Hoffmann's Greek reconstruction of Q 12,8-9 in HEIL (ed.), *Q 12:8-12*, p. 776:

8a   Any one who [may] speak out for me before men,
8b   for him [the son of man] will also speak out before the angels;
9a   but whoever may deny me before men,
9b   'denial' before the angels.

We note again (cf. p. 61) Hoffmann's hesitation regarding 'the Son of man' in v. 8b, its absence in v. 9b, the absence of the genitive 'of God' after 'before the angels' in both vv. 8b and 9b, the clumsy parallelism between v. 8b and v. 9b, the uncertainty regarding the verb of denying in v. 9b.

Scandal and Salt
(Mark 9,42-50 and Q)

The Two Source theory is considered by a large majority of exegetes as the most probable and workable hypothesis for the study of the synoptic gospels. It is generally claimed that the two sources, Mark and Q, are independent of each other. In a number of texts, however, the two sources "overlap"; these texts are notably similar in sense and sometimes in wording. The "source doublets", i.e., those doublets which are not created by the redactional activity of an evangelist but have their origin in the two different sources, remain the object of much investigation. The question can hardly be avoided: which is Mark's source for these overlap texts? Is Mark in these texts independent of Q? For Albert Fuchs a Deutero-Mark employed Q[1]. But could it not be that Mark himself made a selective use of the Q document?

In 1995 Harry T. Fleddermann published *Mark and Q. A Study of the Overlap Texts* where all the overlap sections are examined; he defends the thesis that Mark knew and used the final version of Q[2]. In this brief contribution in honor of a respected colleague and long-standing friend, Albert Fuchs, we propose to analyse a small passage, namely Mk 9,42-50. Because of its connections with 9,33-41 this passage is hardly a self-contained unit[3]. Yet in 9,42 the new topic "scandal" appears and the second person plural of verse 39 and 41 disappears. Moreover, 9,42 may have a Q parallel, the Scandal saying. Another Q parallel is certainly present in 9,50, the Salt saying; verse 50 obviously closes the pericope.

---

1. Cf. his numerous publications listed in the Bibliography of this Festschrift.
2. FLEDDERMANN, *Mark and Q*. For the full reference, see the Bibliography at the end of this contribution, pp. 78-79.
3. The so-called Discipleship Discourse (9,33-50) is interrupted by John's question regarding the strange exorcist in verse 38. The second part properly begins at verse 39. Cf. GUNDRY, *Mark*, p. 507: "The first subsection grows out of a dispute over greatness (vv. 33-37), the second out of a rivalrous confrontation (vv 38-50)". For the analysis of Mark and Q in the whole Discipleship Discourse, see FLEDDERMANN, *Mark and Q*, pp. 153-169 (and bibliography on pp. 221-238; supplement by NEIRYNCK on pp. 304-307), and FLEDDERMANN, "The Discipleship Discourse".

In the following pages we will first try to reconstruct the Q verses and then discuss the Markan composition. In the conclusion we will point out the characteristics of Mark's way of writing and reflect upon our conclusions.

The Reconstruction of the Q Verses

Once should remain duly reserved in reconstructing the exact Greek wording of the Q text as soon as the verbal agreements between Matthew and Luke are missing. This rule of prudence, however, does not weaken the arguments for the presence of a Q text even though doubts remain regarding its exact vocabulary.

Q 17,1-2abc: Scandal

Not everyone is willing to admit that Mk 9,42 possesses a Q parallel[4]. It is believed that Lk 17,2 as well as Mt 18,6 could have their origin only in Mk. Yet several data point to the possibility of a Q text as well.

(1) One might claim that it was the theme "scandal" in Mk 9,42 which caused both Matthew and Luke, independently, to add the saying Q 17,1 (scandals are sure to come, but woe to him by whom they come). This striking coincidence, however, should make one suspicious. There may be another reason, their use of Q 17,2.

(2) Q 17,2 fits in the Q sequence of 17,1 and 3-4 which is also visible in Mt 18,6.15 and 21-22.

(3) The content of Q 17,2 follows that of Q 17,1 in a suitable way. Jesus utters a "woe" to the person who scandalizes; the mention of the severe punishment for that person is, as it were, to be expected.

(4) Between Mt 18,6 and Lk 17,2 there are the following minor agreements. Matthew writes συμφέρει αὐτῷ ἵνα ...; Luke has λυσιτελεῖ αὐτῷ εἰ ... ἢ ἵνα ... In Mk 9,42 the text is καλόν ἐστιν αὐτῷ ... εἰ ... The two verbs immediately followed by the personal pronoun in the dative in Mt and Lk correspond regarding basic meaning; we also note the presence of a ἵνα, although the conjunction is not at the same place and, moreover, differs in sense.

---

4. See, e.g., the hesitation and objections of GUNDRY, *Mark*, p. 523.

The cumulative force of this data makes the presence of the saying in Q most likely, if not certain[5]. Therefore, in Q, it seems reasonable to postulate 17,2 after 17,1. With regard to Q 17,1 one can easily admit that Mt 18,7a is anticipative and redactional. The meaning of what remains is evident: "it is inevitable that scandals come, but woe to the person by whom they come". Q certainly contains the verbs ἐλθεῖν and ἔρχεται, the plural noun σκάνδαλα, and the connection πλὴν οὐαί as well as δι' οὗ. A further reconstruction of the wording would be hazardous and is unnecessary for our purposes.

Even less can be said with certainty about the original vocabulary of Q 17,2. Both Matthew in 18,6 and Luke in 17,2 not only depend on Q but are also heavily influenced by Mk 9,42. Moreover, their minor agreements against Mark are not perfect. So the Q wording of this second saying is, I think, irrecoverable. But a Q saying there was, almost certainly. Its content must have run more or less as that of Lk 17,2abc: "It is better for that person that an ass's millstone be put around his neck and that he be thrown into the sea". There is no reason, it would seem, to presume a content which greatly differs from that in Mk 9,42bcd.

Q 14,34-35ab: Salt

Mt 5,13a, a clause heavily edited and adapted by the evangelist, suggests that in Q 14,34 a statement like that of Lk 14,34a must have been present: "Salt is good" or "salt is a valuable substance". Such a positive qualification of salt is needed for the implicit warning which follows in verses 34bc and 35. Q 14,34a points to a truth which is generally admitted. Therefore, it may have a concessive nuance: "True, salt is good, yet...". It cannot but remain uncertain whether καλόν (cf. Lk 14,34a) is Markan or was also part of Q. There is little doubt with regard to the Greek Q text of 14,34b: "but if salt has lost its taste (μωρανθῇ)". Since ἁλισθήσεται in Mt 5,13c most probably is obtained from Mk 9,49[6] and in Mk, too, is redactional[7], we can assume that in Q 14,34c the verb, opposed to that in Q 14,34b, is ἀρτυθήσεται (like μωρανθῇ also a third

---

5. For the opposite position, see NEIRYNCK, "The Minor Agreements and Q", especially pp. 57-59 with reference to, e.g., SCHLOSSER, "Lk 17,2 und die Logienquelle".

6. According to FLEDDERMANN, *Mark and Q*, p. 167, Matthew assimilates the verb to the word ἅλας in verse 13ab.

7. I think that Mark redacts already under the influence of Q 14,34 which he quotes in verse 50.

person singular, future, passive, and with the same grammatical subject). The clause is a rhetorical question: "by what will it be seasoned?"

We must accept that Q 14,35 contains two parts. Only a few Greek details are common to Mt and Lk: the negation in 35a, the verb "to throw" and ἔξω in verse 35b; these are the Q elements. Perhaps the noun γῆ (Lk 14,35a; cf. Mt 5,13a) also belongs to Q 14,35a. To decide more about the Greek wording of this Q verse, as well as about its original length, would not be wise. However, the sense of Q 14,35 must have been as follows: that salt "is no longer fit for the land; people throw it out"[8].

The Markan Text

Our working hypothesis is that Mark knew and used the Q verses we have tried to reconstruct. The question to be answered in this second part is whether, in that hypothesis, we can explain and better understand Mark's way of composing. Mk 9,42-50 is best divided into verses 42, 43-49 and 50[9].

Mark 9,42

In a rather loose way, by means of a third γάρ, Mark has joined 9,41 to 9,38-40 (the pericope on the strange exorcist): "For whoever gives you a cup of water to drink because you bear the name of Christ, truly I tell you that he will by no means lose his reward". What follows in 9,42 is meant as the opposite to verse 41. In verse 42a the idea of scandal is taken from Q 17,1 but its structure is very much like that of verse 41a: an indefinite noun-clause: ὃς ἄν with the aorist subjunctive. Verses 41 and 42 are connected by καί. The expression "one of these little ones" reminds the reader of "one of such children" in verse 37. By adding in verse 42 the qualification "who believe in me"[10] these little ones are no longer just children; they have become weak believers. Mark links the expression to

---

8. For a discussion of the salt logion in Q, cf. KEA, "Salting the Salt"; HAINZ, "Salzloses Christentum?".

9. In addition to the commentaries, cf., e.g., SCHNACKENBURG, "Mk 9,33-50"; VON WAHLDE, "Mark 9:33-50"; HENDERSON, "'Salted with Fire'" (with 9,42-50, a unit of imprecatory rhetoric in which the Markan Jesus adjures the potential leaders – a strange approach).

10. On the substantial doubt regarding the presence of εἰς ἐμέ in the authentic text of Mk 9,42, see METZGER, Textual Commentary, p. 86: strong attestation but perhaps origin in the Matthean parallel.

what is already supposed in verse 41: the disciples who receive a cup of
water are but humble people, according to verse 42: little ones who
believe in Christ. But does Mark really intend this identification?

The construction καλόν ἐστιν αὐτῷ μᾶλλον εἰ in verse 42b may be a
rather awkward rewriting of Q by Mark. In verses 43, 45 and 47 a dative
and μᾶλλον εἰ are no longer present and the conjunction ἤ ("than")
appears; so in those verses, too, καλόν means "better"[11]. In verse 42b αὐτῷ
refers back to ὅς of verse 42a (and no longer to the person of the woe-
saying of Q). The rest of verse 42b is probably more or less the same as
the text in Q.

The most eye-catching features in Mark's use of Q are the absence of
the idea of the scandals' inevitability and of the "woe"-exclamation[12]. Mark
inserts the saying into his discourse on discipleship: just as you disciples
can be helped, so also little believers (you?) can be scandalized. Mark thus
concretizes the undetermined utterance of Q 17,1a. The person who can
be brought to sin is a believer. Yet, one should admit that verse 42 is somewhat unexpected (just as verse 41 was in its own way). The line of thought
is not smooth. Furthermore, the change from second person plural to the
third person singular and that from "because you bear the name of Christ"
to "one of these little ones who believe" are not without tension.

Mark 9,43-49

A close reading reveals both similarities and differences between, on the
one hand, verse 42 and, on the other, verses 43.45.47. The verb in the subordinate clauses is the same, but the tense of the subjunctive in the last
three clauses is present, the grammatical subject is a member of the body,
and the direct object is three times σέ (second singular over against the
plural in vv. 39 and 41). All three clauses are conditional, each one introduced by καὶ ἐάν. In the main clause we have an identical καλόν ἐστιν
without μᾶλλον; yet, as already indicated, an added ἤ ("than") indicates
that its meaning remains "better". "It is better" is now followed by an

---

11. For καλόν (ἐστιν) + dative + εἰ or ἐάν ("better"), cf. Mk 14,21 and Mt 26,24; 1 Cor
7,8 ("well" or "better"). For καλόν + dative + ἤ + infinitive ("better"), cf. 1 Cor 9,15. For
καλόν ἐστιν + infinitive clause + ἤ ("better"), cf. Mk 9,43.45.47 and Mt 18,8.9. For καλόν
ἐστιν + infinitive or infinitive clause ("well"), cf. Mt 17,4; Mk 9,5; Lk 9,33; Rom 14,21;
1 Cor 7,1.26; Gal 4,18. See further SNYDER, "The *Tobspruch* in the New Testament".

12. Cf. FLEDDERMANN, *Mark and Q*, p. 163: Mark "dropped the clause [i.e., the necessity of scandals] because for him scandal means falling into unbelief so he could never
admit that scandals were necessary" (with a reference to Mk 4,17; 6,3 and 14,27). For a
"woe"-saying similar to that of Q, see 14,21 which Fleddermann discusses on pp. 164-166.

infinitive construction which, as it were, three times expresses a preference for the endurance of bodily mutilation to that of eschatological punishment ("hell") which is more severe than that in verse 42 ("sea").

If one omits the end of verse 43 ("to the unquenchable fire"[13]) as well as the whole of verses 48-49, three highly parallel sentences appear; they consist of an "eventualis" followed by the speaker's opinion in the event that the case should occur. There remains a slight variation of terms through which a certain monotony is avoided. Mark may be at least partially responsible for some of these terms. Some of the terms are conditioned, of course, by the different parts of the body which cause one to sin.

In verse 43 the expression "the unquenchable fire" explains the loan word from Hebrew ἡ γέεννα and is most probably added by Mark himself since for his readers the term is no longer intelligible. Fleddermann takes the expression as "an anticipation of the quotation from Isa 66:24 LXX in v. 48"[14]. By means of that quotation in verse 48 Mark stresses the physical pain and its lasting character. The LXX version of the last verse of the book of Isaiah was adapted to its new context: the added ὅπου refers to hell and, instead of futures, Mark uses present tenses which underline the duration.

There can be hardly any doubt that verse 49 still belongs to this subunit. The γάρ highlights the pain of the punishment; the term "fire" of verses 43 and 48 recurs. In verse 49 the "fire" remains that of judgment and condemnation[15]. The positive notion of purification through fire does not seem to be present[16]. I doubt that Mark intends the small clause of verse 49 to refer to Lev 2,13[17]. The meaning of the verb ἁλισθήσεται is evidently metaphorical. Its origin is most probably to be found in ἅλας of the Salt saying of Q. By this motivating clause Mark again emphasizes the (physical) pain of fire which can be compared with salt in an open wound. "Everyone" (πᾶς) generalizes but is not universalistic; it seems to

---

13. For the variant readings see METZGER, *Textual Commentary*, p. 87.

14 Cf. FLEDDERMANN, "Discipleship Discourse", p. 69.

15. Cf. HAINZ, "Salzloses Christentum", p. III: "Es ist der Gerichtsgedanke, der 9,42ff und 9,49 verbindet". Otherwise, e.g., TAYLOR, *Mark*, pp. 412-414: "the fire of 49 has nothing to do with that of 48" (p. 413).

16. Otherwise TITRUD, "Mark 9:49 Revisited" (salt and fire have both positive and negative effects); LARSEN, "The Use of γάρ and the Meaning of Fire in Mark 9:49".

17. Cf. METZGER, *Textual Commentary*, pp. 102-103. Only in the secondary variants is the reference obvious. Metzger describes the hypothetical history of the text, suggesting that at a very early period a scribe found in Lev 2,13 "a clue to the meaning of Jesus' enigmatic statement" (p. 103).

point to all people who give in to the temptations spoken of in verses 43-48, maybe also to the "scandalizers" of verse 42[18].

That in verses 43, 45 and 47 Mark uses traditional material is confirmed by his addition in verse 43 and his editorial comments in verses 48-49. Most probably the catchword "scandal" brought him to the insertion of these verses[19]. It is not clear what kind of individual temptations Mark has in mind. One should not too easily suppose a sexual context which Matthew in his secondary application in 5,29-30 provides[20]. Notwithstanding Mark's redactional activity, especially towards the end, there remains a serious tension between verses 43-49 and verse 42, both grammatically and regarding content. Mark moves from scandals caused by others to scandals caused by the person himself or herself[21]. We must not try to straighten out the rather bumpy line of thought. Mark's emphasis on hell and its everlasting pain should not go unnoticed. Moreover, the Discipleship Discourse appears to contain somewhat of a catalogue of different dangers for the believers.

Mark 9,50

In view of the text of Luke there seems to be no reason for postulating in Q 14,34a a text different from Mk 9,50a: "Salt is good". Mark borrowed the clause from Q. "Salt" in Mark must be a positive quality. Many interpreters assume a reference to the salt of the covenant (cf. Lev 2,13; Num 18,19; 2 Chr 13,5) and, hence, to "peace" (cf. v. 50d), but this seems to be unfounded and far-fetched. Mark most likely points to the salt's quality of preservation; salt here means the authenticity and perseverance of the disciples.

The Greek text of Q 14,34b is certain (without the Lukan addition of καί). It must have been Mark who altered the verb μωρανθῇ into ἄναλον γένηται[22]. In verse 50c he "also substitutes the active expression αὐτὸ

---

18. GUNDRY, *Mark*, p. 515, prefers the meaning "everyone without exception". True believers may pass the test of the frightful eschatological fire.

19. Cf. FLEDDERMANN, "Discipleship Discourse", p. 71. He comments: in these verses "we can hear the cadences of the spoken word".

20. Cf. COLLINS, *Sexual Ethics*, pp. 62-72; cf. also p. 186: Matthew, "as Mark before him, has preserved the memory of an old tradition that spoke of the evil of child abuse (Matt. 18:6; Mark 9:42)". See also, e.g., GUNDRY, *Mark*, pp. 514-515; DEMING, "A First Century Discussion of Male Sexuality".

21. Cf. GUNDRY, *Mark*, p. 513: "Again, sinning is in view, but sinning caused from within by a member of one's own body, not from without...".

22. Cf. FLEDDERMANN, "Discipleship Discourse", pp. 72-73: "Mark likes alpha-privative adjectives". Fleddermann refers to ἄσβεστον in Mark's addition in verse 43; see also p. 69. KEA, "Salting the Salt", p. 240, and HAINZ, "Salzloses Christentum", pp. 107-107, e.g., assume that ἄναλον γένηται is more original than μωρανθῇ in Q.

ἀρτύσετε for the passive ἀρτυθήσεται. He uses it to lead into his climax" at the end of verse 50[23]. The second person plural reminds us of Jesus addressing the disciples in verses 33 and 39-41. The question form of verse 50c is not without a hidden warning.

The two parallel clauses of verse 50de ("have salt in yourselves, and be at peace with one another") differ in content: "salt" does not mean "peace" and "in yourselves" is not "with one another". Verse 50d most probably refers to genuine strength and firmness in temptations which is so recommended in verses 43-49, while the idea of staying in peace in verse 50e may point back, by way of inclusion, to the missing harmony of the disciples discussing on the way in verses 33-37. The καί between the two clauses is simply connective and does not seem to possess a consecutive value ("and 'so' you will have peace with one another"[24]). We can assume that Mark himself composed the clauses. The two clauses take the place of the two-part Q 14,35 which Mark has omitted. No doubt he knew both salt verses, Q 14,34 and 35[25].

By now it must have become more evident that Q 14,34-35 suggested Mark's choice of the verb ἁλίζομαι in verse 49. The salt image in verse 50, therefore, is not completely new. Yet the reader must reflect upon what the evangelist means by this sudden positive turn in the discourse and his direct address of the disciples. Towards the end the verse is explicitly hortatory. Since it refers back to ideas present in the preceding sections, verse 50 appropriately rounds off the whole of 9,33-50.

Concluding Remarks

Our concluding remarks will begin with comment on Mark 9,42-50. They will cover two separate topics: Mark's editorial activity and his dependence on Q. A methodological reflection will round off this study.

23. FLEDDERMANN, "Discipleship Discourse", p. 73.

24. Otherwise, e.g., GUNDRY, *Mark*, p. 528, who, as many others, sees in verse 50de "a synonomous parallelism in which the prosaic second clause interprets the figurative first clause"; καί has the force of "i.e." and ἐν ἑαυτοῖς of verse 50d means "among yourselves" in agreement with ἐν ἀλλήλοις of verse 50e. It would also seem that SAND, ἅλας, p. 137, detects too much harmony within verses 49-50: "Das Wort vom Feuer (als Mittel der Läuterung…), der sich in der katechetischen Anwendung ausdrückt: 'Habt in euch Salz und haltet Frieden untereinander!'…: d. h. die under dem reinigenden Gericht stehende Gemeinde wird zum Friedensbereitschaft verpflichtet".

25. The negative of Q 14,35, especially ἔξω βάλλουσιν αὐτό, could have influenced Mark in rewriting and expanding verses 43-49 and his emphasis on the eschatological punishment.

Marcus redactor

Mark has been very active indeed in composing the last part of the discourse. He has been rewriting traditional material as well as creatively
expanding it. As far as we can judge, verses 42a, 49 and 50dc are purely
redactional (a Q influence on vv. 42a and 49 is not to be excluded). Mark
has tried to harmonize the content of this small passage and link it with
the context. This clearly occurs in verse 42a ("the little ones who believe in
me"; cf. v. 41 and v. 37) and probably also in verse 50 (the Salt saying
appears, in terms of content, to be connected with vv. 43-49 and vv. 33-
37). Mark utilizes the catchword technique; the most important recurring
words are σκανδαλίζομαι, καλόν ἐστιν, πῦρ and ἁλίζομαι-ἅλας. The traditional material in verses 43, 45 and 47 provided Mark with a threefold
repetition. Between verse 42 and verse 41 a stylistically apt opposition is
created, equally between verse 50 and the preceding text. There also is an
impressive crescendo regarding the punishments: compare verse 42 (sea)
with verses 43-49 (hell).

One should, however, fully recognize that the result is far from perfect. More than one tension is visible in this short text. The grammatical construction in verses 43.45.47 (καὶ ἐάν) differs from that in verse 42
(ὃς ἄν), also regarding tense, subject and direct object. The transition
from verse 42 (a person scandalizing a little one who believes) to verse
43 (your hand scandalizing you yourself) is strained, to say the least. The
reader does not immediately see who are meant by the generalizing πᾶς
in verse 49. The appearance of the salt metaphor in verse 50 and, no less,
the use of the second person plural and its exhortation in the middle of
that verse are unexpected.

As often, tensions may reveal the use of disparate sources. In fact, Mark
successively uses Q 17,1-2 in verse 42, an originally connected traditional
series in verses 43.45.47, Isa 66,24 in verse 48, and Q 14,34-35 in verse 50.
What can be said about his dependence on Q?

Mark's Dependence on Q Material

We presume more than just Mark's reliance on Q in this passage, even
if the probative value of the data is not absolute. Perhaps one should no
longer claim that the Markan text offers no reasons to assume that Q
itself is the source for the overlap sections but, rather, recognize that there
are no reasons to postulate another source for them[26].

26. *Pace* CROOK, "A Test-Case".

It would seem that our analysis almost certainly confirms that 17,2 belongs to Q and that, together with Mt 18,6 and Lk 17,2, Mk 9,42 can be used for the inevitably hypothetical reconstruction of that verse in Q.

It is equally as good as certain that the Greek text of Q 14,34a corresponds with that of Mk 9,50a and Lk 14,34a (without οὖν) and, moreover, that Mark also knew Q 14,35.

This brief study can, of course, not speak of the Q document as a whole nor reveal a great deal about the final or redactional Q and the order of Q or its sections. However, the manner in which Mark uses the Q verses and integrates parts of them in his discourse manifest, I believe, that his text is secondary over against that of Q. Perhaps this study may caution those who in their reconstruction of Q rightly begin with a close comparison of Matthew and Luke. The extension of Q cannot be dogmatically restricted to passages and verses where Matthew and Luke, in context and text, agree against Mark. The investigation of the overlap texts appears to demonstrate this.

Methodological Reflection

By way of reflection on method we may quote the rather strange, not to say unfair, reasoning of I. Dunderberg (I add the numbers for the sake of a reply):

(1) The Markan dependence on Q immediately raises some methodological problems. (2) Even if in a certain section Matthew and Luke seem to follow the Markan pattern, one could no longer conclude that those passages actually derive from Mark ... (3) An extreme, but nevertheless logical consequence of the Markan knowledge of Q would be that *any synoptic passage* having triple attestation by Matthew, Mark, and Luke can derive from Q[27].

Ad (1): Markan dependence exists or does not exist. One cannot change facts by theory or hypothesis. The question of Mark's sources (or traditions) is a real one whatever the answer may be; the overlap texts have to be examined. However, no defender of Markan knowledge of Q claims that in his gospel Mark has used all of Q. But even partial use does raise methodological problems indeed.

Ad (2): A sound methodology will consider only those synoptic sections where Matthew and/or Luke follow the Markan pattern if there exist enough minor agreements against Mark, i.e., cumulative and significative evidence, to postulate a Q influence.

27. DUNDERBERG, "Q and the Beginning of Mark", p. 503.

Ad (3): If the first two replies are duly taken into account, no exegete will consider the extreme (but not logical!) consequence regarding "any synoptic passage".

In this and similar contributions, the Two-Source theory, the most widely accepted hypothesis, remains the framework, the overall basis. Assuming Markan knowledge of Q, I think, helps better to understand and explain a limited number of synoptic texts as well as Q.

Bibliography

COLLINS, R. F., *Sexual Ethics and the New Testament: Behavior and Belief* (Companions to the NT), New York, 2000.

CROOK, Z. A., "The Synoptic Parables of the Mustard Seed and the Leaven: A Test-Case of the Two-Document, Two-Gospel, and the Farrer-Goulder Hypothesis", in *JSNT* 78 (2000) 23-38.

DEMING, W., "Mark 9.42–10.12, Matthew 5.27-32 and *B. Nid.* 13b: A First Century Discussion of Male Sexuality", in *NTS* 3 (1990) 130-141.

DUNDERBERG, I., "Q and the Beginning of Mark", in *NTS* 41 (1995) 501-511.

FLEDDERMANN, H. T., "The Discipleship Discourse (Mark 9:33-50)", in *CBQ* 43 (1981) 57-75.

FLEDDERMANN, H. T., *Mark and Q. A Study of the Overlap Texts. With an Assessment by F. Neirynck* (BETL, 122), Leuven, 1995.

GUNDRY, R. H., *Mark. A Commentary on His Apology for the Cross*, Grand Rapids, 1993.

HAINZ, J., "Salzloses Christentum?", in J. HAINZ, H.-W. JÜNGLING and R. SEBOTT (eds.), *"Den Armen ein frohe Botschaft". FS F. Kamphaus*, Frankfurt, 1997, 107-123.

HENDERSON, J. H., "'Salted with Fire' (Mark 9.42-50): Style, Oracles and (Socio-) Rhetorical Gospel Criticism", in *JSNT* 80 (2000) 44-65.

KEA, P. V., "Salting the Salt: Q 14:34-35 and Mark 9:49-50", in *Forum. A Journal of the Foundations and Facets of Western Culture* 6 (1990) 239-244.

LARSEN, I., "The Use of γάρ and the Meaning of Fire in Mark 9:49", in *Notes on Translation* 8 (1994) 33-39.

METZGER, B. M., *A Textual Commentary on the Greek New Testament*, Stuttgart, ²1994.

NEIRYNCK, F., "The Minor Agreements and Q", in R. A. PIPER (ed.), *The Gospel Behind the Gospels. Current Studies on Q* (SupplNT, 75), Leiden, 1995, 49-72.

SAND, A., ἅλας, ἁλίζω, in *EWNT I*, 136-137.

SCHLOSSER, J., "Lk 17,2 und die Logienquelle", in *SNTU* 8 (1993) 70-78.

SCHNACKENBURG, R., "Mk 9,33-50", in J. SCHMID & A. VÖGTLE (eds.), *Synoptische Studien. FS A. Wikenhauser*, Munich, 1953, 184-206; repr. in R. SCHNACKENBURG, *Schriften zum Neuen Testament*, Munich, 1971, pp. 129-154.

SNYDER, G. R., "The *Tobspruch* in the New Testament", in *NTS* 23 (1976-77) 117-120.

TAYLOR, V., *The Gospel according to St. Mark*, London, 1966.

TITRUD, K., "Mark 9:49 Revisited", in *Notes on Translation* 8 (1994) 30-32.

VON WAHLDE, U., "Mark 9:33-50: Discipleship: The Authority That Serves", in *BZ* 23 (1985) 49-67.

6

The Great Commandment Pericope
(Mark 12,28-34 and Q 10,25-28)

A number of minor agreements are present in Mt 22,34-40 and Lk 10,
25-28. This might suggest the existence of a Q-variant of the Markan
great commandment pericope. Yet nothing of such a possibility is mentioned in the more recent Q synopses of, e.g., A. Polag, J. S. Kloppenborg
and F. Neirynck[1]. Is this possibility or hypothesis not worth considering?
We think it is, for several reasons. If the existence of a Q pericope
becomes probable, not only can more insight be reached regarding Luke's
redaction within 10,25-28 and that of Matthew in 22,34-40, but the question must also be asked whether or not Mark himself has known that Q
text[2]: in view of a (hypothetical) dependence on Q, does his redaction
of 12,28-34 perhaps become more comprehensible?

1. A. POLAG, *Fragmenta Q. Textheft zur Logienquelle*, Neukirchen-Vluyn, 1979;
J. S. KLOPPENBORG, *Q Parallels: Synopsis, Critical Notes and Concordance*, Sonoma, 1988;
F. NEIRYNCK, *Q-Synopsis. The Double Tradition Passages in Greek*, Leuven, 1988. See also,
however, G. SELLIN, "Lukas als Gleichniserzähler: Die Erzählung vom barmherzigen
Samariter (Lk 10,25-37)", in *ZNW* 65 (1974) 166-189; 66 (1975) 19-60, especially pp. 20-23;
R. H. FULLER, "Das Doppelgebot der Liebe. Ein Testfall für die Echtheitskriterien der
Worte Jesu", in G. STRECKER (ed.), *Jesus Christus in Historie und Theologie. FS H. Conzel-
mann*, Tübingen, 1975, 317-329; R. PESCH, *Das Markusevangelium. II* (HTKNT), Freiburg – Basel – Wien, 1977, pp. 244-248.

2. Cf. D. LÜHRMANN, *Das Markusevangelium* (HNT), Tübingen, 1987, p. 205: "Könnte man daraus [= aus den Übereinstimmungen] schliessen, dass Mt und Lk an dieser
Stelle nicht nur den Mk-Text, sondern ausserdem eine parallele Überlieferung (vielleicht Q)
zur Verfügung hatten, wäre gesichert, dass Mk die Szene als ganze im wesentlichen
vorgelegen hat". I have tried to demonstrate Mark's knowledge and use of Q in several
pericopes. See "Die Logia-Quellen von Markus 13", in *Bib* 47 (1966) 321-360; *Die Redaktion der Markus-Apokalypse. Literarische Analyse und Strukturuntersuchung* (AnBib, 28),
Rome, 1967; *Marcus interpretator. Stijl en boodschap in Mc. 3,20–4,34*, Brugge, 1969;
"Redaction and Theology in Mk. IV", in M. SABBE (ed.), *L'Évangile selon Marc. Tradition
et rédaction* (BETL, 34), Leuven, 1974, ²1988, 269-308; "Jesus and the Law: An Investigation of Mk 7,1-23", in *ETL* 53 (1977) 24-82, reprinted in J. DUPONT (ed.), *Jésus aux origi-
nes de la christologie* (BETL, 40), Leuven, ²1989, 358-415 and 428-429; "Q-Influence on
Mark 8,34–9,1", in J. DELOBEL (ed.), *Logia. Les paroles de Jésus – The Sayings of Jesus*
(BETL, 59), Leuven, 1982, 277-303; "John the Baptist and Jesus in Mark 1.1-15: Markan
Redaction of Q?", in *NTS* 37 (1992) 357-384, reprinted in this volume, pp. 14-42.

It would seem that in this investigation three steps have to be taken. First, it is necessary to have a clear view of Luke's editorial activity in 10,25-28. Then, the minor agreements between Mt 22,34-40 and Lk 10,25-28 should be brought together and carefully analyzed. If this analysis leads us to the postulate of a Q text and, therefore, to its reconstruction, then, in a final section, the possibility of Mark's knowledge of this Q passage and his use of it in 12,28-34 must be examined.

Lukan Redaction in 10,25-29

In Lk 10,25-37 there are two sections of dialogue (vv. 25-29 and 36-37) separated by a monologue, i.e., the parable about the good Samaritan (vv. 30-35)[3].

Lukan Creative Activity

We focus here mainly on verses 28-29. "*Do* this, and you will *live*" in v. 28 constitutes an eye-catching inclusion with v. 25 "what shall I *do* to inherit eternal *life?*"[4] The verb "to do" (ποιέω), moreover, is employed twice in the final verse 37: "the one who *did* mercy" and "go and *do* likewise". Such frequency is most probably the result of Luke's editorial activity[5].

V. 29 also appears very Lukan. First of all, there is the striking fact that the idea of the lawyer's "desiring to justify himself" occurs in the gospels only here and in another Lukan text, 16,15, where it is said that the Pharisees justify themselves before others. What is decisive, however, in leading us to view this transitional v. 29 as a purely Lukan creation is the question which it contains: "And who is my neighbor?" This question stands in a certain tension with that of v. 36: "Which of these three became neighbor to the man...?" Verse 29 is evidently formulated by the same redactor who had just previously written at the end of v. 27, "(Love) your neighbor as yourself", and who, with this commandment in mind,

---

3. In what follows in "Lukan Redaction in 10,25-29" and in the first paragraph of "Minor Agreements and Q", I have utilized my *Once More Astonished: The Parables of Jesus*, New York, 1981, ²1983, pp. 57-68.

4. Cf., e.g., J. KIILUNEN, *Das Doppelgebot der Liebe in synoptischer Sicht. Ein redaktionskritischer Versuch über Mk 12,28-34 und die Parallelen* (Annales Academiae Scientiarum Fennicae, B/250), Helsinki, 1989, p. 68: "Die Inklusion ist vollkommen".

5. According to M. D. GOULDER, *Luke: A New Paradigm* (JSNT SS, 20), Sheffield, 1989, p. 485, Luke "reformulates the man's question ..., replacing the Jewish-theoretical interest with a Lucan, practical one". Cf. also, e.g., KIILUNEN, *Doppelgebot*, pp. 57-58.

reads the parable about the good Samaritan and wishes to use it as a commentary on that commandment, its clarification. Luke makes the lawyer ask: Who, concretely, is my neighbor? The expected answer is: the wounded traveller. But later, at the end (v. 36), comes the other question, Jesus' question: Which of these three – priest, Levite or Samaritan – became a neighbor? The answer now is: the good Samaritan.

What can be concluded from these remarks? Since verses 28 and 29 appear to be highly redactional transitions from dialogue to parable, since verse 28 constitutes a redactional inclusion with v. 25 and the editorial verse 29 stands in a certain tension with v. 36, and since verse 30 contains the phrase "a certain man" with which many other originally independent parables in Luke begin, it seems best to ascribe the connection between dialogue and parable to Luke himself. The evangelist realized that he could explain and illustrate the commandment of love of neighbor by means of the parable about the good Samaritan. As he wrote, however, he may not have noticed that his parable commentary actually explains only the second commandment and not the first concerning the love of God.

Luke's Dependence on Lk 18,18-20 (= Mk 10,17-19)

It would seem that Luke's use of "to do" and "life" is not purely redactional. In v. 25 he writes, διδάσκαλε, τί ποιήσας ζωὴν αἰώνιον κληρονομήσω;[6] The formulation of this question is verbally almost the same as that of Lk 18,18 in the pericope of the rich man: "(Good) Teacher, what shall I do to inherit eternal life?" (cf. Mk 10,17)[7]. In Lk 10,26 Jesus answers: "What is written in the law?[8] How do you read?[9]" In the pericope about the rich man Jesus says: "you know the commandments" (Lk 18,20 = Mk 10,19)

6. Cf. T. SCHRAMM, *Der Markus-Stoff bei Lukas. Eine literarkritische und redaktions-geschichtliche Untersuchung* (SNTSMS, 14), Cambridge, 1971, p. 48: "Gut lukanisch wird die theologisch-spekulative Frage durch eine solche nach dem praktischen Tun ersetzt". Schramm admits in Lk 18,25 "eine Nicht-Mk-Traditionsvariante" (p. 49).

7. The texts of the questions in Lk 10,25 and 18,18 are strictly identical except for the qualification ἀγαθέ in 18,18 which is absent in 10,25. In Mk 10,17 "to do" is the main verb: διδάσκαλε ἀγαθέ, τί ποιήσω ἵνα ζωὴν αἰώνιον κληρονομήσω;

8. νόμος is absent in Mark's gospel. For the connection of "what is written" and "law" in Luke, see 2,23 (cf. 2,24: κατὰ τὸ εἰρημένον ἐν νόμῳ κυρίου) and 24,44.

9. For ἀναγινώσκω, see Lk 4,16 and 6,3. In Acts Luke employs the verb quite frequently: 8,28.30 and 32 (Isaiah the prophet); 13,27 (the prophets); 15,21 (Moses); 15,31 (a letter from the Jerusalem authorities); 23,34 (a letter of the tribune). The question πῶς ἀναγινώσκεις is probably Lukan. Otherwise I. H. MARSHALL, *The Gospel of Luke* (NIGTC), Exeter, 1978, p. 441.

and cites the law (Ex 20,13-16 and 12 = Deut 5,17-20 and 16). Twice, thus, in Lk 10 and 18, we have also a reference to scripture.

One can hardly avoid the impression that in his editing of 10,25-28 Luke was influenced by the beginning of the pericope of the rich man[10] which he presents in 18,18-30.

Luke's Use of Mk 12,28-34

"The crucial problem in the [= Luke's] narrative is its relationship to Mk 12:28-34"[11]. There are a great many differences between Lk 10,25-28 and Mk 12,28-34. For a moment, however, we should focus our attention on Luke's dependence on Mark since Luke "enthält Elemente aus Mk 12,28ff. und zwar aus höchstwahrscheinlich *redaktionellen* Wendungen"[12]. In regard to Lk 10,25-28 (and 20,39-40) five items must be mentioned.

(a) It cannot but strike the reader that, between Lk 20,39 and 40 (or 40 and 41), the Markan pericope of the great commandment is missing. The most probable explanation of this fact is that Luke wants to avoid a repetition here[13]. He must have realized that 10,25-28 is much the same as that Markan pericope[14]. Therefore he omits it in chapter 20.

(b) Lk 20,40 concludes the Sadducees' question concerning the resurrection: οὐκέτι γὰρ ἐτόλμων ἐπερωτᾶν αὐτὸν οὐδέν. The fact that one does not easily see how the motivation (γάρ) properly functions may point to a somewhat clumsy Lukan editing; two verses have been linked which originally did not belong together[15]. It would seem that Luke has taken this verse from Mark's conclusion of the great commandment passage, 12,34c: καὶ οὐδεὶς οὐκέτι ἐτόλμα αὐτὸν ἐπερωτῆσαι. It should be noted that already in 20,39 Luke is influenced by Mark's pericope of the

---

10. There can scarcely be any doubt that the question which Luke takes over from Mk 10,17, is more original in the pericope about the rich man (18,18) than in Lk 10,25.

11. MARSHALL, *The Gospel of Luke*, p. 440. Cf. FULLER, "Doppelgebot", p. 318; and SELLIN, "Lukas als Gleichniserzähler", p. 20: Lk 10,25-28 "stellt in seinem Verhältnis zu Mk 12,18-34 / Mt 22,34-40 immer noch ein literarkritisches Rätsel dar".

12. SELLIN, "Lukas als Gleichniserzähler", p. 20.

13. Although the so-called consistent avoidance of "doublets" ("Dublettenvermeidung") by Luke must not be accepted without qualification, it provides, I think, an adequate reason for the absence of the great commandment pericope in chapter 20. Cf., e.g., J. A. FITZMYER, *The Gospel According to Luke (X-XXIV)* (AB), Garden City, NY, 1985, p. 877.

14. Cf. MARSHALL, *The Gospel of Luke*, p. 440: "... it is incontestable that Luke knew Mark's form of the story and regarded his own as an equivalent to it".

15. Cf. KIILUNEN, *Doppelgebot*, pp. 29-32. One more detail strikes the reader, at least at first sight: "In dem V. 40 fällt ... das Adverb οὐκέτι auf. Dass die Schriftgelehrten keinen Mut zu weiteren Fragen hätten, ist befremdlich, denn nicht sie, sondern die Sadduzäer haben im vorangehenden Abschnitt 20,27-38 Jesus befragt" (p. 30).

great commandment. Compare not only v. 39b with Mk 12,32b but also τινὲς τῶν γραμματέων in v. 39 with εἷς τῶν γραμματέων in Mk 12,28 and καλῶς in both these verses[16].

(c) In Lk 10,27, it is the lawyer who answers and quotes the double commandment of love of God and neighbor; in Mk 12,29-31, it is Jesus who does so. In Mk, the two commandments are neatly separated into the first (see πρώτη in Mk 12,28 and 29; verses 29-30 cite Deut 6,4-5, love of God) and the second (see δευτέρα in Mk 12,31; here Lev 19,18 is quoted, love of neighbor). These two facts – that in Luke's text the two Old Testament quotations are fused into a single sentence and that it is the lawyer and not Jesus who makes the daring equation of the two commandments – strongly suggest that the Lukan text is less original than its Markan parallel[17]. It is not impossible that in "fusing" the two quotations Luke was influenced by Mk 12,33 since in this Markan verse the scribe combines Jesus' twofold answer: it becomes one long sentence[18]. Two small agreements may point to a Lukan dependence on Mk 12,29. The prepositional phrase referring to the first faculty in Lk 10,27 has ἐξ (the others have ἐν); also Lk 10,27 possesses the same four faculties (not three as in the Septuagint) as in Mark, be it in a different order.

(d) Jesus' reaction in Lk 10,28b, "You have answered rightly", is reminiscent of Mk 12,34a, "And when Jesus saw that he answered wisely". Luke must have been influenced by this Markan statement. Further, in Lk 10,28, as in Mk 12,34, "Jesus behält das letzte Wort"[19].

(e) The idea of illustrating the quotation in Lk 10,27 – above all Lev 19,18: "and your neighbor as yourself" – by the parable about the good Samaritan perhaps came to Luke's mind from reading Mk 12,33b: "And 'to love one's neighbor as oneself', this is much more important than all whole burnt offerings and sacrifices"[20].

---

16. Cf. KIILUNEN, *Doppelgebot*, pp. 31-32: "Beide Verse stammen aus dem sonst ausgelassenen Mk 12,28-34, während die Konjunktion γάρ – in schwerfälliger Weise – versucht, das ausgelassene Textstück zu überbrücken".

17. Cf. SELLIN, "Lukas als Gleichniserzähler", pp. 22-23: "die ursprünglich pointierte Verbindung von Dtn 6,5 und Lev 19,18 wird schon als überliefert und bekannt vorausgesetzt" (p. 22). GOULDER, *Luke*, p. 485, notes: "this reversal of the position, with Jesus asking the question and the scribe answering, enables Luke to let down the guillotine ['You have answered right', 10,28] as at 7.42ff." (see also p. 490).

18. Cf. FULLER, "Doppelgebot", p. 319.

19. SELLIN, "Lukas als Gleichniserzähler", p. 21. Cf. K. KERTELGE, "Das Doppelgebot der Liebe im Markusevangelium?", in *À cause de l'Évangile. FS J. Dupont* (LD, 123), Paris, 1985, 304-322, especially p. 306. See also GOULDER, *Luke*, p. 487: "ὀρθῶς ἀπεκρίθης echoes Mk 12.34 νουνεχῶς ἀπεκρίθη".

20. Cf. FULLER, "Doppelgebot", p. 319.

We may conclude this analysis as follows: Lk 10,25-28 has most probably not been written without the influence of Mk 12,28-34, a pericope·
which Luke omits in his parallel chapter 20[21]. In using the Markan text
Luke betrays himself as redactionally secondary.

Minor Agreements and Q

It is clear that the evangelist Luke has not mechanically or blindly reproduced the traditions which he received. In respect to this pericope, he was
perhaps more active as a redactor than might be apparent in a first reading. It would, however, be wrong to conclude from the literary data just
mentioned that Luke merely transposed and rewrote Mk 12,28-34[22] with
a view to using it in his gospel as an introduction to the parable about the
good Samaritan. A comparison with Mt 22,34-40 seems to indicate that
Luke had access to a second source which was more or less similar to the
version known to him from Mark's gospel. The reason for postulating this
second source is that Matthew and Luke exhibit a number of quite remarkable agreements in this passage against the Markan parallel text which can,
it would seem, only be explained in terms of a second common source.

Agreements

The points on which Matthew and Luke agree with one another and
at the same time differ from Mark are the following[23]:

21. C. BURCHARD, "Das doppelte Liebesgebot in der frühen christlichen Überlieferung", in E. LOHSE (ed.), *Der Ruf Jesu und die Antwort der Gemeinde. FS J. Jeremias*, Göttingen, 1970, 42-43, is (too) minimalist: "Abgesehen von Lk 20,39f. scheint die Markusfassung im dritten Evangelium keine oder nur geringe Spuren hinterlassen zu haben".
22. Cf., e.g., G. SCHNEIDER, *Das Evangelium nach Lukas. Kapitel 1-10* (ÖkTKNT),
Gütersloh – Würzburg, 1984, p. 247: "Für die Annahme, dass Lukas in den VV 25-28
Mk 12,28-34 und keine Sondervorlage benutzt hat ... gibt es wohl die besten Argumente".
J. GNILKA, *Das Matthäusevangelium. II* (HTKNT), Freiburg – Basel – Wien, 1988, p. 257,
writes about Mt 22,34-40: "Die traditionskritische Analyse bereitet besondere Schwie-
rigkeiten". He refers to "Gemeinsamkeiten des Mt mit dem Lk Text" and mentions that
"vielfach die Auffassung vertreten [wird], dass neben der Mk-Vorlage noch eine zweite
Vorlage der Perikope existiert habe, von der Mt und Lk zusätzlich abhängig seien". Yet
he states:"Hier soll die Auffassung von der zweiten Vorlage nich übernommen werden".
– As is well known, GOULDER, *Luke*, pp. 484-487, believes that Luke is dependent on
(both Mark and) Matthew.
23. For a similar list see BURCHARD, "Das doppelte Liebesgebot", p. 41 n. 4; FULLER,
"Doppelgebot", p. 318; PESCH, *Markusevangelium*, pp. 244-245; KERTELGE, "Doppelgebot", p. 308; KIILUNEN, *Doppelgebot*, pp. 18-19. We should not forget the old, but not
dated, discussion in J. SCHMID, *Matthäus und Lukas* (BSt, 23,2-4), Freiburg [Breisgau],

(1) Unlike Mk 12,29, their quotation of the first commandment, does not begin with "Hear, O Israel: the Lord our God, the Lord is one".

(2) Both Matthew and Luke offer a much shorter version. They have no parallel to Mk 12,32-33. This means that they do not offer a monotheistic comment (cf. Mk 12,32: "there is no other than he") nor a critique on sacrifices (cf. Mk 12,33: "much more than all whole burnt offerings and sacrifices").

(3) Jesus is initially addressed as διδάσκαλε ("teacher"), a title not found at the beginning of the Markan pericope (12,28) but only subsequently in 12,32.

(4) The question in Mt 22,35 and Lk 10,25 is asked by a νομικός ("lawyer")[24], whereas in Mk 12,28 it is posed by εἷς τῶν γραμματέων ("one of the scribes").

(5) By his question the lawyer intends to put Jesus to the test (Mt 22,35: πειράζων and Lk 10,25: ἐκπειράζων), while Mark's scribe questions Jesus "seeing that he answered them [= the Sadducees] well" (12,28c; cf. Lk 10,28b). The scribe in Mark appears to be well-disposed toward Jesus.

(6) Both Matthew and Luke have the expression ἐν τῷ νόμῳ, be it in a different context. Compare Mt 22,36, "Teacher, which is the great

---

1930, pp. 142-147. After mentioning most of the "minor" agreements, he writes: "Eine solche Häufung von an sich geringfügigen Übereinstimmungen ist jedenfalls beachtenswert" (p. 145).

24. "Die Ursprünglichkeit des Terminus" in Mt 22,35 "kann textkritisch nicht restlos gesichert werden" (KIILUNEN, *Doppelgebot*, p. 37 n. 9). Cf. B. M. METZGER, *A Textual Commentary on the Greek New Testament*, London – New York, 1975, p. 59. In Mt 22,35 family 1 and "widely scattered versional and patristic witnesses" omit the term νομικός. Since, in addition, "Matthew nowhere else uses the word" the Committee is of the opinion that "it is not unlikely, therefore, that copyists have introduced the word here from the parallel passage in Lk 10.25". Yet there "seems to be an overwhelming preponderance of evidence supporting the word" so that "the Committee was reluctant to omit the word altogether, preferring to enclose it within square brackets". GNILKA, *Matthäusevangelium II*, p. 258, clearly underestimates the testimony for the presence of νομικός: "trotz relativ guter Bezeugung". R. GUNDRY, *Matthew: A Commentary on His Literary and Theological Art*, Grand Rapids, 1982, p. 448, more correctly speaks of "the relative weakness of the support for omission". W. SCHENK, *Die Sprache des Matthäus. Die Text-Konstituenten in ihren makro- und mikrostrukturellen Relationen*, Göttingen, 1987, p. 65, mentions possible Q-influence. See now the lengthy discussion of νομικός in Mt and Lk in F. NEIRYNCK, "Luke 14,1-6. Lukan Composition and Q Saying", in *Evangelica II* (BETL, 99), Leuven, 1991, pp. 183-204, especially pp. 190-193: νομικός does not belong to the Q vocabulary; all occurrences in Lk are Lukan; in Mt 22,35 the term is either not authentic or due to Matthean editing. Once more, a minor agreement is explained away.

According to BURCHARD, "Das doppelte Liebesgebot", p. 43 n. 14, νομικός is "bei Matthäus ... wohl Adjektiv". It is better taken as a noun in the so-called attributive position (Schenk: "eine nachgestellte Apposition"): "one of them, a lawyer".

commandment 'in the law'?" with Lk 10,26, "(Jesus) said to him, What is written 'in the law'?"[25] The expression ἐν τῷ νόμῳ is not present in Mark.

(7) In the enumeration of Mt 22,37 and Lk 10,27, both evangelists use the preposition ἐν, while Mark in 12,30, as well in 33, always writes ἐξ[26].

(8) Both Matthew and Luke end the series of human faculties on διανοία ("mind"). Mark has ἰσχύς ("strength") as the fourth and last term.

(9) Matthew and Luke agree in that they have, respectively in 22,37a and 10,26a, ὁ δέ (without "Jesus"), a verb of saying and the indication of the addressee: compare ὁ δὲ ἔφη αὐτῷ (Matthew) with ὁ δὲ εἶπεν πρὸς αὐτόν (Luke). In Mk 12,29a we read: ἀπεκρίθη ὁ Ἰησοῦς. This last agreement, thus, is threefold.

(10) Both Matthew and Luke have Jesus' answer in direct speech without a ὅτι which we find in Mk 12,29a[27].

A Second Version

The number of agreements in these four verses of Luke is very impressive indeed. Of course, some of them are very minor (e.g., 6, 7, 8, 9, 10) and, without a common second version, could have been the result of mutually independent but identical or similar rewriting of the Markan text. Further, if there were only two or three items, one would be justified in reckoning with accidental correspondence. For the isolated agreement, a possibility of independent redaction of Mark's text can almost always be brought forward, however stretched and strained the reasoning sometimes appears.

The number of the agreements, however, is too high and several of them (e.g., 1, 2, 4, 5) are really too striking to be explained by mere coincidence. It is not very likely that Matthew and Luke would have, independently of a second source, made all these similar editorial

25. Cf. BURCHARD, "Das doppelte Liebesgebot", p. 60: "Matthäus hat schon in die Frage des Schriftgelehrten V. 36 ἐν τῷ νόμῳ eingefügt, möglicherweise nach der auch bei Lukas vorliegenden Überlieferung".

26. Actually, Luke follows Mark in beginning with ἐξ, but immediately after the first faculty, probably under Q influence, switches to ἐν. N[26] and the Synopsis of Huck-Greeven accept in Lk 10,27 four nouns, of which the first is introduced by ἐξ, the other three by ἐν. There are, however, minor variants regarding the nouns, their number (three or four) and their prepositions. Cf. KIILUNEN, *Doppelgebot*, pp. 43-45 and 64-67; K. J. THOMAS, "Liturgical Citations in the Synoptics", in *NTS* 22 (1975-76) 205-214, especially pp. 205-206 and 209-215.

27. In Mk 12,29 it could also be direct speech, but with ὅτι this remains uncertain.

changes to the common Markan text. For these sometimes verbatim agreements they most probably are indebted to a competing version from Q. One should concede, however, that, to a certain extent, the judgment in such matters remains the result of a personal evaluation and prudential assessment. Moreover, the existing texts scarcely allow a rigorous proof.

Quite recently, J. Kiilunen analyzed in great detail all agreements of the great commandment pericope. He is convinced that the way in which Matthew and Luke, each according to his own style and concerns, rewrote the Markan text adequately explains their versions: "als selbständige Redaktionsarbeit des Matthäus und Lukas an der Mk-Vorlage erklärbar"[28]; no second source-text is needed. Yet it must be repeated: even though each of these agreements, taken separately, could be regarded as independent Matthean and Lukan redactions of the Markan text alone, this type of solution hardly works for all of them taken together. Could two independent redactors agree so often? This is hardly believable. It would seem that here coincidence no longer is acceptable.

There must have been, therefore, in addition to the Markan great commandment pericope, another text telling a similar story. Both Matthew and Luke must have known this second version which most probably belongs to Q. Each in his own way realized that both accounts dealt with the same incident and, therefore, both evangelists narrated it only once in their respective gospels. In their redactions, however, they clearly drew upon both sources, Mark and Q[29].

---

28. KIILUNEN, *Doppelgebot*, quotation on p. 19. Cf. P. J. FARLA, *Jesus' oordeel over Israël. Een form- en redaktionsgeschichtliche analyse van Mc 10,46–12,40*, Kampen, 1980, pp. 240-271, especially pp. 241-254; J.-G. MUDISO MBÂ, *Jesus und die Führer Israels. Studien zu den sog. Jerusalemer Streitgesprächen* (NTA, 17), Münster, 1984, pp. 110-233, especially pp. 110-119: "Es dürfte also klar geworden sein, dass es sich unter literarkritischen, kompositorischen und redaktionskritischen Gesichtspunkten plausibel machen lässt, dass Lk und Mt über keine andere Vorlage als Mk verfügen" (p. 119); F. NEIRYNCK, "Paul and the Sayings of Jesus", in A. VANHOYE (ed.), *L'apôtre Paul. Personnalité, style et conception du ministère* (BETL, 73), Leuven, 1986, 265-321, reprinted in NEIRYNCK, *Evangelica II* (BETL, 99), Leuven, 1991, p. 504 n. 150: the author agrees with those "who explain the version of Mt 22,34-40 and Lk 10,25-28 as relying on the sole basis of Mark"; GNILKA, *Matthäusevangelium II*, pp. 257-258.
The fact that elsewhere in his gospel Mark has utilized Q heightens the probability of his knowledge of the pericope about the great commandment in Q as well. In my article "John the Baptist" (see note 2) I mentioned, moreover, the corroborating or confirmative factor that in Mt 3–4 = Lk 3–4 numerous minor agreements are present in a cluster of pericopes.

29. We may quote KERTELGE, "Doppelgebot", p. 310: "Die Übereinstimmungen zwischen Matthäus und Lukas gegen Markus sind nicht ohne weiteres durch voneinander unabhängige Redaktionen der beiden Evangelisten zu erklären". After having considered

Reconstruction

The Markan and Q versions almost certainly narrate the same incident[30]. Which of the two is older and, perhaps, more original? Within the most obvious working hypothesis we postulate that it is Q[31]. Moreover, as a second hypothesis in this paper, we presume that Mark has known Q, and that he thus may have used and rewritten the Q-text about the great commandment and integrated it into his gospel. In order to investigate Mark's editing we must, therefore, first try to reconstruct the Q version of this pericope.

Within the reconstructed text of Q the common elements of Matthew and Luke should certainly find a place. Since the two evangelists, however, did their own rewriting, it is possible that some features of Q have been preserved only in Mark.

a) Basic Structure

The original structure is decidedly that of Matthew / Luke (without Mk 12,32-34): the inimical question addressed to Jesus by a lawyer and

all data, F. W. BEARE, *The Earliest Records of Jesus*, Oxford, 1962, pp. 158-159, concludes: "This would indicate that the Lucan version comes from 'Q'...; and that Matthew has conflated Mark with the 'Q' story". Cf. K. BERGER, *Die Gesetzesauslegung Jesu. Ihr historischer Hintergrund im Judentum und im Alten Testament. I: Markus und Parallelen* (WMANT 40), Neukirchen-Vluyn, 1972, pp. 56-208 (without mentioning Q: "eine für Mt und Lk gemeinsame Tradition", p. 203).

See also G. BORNKAMM, "Das Doppelgebot der Liebe", in W. ELTESTER (ed.), *Neutestamentliche Studien für Rudolf Bultmann* (BZNW, 21), Berlin, ²1957, pp. 85-93; also in BORNKAMM, *Geschichte und Glaube. I* (BEvTh, 48), München, pp. 37-45: Matthew and Luke each had before him "eine eigene Variante unseres Mk-Textes" (p. 44); SCHRAMM, *Markus-Stoff*, p. 47: "Die Unterschiede zu Mk 12,28-34 sind evident und am besten erklärt, wenn man Lk aus einer Mk-fremden Tradition schöpfen lässt..."; FITZMYER, *Luke*, pp. 877-878, who admits another version but ascribes it to "L" (Luke's special material); MARSHALL, *The Gospel of Luke*, p. 444.

R. BULTMANN, *Die Geschichte der synoptischen Tradition*, Göttingen, 1970, p. 22, postulates a second version for, it would seem, a less appropriate reason: "Möglicherweise ist diese Kombination [10,25-28 and the Good Samaritan] schon vor Lk vollzogen gewesen; denn die Formulierung der Frage und die Gegenfrage (Lk 10,25f.) scheinen zu zeigen, dass hier eine andere Fassung des Textes benutzt ist als die Mk Redaktion".

30. Cf., however, the cautious opinion of FITZMYER, *Luke*, pp. 876-879: "Whether the Marcan and Lucan forms of the story go back to the same incident in the ministry of Jesus is hard to say" (p. 876). Yet "it is more likely that the different forms ... emerged in the post-Easter transmission ..." (p. 878). MARSHALL, *The Gospel of Luke*, pp. 441-442, with reference to T. W. Manson, M.-J. Lagrange and J. Jeremias, seems to opt for different incidents: "There is nothing surprising in the question being asked on more than one occasion, since it was a rabbinic theme" (p. 442).

31. Otherwise, V. TAYLOR, *The Gospel According to St. Mark*, London, 1952, p. 484 (with reference to Bultmann and M. Albertz).

the double answer given by Jesus who connects "love of God" with "love of neighbor"[32]. This is the backbone of the fairly simple pericope.

Luke has rewritten the text in view of the parable about the good Samaritan. As long as the pericope of the great commandment stood alone, it was, logically speaking, Jesus himself who in his answer must have made this connection between the two commandments and thus created a challenging new way of behavior. Luke's attention was, however, so exclusively focused on what he wanted to illustrate by the parable about the good Samaritan that, in his introductory presentation, he did not hesitate to place the connection on the lips of the lawyer. Jesus' reaction to the lawyer's question now is: "What is written in the law? How do you read?" The lawyer answers and quotes, within the same long sentence, both commandments; he only once uses the verb ἀγαπήσεις: "You shall love the Lord your God with all your heart, and with all your soul and with all your strength, and with all your mind; *and* your neighbor as yourself".

b) Vocabulary

The reconstruction of words, phrases and whole sentences cannot be completely effected because of the mixed state of the existing texts. We must proceed cautiously and indicate what of the evangelists is either present or absent in the Q pericope. We do intend to engage in a word-by-word reconstruction of the entire hypothetical Q-text[33].

Q 10,25a: It must be assumed to be as good as certain that the introductory clause contained the noun νομικός (most probably without τις[34])

---

32. LÜHRMANN, *Markusevangelium*, p. 206, notes: "Da eine solche Verbindung ... nur in der sich im griechischen Horizont definierenden jüdischen Überlieferung nachzuweisen ist, geht die Szene nicht auf die historische Situation Jesu zurück" (cf. also p. 207). See in the same sense, e.g., BURCHARD, "Das doppelte Liebesgebot", pp. 51-62; SELLIN, "Lukas als Gleichniserzähler", p. 21. Otherwise, however, FULLER, "Doppelgebot", p. 329; PESCH, *Markusevangelium*, p. 246: "Gegen die Herkunft dieser Beantwortung einer prüfenden Frage eines Schriftgelehrten von Jesus selbst lassen sich keine durchschlagenden Bedenken mehr erheben".

33. See for a reconstruction of the text in Greek, FULLER, "Doppelgebot", p. 322; and in German, PESCH, *Markusevangelium*, pp. 245-246. Cf. the discussion of these reconstructions in KIILUNEN, *Doppelgebot*, pp. 81-84.

In this study the Lukan versification is used for designating the Q text.

34. For its Lukan character, cf., e.g., SELLIN, "Lukas als Gleichniserzähler", pp. 21-22 and n. 110: "einem Substantiv nachgestelltes τις: Nie in Mt, 1mal in Mk, 29mal in Lk, 39mal Act". FULLER, "Doppelgebot", p. 321, and PESCH, *Markusevangelium*, p. 445, are of the opinion that the Semitism εἷς ἐκ (Mt 22,35) belongs to Q; but see also KIILUNEN, *Doppelgebot*, pp. 36-37.

and the participle (ἐκ)πειράζων³⁵. Much uncertainty remains concerning the expression καὶ ἰδού at the beginning³⁶ and in regard to the main verb³⁷. It is quite possible that the name Jesus was mentioned in this introduction.

Q 10,25b: This clause is a question in direct speech. Its first word is the vocative διδάσκαλε. Then, for what follows, we must perhaps turn to Matthew: "Which commandment is great [= the greatest] in the law?"³⁸. Instead of ποία, the interrogative pronoun τίς may be preferable for Q. Most probably the expression ἐν τῷ νόμῳ was part of the same question³⁹.

Q 10,26a: The clause which introduced Jesus as speaker contained ὁ δέ, a verb of saying and the indication of the lawyer by means of (presumably the dative of) αὐτός⁴⁰.

(Lk 10,26b-27a must, of course, be omitted.)

Q 10,27bc: This long clause, the citation of Deut 6,5, immediately follows Q 10,26a. The question "Which commandment...?" is followed by

35. We may prefer here the simplex since Luke seems to prefer compound verbs. However, Q employs both πειράζω (Mt 4,11 = Lk 4,2; Mt 16,1 = Lk 11,16) and ἐκπειράζω (Mt4,7 = Lk4,12). The compound is also present in Deut 6,16.

36. We have the Septuagintism καὶ ἰδού certainly twice in Q (Mt 12,4: Lk 11,32 and Mt 12,42 = Lk 11,31) and ἰδού occurs seven times in Q (Mt 10,16 = Lk 10,3; Mt 11,8 = Lk 7,25; Mt 11,10 = Lk 7,27; Mt 10,19 = Lk 7,34; Mt 23,38 = Lk 13,35; Mt 24,26 = Lk 17,23 [twice]). According to SELLIN, "Lukas als Gleichniserzähler", p. 21, the phrase here is decidedly Lukan. He may be right. See also GOULDER, Luke, p. 486; KIILUNEN, Doppelgebot, pp. 54-55; FULLER, "Doppelgebot", p. 320 (with reference to SCHRAMM, Markus-Stoff, pp. 91-92): "eine lukanische Einführung ..., nach dem Stil seines Sondergutes gefasst".

37. It may have been a simple verb of coming or approaching or, perhaps, as in Lk 10,25 ἀνίστημι (cf. for Q: Mt 12,41 = Lk 11,32). For FULLER, "Doppelgebot", p. 320, this last verb is pleonastic and Lukan redaction. Moreover, FULLER (pp. 320-321) and PESCH, Markusevangelium, p. 245, reconstruct the "Semitic" sequence: verb-subject.

38. Cf. PESCH, Markusevangelium, p. 245, who, again, points to Semitisms: "Verwendung des Positivs stalt des Superlativs" and "Fehlen der Kopula"; see also FULLER, "Doppelgebot", p. 321. Otherwise KIILUNEN, Doppelgebot, pp. 40-42, who with a not very convincing reasoning defends the meaning "great". The use of μείζων by Mark in 12,31 seems to indicate that he, too, read μεγάλη in his source.

39. However, Matthew's interest in the law within this pericope is most evident from 22,40, and Luke has "You know the commandments" in Lk 18,20 almost immediately after 18,18, the very verse he used in 10,25. Cf., e.g., GOULDER, Luke, p. 486; GNILKA, Matthäusevangelium II, p. 258: "die Wendung ἐν τῷ νόμῳ ... hat jeweils einen anderen Bezug und ist beiden Evangelisten auch sonst vertraut". On the other hand, redactional tendencies do not exclude (supplementary) Q influence. Moreover, it is possible that Matthew retained νομικός (a hapax legomenon in his gospel) precisely because of the presence of ἐν τῷ νόμῳ in Q 10,25b.

40. As is well known, Luke often uses πρός plus accusative after a verb of saying for the addressee(s). Cf., e.g., GOULDER, Luke, p. 487; KIILUNEN, Doppelgebot, p. 58; SELLIN, "Lukas als Gleichniserzähler", p. 22, n. 122: "εἶπεν πρός ist Lukanismus (Lk: etwa 75mal; Mk: 6mal; Mt: nur 3,15)".

the answer which cites the commandment. The repeated preposition within the Old Testament quotation is, in the Septuagint, ἐν plus dative. In Q, as in Mt 22,37, most probably three nouns (heart, soul, mind) were present[41]. We may accept that in Q καὶ ἐν ὅλῃ διανοίᾳ concluded the enumeration[42]. Pesch thinks that the first question was followed by "This (is) the great [= greatest] commandment" (v. 27c)[43].

Q 10,27de: Was the second part of Jesus' answer separated from the first by an introductory formula as we find it in Mt 22,39: "and a second [is] like it" (v. 27d)?[44] This is not impossible. Then, in v. 27e, the quotation of Lev 19,18 follows. In Q, as in both Mt 22,39 and Mk 12,31, the verb ἀγαπήσεις is repeated.

Q 10,27f: It would seem that Jesus' answer also contained a concluding statement similar to the one present in Mk 12,31c: "There is no other commandment greater than these". Was this the end of the pericope, as Matthew suggests? We cannot be completely certain, although the continuations of Mk 12,32 and Lk 10,28 each introduce a secondary addition.

All in all, not too much guesswork is necessary. In Q 10,25a we hear about a (certain) lawyer who came to Jesus to test him; in v. 25b he asks

---

41. Cf. PESCH, *Markusevangelium*, p. 245.

42. We may refer to the extensive discussion in BERGER, *Gesetzesauslegung*, pp. 177-183 and also draw the following synopsis:

LXX Dt 5,5	Mk 12,30	Mk 12,33	Mt 22,37	Lk 10,27
καρδία	καρδία	καρδία	καρδία	καρδία
ψυχη	ψυχή	ψυχή	ψυχή	ψυχή
	διάνοια			ἰσχύς
δύναμις	ἰσχύς	ἰσχύς	διάνοια	διάνοια

A variant of the first noun in the LXX is διάνοια.

Cf. LÜHRMANN, *Markusevangelium*, p. 206: "Drücken die drei ursprünglichen Substantiva [= die drei anthropologischen Grundbegriffe] die Totalität der Gottesbeziehung aus, so tritt im griechischen Sprachbereich der Verstand hinzu, diese Totalität zu wahren"; PESCH, *Markusevangelium*, p. 240, comments: "Vermutlich sind in der viergliedrigen Formel die beiden ersten Glieder (Herz-Seele) als Benennung der ganzen, ganzheitlichen personalen Existenz und die beiden letzten Glieder (Denke-Kraft) als zur Hervorhebung der all-umfassenden Kräfte einander zuzuordnen". See, however, also, e.g., E. P. GOULD, *The Gospel According to St. Mark* (ICC), Edinburgh, 1907, p. 232: "There is no attempt at classification, or exactness of statement, but simply to express in a strong way the whole being".

43. Cf. PESCH, *Markusevangelium*, p. 245, n. 26. Again Semitisms: no "Kopula"; "great" in the sense of "greatest".

44. So PESCH, *Markusevangelium*, p. 245, n. 26. The adjective ὅμοιος, although (together with its cognates) very much favored by Matthew, is also present in Q (cf. Mt 11,16 = Lk 7,32; Mt 13,31 = Lk 13,18; and Mt 13,33 = Lk 13,21).

his question probably as follows: "Which commandment is the greatest in the law?" Jesus is introduced as replying in v. 26a; the first part of the answer follows in v. 27b, the second part in v. 27e. The Greek Q text of v. 27b and v. 27e can to a great extent be recovered. If the clauses of v. 27c, d and f are present in Q – which is somewhat doubtful – their vocabulary remains uncertain. This applies to v. 25b to a lesser extent as far as the vocabulary is concerned. We may summarize our findings in the following tentative text (the square brackets indicate our hesitation):

Q *10,25a*	A lawyer stood up to put Jesus to the test,
b	"Teacher, [which commandment is the greatest in the law?]"
26a	He said to him,
27b	"You shall love the Lord your God with all your heart, and with all your soul, and with all your mind.
c	[This is the greatest commandment.]
d	[And a second is like it,]
e	You shall love your neighbor as yourself.
f	[There is no other commandment greater than these]".

Place in the Q Document

To determine the original place of Q 10,25-28 in Q is quite a difficult, if not an impossible, task. Matthew is of no help here since he follows the Markan disposition. Insofar as Mark utilizes Q elsewhere, he does not seem to respect its order to any great degree. In Luke the great commandment pericope follows the section on "Discipleship and Mission" (Q 9,57–10,24)[45] and could be the concluding pericope of this section, or the pericope might belong to the cluster "Controversies with this Generation" (Q 11,14-52 and 13,34-35). The pericope of Q 10,25-28 stands in fairly close proximity to this cluster, and within it, in Q 11,46 and 52, the noun νομικός is present.

To be sure, Lukan disposition is always a valuable argument in the matter of Q's order[46]. To a lesser extent, the controversial character of our pericope could also be helpful in determining its position in Q.

---

45. For the titles and the extension of this "cluster" and the following, see KLOPPEN-BORG, *Q Parallels*, pp. xxxi-xxxii.

46. Cf., e.g., V. TAYLOR, "The Order of Q", in *JTS* (1953) 27-31; and "The Original Order of Q", in A. J. B. HIGGINS (ed.), *New Testament Essays. Studies in Memory of T.W. Manson*, Manchester, 1959, 246-269. Both studies are reprinted in TAYLOR, *New Testament Essays*, London, 1970, pp. 90-94 and 95-118.

The reappearance of νομικός, however, is hardly an indication of order. Moreover, we must not forget that the pericope is employed by Luke in function of the parable. Such a secondary adaptation may have caused a transposition.

In regard to the precise position of the great commandment pericope in Q, it would perhaps be better simply to confess our ignorance because of lack of clear data. A similar ignorance is to be admitted regarding the stage of Q into which the pericope was integrated[47].

Markan Redaction of Q

Is there any ground for positing another text than the reconstructed Q version as the immediate source of Mark[48]? The main reasons which are brought forward to postulate a pre-Markan text different from Q are the following[49].

(1) There is a certain tension between v. 34c and what precedes: "Dass niemand mehr Jesus eine Frage zu stellen wagt, bezieht sich nur einschlussweise auf diese Gesprächsszene, sachlich gesehen aber eher auf die vorhergehenden Konflikte..."[50].

(2) That Jesus and the scribe agree is unlike the picture of the scribes which Mark presents elsewhere in his gospel.

(3) The criticism contained in the preference of love of neighbor to sacrifices is better understandable in a Jewish-Christian than in a (Markan) Gentile-Christian setting.

But do these reasons really force us to admit a pre-Markan text which could then be seen as an intermediate stage between Q and Mark?

If one accepts (as a working hypothesis) Mark's knowledge of this Q pericope, then his editorial activity, it would seem, becomes more evident and understandable. To be sure, Mark quite heavily rewrote and expanded

---

47. For the stages in Q, see, e.g., my remarks in "Q-Influence" (see note 2 above), pp. 298-304. A consideration such as that of Lührmann (see note 32 above), if correct, seems to plead for a rather late stage.

48. BURCHARD's position ("Das doppelte Liebesgebot", p. 43) is diametrically opposed to our hypothesis. The "zweite Fassung [= Q] mag Matthäus oder Lukas oder beiden vorgelegen haben ... Wie dem auch sei, die Fassung hat jedenfalls mit Markus literarisch nichts zu tun, auch nicht über eine gemeinsame Vorlage, sondern fusst auf einer mündlichen Einzelüberlieferung"; Mk 12,28-34 hat "keine literarische Vorgeschichte".

49. Cf. KERTELGE, "Doppelgebot", pp. 311-324.

50. *Ibid.*, p. 306.

the pericope of the great commandment[51]. He made it the last of the three questions (12,13-17; 12,18-27 and 12,28-32) addressed by non-disciples to Jesus in the temple complex after he told the parable about the vineyard (12,1-12)[52]. "Ein Gesetzesapophthegma aus Q ... wird von Mk erweitert in eine Art Lehrgespräch"[53]. We may go into greater detail[54].

Markan Rewriting

Mk 12,28: The first clause is a thorough rewriting of Q 10,25a. Mark does not employ νομικός. The genitive construction with γραμματεύς, "one of the scribes", can be compared with 2,6 and 7,1 ("some of the scribes")[55]. According to Mark's narrative, the scribes have been present since 11,27. The construction of 12,28a: καὶ προσελθὼν εἷς τῶν γραμμα-τέων ... ἐπηρώτησεν αὐτόν, is very similar to that of 10,2a: καὶ προσελ-θόντες Φαρισαῖοι ἐπηρώτων αὐτόν. This is all the more striking because in 10,2 Mark has πειράζοντες, the negative participle from Q which he omits in 12,28. He wants to depict the scribe as a sincere person. At the end of the pericope the Markan Jesus will even praise him (see 12,34). This is at first sight strange enough since in Mark's gospel the scribes are

51. Cf. LÜHRMANN, *Markusevangelium*, p. 205: "Der markinische Anteil ist ... höher zu veranschlagen, als das üblicherweise geschieht". As can be expected, PESCH, *Markus-evangelium*, p. 236, sees Mark's editing as mimimal: "Der Konservative Redaktor Markus greift in die Überlieferung selbst nicht ein".

52. According to PESCH, *Markusevangelium*, p. 236, the connection with 12,18-27 is "vormarkinisch".

53. SELLIN, "Lukas als Gleichniserzähler", p. 21. Cf. KERTELGE, "Doppelgebot", p. 307: "Der Schriftgelehrte wird zum gelehrigen Schüler des Meisters Jesus". BURCHARD, "Das doppelte Liebesgebot", pp. 49-50, pleads for the opposite evolution: from "Schulge-spräch" to "Streitgespräch", i.e., from "apologetisch-missionarische Theorie" to "christliche Paränese". Cf. also FULLER, "Doppelgebot", p. 323 (with reference to Bultmann): "Nach den Erkenntnissen der Formgeschichte ist das Streitgespräch gegenüber dem Schulge-spräch sekundär". M. KINGHARDT, *Gesetz und Volk Gottes. Das lukanische Verständnis des Gesetzes nach Herkunft, Funktion und seinem Ort in der Geschichte des Urchristentums* (WUNT II/32), Tübingen, 1988, pp. 137-139, does not accept the hostile character of the verb here: "Trotz das (ἐκ)πειράζων der Mt-Lk Fassung ist nicht ersichtlich, dass es sich dabei um ein Streitgespräch gehandelt hat" (p. 137). This is hardly correct.

54. See, e.g., KERTELGE, "Doppelgebot", pp. 314-321.

55. Within Mark's gospel the scribes are very prominent and active. Twice it is stated that some of them come down from Jerusalem to Galilee (see 3,22 and 7,1). In 3,22 Mark, too, most probably inserted "scribes" into a Q-pericope (cf. Lk 11,14: οἱ ὄχλοι; 11,15: τινὲς δὲ ἐξ αὐτῶν). See LÜHRMANN, *Markusevangelium*, p. 51: "Von allen jüdischen Grup-pierungen eigneten sich die Schriftgelehrten am meisten als Identifikationsfiguren für aktuelle Auseinandersetzungen mit den Juden". Cf. PESCH, *Markusevangelium*, p. 243.

consistently Jesus' opponents: "Nicht die Pharisäer, sondern die Schriftgelehrten sind ... die Hauptgegner Jesu bei Mk und – so möchte ich
folgern – die aktuellen Gegner der Gemeinde des Mk von jüdischer
Seite"[56].

There can hardly be any doubt that verse 28bc has been added by
Mark. The two clauses refer to the preceding pericope, the controversy
of Jesus and the Sadducees about the resurrection: "having heard them
disputing and knowing that he answered well". The scribe apparently
admires Jesus. His question, in its essence taken over from Q, could no
longer be brought forward in order to test or entrap Jesus. Not in an
adversary sense, but being well-intentioned, he asks: "Which commandment
is the first of all?" Since the scribe uses διδάσκαλε in v. 32, nothing can
be deduced from its omission in v. 28. Mark writes "first" instead of
"great" (= greatest), probably influenced by "second" in Q 10,27d (at least
if this term was present in Q, cf. Mt 22,39); he "numbers" the commandments, more than his source. Mark, who in his gospel does not use νόμος,
replaces "in the law" by "of all (commandments)"[57]. The adverb καλῶς is
most probably Markan (see 7,6.9.37 and 12,32). It is widely recognized
that ἐπερωτάω is a favorite verb of Mark[58]. "Die einleitende Fragepar-
tikel ποία ersetzt ein τίς, hebt zugleich aber auch auf die *Qualität* des
'ersten Gebotes' ab"[59].

Mk 12,29: Jesus is introduced explicitly as "answering". Mark adds ὅτι
πρώτη ἐστιν which corresponds to his question of v. 28. The double
use of "first" betrays a "Systematisierung im markinischen Text, wo die
Gebote als erstes und zweites eingeführt werden"[60]. The origin of the
addition of v. 29b, "Hear, O Israel: the Lord our God, the Lord is one"
is disputed. It was not present in the Q pericope. It does not seem impossible that Mark himself inserted the "Hear, O Israel", perhaps under

56. D. LÜHRMANN, "Die Pharisäer und die Schriftgelehrten im Markusevangelium",
in *ZNW* 78 (1987) 169-185, p. 183. Cf. ID., *Markusevangelium*, p. 51: "Dass mit einem
einzeln Schriftgelehrten Jesus gegenseitige Übereinstimmung erzielen kann ..., was nie
von den Pharisäern gesagt wird, zeigt, wie nahe sich ein solches von den Schriftgelehrten
vertretenes Diaspora-Judentum und das Christentum der Leser des Mk standen". See
also the same author in the preceding note.

57. πάντων may be feminine (cf. ἐντολή). The numeral πᾶς is becoming indeclinable:
cf. M. ZERWICK, *Biblical Greek*, Rome, 1963, number 12.

58. ἐπερωτάω is used 25 times in Mk, 8 times in Mt and 17 times in Lk. We cannot
accept FULLER's reconstruction of "die früheste erreichbare Form" (= older than Q): καὶ
ἐπηρώτησεν εἷς τῶν γραμματέων ("Doppelgebot", pp. 322-324), which retains both ἐπερωτάω and γραμματεύς.

59. KERTELGE, "Doppelgebot", p. 315.

60. PESCH, *Markusevangelium*, pp. 238 and 245, n. 26 (but on the pre-Markan level).

some Jewish-Hellenistic influence in his community[61]. Monotheism is thus stressed. We will see how, in v. 32, Mark comments on that sentence.

12,30: Mark alters the first citation through the minor shift from ἐν back to the Septuagintal ἐκ[62] and through the replacement of δύναμις by (διάνοια and) ἰσχύς[63].

12,31: If verse 27d ("and a second [is] like it") was present in Q 10, Mark retains δευτέρα, adds the announcing demonstrative αὕτη, but omits ὁμοία αὐτῇ. As the introductory clause now stands, it could suggest a rather subordinating nuance: Love of neighbor is only the second commandment. This, however, is hardly Mark's idea. The second quotation (Q 10,27e = Lev 19,18) is taken over and, probably, also "there is no other commandment greater than these" (Q 10,27f).

12,32-33: Verses 32-34 constitute a most impressive Markan expansion of Q. A first remark should focus on the function of the repetition of the O.T. quotations in vv. 32-33. Since the figure of the scribe in Mark remains thoroughly positive throughout the pericope, this repetition is needed from a narrative point of view. By his reaction the scribe must, as it were, manifest his agreement with Jesus, so that he can be praised by Jesus in v. 34.

In vv. 32-33 we must appreciate "the evident enthusiasm with which the Scribe received the statement of Jesus, and his ability to enter into the spirit of it so as to develop it in his own way"[64]. The Markan scribe "wiederholt zustimmend und weiterführend Jesu Antwort"[65] and thus provides a double comment. The first explains the "Hear, O Israel…"; the second deals with the two commandments[66].

---

61. Cf. FULLER, "Doppelgebot", p. 323: "offentsichlich für heidnische Leser hinzugefügt" (by Mark?). According to PESCH, *Markusevangelium*, p. 239, the clause is inserted before Mark. J. GNILKA, *Das Evangelium nach Markus. II* (EKK), Zürich – Neukirchen-Vluyn, 1979, p. 165, writes: "Wenn Markus … mit der Zitierung von Dtn 6,4 auf die Einzigkeit Gottes abhebt, wird erneut der hellenistische Grund erkennbar". BORNKAMM, "Doppelgebot", pp. 39-40, assumes the presence of 12,29b in the Jewish-Palestinian pre-Markan pericope but states that its sense must have been changed in a Jewish-Hellenistic milieu.

62. Deut 6,5 (LXX): καὶ ἀγαπήσεις κύριον τὸν θεόν σου ἐξ ὅλης τῆς καρδίας σου καὶ ἐξ ὅλης τῆς ψυχῆς σου καὶ ἐξ ὅλης δυνάμεώς σου.

63. Cf. GNILKA, *Markus*, p. 165: "… zwei aus dem rationalen bzw. psychologischen Bereich stammende Begriffe". For Gnilka διάνοια is "die Verstandeskraft". "ἰσχύς wurde zu einem psychologischen Term, der die Gesamtkraft der Seele bezeichnet". See also note 42 above.

64. GOULD, *Mark*, p. 234.

65. LÜHRMANN, *Markusevangelium*, p. 205.

66. Cf. BORNKAMM, "Doppelgebot", pp. 38-39: "Man wird an der Formulierung V 3 beachten müssen, dass sie Jesu Wort in zwei Sätze zerlegt, und zwar nicht, wie man erwarten sollte, den beiden Geboten … entsprechend".

For the editorial καλῶς, see v. 28. As already mentioned above, the vocative διδάσκαλε is transferred from Q 10,25b. For the expression ἐπ' ἀληθείας (and διδάσκαλε), see 12,14 which is also of interest as to its content: "... you truly (ἐπ' ἀληθείας) teach the way of God...". Is this not what takes place in 12,28-31 as well?

Within the resumption in v. 32, neither the first two words ("Hear, O Israel") nor "God" and "Lord" are repeated. The end of v. 32 ("and there is no other but he") quotes Deut 4,35 and explains how we have to understand the term εἷς in vv. 29 and 32: "one", in the sense of "unique: foreign gods do not exist"[67].

In v. 33 σύνεσις seems to replace διάνοια. Only three faculties remain; the second of v. 30, ψυχή, is omitted[68]. Mark twice "substantivizes" the verb "you shall love": τὸ ἀγαπᾶν. Although both τὸ ἀγαπᾶν-clauses function in this long sentence as the grammatical subject, the predicate ("is much more than all whole burnt offerings and sacrifices") apparently refers more particularly to the second clause. We must understand: love of neighbor is better than all sacrifices; love of neighbor is by far the best proof of true love of God[69]. K. Kertelge comments: "Die 'Ethisierung' des Gottesdienstes und damit verbunden die Entwertung des Opferkultes entspricht einer gesetzeskritischen Tendenz, die Markus auch an anderen Stellen seines Evangeliums erkennen lässt"[70].

12,34: Notwithstanding the fact that the adverb νουνεχῶς is a *hapax legomenon*, the construction of v. 34a is almost certainly Markan. We may compare ἰδών ... ὅτι νουνεχῶς ἀπεκρίθη with what we have in v. 28: ἰδών ὅτι καλῶς ἀπεκρίθη[71]. Not only among Hellenistic Jewish Christians but also in a Gentile Christian setting is this reaction possible. Mark himself could have composed it. Together with the verb ἐπερωτάω (in both vv. 28 and 34) the clause forms an artful inclusion of the whole pericope.

This pericope is the only place in Mark's gospel where the evangelist presents a scribe in a positive way. However, for Jesus' appreciative

---

67. In the Old Testament other senses of εἷς have been proposed, e.g., the only God worshipped in Israel (other nations have their own god or gods).

68. σύνεσις, perhaps, replaces both ψυχή and διάνοια. According to GNILKA, *Markus*, p. 166, the new term again emphasizes "das Verstandesmässige".

69. Cf. in the Old Testament 1 Kings 15,22 and Hos 6,6.

70. KERTELGE, "Doppelgebot", p. 520. He refers to Mk 2,18-22; 2,23-28; 3,1-6; 7,1-23; 11.15-19, 14.58.

71. A variant reading in v. 28 has εἰδώς. Cf. LÜHRMANN, *Markusevangelium*, p. 206: "Die Bezeugung ... ist etwa gleichwertig; das textkritisch unumstrittene ἰδών in 34 könnte zu einer Änderung von ursprünglichem εἰδώς geführt haben".

statement ("you are not far[72] from the kingdom of God"), we may refer to 15,43 where Joseph of Arimathea is called εὐσχήμων βουλευτής and qualified as follows: "he was himself looking for the kingdom of God". This last verse, moreover, has, like 12,34, the verb τολμάω. For Mark the "kingdom of God" is the central theme of Jesus' proclamation (cf. Mk 1,14-15). The expression is here used ecclesiastically rather than eschatologically[73]. Does the litotes "not far from" [= within reach] imply that the scribe refuses to accept this proclamation[74]? Hardly. Further, because this sympathetic scribe is an exception in Mark, we should not conclude too easily that for this presentation Mark depends on a non-Q tradition[75].

"And after that no one dared to ask him any question" (v. 34c) is the conclusion not only of this pericope but of the three controversies together (12,13-34ab) and even of the whole section 11,27–12,34ab. One must therefore not exaggerate the so-called tension between the pericope proper and verse 34c. The clause marks a pause in the narrative.

Markan Context and Content

Through comparing Mk 12,28-34 with its probable source, Q 10,25-28, we are able, it would seem, to reach a better insight into Mark's thorough rewriting and editing. First of all, the evangelist integrated the Q text into his gospel. He provided it with a particular controversy-context. The pericope became the third and final discussion while Jesus, during the last days of his public life, was teaching in the temple. After Jesus has spoken the parable of the workers in the vineyard, some Pharisees and Herodians are sent to entrap Jesus by means of the question about paying taxes to Caesar (12,13-17). Then, some Sadducees come to him with their question about rising from death (12,18-27). Finally, one of the scribes approaches Jesus and asks the question about the greatest commandment. At the close of this third discussion nobody dares to ask Jesus any more questions[76].

---

72. The adverb μακράν is a *hapax legomenon* in the N.T. For Markan preference for μακρόθεν, cf. 5,6; 8,3; 11,13; 14,54; 15,40; see also the neutral plural μακρά in 12,40.

73. Cf. PESCH, *Markusevangelium*, p. 244.

74. Cf. LÜHRMANN, "Die Pharisäer", p. 184, and *Markusevangelium*, p. 207: "Trotz aller Nähe bleibt also ein unüberbrückbarer Gegensatz". Contrast KERTELGE, "Doppelgebot", p. 320: "Dieses Wort schränkt die Anerkennung Jesu für den Schriftgelehrten nicht ein, sondern setzt sie voraus".

75. So TAYLOR, *Mark*, p. 485.

76. Cf. KERTELGE, "Doppelgebot", pp. 305-306.

What must strike everyone who knows the Q pericope, as well as
everyone who takes into account its present Markan context of controversy, is the presentation of the scribe as a sincere and receptive person.
As already mentioned above, in the Markan gospel itself such a scribe is
an exception (but see "the respected member of the council" in 15,43).
The scribe comes to Jesus because he is convinced that Jesus has given
the Sadducees a good answer. Otherwise than in Q, he asks his question
out of a sincere disposition. By expressing his assent ("you are right,
Teacher", 12,32) and by resuming Jesus' answer, the scribe proves that he
is in accordance with what Jesus proposes. Jesus notices that the reaction
of the scribe is wise and does not hesitate to say: "You are not far from
the kingdom of God" (12,34b). That is to say: not far from what Jesus
himself preaches in his gospel. "Dass der 'Schriftgelehrte' im zweiten Teil
in die Nähe der Gottesherrschaft gerückt wird, verrät eine werbende
Absicht missionarischer Bemühung im jüdisch-hellenistischen Milieu"[77].

By inserting "Hear, o Israel: The Lord our God, the Lord is one" at
the beginning of the first quotation (that from Deuteronomy), Mark
stresses the uniqueness of God. The scribe reacts to Jesus: you are right
in saying that there is only one God, that there is no other god but he
(cf. 12,32). Apparently, monotheism matters to Mark.

Mark has added, in v. 29, "the first is". It remains somewhat uncertain
whether, in v. 31, he underlined the numbering by "the second is this".
Probably a clause such as "there is no other commandment greater than
these" was already present in Q. In Mark, as in Q, the two commandments are joined together. However, one could argue that the second is
but the second. Does this involve a subordinating nuance which differs
from the coordinating one in Mt 22,39 and, possibly, in Q: δευτέρα δὲ ὁμοία
αὐτῇ[78]? Most probably not, since, in the scribe's comment of v. 33, Mark
emphasizes the importance of the second command, love of neighbor[79].

---

77. PESCH, *Markusevangelium*, p. 248.

78. See GUNDRY, *Matthew*, p. 449: In Matthew "'second' refers ... to order in quotation, not to order of importance". According to Matthew the second commandment is
equal to the first in importance. The same applies to Q. However, BURCHARD, "Das doppelte Liebesgebot", p. 61, presents an interesting comment on Mt 22,39a: "Das bedeutet
mehr, als dass beide Gebote gleichgeordnet werden. Es ist Gleichordnung trotz Differenz.
Obwohl das Gebot der Liebe zu Gott das grösste und erste ist, und nur eins kann das
sein, ist das Gebot der Liebe zum Nächsten ihm gleich".

79. For Mark, cf. GNILKA, *Markus*, p. 165: "Zwar ist dieses [= the second command-
ment] bei Markus dem ersten nicht gleichgestaltet wie bei Mt 22,39 ..., aber das neben-
einander beider bereitet die Gleichwertung vor"; PESCH, *Markusevangelium*, pp. 238-239
(however, on the pre-Markan level).

By themselves, sacrifices should manifest the respectful, submissive and loving attitude towards God. The scribe, however, rightly concludes from Jesus' words that "to love one's neighbor as oneself" is a true manifestation of love of God, much more and much better "than all whole burnt offerings and sacrifices".

Conclusions

Three important conclusions can be drawn from this investigation.

a) It appears impossible to adequately explain Lk 10,25-28 and Mt 22,34-40 without the postulate of a second source, a text which is different from Mk 12,28-34, the first source of Matthew and Luke. The second text can be reconstructed in its outline and even, to a great extent, with its vocabulary. There is no reason why this text should not be called a Q passage. Its place in the Q document, however, is difficult to determine. As to its content, the main point of the Q pericope is Jesus' joining of love of God with love of neighbor. Notwithstanding the brevity of the passage, Jesus' answer is a radical and truly revolutionary statement. We must also note the negative, "testing" intention of the lawyer who asks the question.

b) The two texts, Q 10,25-28 and Mk 12,28-34, apparently deal with the same incident. Ultimately they must go back to one and the same narrative. But, as far as Mark is concerned, must we look for a narrative different from that of Q? Other Markan texts strongly suggest that Mark knew sections of Q. The analysis of Mark's version of the great commandment leads to the conclusion that there is no need for supposing another text as source for Mark than the Q passage itself. Mark has most probably known and used this Q pericope as well.

c) Once again, by detecting how Mark radically edited Q, while incorporating sections of it into his gospel, we have encountered the evangelist whom we may still call *Marcus interpretator*, to be sure, not so much as Peter's translator or interpreter, but more the explaining and actualizing *interpretator* of older traditions, Q included.

Peace on Earth or Peace in Heaven?
(Luke 2,14 and 19,38)

The title of this contribution is taken from two expressions of praise in the gospel of Luke. In 2,14 the angels sing: "Glory to God in the highest heaven, and on earth peace among those whom he favors!" (NRSV translation). As Jesus was approaching the path down from the Mount of Olives, "the whole multitude of disciples began to praise God joyfully with a loud voice for all the deeds of power that they had seen, saying, 'Blessed is the king who comes in the name of the Lord! Peace in heaven, and glory to the highest of heaven!'" (19,37-38). Why does the gospel text speak of peace on earth at the birth of Jesus while at Jesus' entry into Jerusalem it refers to peace in heaven?

Let us first compare the slightly more literal RSV translation of the two verses:

> 2,14a Glory to God in the highest,
>   b and on earth peace among men with whom he is pleased.

> 19,38a Blessed is the King who comes in the name of the Lord!
>   b Peace in heaven,
>   c and glory in the highest.

Just as in 2,14a, one finds in 19,38c "glory in the highest". The rest of the two verses contains differing or even contrasting elements. The attention of this contribution will be devoted to peace on earth and peace in heaven. One preliminary remark. The new common translation of ἐν ἀνθρώποις εὐδοκίας at the end of 2,14b ("among men with whom he is pleased" or "among those whom he favors") instead of the traditional *hominibus bonae voluntatis* ("'men' of good will") no longer needs a defense.

Two Different Narratives

The praise of 2,14 is sung by a choir of angels, that of 19,38 by the disciples. The two verses belong to highly diverging units, 2,1-21 and 19,28-46.

The first passage depicts the birth of Jesus and can be taken as the fifth pericope of the seven narratives which constitute the infancy gospel of Luke (1,5–2,52); the second passage is the conclusion of the lengthy Lukan travel narrative (9,51–19,46) which ends at Jerusalem in the temple.

The Birth of Jesus at Bethlehem (2,1-21)

This pericope portrays Jesus' birth (vv. 1-7), the experience of the shepherds (vv. 8-20) and the circumcision as well as the naming of the child (v. 21). The pericope shows some parallelism with the preceding narrative about the birth of John (1,57-80). The scene of the angels with the song of praise in 2,14 (the beginning of the "Gloria") and with the shepherds' praise of God in 2,20 appears to correspond to the long hymn of Zechariah in 1,68-79 (the "Benedictus").

It must strike the reader that by means of this composition Luke, together with this symmetry, also wishes to underline the superiority of the second child, Jesus. John is (only) the precursor, the one who prepares the road (1,76); Jesus is the Savior, Christ the Lord (2,11). To be sure, John was himself already a "wonder-child": his aged mother, who had been deemed barren, experiences God's great mercy; the child receives a special name in accordance with God's will; eight days after his birth his dumb father can speak again and, filled with the Holy Spirit, utters prophetic words. But all this is by far surpassed by what happens in connection with the birth of Jesus. His mother had conceived him and remained a virgin. The good tidings of his birth are brought by an angel of the Lord to the shepherds and a great host of angels sings praise to God. This child too is given a special name, Jesus, in accordance with the angel's command before his conception (2,21). And when the child is presented to the Lord in the temple of Jerusalem, two prophetic figures, the man Simeon and the woman Anna, witness to this Jesus: a light to the Gentiles and the glory of his people Israel (cf. 2,22-39).

"In those days a decree went out from Emperor Augustus that all the world should be registered" (2,1). This opening sentence is formulated in a deliberately solemn way. By his worldly decree the Roman emperor sets a movement in motion. His subjects have to comply. Joseph too obeys. Together with Mary, who is with child, he goes to Bethlehem to register. And there it happens that Mary gives birth to a son. She wraps the child in swaddling clothes and lays him in a manger; there was no room for them in the inn. One event follows another; the facts are simply narrated (vv. 2-7).

Were there not the second section, that concerning the shepherds (vv. 8-20), the birth of Jesus would have passed almost unnoticed as that of a poor, ordinary human being, and yet Luke has related his virginal conception and situated his birth with much care in the course of world history. But now the heavens open and a messenger of God appears: the glory of the Lord shines over the shepherds who are watching their flocks by night. The angel brings them good news which will be a great joy to all the people. "To you is born this day in the city of David a Savior, who is Messiah, the Lord" (v. 11).

In the first half of the shepherd narrative (vv. 8-14) everything is miraculous and apocalyptic. Not only are there the angels and the heavenly glory, but also the structural elements of what is called a "revelation story" are present. In such a literary composition, the recipients of the apparition are frightened; the angel then says "do not be afraid" and delivers his message from heaven. The giving of a sign also pertains to such a story. Finally, alongside the one angel who had proclaimed to the shepherds in God's name the significance of Jesus' birth, a great host of angels suddenly appears acclaiming and singing praise to God: "Glory to God in the highest, and on earth peace to men with whom he is pleased" (v. 14).

Proclamation and acclamation likewise recur in the second half of the narrative (vv. 15-20). The angel and the angels provide as it were the pattern according to which the shepherds will respond. The shepherds announce what was said to them concerning the child (v. 17); they thus transmit the message of the angel; in their turn they become proclaimers of the good news. The same shepherds also glorify and praise God (v. 20), and in this response they resemble the angels who appeared at the end of the first half of the story.

For the composition of this pericope Luke most probably did not utilize a written source, but rather traditions about Joseph and Mary and their place of residence at Nazareth, about the birth of Jesus at Bethlehem, and perhaps also a vague tradition about a census with which Jesus' birth was connected. Yet the composition of the narrative is clearly the work of the evangelist: the solemn mention of the Emperor's decree, the journey from Nazareth to Bethlehem, the manger, the shepherds, the angels.

Jesus' Entry into Jerusalem and the Temple (19,28-46)

In 9,51 Luke refers to the beginning of Jesus' going up to Jerusalem: "When the days drew near for him to be taken up, he set his face to go

to Jerusalem". In 18,31, at his third prediction of the passion, Jesus emphasizes his intention: "Then he took the twelve aside and said to them,
'See we are going up to Jerusalem, and everything that is written about
the Son of Man by the prophets will be accomplished'". The journey to
Jerusalem approaches its end. The references to the route and the drawing near to the city follow one another: "as he approached Jericho" (18,35);
"he entered Jericho and was passing through it" (19,1); in the house of
Zacchaeus he went on to tell a parable "because he was near Jerusalem,
and because they [= the disciples] supposed that the kingdom of God was
to appear immediately" (19,11); after this "he went on ahead, going up
to Jerusalem" (19,28); "when he had come near Bethphage and Bethany,
at the place called the Mount of Olives" (19,29); "as he was now
approaching the path down from the Mount of Olives..." (19,37); "as he
came near and saw the city..." (19,41); "then he entered the temple..."
(19,45).

There is, however, one clear interruption. At Jericho, Jesus stays at
Zacchaeus' house, and there, moreover, he narrates the parable of the
pounds (19,12-27) because – as already said – it was thought that at
Jerusalem the kingdom of God would appear immediately (cf. 19,11).
However through that parable Jesus explains that he has first to depart
to a far country; only after this absence will he return as a king. Jesus thus
announces his death as well as his glorification and equally, at his return,
the coming of God's kingdom. No further interruptions will occur after
19,28.

The pericope of the entry, 19,29-46, is comprised of four small units:
two disciples bring the colt and Jesus rides on it (vv. 29-36); the disciples praise God but some of the Pharisees react negatively (vv. 37-40);
Jesus weeps over Jerusalem (vv. 41-44); Jesus enters the temple and drives
out those who are selling things there (vv. 45-46). For this study the
second unit is of special interest; here Luke rewrites Mark, his source
text, and expands it considerably.

Lukan Redaction in 19,37-40

It is worthwhile first to provide the more literal RSV translation of
Mk 11,9-10 and then that of Lk 19,37-40:

Mk 11,

 9a And those who went before and those who followed cried out,
  b "Hosanna! Blessed is he who comes in the name of the Lord!

10a   Blessed is the kingdom of our father David that is coming!
  b   Hosanna in the highest!"

Lk 19,
37a   As he was now drawing near, at the descent of the Mount of Olives,
  b   the whole multitude of the disciples began to rejoice and praise God
       with a loud voice for all the mighty works that they had seen,
38a   saying, "Blessed is 'the King who comes' (lit.: 'the coming one, the
       King') in the name of the Lord!
  b   Peace in heaven
  c   and glory in the highest!"
39a   And some of the Pharisees in the multitude said to him,
  b   "Teacher, rebuke your disciples".
40a   He answered,
  b   "I tell you, if these were silent,
  c   the very stones would cry out".

Brief Discussion

Luke's text is evidently much longer than that of Mark. Luke adds the topographical information (v. 37a), the Pharisees' reaction (vv. 39-40) and the weeping over Jerusalem (vv. 41-44). He rewrites the Markan "those who went before and those who followed" (Mk 11,9a) and expands it to what is present in verse 37b. In verse 38a he omits "hosanna"; after "the coming one" he inserts "the King". In view of the reference to Jesus' kingship in the added parable of the pounds (19,12-27), the insertion of "the King" is not strange, except for its position in the sentence. Luke also omits "the coming kingdom of our father David" from Mk 11,10a; he replaces this clause by "peace in heaven" (v. 38b). The praise "hosanna in the highest" of Mk 11,10b becomes "and glory in the highest" in verse 38c.

In the Lukan passage the acclamation of the disciples is followed not only by the reaction of some of the Pharisees and Jesus' reply (vv. 39-40) but also by Jesus' lament over Jerusalem, a passage that is peculiar to Luke:

> 19,41 And when he drew near and saw the city he wept over it, 42 saying, "Would that even today you knew the things that make for peace! But now they are hid from your eyes. 43 For the days shall come upon you, when your enemies will cast up a bank about you and surround you, and hem you in on every side, 44 and dash you to the ground, you and your children within you, and they will not leave one stone upon another in you; because you did not know the time of your visitation.

After the acclamation in Mk Jesus enters Jerusalem and the temple. Having inspected everything, Jesus departs from the temple and goes to Bethany (Mk 11,11). Only the following day is the temple cleansed (11,15-17).

In Lk 19,45, immediately after the lament, it is said: "And he entered the temple and began to drive out those who sold". According to Luke the cleansing takes place on the same day as the arrival at Jerusalem.

Comparison with Lk 2,13-14

After the Lukan rewriting, 19,37b is very similar to 2,13: "And suddenly there was with the angel a multitude of the heavenly host praising God and saying". In 19,37b, too, Luke speaks of "a multitude" and of "praising God". It may also be noticed that the χαρά ("joy") which the angel announces in 2,10 recurs in the verb χαίροντες ("rejoicing") of 19,37b. The parallelism between 2,14 and 19,38bc is even more striking. Both verses are characterized by a twofold somewhat chiastic structure:

δόξα ἐν ὑψίστοις θεῷ // ἐπὶ γῆς εἰρήνη... (2,14)
ἐν οὐρανῷ εἰρήνη // δόξα ἐν ὑψίστοις (19,38bc)

"glory to God in the highest // on earth peace..." (2,14);
"in heaven peace // glory in the highest" (19,38bc).

The absence of "to God" in 19,38c is the only difference. In 2,14 "glory" and "peace" are respectively at the beginning and (almost) at the end, "the highest" and "earth" in the center. In 19,38bc "heaven" and "the highest" form the extreme parts while "peace" and "glory" are in the center. Of course, the speakers – angels and disciples – differ.

All these data point to deliberate editing by the evangelist. Thus, when he speaks of "the whole multitude of the disciples" who at the triumphal entry of Jesus in Jerusalem praise God with a loud voice, Luke intends to remind his readers of "the multitude of the heavenly host" praising God at the birth of Jesus in Bethlehem. Because of this parallelism the question becomes even more pressing: why that difference between "in heaven peace" (19,38b) and "on earth peace" (2,14b)? It is necessary to scrutinize texts and contexts more closely.

The Eschatological Peace of Christ

Both in 2,13-14 and 19,37-38 the praising of God relates to peace: peace on earth, peace in heaven. The first time it is the angels who sing God's praise; the second time the disciples glorify God. The first time "glory to God in the highest" precedes the peace saying, while the second time "glory in the highest" follows it.

In 2,20 the returned shepherds likewise glorify and praise God. Except for the uncertain variant in the final verse (24,53) the expression "praising God" does not occur further on in the gospel, i.e., after 19,37-38. It recurs in Acts 2,47 (the first Christians) and 3,8-9 (the man who had been lame from birth), but no words of praise are cited in these two passages (nor in the variant reading of 24,53).

The Song of Praise of 2,14

Clauses 14a and 14b contain some reverse parallelism in regard to content, but "glory to God in the highest" (v. 14a) and "on earth peace among men with whom he is pleased" (v. 14b) differ among themselves in more than one aspect. There is not only the contrast of God and humankind, of glory and peace, of the highest (heaven) and earth, but owing to the expression "among men pleasing to him" verse 14b is considerably longer than verse 14a with "to God". The expression ἐν ἀνθρώποις εὐδοκίας refers to God's pleasure, to the election and sovereign grace by which God will bring about peace among these men and women on earth. Whether Luke also reflects upon human openness and responsiveness is difficult to ascertain.

In both 14a and 14b the verb is omitted; the clauses are elliptic. Which verb needs to be supplied? Verse 14a most probably should be regarded as a wish-prayer: glory "be" to God who is in heaven. The angels thus glorify and praise God because of the birth of Jesus his Son. "Praising God" recurs in Lk 17,18 where only the Samaritan, the foreigner among the ten lepers, returns to give praise to God.

In verse 14b, however, the ellipsis does not seem to represent a wish but rather an intention to convey information. The angel announces that through the birth of Jesus God makes peace on earth among those whom he favors. While verse 14a contains an acclamation, verse 14b consists of a proclamation of peace. So, once again, the difference between the two partly parallel clauses is apparent.

Can one step further be taken and a nuance of motivation be assumed in verse 14b? Glory to God in the highest, first of all because of the birth of the Savior, the Messiah, the Lord (v. 11), but also "because" the eschatological peace among those whom God favors becomes a reality on earth? Yet this may go too far. The two clauses of verse 14 constitute two independent halves, to be sure connected by "and"; they are contrasting clauses: heaven-earth, God-humankind and glory-peace. While in meditation and prayer one may easily "impose" a motivating nuance, most likely the text itself does not contain it.

The Praise of 19,38

First a note on 19,37. According to this verse the praise of God is sung by "the whole multitude of the disciples". The disciples do this rejoicing; with a loud voice they praise God for all Jesus has done, "for all the mighty works that they have seen".

Only then, in 19,38, do the words of the praise follow. However, they contain more than just verse 38bc. The praise already begins with verse 38a: (literally) "Blessed the coming one, the King, in the name of the Lord!" In the original Greek text the insertion of "the King" visibly separates what originally belongs together. The expression "in the name of the Lord" goes with "the coming one", as Mk 11,9b shows. How must the ellipsis be solved? The verb "is" must be added, for the disciples mean that Jesus, who as King comes in the name of the Lord, "is" really blessed. Verse 38b, a Lukan addition, is best taken as a solemn declaration: "peace (is) in heaven (with God)". But in verse 38c one has, just as in 2,14a, a wish-prayer: "glory (be) (to God) in the highest!"

For Jerusalem on earth no peace is announced: "would that even today you knew the things that make for peace!" (19,42). Jesus predicts the surrounding of the city and its complete destruction: not a single stone will be left in its place "because you did not know the time of your visitation" (v. 44; probably: the time that God comes to visit you). Pharisees condemn the acclamation; on the very day of Jesus' entry into Jerusalem the city rejects what would bring peace to her; and on this very day Jesus drives out the merchants. Therefore, in chapter 19 Luke could not have written: "peace on earth".

Yet, "peace in the highest heaven" is seen by the Lukan Jesus as the program for earth. As King making peace he comes in the name of the Lord and as such he is acclaimed by the disciples: blessed by God. This supposes that the eschatological peace is already present on earth, at least in his person. While all this is not stated explicitly in the praise of 19,38, such a vision certainly dominates the mind of Luke.

Conclusion

The main results of this study can be summarized in a threefold conclusion.

1. Luke intended to create a connection between 2,14 and 19,38. In 19,38 he wanted to resume the acclamation of 2,14. The alterations which he made to his source text (Mk 11,9-10), as well as his own additions, do not

leave any doubt about that. In both passages angels or disciples sing "glory to God"; heaven and earth are brought together. In both passages (or their context) Jesus is presented as King: to him will be given the throne of his father David (1,32); he is the Savior, Christ the Lord (2,11); he is the King who comes in the name of the Lord (19,38); he will return for judgment as King (cf. 19,15). In both passages the theme of peace is very much emphasized.

2. At closer inspection there is no real opposition between peace on earth (2,14) and peace in heaven (19,38). The peace that both acclamations mention is the eschatological peace which God realizes through the sending of his Son and which should be received by the whole of humankind. According to 19,29-44 Jesus enters Jerusalem as the King who brings that peace from heaven, but some of the Pharisees, as well as Jerusalem with its temple, refuse to recognize what is needed for peace. According to 2,1-21 there is peace among those whom God favors; yet God's favor supposes human responsivity. Thus the two pericopes appear to be complementary. In chapter 2 God is in the forefront. In chapter 19 attention is rather devoted to the human reaction; in this chapter Luke explains that on earth peace is not received by all: see the parable of the pounds, the Pharisees' reaction, Jesus' lament over Jerusalem and his cleansing of the temple.

In Acts 10,34-36 Peter says:

> I truly understand that God shows no partiality, but in every nation anyone who fears him and does what is right is acceptable to him. You know the message he sent to the people of Israel, preaching peace by Jesus Christ – he is the Lord of all.

It is evident that God's plan of universal salvation as well as Christ's gospel of peace stand out. Yet Israel and all nations alike must fear God and do what is right; they all must become acceptable to God. In the sending of the seventy in Lk 10,1-12 something similar occurs. Whenever they go into a house the first word they speak shall be: "peace be with this home" (v. 5). Yet the messengers must be received.

That Luke intended to oppose "peace on earth" of 2,14b to the "pax Romana", the political peace within the Roman Empire, is doubtful. Still more doubtful is the opinion that by means of "peace in heaven" he wanted to contrast that heavenly peace with the Jewish War that tragically ended in the fall of Jerusalem[1].

---

1. These views are defended by Günter KLEIN, in "Eschatologie und Schöpfung bei Lukas. Eine kosmische Liturgie im dritten Evangelium", which is published in M. EVANG,

3. The two texts, 2,14 and 19,38, are commonly called praises or acclamations. Yet in them there appears to be a wish ("glory be to God") and
an announcement or proclamation ("there is peace thanks to the coming of Jesus"). The two clauses are different and separated. However, one
can prayerfully make a causal connection between wish and proclamation. The wish then becomes, almost by itself, an imperative: God must
be glorified and praised because out of heaven God has brought peace
on earth through his Son Jesus Christ.

H. MERKLEIN, M. WOLTER (eds.), *Eschatologie und Schöpfung. FS E. Grässer* (BZNW, 89),
Berlin – New York, 1997, 145-194. This article prompted me to write this brief study.

8

The Parable of the Throne Claimant
(Luke 19,11-27)

The version of Matthew's parable of the talents (Mt 25,14-30) in Luke's gospel is often called the parable of the pounds. It would seem that "the claimant to the throne" is a better title[1]. How does the evangelist Luke understand this parable? The aim of this study is to examine how Luke's view of salvation history corresponds with the placement of the parable in the gospel as well as its rewriting. The first part will be devoted to the state of the question. In the second part I will try to connect the so-called diachronical and synchronical approaches. Some hermeneutical considerations will constitute the content of the third part.

Text, Context and Luke's Salvation History

For the state of the question regarding Luke's claimant to the throne I summarize here the conclusions of two of my previous studies (1981 and 1985) and those of an excellent article by Vittorio Fusco (1992)[2].

---

1. Compare similar titles "the parable of the pretender to the throne"; "the Lukan kingship parable"; and "the royal parable of the pounds". – It is for me a joy to contribute an article in honor of R. Jesu Raja, S.J., colleague and friend.
2. The first study is part of J. LAMBRECHT, *Once More Astonished: The Parables of Jesus*, New York, 1981, pp. 167-195: "The Talents and the Pounds". This work is a revised edition of *Parables of Jesus: Insight and Challenge*, Bangalore, 1978, which is a translation from the Dutch *Terwijl Hij tot ons sprak. Parabels van Jezus*, Tielt – Amsterdam, 1976. A newly reworked version is present in *Out of the Treasure: The Parables in the Gospel of Matthew* (LTPM, 10), Leuven, 1994, pp. 217-244. The quotations are taken from this last publication.
The second study is J. LAMBRECHT, "Reading and Rereading Lk 18,31–22,6"; it appeared in *À cause de l'Évangile. Mélanges offerts à Dom Jacques Dupont* (LD, 123), Paris, 1985, 585-612.
The article by V. FUSCO is entitled "'Point of View' and 'Implicit Reader' in Two Eschatological Texts (Lk 19,11-28; Acts 1,6-8)" and is published in F. VAN SEGBROECK, C. M. TUCKETT, G. VAN BELLE, J. VERHEYDEN (eds.), *The Four Gospels. FS Frans Neirynck* (BETL, 100B), Leuven, 1992, 1677-1696. For the bibliography we may refer to these

The Text

One could call the analysis of the first study mainly "diachronical". A sort of basis text (Q) is reconstructed which has provided the (hypothetical) starting point for the later divergent gospel texts of Matthew and Luke. It is further stated that the Q text does not yet offer the parable as it was spoken by the earthly Jesus; a still earlier version must be distinguished. Only then, after the analytical search, can the original parable of Jesus, its Q version and the two gospel texts be explained one after the other.

Most probably both Matthew and Luke were editorially very active. It would seem that the Q version spoke of pounds, not talents, and of only three servants who received either five pounds, two or one pounds. Their reward is "to be set over much" because they have been faithful over "little". From the servant who has received the one pound and hid it in the ground, that pound is taken and given to the servant who has the ten pounds. Already in Q the wisdom saying "to every one who has will more be given; but from him who has not, even what he has will be taken away" (19,26) was added by Christians at an early stage.

In our opinion Luke himself is responsible for the introductory verse (19,11) and for expanding the Q parable of the pounds with the data about the throne claimant; therefore, also verses 14 and 27 are due to his redaction. The end of verse 13, the second part of 15, verse 22a and the whole of verse 25 are equally secondary. We added, however: "it is not necessary to hold, at all cost, to the position that Luke works with the 'bare' parable of the source-text which we think we have been able to reconstruct"[3]. Nonetheless, the Q parable has been altered in a remarkable way. "Luke's version … can be described with three terms: it reflects allegorizing, de-eschatologizing, and moralizing"[4].

The reader of Luke's gospel has to interpret the parable in a radically allegorical way[5]. The master is no longer God; the man of noble birth is Christ who leaves and disappears. The far country is heaven and the journey is Christ's ascension. There Christ will be enthroned as king, and it is as king that he will return for judgment. His Jewish compatriots who rejected him will be severely punished (= fall of Jerusalem in 70 AD). His

studies. More recent commentaries on the gospel of Luke include those by L. T. JOHNSON, J. NOLLAND and J. B. GREEN.

3. LAMBRECHT, *Out of the Treasure*, p. 236.
4. *Ibid.*
5. Cf. *ibid.*, pp. 236-240.

servants – all Christians – will have to give an account of what they have done with what has been entrusted to them (= Last Judgment).

"In light of the gospel context, and more particularly of the statement in 19,11, this allegory is intended to show that the kingdom will not be manifested at the time of Jesus' entry into Jerusalem. A certain misconception on this point must be dispelled. Jesus must first die and ascend to heaven. Only thereafter will he return as king. In the meantime, active service is called for"[6]. The allegory is especially meant for Jesus' disciples. "But through the disciples the evangelist also has his contemporaries, his fellow Christians, in mind. Luke thus de-eschatologizes, that is, he explains why the kingdom of God has not yet been manifested. He uses the allegory to combat the enthusiastic expectation of the end, the *Naherwartung*, among his Christian community (or to alleviate their disappointment at the long delay of the parousia)"[7].

During the period of absence, the believers must engage themselves in the task of trading with the money entrusted to them. Luke inserts an explicit command into his text (see 19,13). In view of the return of the king and the coming judgment this is now their urgent duty. According to Luke, that judgment is not far off. The fall of Jerusalem in the recent past proves this. So, in a certain sense, for the fellow Christians Luke insists on readiness and watchfulness: "this generation will not pass away till all has taken place" (21,32)[8]. Just as with his allegorizing rewriting, the so-called delay character of the parable manifests a parenetic and moralizing intention.

The Context

A threefold "synchronical" reading of Lk 18,31–22,6 takes into account Luke's use of sources (Mk, Q and his special material) and his compositional skill. The first reading shows how in this gospel section Luke deliberately concentrates and unifies the geography. He emphasizes Jesus' drawing near to Jerusalem; he presents Jesus' final teaching ministry in the same place (the temple) and within one period of time. Luke clarifies the real meaning of Jerusalem, and even more, the exact sequence of the future events. The second reading, therefore, focuses on Luke's eschatology, his view of the longer period of waiting between Jesus' death and

6. LAMBRECHT, *Out of the Treasure*, p. 237.
7. *Ibid.*, p. 238.
8. So Luke's "de-eschatologizing" is not complete.

return, but also his conviction that with the fall of Jerusalem the end was at hand. The third reading pays special attention to the Jewish people and their authorities. Within this lengthy passage Luke is almost completely absorbed by the guilt of Israel and her leaders, by the fate of the city and its temple, so that the role of the Gentiles remains negative and, for the time being, Luke's universalism seems forgotten[9].

In 18,31–19,27 it is best to distinguish only three pericopes: the prediction of the passion (18,31-34), the healing of the blind man (18,35-43), and Jesus in the house of Zacchaeus (19,1-27). In the prediction of the passion the Lukan Jesus states: "Behold, we are going up to Jerusalem, and everything that is written of the Son of Man by the prophets will be accomplished" (18,31). The other two pericopes begin with a topographical indication: "As he drew near to Jericho" (18,35) and "He entered Jericho and was passing through" (19,1). "Jericho" calls for attention. There is no serious reason for making the parable a separate pericope. It is told in the house of Zacchaeus. Those present who have murmured "He has gone in to be the guest of a man who is a sinner" (19,7) can hear Jesus speaking. Moreover, Luke states that Jesus adds the parable to what he has already said: "As they heard all these things, he proceeded to tell a parable" (19,11). Yet one must concede that the third pericope has become rather long. Therefore, in 19,28 Luke must repeat the travel motif: "And when he [= Jesus] had said this, he went on ahead, going up (ἀναβαίνων, same verb in 18,31) to Jerusalem". From 19,11, the verse which introduces the parable, it is clear that "Jerusalem" seemingly occupies the mind of the Lukan Jesus. The reason why Jesus tells the parable is that he is near Jerusalem. Just as the prediction of the passion informs the readers as to the real meaning of Jerusalem, so the parable of the throne claimant explains which events will be connected with the city. Jerusalem is not only the place of suffering and resurrection but also of Jesus' departure for a temporary absence; only later will Jesus return, installed as king, and only later will the kingdom of God be manifested[10].

In 18,34 Luke notes that the twelve have not understood the prediction of the passion: "this saying was hid from them, and they did not grasp what was said". One can regard 19,11 as an illustration of this lack of understanding. The twelve, too, suppose that the arrival at Jerusalem will mean the glorious appearance of the kingdom of God. Luke himself probably expands the parable by adding the story about the nobleman who wants to receive a kingdom. By such a conflation the parable

9. Cf. the conclusion in LAMBRECHT, "Reading and Rereading", p. 612.
10. Cf. *ibid.*, pp. 590-591.

becomes a rather complicated narrative. There are hostile compatriots who, by sending an embassy after the throne-pretender, try to prevent his becoming a king. As in the original parable, however, there are also servants. According to Luke, during the absence of their lord they must trade with the money they receive. At his return the king wants to know what his servants have done with the money; then comes the punishment of those who refused his rule. Luke thus reworks the parable into a moralizing allegory with which he discusses a period of Church history. Jesus must first die and go into a far country, i.e., heaven. Only then will he come back, installed as king. In the meantime his disciples have to trade with their pounds. The Jews who do not recognize Jesus as Messiah should not think that he will remain powerless and inactive forever. He will return as a mighty king and he will judge them severely[11].

Three times in the gospel of Luke (17,20; 19,11; 21,7) and once in Acts (1,6), a question is asked about the end events. It would seem that the Lukan Jesus has to correct false time conceptions. The Son of man must first suffer and be rejected by this generation (17,25); the kingdom of God will not "appear" immediately after Jesus' arrival at Jerusalem (19,12-27). The kingdom will not be "restored" immediately after the resurrection (Acts 1,7-11). Neither will the kingdom "come" at the moment of Jerusalem's fall, before the times of the Gentiles are fulfilled (Lk 21,20-28). Yet, as far as the destruction of Jerusalem and the desolation of the temple are concerned, it should be emphasized that Luke situates this catastrophe within the period leading up to the end. No doubt he himself already looks back at that destruction, but this by no means implies that for him the coming of the Son of man lies in a far-off, distant future. Luke, like Mark, still lives in a sphere of *Naherwartung*; he eagerly expects a fast-approaching end to this world. That is why he exhorts his fellow-Christians to watchfulness (Lk 21) and diligent activity (Lk 19) with such insistence. He supports his admonition by means of the consideration that the end time is near and that the "day" will come upon all suddenly (cf. 21,34-36). This period of waiting should be spent and utilized in a responsible way[12].

Lukan Salvation History

At the beginning of his study, V. Fusco refers to the same four Lukan texts. For Luke there is a close link between the messianic kingdom and

---

11. Cf. LAMBRECHT, "Reading and Rereading", pp. 600-601.
12. Cf. *ibid.*, pp. 598-600 and 602-605.

Jerusalem. No doubt the Messiah is identified with Jesus himself. The coming of the kingdom is not different from the coming of the Son of man at his parousia. Fusco claims that the Lukan Jesus in no way corrects an earthly or nationalistic conception. Even the chronological questions are not refused nor blamed. In the four texts, "the hope of a prompt coming at that moment is rejected: not only in a negative way, reassessing the impredictability of the end (17,20-37; 21,34-36; Acts 1,7); but also in a more positive way, explaining that the delay is due to certain events which should have occurred before. And it is very interesting to notice what these events are and how they follow one another: first of all the passion (Lk 17,25), then a time of absence of the Lord after his ascension (Lk 19,11-28) and, during this time, the destruction of Jerusalem followed by the 'times of the Gentiles' (Lk 21,24b), and finally the witness to the end of the earth (Acts 1,8)"[13].

Hermeneutical considerations form part of this study. Fusco deals with "the point of view" in the eschatological texts of Luke. One must distinguish between the point of view within the narration (the Lukan Jesus predicts future events) and the real setting of Luke and his readers (the evangelist probably wrote after the destruction of Jerusalem)[14]. Why then does Luke mention events which for him certainly belong to the past? Fusco's answer contains a number of not exclusive possibilities: "there might have been the need to interpret all these events theologically, to solve problems they had left unsolved; if those experiences had left behind them a sequel of dangerous misunderstanding and disappointment, this had to be eliminated. Besides, the more one recalled Jesus' prophecies that had already come true, the stronger became the certainty that all the other prophecies would certainly be fulfilled in due time. Since the ultimate fulfillment could not take place without all the previous stages, reminding them becomes quite necessary in order to keep the expectation alive. Still more: assessing that they are *all* fulfilled, might even mean ... that the goal is almost reached"[15].

Fusco very much emphasizes that for Luke's readers the destruction of Jerusalem is not fully "de-eschatologized". The connection of this past event and the still future parousia is not broken. Of course, the Christians experienced a delay, but a short-term expectation coexisted. "For the

---

13. Cf. "'Point of View' and 'Implicit Reader'", pp. 1679-1680.
14. See *ibid.*, pp. 1682-85. There is also "the literary point of view chosen by the narrator" (cf. p. 1683). For this Fusco points to the time of Paul's imprisonment narrated in Acts 28,30-32. However, in Luke's case, "it is not necessary to separate the real from the literary setting" (p. 1684); the readers must have known that the evangelist had written after the destruction of Jerusalem.
15. *Ibid.*, pp. 1684-1685.

first Christian generations perhaps there never was an expectation which
was not an imminent expectation, although this does not necessarily
mean that it either reached a feverish intensity or became the center of
faith"[16].

By the mention of the opinion concerning the appearance of the kingdom in 19,11 Luke specifies the function of the ensuing parable at the
juncture of his gospel. The entry in Jerusalem will not coincide with the
appearance of the kingdom. The return of the king, i.e., Jesus' parousia,
will be the Last Judgment. The punishment of the rebels (19,27) points
to the catastrophe of 70 A.D., the destruction of Jerusalem. One must not
see too great a difficulty in the fact that the parable suggests that the
return of the king, the reward of the servants, and the punishment of the
enemies are simultaneous. Fusco maintains: "the only possibility of bringing both the punishment together with the events of 70 A.D. and the
reward of the servants together with the parousia is to admit that for
the evangelist the span between the two events is short enough to take
them as a whole". According to Fusco the parable does not weaken "the
hypothesis of an imminent expectation still persistent in Luke-Acts". In
no way should one interpret the departure "into a far country" (19,12) as
referring to an endless delay of the parousia[17].

Discussion

This retrospective overview of three studies cannot but lead to a reflection. Should one oppose the two approaches, the diachronical and the
synchronical, and manifest a preference for one of them? And, after all,
how is Luke's view of salvation history to be related to his eschatological conviction? In this second part no effort is given to a further analysis of the detailed exegesis in the previous studies. The sole aim is a more

---

16. Cf. FUSCO, "Point of View", pp. 1685-1686. Fusco here employs the terminology
of "implicit" reader.

17. Cf. *ibid.*, pp. 1687-1693; quoted texts on p. 1689. The parable also possesses an
apologetical-christological interest ("... although Jesus' entry into Jerusalem did have
something triumphal about it ..., it could not establish the Kingdom immediately: the
responsibility fell on Jerusalem itself ...", p. 1191) and a parenetical note ("for unbelievers ... a threat, for Christians an encouragement and an appeal ...", *ibid.*).

On pp. 1688-1689 Fusco critically deals with the studies of L. T. JOHNSON, "The Lukan
Kingship Parable (Lk 19,11-27)", in *NT* 24 (1982) 139-159 and I. DE LA POTTERIE, "La
parabole du prétendant à la royauté (Lc 19,11-28)", in *À cause de l'Évangile. FS J. Dupont*
(LD, 123), Paris, 1985, 613-641. Be it in partly differing ways, these two authors refuse to
see a reference to the parousia in this parable.

precise insight into the area of methodology and a better grasp of the Lukan convictions.

Two Complementary Approaches

It would seem that a diachronical investigation as well as a synchronical analysis are useful and that both approaches appear to be complementary.

The diachronical approach compares Luke's parable with that of the talents of Matthew and reconstructs a source-text. Next to the possibility of a better understanding of what the more original parable – and perhaps the earthly Jesus by means of it – intended, such a comparison clearly shows the secondary character of Luke's fusion of two stories, that of the claimant and that of the pounds. By looking at the source-text one finds an explanation for what appears to be a too greatly expanded part of the account (vv. 15-26). Furthermore, the attentive reader senses that Luke was not completely free nor entirely consistent in his editing. A consideration of the ten servants and the fact that only three of them are heard at the return of the king makes this evident. Finally, to a certain degree Luke appears to want to remain faithful to his source-text: see, e.g., his redactional verse 25 which introduces the strange saying of verse 26 that is retained.

In the Q-material, the parable of the pounds may have followed that of the faithful or wicked servant (cf. Mt 24,45-51 and 25,14-30, thus separated in Matthew only by the *Sondergut* of the parable of the ten virgins, 25,1-13). Luke presents the parable of the faithful or wicked servant in 12,42-46. In 12,47-48 he himself adds: "And that servant who knew his master's will, but did not make ready or act according to his will, shall receive a severe beating. But the one who did not know, and did what deserves a beating will receive a light beating. From everyone to whom much has been given, much will be required; and from the one to whom much has been entrusted, even more will be demanded". It is not impossible, in fact it seems likely, that Luke wrote these verses after reading the parable of the pounds which followed next in his Q-source (on this hypothesis, he did not wish to use the parable of the pounds immediately in chapter 12 but reserved it for his chapter 19). To know God's will and yet not to act according to it deserves severe chastisement. From those to whom much is entrusted more will be demanded. In 12,47-48 Luke is thinking about levels of responsibility and he does so probably under the influence of the parable of the pounds. Then, in chapter 19, when he comes to edit that parable itself, he probably still has the reflection of 12,47-48 in mind[18].

On the other hand the synchronical investigation convincingly shows why the original parable is expanded by that of the throne claimant and why Luke places it on the way in Jericho, i.e., before Jesus' arrival in Jerusalem. The allegorization of the parable functions within the broader context: the temporary absence of the claimant (after Jesus' death), his installation as king (ascension), and his return (parousia with judgment). As king Jesus is present in the parable (19,12 and 15), but also during the entry into Jerusalem (19,38) and during the passion (23,2-3 and 37-38). That the harsh punishment of 19,27 refers to the destruction of Jerusalem becomes almost undeniable in the light of parallel texts such as 19,41-44; 21,6.20-24; and 23,27-31. The delay of the parousia is confirmed by 17,25; 21,8-9 and Acts 1,7-11.

It is evident that the two approaches enrich each other; they control each other and they provide a mutual confirmation of the insight into Luke's salvation historical conception.

De-eschatologizing?

Fusco does not want to assume that Luke describes the Jewish expectations as too earthly and nationalistic nor that Jesus rectifies them: "there is no trace of such reproach or correction"[19]. However, the point of view within the narration, obviously different from Luke's own setting, should be taken into account. This distinction is rightly put forward by Fusco himself. Within the gospel narration the twelve are full of misunderstanding with regard to Jesus' going to Jerusalem (see 18,34). The twelve and other people and even Pharisees ask questions which betray their expectation of an imminent appearance of the kingdom that presumably is thought of in a worldly form (see 17,20; 19,11; 21,7; Acts 1,6). Jesus has to correct their views over and over again. In this sense, he de-eschatologizes his arrival in Jerusalem as well as his passion, resurrection and ascension.

For the real setting of Luke and his readers the situation is different. What, according to the narration, is corrective prophecy becomes later an assessment *post eventum*. Luke and his readers can look back on Jesus' entry, his death, resurrection and ascension, on initial persecutions of Christians and most probably also on the destruction of Jerusalem. The Lukan

---

18. Cf. LAMBRECHT, *Out of the Treasure*, pp. 238-239.
19. FUSCO, "Point of View", p. 1679.

Jesus places these events within salvation history and explains them. He strongly moralizes: in between his departure and his return Christians must "trade" with the money they receive; opposition on the part of the enemies will be punished severely. Yet, as far as Luke's actual readers are concerned, no de-eschatologizing is present.

Luke's Expectation

It is in the eschatological discourse of chapter 21 that Luke provides a rather detailed overview of future events. A threefold division of this discourse can be assumed: verses 5-9, 10-28, and 29-36. In verses 5-9, after the prediction of the passion, Jesus is asked when the destruction of the temple will take place and what will be the sign when this is about to occur (cf. v. 7). Verse 9 makes evident that the Lukan Jesus connects all this with the "end". In verses 8-9 Jesus issues a warning. One must not follow after the pseudo-messiahs who come in his name and also say: "the time is at hand". Nor should rumors of wars terrify the disciples. "These things" must take place, but the end will not follow immediately. A time period of wars and pseudo-messiahs also lies before the destruction of the temple.

Luke provides still more explanation in verses 10-28. In verses 10-11 Jesus considers the questions of verse 7 (when and what sign?) in greater detail. The fight of the nations, the catastrophes on earth and the terrifying signs in heaven constitute the answer. All this is the "sign". Then (or immediately after all this) the destruction of the temple will take place and the end will follow. But within this passage, in verses 12-19, Jesus again deals with the period which precedes that end, a period in which the disciples will be heavily persecuted. Jesus promises help and, as in verses 8-9, encourages them and exhorts them to persevere in their endurance. In verses 20-28 he again returns to the questions of verse 7 and the answer already given in verses 10-11. Regarding timing, the signs and the distress in verses 25-26 correspond to those in verses 10-11. Verses 20-28 should be regarded as a sort of unit. The whole leads up to the end. Jerusalem's destruction (vv. 20-24) on the one hand and the signs and coming of the Son of man (vv. 25-27) on the other cannot be totally distanced from each other. Moreover, verse 28 links all this to the very end: "Now when these things begin to take place, look up and raise your heads, because your redemption is drawing near". To be sure, verse 24 indicates that the dispersion of the Jews and the cruelties of the Gentiles will last a certain period, namely "until the times of the Gentiles are fulfilled", but it would be wrong to radically separate verses 20-24 from verses 25-28 as far as time is concerned. For Luke, the destruction of the city is the beginning of the end. By means of "and there will be signs in sun and moon and stars" in verse 25 Luke continues speaking of the time period already dealt with in verses 20-24. What might have seemed to be a rather accidental link between the destruction of the temple and the end of ages in verses 5-9 is thus strongly confirmed by the connection present in the composition of verses 20-28.

A time connection is also emphasized in the last pericope, verses 29-38. "When you see these things taking place, know that the kingdom of God is already near" (v. 30). "These things" (cf. "all" in v. 32) are most probably the signs and events depicted in verses 10-11 and 25-28; but they also contain – be it separated by a certain period from these signs – the fall of Jerusalem and the destruction of the temple (vv. 6 and 20-24). In the time before the end the disciples must take heed and be watchful (vv. 34-36, a Lukan composition)[20].

Fusco, too, rightly emphasizes Luke's expectation of Jesus' imminent return, his parousia[21]. For Luke and his fellow believers, there may have been experiences of delay, but it is Luke's firm hope that the basic content of their eschatological hope, Jesus' parousia, does not vanish into a far-distant and indefinite future.

Eschatology Today

The exegetical task is not completed as long as the question of the relevance of the text for believers today is not answered. Does Luke's salvation historical conception as outlined above retain its significance for this planet that is part of the cosmos, notwithstanding a substantially altered view of history?

Better Insight

Thanks to the double exegetical approach a better insight into the interpretation of events and situations by Luke can no doubt be obtained. One cannot but admire the great compositional daring of the evangelist. By means of the allegorized throne claimant narrative, he redefines his eschatology. Christ's passion, resurrection and ascension, the persecutions undergone by the Christians, the punishment and destruction of

---

20. Cf. LAMBRECHT, "Reading and Rereading", pp. 602-604.
21. Cf. FUSCO, "'Point of View'", e.g., pp. 1682, 1684-1685, 1686 and 1695-1696.

unfaithful Jerusalem: all this already belongs to the past. Nevertheless, these events of the past, instead of relaxing the expectation of the end, function in Luke's view as a guarantee for the hope of Christ's speedy return. For Luke Christ is the expected King-Judge. The fate of Jerusalem remains a warning for the enemies. For the individual believer a responsible devotion to the task until the parousia is insisted upon. All Christians have to watch at all times and to pray so that they can stand before the coming Son of man (cf. 21,36). The apostles have received the power of the Holy Spirit to be Christ's witnesses to the end of the earth (cf. Acts 1,8). By all means Luke's vision is grandiose.

Critical Evaluation

Notwithstanding the Lukan endeavor and adaptation a double critical reflection cannot be omitted. First of all, it has to be fully recognized that the parousia is delayed. Centuries have passed; the end has not come. No sign indicates that history will not continue for centuries to come.

But there is much more. The dimensions of time and space are for us, as it were, broken open. There is the almost immeasurable past of the cosmos, the hidden and far away origin of life and humanity. Our view of history is radically different from that of Luke and his contemporaries. And what about the world in that history, our earth in the midst of galaxies? Furthermore, most of India, the whole of China and the rest of Asia, great parts of Africa and the two Americas were unknown in the first century. There was no idea at all of the nearly countless human beings of past and present times, human beings with their respective religions[22].

So the question cannot be avoided: What is today the lasting value, what was and is for all of us the relevance of Luke's eschatological message?

Actualization

Luke adapted the original parable of the pounds taking into account those events which for him and his readers already belonged to the past. In his rewriting he was, of course, also conditioned by the then limited knowledge of world and history. Therefore today's Christians have to adjust Luke's vision. How in the eschaton the Kingdom in its universal and cosmic dimensions will "appear" remains a mystery. Without giving

---

22. From 1990 until 1995 I was a witness to how Fr. Raja has been acutely sensitive to such wordwide problems during the meetings of the Pontifical Biblical Commission.

up their eschatological hope of a final completion in Christ, Christians should certainly avoid all speculations about the date of the end. It simply is not for us to know times and periods that the Father has set by his own authority (cf. Acts 1,6). Although here, too, the term "de-eschatologizing" proves less appropriate, each form of *Naherwartung*, of a feverish expectation of the imminent end, is altogether wrong, especially around the turn of a millennium.

Of course, parabolic or allegorical language should not be interpreted too literally. Departure to a far country and return from it, as well as the installation of a king, are images or metaphors; they must not be understood realistically. Although the harsh words in Lk 19,27 ("But as for these enemies of mine, who did not want me to reign over them, bring them here and slay them before me") can perhaps be better received when examples in the Old Testament (cf., e.g., 1 Sam 15,33) and everywhere in history are remembered, the image of a vindictive judge disturbs our view of Christ.

Yet a much greater difficulty lies in Luke's identification of the brutal action of the king with the fall of Jerusalem. Can such an intramundane catastrophe be seen as God's punishment because Israel – part of it! – rejected her Messiah? Nowadays, most commentators will hesitate to answer this question positively, and it would seem rightly so.

For Christian life, however, an eschatological spirituality remains fundamentally sound. There is the Christian hope of the coming, appearance and restoration of God's kingdom (Lk 17,20; 19,11; Acts 1,6), of the return of Jesus (Acts 1,11), i.e., the coming of "the Son of man in a cloud with power and great glory" (Lk 21,27). This will be, perhaps still far away, the eschaton in the strict sense. There also is, however, a nearer eschatological dimension for each of us. Why not say it plainly? Not too many years separate the believers from death, i.e., from their encounter with Christ, their Savior and Judge. The nobleman of the parable orders his servants to trade with the money he has given them (Lk 19,13); the risen Lord instructs the apostles to bear witness for him in Jerusalem, and all over Judea and Samaria, and away to the ends of the earth (Acts 1,8). Who among us, listening to these commands, cannot fill in his or her own particular vocation? For all of us hope that at that final encounter we hear the approval from Christ: Well done, you are a good, trustworthy servant (Lk 19,17)[23].

---

23. A slightly adapted Italian version of this study is published in E. FRANCO (ed.), *Mysterium Regni, Ministerium Verbi. Scritti in onore di mons. Vittorio Fusco* (SupplRivBib, 31), Bologna, 2001, 379-390: "La parabola del pretendente al trono (Lc 19,11-27)". V. Fusco died on July 11, 1999.

9

The Lame Man's Trust or Peter's Faith?
(Acts 3,12-16)

The Greek text of Acts 3,16 reads:

a καὶ ἐπὶ τῇ πίστει τοῦ ὀνόματος αὐτοῦ τοῦτον ὃν θεωρεῖτε καὶ οἴδατε, ἐστερέωσεν τὸ ὄνομα αὐτοῦ,
b καὶ ἡ πίστις ἡ δι' αὐτοῦ ἔδωκεν αὐτῷ τὴν ὁλοκληρίαν ταύτην ἀπέναντι πάντων ὑμῶν.

In his commentary Joseph A. Fitzmyer (*The Acts of the Apostles* [AB, 31], New York, 1998) translates this verse as follows:

a Indeed, because of faith in his name, that name has made this man strong whom you see and know well.
b The faith that comes through Jesus has given him the perfect health that is present before all of you (p. 281).

He notes: "This sentence is not well written..." (p. 286); he further-more asserts:

It is not clear whose faith is involved. One might think that it is the beg-gar's faith, but that is not expressed, save indirectly in his subsequent praise of God (3:8-9). So it might refer to the faith of Peter and John who, believ-ing in the power of Jesus' name, were able to cure the lame beggar. In any case, *pistis* expresses an effective allegiance to the risen Christ and through it the miracle has taken place (ibid.).

However, if Luke has in mind the beggar's faith, it is difficult to see how such faith could express "an effective allegiance to the risen Christ through which the miracle has taken place". That faith would be little more than initial trust or confidence.

There can no doubt that in the Lukan gospel faith often is that of the sinner or the sick person. In *The Gospel According to Luke I–IX* (AB, 28), New York, 1981, p. viii, Fitzmyer aptly distinguishes among three stages in his discussion of the Lukan text:

Stage I is concerned with what the historical Jesus of Nazareth did and said; Stage II with what was preached and proclaimed about him after the resurrection; and Stage III with what NT writers decided to put in writing concerning him.

With regard to faith in Luke's gospel one has to reckon with these stages: "... in stage I *pistis* would hardly have had the full sense of post-resurrection faith in Jesus. But in stage III, on the level of Lucan composition, it may well carry that connotation" (p. 236).

So in Lk 5,20 ("when he saw their faith"), in Stage I faith would have meant "that Jesus would be able to do something for the man's condition, a sense of confidence in the power manifest in Jesus" (p. 582; cf., e.g., p. 692 on 7,50: "Your faith has brought you salvation"). In stage I faith thus means confidence, trust.

In the Dutch Roman Catholic revised *Willibrordvertaling* (1995) of Luke's gospel one finds four times "uw vertrouwen is uw redding", "your trust is your rescue" (7,50; 8,48; 17,19 and 18,42). The first Greek word is πίστις. The expression "is ... redding" renders the perfect σέσωκεν of the verb σώζω ("to rescue, to save"). English versions currently render ἡ πίστις σου σέσωκέν σε by "your faith has saved you". Of course, one can claim that before Jesus' resurrection the sinful or sick people could not really have Christian faith. They manifested their trust in Jesus. They placed their confidence in the wonderworker. However, the problem is whether the evangelist Luke makes the distinction between Fitzmyer's stages I and III. Does Luke suppose such a distinction to be present in the mind of his readers? I do not think so.

Two Translations of Acts 3,12-16

The problems are even more complicated in the first part of Peter's discourse in The Acts of the Apostles after the healing of the beggar at the gate of the temple. Peter and John have gone to the temple. There a lame man asks for alms. Peter addresses him saying: "I have no silver or gold, but what I have I give you; in the name of Jesus Christ of Nazareth, stand up and walk" (3,6). Even though in Acts the pre-paschal stage I is no longer present, the beggar's approach can be compared to it: he must have had confidence in Peter and John and, equally, an initial trust in Jesus Christ.

Peter's long discourse begins in 3,12 and ends at 3,26. For this note only verses 12-16 are of interest. This is the NRSV translation:

12   You Israelites, why do you wonder at this, or why do you stare at us,
      as though by our own power or piety we had made him walk?
13   The God of Abraham, the God of Isaac, and the God of Jacob, the
      God of our ancestors has glorified his servant Jesus, whom you handed

over and rejected in the presence of Pilate, though he had decided to release him.

14　But you rejected the Holy and Righteous One and asked to have a murderer given to you,

15　and you killed the Author of life, whom God raised from the dead. To this we are witnesses.

16a　And by faith in his name, his name itself has made this man strong, whom you see and know;

　b　and the faith that is through Jesus has given him this perfect health in the presence of all of you.

The miracle that Peter and John have worked has not been accomplished by their own power or piety (v. 12). It is the name of Jesus Christ, or the faith in that name, which has given the man physical strength and perfect health (v. 16). Apparently that faith is brought about by Jesus Christ himself: "the faith that is through Jesus" (v. 16). The question cannot be avoided: whose faith? That of Peter and John or that of the lame man?

The revised *Willibrordvertaling* renders Acts 3,16 as follows: "Op grond van het vertrouwen in de naam Jezus Christus kwam er weer kracht in deze man hier, die u allen kent; dat vertrouwen heeft hem, waar u allen bij was, weer helemaal gezond gemaakt". We may translate this simplifying and somewhat paraphrasing version: "Because of the trust in the name Jesus Christ strength has returned in this man here, whom you all know; that trust has made him, before you all, completely healthy again". This translation of verse 16 merits our attention. It differs in three ways from the Greek original and the NRSV translation. (1) The translation of πίστις is "trust" (twice); (2) it is no longer said that the πίστις is δι' αὐτοῦ ("through him"); (3) "His name" is no longer the grammatical subject of the verb in v. 16a: "because of the trust in the name Jesus Christ strength has returned in this man here". The Greek text has: τοῦτον ... ἐστερέωσεν ... τὸ ὄνομα αὐτοῦ ("this [man] his name made firm"). The NRSV repeats "name" as the Greek text does: "And by faith in his name, his name itself has made this man strong".

Through the omission of the grammatical subject (3) the Dutch translator avoided the repetition of "name" and its awkward change of grammatical function; the Dutch sentence is also more simple and less rough than the Greek because of the absence of δι' αὐτοῦ (2). Yet preference should be given, I think, to the more literal NRSV. But what must be said about "trust" instead of "faith" (1)?

The revised English translation does not explicitly indicate that πίστις here is the trust of the lame man. Is the trust of Peter and John perhaps referred to? Yet in Peter and John one can hardly suppose the presence of trust in a wonderworker, rather than their faith in the risen Christ. So the readers of the new *Willibrordvertaling* think of the trust ("vertrouwen") of the beggar, quite spontaneously. But one must admit at once that "trust in the name" remains strange, and it is even stranger that such a trust can bring about the perfect health of the beggar. One could be tempted to refer to the clause "your trust is your rescue", but although *Willibrord* writes "has made him ... completely healthy again", the verb in v. 16 is not σῴζω but στερεόω ("to make firm"). Moreover, the context of v. 16 makes it clear, I think, that Luke means Peter's faith (and that of John). The following section will attempt to demonstrate this.

The Faith of Peter

In Peter's discourse the noun πίστις occurs only in 3,16 (twice). Neither the verb "to believe" nor the adjective "believing" are employed. In support of faith or trust of the lame man one could refer to 14,9-10. In Lystra there was a man who could not use his feet from birth. He listened to Paul, and Paul, "looking at him intently and seeing that he had faith to be healed (ὅτι ἔχει πίστιν τοῦ σωθῆναι), said in a loud voice, 'Stand on your feet'". Undoubtedly here the crippled man's faith or trust is meant, his confidence that he will be healed. Why not also in 3,16? It would seem that the five following reasons, taken together, require a negative answer to this question.

a) Perhaps the doing of a miracle not by the apostles' own power and piety (3,12) is contrasted with God who through that miracle glorifies his servant Jesus (v. 13). It is possible that "to glorify" refers here solely to God's raising of Jesus from the dead and verse 13a thus constitutes an inclusion with verse 15b. If so, then the double mention of Jesus' resurrection ("to glorify" in v. 13a and "to raise" in v. 15b) frames the sharp accusation against the Israelites (vv. 13b-15a): they handed Jesus over to Pilate, they rejected him in the presence of Pilate; they asked Pilate to have a murderer given to them; they killed the Author of life. Be this as it may, verse 16a ("by faith in his name") stands in contrast to v. 12a ("as though by our own power or piety"). Peter and John are convinced that, as matter of fact, they did not work the wonder by their own power but by the name of Jesus, that is Jesus himself. In this context the mention of the lame man's faith or trust would by no means be appropriate. This is confirmed by 3,6 where Peter says: "In the name of Jesus Christ of Nazareth, stand up and walk".

b) To the question who in fact is working the wonder and through what kind of agency it occurs, the answer is strikingly manifold. Peter performs the miracle, but in the name (ἐν τῷ ὀνόματι) of Jesus (3,6). In point of fact God himself performs it and thus glorifies his servant Jesus (3,13). The miracle is also said to be accomplished ἐπὶ τῇ πίστει τοῦ ὀνό-ματος αὐτοῦ ("'on the basis', 'upon' the faith in his name"); it is equally the name itself, or the faith in that name, which made the man strong (3,16). In 4,10 it is reiterated that "by the name (ἐν τῷ ὀνόματι) of Jesus Christ of Nazareth" this man is standing before the authorities in good health. In 4,12 the identification of the name with Jesus occurs explic-itly: "There is salvation in no one else, for there is no other name under heaven given among mortals by which (ἐν ᾧ) we must be saved". The name is Jesus himself, indeed. Finally, in 4,16 the miracle is ascribed to Peter and John as mediators: "a notable sign has been done through them (δι' αὐτῶν)". God himself, Jesus Christ, his name, Peter (and John) by, in or "upon" the name of Jesus. It would, therefore, seem that in 3,16 Luke most probably deals with Peter's faith, not that of the beggar. Given all these affirmations it would be utterly strange that it is the faith of this man that has occasioned the miracle.

c) At the end of 3,15 Peter states that God raised Jesus from the dead. It is somewhat unexpected that he immediately adds: "To this we are witnesses". Apparently God raising Jesus is the source of the apostle's faith; through Jesus' resurrection they continue to believe in his name. In the middle of 3,16 one comes across the surprising clause ἡ πίστις ἡ δι' αὐτοῦ, literally "the faith, the one through him" (= the faith that is through Jesus, that took its origin in Jesus). One surmises that this expres-sion refers to the appearances of Jesus: they gave birth to the faith of the disciples. To suppose here that the faith of the lame man is meant would really upset the context.

d) Grammatically as well as logically a reading of 3,16b with the lame man's faith as subject is nearly impossible. One would have to construe and interpret the text as follows: "his faith (= that of the lame man), that has its origin in him (= Jesus), has given him (= the man) perfect health". For the secondary "improvement" of the verse in the Western text, see Fitzmyer, *Acts*, p. 286.

e) A final reason for concluding that Luke's mention of faith in the name of Jesus points to Peter's faith can be found in the broader context of the narrative in Acts. Nothing in the first discourse of Peter in chap-ter 3 indicates that the beggar knows anything regarding Jesus Christ and his message. Where would his faith in Christ have come from?

The lame man has been carried to the gate of the temple every day. There he sees Peter and John who are entering the temple and he asks them for alms. At Peter's command, "Look at us", the man fixes his attention on them and expects to receive something from them. Without any further preparation he hears Peter say: "In the name of Jesus Christ of Nazareth" (cf. 3,1-6). Evidently, Peter speaks and acts out of his faith in Christ.

In conclusion: faith or trust of the lame man before his cure is out of the question. In Acts 3,16 Luke, be it in a logically and stylistically odd sentence, must have had in mind Peter's faith, rather than the faith of the beggar.

Cure or Salvation?

Chapter four of Acts goes on to deal with this miracle. Peter and John are arrested the same day; the next day they stand before the Jewish authorities. Peter, full of the Holy Spirit, speaks to them (see 4,8-12). Special attention must be devoted to verse 9 and verse 12. Peter and John are questioned because of a good deed done to someone who was sick: "how this man has been healed", how he was made well (v. 9). The verb is σῴζω ("to rescue, to save"). In verse 12 we read the solemn declaration which contains the same verb as well as the noun (σωτηρία): οὐκ ἔστιν ἐν ἄλλῳ οὐδενὶ ἡ σωτηρία, οὐδὲ γὰρ ὄνομά ἐστιν ἕτερον ... ἐν ᾧ δεῖ σωθῆναι ἡμᾶς ("There is salvation in no one else, for there is no other name ... by which we must be saved". Clearly more than healing, more than recovery or cure is meant here.

Luke thus employs the same verb σῴζω for the physical healing of the beggar as well as for spiritual salvation. The conclusion is justified: for Luke the cure of the body points to the religious deliverance of the whole person; the miracle of healing symbolically refers to eschatological salvation.

Above, the last reason that is given why we should not find in 3,16 the lame man's faith or trust in Jesus Christ refers to his lack of acquaintance with Jesus. Before his cure, that man could certainly not have had faith in the risen Jesus. Could an analogous reasoning be applied to the clause "your faith has saved you"? Those in the gospel who implore forgiveness or healing can, of course, not yet possess the postpaschal faith. Must, therefore, in those Lukan passages "trust" or "confidence" be preferred? Probably not, not only because Luke is writing after Easter and his readers spontaneously interpret πίστις as the postpaschal christological faith of the disciples, but also because the confidence of sinners and trust of the sick symbolically refer to that faith, because their forgiveness or recovery anticipate the eschatological salvation which Jesus proclaimed.

There can be no doubt, however, that christological faith implies more than just intellectual knowing the truth. Trust is an integral part of it. Without trust and confidence no real faith exists; yet faith in the risen and glorified Jesus Christ is much richer and fuller than initial trust in the earthly Jesus.

Jesus Christ Is the Lord of All
(Acts 10,34-43)

Peter's so-called last mission discourse in Acts (10,34-43) is rather brief; its Greek syntax rough and uneven, at some places irregular[1]. Yet because it is Peter's last speech and, moreover, given its position in the book of Acts, this discourse merits a close reading. One should probably not look for a source text; the composition of this speech appears to be completely Lukan[2]. The many emphases present in it may at first appear confusing, but they prove to be remarkably rich and they ultimately support one another[3].

The passage belongs to the larger unit of 10,1–11,18, which, in great detail, deals with the conversion of Cornelius in Caesarea and the initiation of the mission to the Gentiles. Cornelius was a Gentile, a centurion of the Italian Cohort, "a devout man who feared God with all his household; he gave alms generously to the people and prayed constantly to God" (10,1-2). Cornelius has a vision and is told by the angel of God to send for Peter who is at Joppa. Peter comes to Caesarea and enters the house of Cornelius. After both have explained what happened to each of them, Peter speaks to Cornelius and all those present in the house.

---

1. Cf. B. M. METZGER, *A Textual Commentary on the Greek New Testament*, Stuttgart, ²1994, p. 333 (on vv. 36-38): "In several respects the Greek of the Alexandrian text is harsh…".

2. See the recent commentaries, as well as F. NEIRYNCK, "Actes 10,36-43 et l'Évangile", in ID., *Evangelica II* (BETL, 99), Leuven, 1991, pp. 227-236 (repr. 1984); G. SCHNEIDER, "Die Petrusrede vor Kornelius. Das Verhältnis von Tradition und Komposition in Apg 10,34-43", in ID., *Lukas, Theologe der Heilsgeschichte. Aufsätze zum lukanischen Doppelwerk* (BBB, 59), Bonn, 1985, pp. 253-279; A. WEISER, "Tradition und lukanische Komposition in Apg 10,36-43", in *À cause de l'Évangile. FS J. Dupont* (LD, 123), Paris, 1985, 759-767; R. C. TANNEHILL, "The Function of Peter's Mission Speeches in the Narratives of Acts", in *NTS* 37 (1991) 400-414.

3. This contribution is written in gratitude to David L. Dungan for editing, together with William R. Farmer (†), Sean McEvenue and Armando J. Levoratti, the one-volume *The International Bible Commentary. A Catholic and Ecumenical Commentary for the Twenty-First Century*, Collegeville, The Liturgical Press, 1998.

Four Evident Points

It would seem that the attentive readers of Peter's discourse will agree that the following four accents should not be missed.

God Shows No Partiality

The first emphasis is evident from the very beginning. Peter has been described by Luke as having been in a trance and having seen the sheet with animals and reptiles; he has heard God's command to kill and to eat: "what God has cleansed, you must not call common" (10,9-16). Peter has also heard about the vision that Cornelius experienced. So now he can say: "I truly understand that God shows no partiality, but in every nation, anyone who fears him and does what is right is acceptable to him" (10,34-35).

At the end of verse 36 Jesus Christ is said to be "the Lord of all"; because of the context πάντων is almost certainly masculine, not neuter[4]. In verse 42b Peter states that Jesus is ordained by God "as judge of the living and the dead"; this is a clearly comprehensive divine appointment. The universality of God's salvation is again pointed to at the very end of the discourse: "everyone who believes in him [= Christ] receives forgiveness of sins through his name" (v. 43b).

Already in verse 28 Peter had explained to Cornelius and the people around: "God has shown me that I should not call anyone profane or unclean". After the discourse, when the Holy Spirit fell upon all who heard it, the circumcised believers who had come with Peter could not but be astounded "that the gift of the Holy Spirit had been poured out even on 'the Gentiles'" (v. 45).

According to the author of Acts it is Peter, not Paul, who initiates the mission to the Gentiles. However, the second part of the book of Acts will abundantly illustrate how, above all, Paul is involved in that work of universal salvation. The ultimate reason for this universalism is that God shows no partiality.

The Fulfillment of the Scriptures

A second point is not so explicit but can hardly be neglected by the readers. The message sent to the people of Israel is cast in a language

---

4. Cf., e.g., J. DUPONT, "'Le Seigneur de tous' (Ac 10:36; Rm 10:12): Arrière-fond scripturaire d'une formule christologique", in G. HAWTHORNE *et al.* (eds.), *Tradition and Interpretation in the New Testament. FS E. E. Ellis*, Grand Rapids – Tübingen, 1987, 229-236.

which is clearly borrowed from Isaiah and thus presents itself as the fulfillment of what the prophet announces. Isa 61,1 reads: "The spirit of
the Lord God is upon me, because the Lord has anointed me; he has sent
me to bring good news to the oppressed…". Compare Acts 10,36-38: in
addition to the content there is the vocabulary of ἀποστέλλω, εὐαγγελίζομαι, χρίζω, πνεῦμα, ἰάομαι (cf. also the quotation in Lk 4,18-19)[5]. Peter
explains to Cornelius that the message preached by Jesus Christ to "the
sons of Israel" has spread throughout Judea (beginning in Galilee) and
ended in Jerusalem (see vv. 37-39).

Peter further indicates that the witnesses of the risen Lord are commanded to declare that Jesus is appointed as the future judge of the living
and the dead (vv. 40-42). Peter stresses that "all the prophets testify"
about Jesus Christ concerning forgiveness for everyone who believes in
him (see v. 43). Salvation history is certainly present here: Jesus announced
by the prophets, Jesus the Messiah of Israel, the risen Jesus manifested
and proclaimed, finally Jesus the universal judge.

God Has the Overall Initiative

The fact that Peter begins his discourse with God showing no partiality and that anyone in every nation fearing God and doing what is
right is acceptable to God is in itself and within the context not so
strange. Yet attentive readers will notice how Peter continues to stress
that God has taken the initiative over and over again. God "sent the message to the people of Israel, preaching peace by Jesus Christ" (v. 36b). God
anointed Jesus of Nazareth with the Holy Spirit and with power (v. 38a).
God was with always with Jesus (cf. the end of v. 38). God raised Jesus
on the third day (v. 40a). God allowed him to appear to the apostles
(vv. 40b-41). Most probably it is also God (and not Jesus Christ) who
commanded them to preach to the people and to testify that Jesus is the
future judge (v. 42).

God transcends time. Of course, Isaiah and all the prophets are his
servants. He chose the apostles in advance (προχειροτονέω) as witnesses
(v. 41a), and from eternity he designated (ὁρίζω) Christ as judge of the
living and the dead (v. 42b) at the close of the age. Past, present and
future are encompassed.

This emphasis on God's repeated initiative is by no means casual. The
readers may be somewhat surprised that it is God who preaches the good

---

5. Moreover, in Isa 52,7 one reads not only εὐαγγελίζομαι but also εἰρήνη.

news by Jesus Christ (v. 36b; a strange present participle), that it is God who anoints Jesus (v. 38a), who allowed Jesus to appear (v. 40b) and, most probably, also God who orders the apostles to proclaim and testify (v. 42a). Moreover, the Greek of the expression that God ἔδωκεν αὐτὸν ἐμφανῆ γενέσθαι (v. 40b) is laborious and rather odd.

Peter and the Apostles: Witnesses

The relatively lengthy qualification of verse 41 interrupts the line of thought. The number of those who received an appearance of the risen Lord is limited: "not to all people but to us who were chosen in advance by God as witnesses"; the text continues: (to us) "who ate and drank with Jesus after he rose from the dead". The emphasis is on the status and specific function of the apostles. Because of this interruption of verse 41, the preceding clause "we are witnesses to all that he did" (v. 39ab) is equally not without emphasis. The same applies to the theme of witnessing in what follows: "He commanded us to preach to the people and 'to testify'..." (v. 42a).

The witness-vocabulary appears to be important. All the prophets have testified about Jesus Christ (v. 43a: μαρτυροῦσιν). Since the apostles are the witnesses both of the earthly Jesus (cf. v. 39a: μάρτυρες) and the risen Christ (cf. 41a: μάρτυσιν τοῖς προκεχειροτονημένοις ὑπὸ τοῦ θεοῦ), they themselves must now testify (v. 42a: διαμαρτύρασθαι) that "he is the one ordained by God as judge of the living and the dead" (v. 42b).

God's commandment is to preach to the Jewish people (v. 42a: τῷ λαῷ), but in verse 33 Cornelius says: "all of us are here in the presence of God to listen to all that the Lord has commanded you to say". Peter's addressees now include Gentiles as well; they will receive the Holy Spirit and be baptized (see vv. 44-48: τὰ ἔθνη).

Jesus Christ

In his brief discourse Peter is certainly presented by Luke as focusing on the four points discussed above, be it each in its own way. Yet the most visible and important emphasis is yet to be mentioned: it is no doubt that on Jesus Christ. It would seem that this emphasis even affects his language and syntax as well as his style. We will consider sentence after sentence and thus distinguish the grammatical units. Jesus Christ is mentioned for the first time after the statement of God's impartiality in verses 34-35.

Verse 36

Verse 36 is best taken as an incomplete sentence, an anacolouthon. After the parenthesis "this (Jesus Christ) is the Lord of all" (v. 36c) verse 37 begins with "you know that". The most probable reading at the beginning of verse 36 is the accusative followed by the relative pronoun: τὸν λόγον ὅν (the word, i.e., the message which God sent). Since because of the anacolouthon the noun in the accusative has no clear grammatical function in the sentence, the omission of the relative pronoun in some manuscripts can be taken as a later scribal effort at amelioration of the text. Without that pronoun the noun itself becomes the direct object of "to send". This is, of course, a much easier reading[6].

One would expect that Jesus Christ is the subject of the verb "to announce the good news of peace". Yet the participle εὐαγγελιζόμενος strangely goes with God who sent. However this is followed by the specification, not without emphasis, "by means of Jesus Christ" (διὰ Ἰησοῦ Χριστοῦ) and the parenthesis which qualifies Christ: οὗτός ἐστιν πάντων κύριος. This parenthesis breaks off the sentence in verse 36 which is not continued later. It is not the title "Lord" that is special but its qualification by the genitive: "Lord of all". In Peter's speech, "all" is almost certainly grammatically masculine, not neuter, and means: not only of the Jews but also of the Gentiles. The demonstrative οὗτος, in most translations nearly invisible, underlines the identification. "This" Jesus Christ, just mentioned, is the Lord of all.

The concern with Jesus Christ is so strong at the end of verse 36 that the grammar appears to be forgotten. Which was the main verb that the author of Acts had in mind at the start of this verse? It may well have been an οἴδατε or a similar verb; if so "the word" was thought of as a direct object (not as an accusative of respect[7]): you know the word that God... Yet τὸν λόγον of verse 36a does not depend on ὑμεῖς οἴδατε of verse 37a. "You know", after the anacolouthon, is the beginning of a new sentence.

Verses 37-38

"God preaching peace by Jesus Christ" in verse 36 constitutes a quite brief and most general description of the work of Christ. The following

---

6. Cf. the brief discussion in METZGER, *A Textual Commentary*, pp. 333-334.
7. So, e.g., F. NEIRYNCK, "Acts 10,36a ΤΟΝ ΛΟΓΟΝ ΟΝ", in ID., *Evangelica II*, pp. 236-242 (= ¹1984).

grammatical unit will provide details. Jesus Christ is the very center of verses 37-38. The unit ends on the statement "for God was with him" (v. 38c) which can be compared with the parenthesis at the end of verse 36c ("this [Jesus] is Lord of all").

Visibly the expression τὸ γενόμενον ῥῆμα, direct object of "you know" in verse 37a, refers not only to the word (cf. τὸν λόγον and εὐαγγελιζόμενος in v. 36ab) but also to the things that happened throughout all Judea, the whole of Jesus' ministry, death and resurrection appearances (see vv. 37-42). It is not impossible that Luke, as elsewhere in Acts (see 1,22; 8,35 and 11,5), writes ἀρχόμενος as a real nominative which here refers to the beginning activity of Jesus – admittedly a grammatically disturbing *constructio ad sensum*[8]. Peter seems to correct what he has just said by means of "throughout the whole of Judea". Jesus' ministry actually began in Galilee; it began after the baptism that John preached. Then, personalizing the ῥῆμα of verse 37a, the text, with much emphasis and by the addition of an accusative also depending on "you know"[9], refers to Ἰησοῦν τὸν ἀπὸ Ναζαρέθ in verse 38a. The expression "Jesus, the one from Nazareth" is a hapaxlegomenon in Acts (and Luke)[10]. "From Nazareth" may be intended to recall "beginning from Galilee". The chronological and geographical order of the sketch of Jesus' life which Peter presents in verses 37-42 appears to be in conformity with what is presented in the gospels (cf. Acts 1,22; 13,31).

The content of verse 38a and b is wholly centered on Jesus: "how God anointed him with the Holy Spirit and with power" (probably at his baptism) and "(Jesus) who went about doing good and healing all who were oppressed by the devil". Grammatically these two heavy clauses (ὡς ἔχρισεν αὐτὸν ὁ θεός ... and ὃς διῆλθεν εὐεργετῶν καὶ ἰώμενος...) qualify the initial "Jesus the one from Nazareth". Thus much attention is devoted to Jesus' ministry; this is once more stressed by the motivation that is added at the end in verse 38c: ὅτι ὁ θεὸς ἦν μετ' αὐτοῦ. Because God is with him Jesus is able to free all who are overpowered by the devil. After the mention of God's anointment of Jesus with the power of the Spirit the logic of this iterative is relatively surprising.

---

8. Otherwise the committee of METZGER, *Textual Commentary*, p. 334. They see the participle as a pendent nominative and take it in a quasi-adverbial sense. Cf., e.g., J. A. FITZMYER, *The Acts of the Apostles* (AB, 31), New York, 1998, p. 464: "Possibly the nominative participle *arxamenos*, 'starting,' represents a frozen, pre-Lucan formula, which originally applied to Jesus, but in this context it can refer only to 'the Word,'...".

9. Yet see the free rendering by FITZMYER, *Acts*, p. 458: "how God anointed Jesus of Nazareth...".

10. We often find "Jesus (Christ), ὁ Ναζωραῖος": see Acts 2,22; 3,6; 4,10; 6,14; 22,8; 24,5; 26,9; Luke 18,37.

Verse 39ab

Most probably the opposition between ὑμεῖς οἴδατε (v. 37a) and καὶ ἡμεῖς μάρτυρες (v. 39a), between the addressees ("you") and Peter ("we", i.e., Peter and the other apostles), is intentional. In verse 39ab Peter stresses the apostles' presence during Jesus' ministry. They have been and remain the witnesses of all that Jesus did in the country of the Jews. The reference to the deeds of Jesus in the country of the Jews summarizes what has already been stated in verse 38ab. The addition of Jerusalem prepares for the end phase: passion, crucifixion and resurrection.

It may be noted that in verse 39a the main verb is lacking. Peter's words are in the form of a nominal clause: "And we (were/are) witnesses of all". Immediately after this affirmation attention in verse 39b is again directed to Jesus Christ.

Verses 39c-42

There can be no doubt that the two accusatives at the beginning, namely ὅν in verse 39c and τοῦτον in verse 40a, continue to put the emphasis on Christ. Grammatically speaking, verse 39c can perhaps be taken together with what follows in verse 40: "(Jesus Christ) whom they put to death by hanging him on a tree, this (Jesus Christ) God raised on the third day and made him manifest"[11]. The syntactical unevenness strengthens the emphasis. The subject of ἀνεῖλαν (v. 39c) must be supplied from verse 39b: Jews or (the Jewish leaders in) Jerusalem[12].

The sentence continues until the end of verse 42. It is as it were too long and becomes somewhat unclear: one could ask who is the grammatical subject of παρήγγειλεν (v. 42a). This is caused, above all, by the interrupting verse 41 which tells us that not all the people saw the risen Lord, only the chosen apostles. The content of what is said about Jesus Christ goes from his crucifixion to his resurrection and appearances, and then – by way of an argumentative twist – from the postpaschal proclamation to the people (of Israel) to the mention of his already fixed appointment as future universal judge. Although God is the subject of the main verbs, thus most probably also of the third one (ἤγειρεν,

---

11. Notwithstanding the use of δίδωμι + verb in 14,3 and in the quotation of Ps 15,10 (LXX) in 2,27 and 13,35, the clause καὶ ἔδωκεν αὐτὸν ἐμφανῆ γενέσθαι remains strange.
12. Cf. 2,23-24 and, e.g., R. PESCH, *Die Apostelgeschichte* (EKK, V/1), Zürich – Neukirchen-Vluyn, 1986, p. 343.

ἔδωκεν, παρήγγειλεν)[13], the verses really deal with Jesus Christ. The last qualification ("judge of the living and the dead", v. 42b) is not without its special emphasis; it stresses the universality (all: living and dead, Jews and Gentiles); moreover, it points to the end of history.

It may also be noted that in verse 40a Peter says theologically that God "raised" (ἐγείρω) Christ, while at the end of verse 41b he refers to the same event by christologically stating that Christ himself "rose" (ἀνίστημι) from the dead.

Verse 43

In the last verse of the discourse God is no longer explicitly mentioned. Perhaps one has to mentally supply after "receives forgiveness" the idea "from God". However in the verse itself it is Christ who is referred to explicitly, three times: all the prophets testify "about him" (emphatic position of τούτῳ at the beginning); through "his" name (διὰ τοῦ ὀνόματος αὐτοῦ); and, at the very end, everyone who believes in "him" (πάντα τὸν πιστεύοντα εἰς αὐτόν). The universalism of the end of verse 42 recurs.

A last syntactical irregularity should not go unnoticed. Without the second part of verse 43 all would agree to take the pronoun τούτῳ as referring to Christ. However, the infinitive construction after μαρτυ-οῦσιν could suggest to the readers that the initial pronoun is a neutral singular and announces what follows: "all the prophets bear witness to 'this'", namely, "that everyone who believes in him receives through his name the forgiveness of sins"[14]. Yet the context as well as the focus on Christ elsewhere in the discourse strongly argue in favor of keeping the pronoun as masculine, against a purely grammatical consideration: To this [= Jesus Christ] all the prophets testify[15].

Emphasis

It can be maintained that the fact that Peter's attention is fixed on Jesus Christ has caused the main grammatical unevennesses in Luke's composition of his discourse. It can, on the other hand, equally be claimed that those syntactical irregularities enhance the emphasis on

13. Regarding the subject of παρήγγειλεν, God, see C. K. BARRETT, *The Acts of the Apostles. Vol. I* (ICC), Edinburgh, 1994, p. 527.

14. *Ibid.*, pp. 489 and 528.

15. See the hesitation of BARRETT, *ibid.*, p. 528 and, at the end, his preference for the neuter.

Christ. We mention (1) the anacolouthon between verse 36 and verse 37, (2) the masculine direct object at the beginning of verse 38 joined to the neutral object of verse 37, (3) the use of a relative pronoun in verse 39c without a grammatically expressed antecedent, and (4) the masculine demonstrative pronoun at the beginning of verse 43.

Emphasis is certainly also produced by the accusative or dative at the beginning of a sentence: see verse 36a (τὸν λόγον), verse 39c (ὅν), verse 40a (τοῦτον) and verse 43a (τούτῳ).

The qualifications (and/or titles) at the end of a sentence very much add to the importance given to Jesus Christ. We must take note of (1) the parenthesis at the end of verse 36 ("this is the Lord of all"), (2) the causal clause at the end of verse 38 ("for God was with him"), and (3) that which the apostles must testify: "that this [= Jesus Christ] is the one ordained by God to be judge of the living and the dead" (v. 42b).

Finally, all that is said about the career of Jesus Christ indicates his unique stature. Through him God preaches the good news of peace (v. 36b). The places of his origin and activity (after John's baptism) are mentioned: Nazareth, Galilee, Judea, Jerusalem. God anointed him with the Holy Spirit and power. He went about doing good and healing all that were oppressed by the devil. His crucifixion, his resurrection on the third day and his appearances are recorded. His final function of universal judge must be announced and, by way of climax, it is stated that in his name forgiveness of sins will be obtained by all who believe in him.

Concluding Consideration

While Peter is still speaking, the Holy Spirit falls upon all the listeners in Cornelius' house at Caesarea. The circumcised believers who have come with Peter are astounded that the gift of the Holy Spirit is poured out even on the Gentiles. However Peter orders these Gentiles to be baptized "in the name of Jesus Christ" (10,44-48). Back in Jerusalem Peter defends himself against the criticism of the circumcised believers (11,1-18). "And as I began to speak", he says, "the Holy Spirit fell upon them [= the Gentiles] just as it had upon us at the beginning ... If God gave them the same gift that he gave us when we believed in the Lord Jesus Christ, who was I that I could hinder God?" (11,15 and 17). The readers of Acts will certainly remember how Peter's discourse began: God shows no partiality (10,34b). Yet a new emphasis appears, that on (the gift of) the Holy Spirit.

There are, no doubt, different emphases in this God-centered discourse; in comparison, the emphasis on Jesus Christ is the greatest. The discourse, however, constitutes a tight unit and its function within the broader context of Acts is central as to Luke's view of the history of universal salvation. Peter stresses the Jewishness of Jesus, but, according to the same Peter, God's ultimate plan with Jesus is his lordship over both Jews and Gentiles. The witnesses of the earthly Jesus and the risen Lord are chosen and commanded to testify that he is ordained by God as the future judge of all. Everyone who believes in Jesus Christ receives forgiveness of sins. For Luke, the author of Acts, Peter thus initiates the mission to the Gentiles which will be carried out especially by Paul (cf. chapters 13–28). Christ's good news is for all.

Additional Note

See the recent publication by M. GOURGUES, "Du centurion de Capharnaüm au centurion de Césarée. Luc 7,1-10 et sa fonction proleptique par rapport à Actes 10,1–11,18", in C. NIEMAND (ed.), *Forschungen zum Neuen Testament und seiner Umwelt. FS Albert Fuchs* (Linzer philosophisch-theologische Beiträge, 7), Frankfurt am Main, 2002, 259-270: "Vu les similitudes accentuées par Luc entre les deux épisodes, le lecteur, en lisant le récit du centurion de Césarée, n'était-il pas amené tout naturellement à effectuer le rapprochement avec celui du centurion de Capharnaüm en ainsi à enraciner dans l'attitude d'ouverture de Jésus l'attitude d'ouverture de l'Église?" (p. 268).

Justification by God and Human Faith
(Romans 1,17)

The NRSV translates Rom 1,17 as follows: "For in it the righteousness of God is revealed through faith for faith; as it is written, 'The one who is righteous will live by faith'". This is a long sentence, especially when the semicolon is justly replaced by a comma. The comparative clause cites Hab 2,4 which Paul has altered slightly. The reader gets the impression that Paul places two different accents in 1,17: the revelation of God's righteousness and the justification of human beings by faith. The double emphasis concerns first God and then human beings. God justifies believers.

The correctness of our impression should become evident first by an analysis of the immediate context and then by the investigation of verse 17 itself. A conclusion will end this brief study.

Romans 1,15-19: The Context

Paul has often intended to come to Rome and to visit the Roman Christians, but thus far he has been prevented (v. 13). In verse 14 he says: "I am a debtor both to Greeks and to barbarians, both to the wise and to the foolish". Then follows the context needed for the analysis. The following text is mainly that of the NRSV:

15   Hence my eagerness to proclaim the gospel to you also who are in Rome,
16a   for I am not ashamed of the gospel,
  b   for it is the power of God for salvation to everyone who has faith, to the Jew first and also to the Greek,
17a   for in it the righteousness of God is revealed through faith for faith,
  b   as it is written, "The one who is righteous will live by faith",
18   for the wrath of God is revealed from heaven against all ungodliness and wickedness of those who by their wickedness suppress the truth,
19a   because what can be known about God is plain to them,
  b   for God has shown it to them.

In this translation full stops and semicolons are omitted; the literal translation of the particles γάρ ("for") and διότι ("because") is preferred. It is not evident that while reasoning Paul interrupts his motivating style. Even "as is written" probably has a causal, grounding nuance. Where does a new sentence begin? In v. 20 another γάρ appears and in v. 21 another διότι, but verses 15-19 constitute the immediate context, sufficient for interpretation, of v. 17.

The three questions which the use of γάρ in vv. 16-17 each time first suggests and then explicitly answers are: (1) Why is Paul eager to proclaim the gospel? Because he is not ashamed of it. (2) Why is he not ashamed of the gospel? Because it is God's power for salvation for all who believe. (3) Why can one claim that the gospel is God's power? Because in it the salvific righteousness of God is revealed. Verses 16-17 logically follow on verse 15.

There is no real break between v. 17 and v. 18, no caesura but rather a contrasting connection. After the lengthy v. 17 the reader will ask: "Why must that righteousness be revealed (now)"? The answer is: "because (to this day) God's wrath is revealed against all human wickedness". In verses 17-18 the general ungodliness "to this day" of human beings is contrasted to the "now" of God's new initiative (cf. 3,21-26). The explanatory motivation of v. 19 does not cause any difficulty.

A provisional conclusion can be drawn from this summary discussion of the context. After the decision announced in verse 15 a number of motivating or explicating sentences follow one after the other. Paul develops his reasoning step after step, without interruption. Again and again he grounds and further explains his ideas. It must be noted that, grammatically speaking, all "for"- and "because"-clauses are dependent on the immediately preceding clauses. Between v. 17 and v. 18 it is necessary to mentally reconstruct a question which reveals the contrast between the two verses. However, even verse 18 is not a new beginning; it is subordinate to the preceding verse 17.

Romans 1,17

In verse 16 the gospel of which Paul is not ashamed is called "the power of God for salvation". All believers, both Jews and Greeks (but the Jew first) can receive that salvation. Yet in verse 17 this last idea, that of God's universal salvific plan, is not further elaborated. What is the precise content of this particular verse?

Verse 17a

δικαιοσύνη γὰρ θεοῦ ἐν αὐτῷ ἀποκαλύπτεται ἐκ πίστεως εἰς πίστιν,

Paul first asserts that God's righteousness is revealed (ἀποκαλύπτω) by the proclamation of the gospel. This revelation is decidedly more than a mere publication. It contains God's involvement in justification. This also applies to verse 18 where the same verb ἀποκαλύπτω returns: the revelation of God's wrath includes God's punishment. Thus in verse 17 Paul means that in the proclamation of the gospel God's justification is at work and efficient. Revelation brings about a new order of being. Publication is at the same time realization.

Through the preaching of the gospel God's new initiative is revealed. To this very day his punitive wrath was at work, but now his merciful, forgiving and salvific righteousness comes into force. Most probably the expression εἰς σωτηρίαν of v. 16 carries an eschatological overtone. God's ultimate aim is final salvation.

In v. 17a, however, the attention shifts from God to human beings and, at the same time, from the divine revelation to the condition that must be fulfilled by human beings so that the justification can take place. The mysterious expression ἐκ πίστεως εἰς πίστιν at least includes the notion: on the condition that there is faith, but this does not seem to be its full meaning. By means of this expression Paul speaks of more and more faith, a constantly increasing faith. "Through faith for faith" strongly emphasizes an open attitude on the part of human beings, the necessary responsiveness to what God will do. After justification has occurred this responsiveness keeps growing. It is a continually increasing faith.

In what way does God's righteousness reveal itself? How is this righteousness "revealed" and visible in the world? This occurs in the first place by the existential change in the believers themselves and through their altered behavior. They have become "a new creation" (2 Cor 5,17; Gal 6,15).

Verse 17b

καθὼς γέγραπται, Ὁ δὲ δίκαιος ἐκ πίστεως ζήσεται.

The citation of Hab 2,4 also emphasizes faith. Paul has already employed this quotation in his letter to the Galatians. In Gal 3,11 he writes: "Now it is evident that no one is justified before God by the law; for 'The one who is righteous will live by faith'". Here "by faith" is opposed to "by the law". In the context of Galatians "will live" means "will be justified" (the future is more logical than temporal); the expression "by faith" stresses "not by the works of the law" (cf. 3,10), i.e., *sola fide*, by faith alone.

Does the citation in Romans have exactly the same meaning as in Galatians? One may doubt this. (1) According to Paul ἐκ πίστεως ("by faith") of Rom 1,17b certainly means, as in Gal 3,11, by faith alone and not by the works of the law (cf. Rom 3,22). Yet in v. 17b "by faith" cannot be interpreted without taking into account ἐκ πίστεως εἰς πίστιν of v. 17a where Paul points to a constantly increasing faith. (2) The future tense of the verb (ζήσεται) seems to retain its temporal force and to resume the future nuance present in εἰς σωτήριαν of v. 16b. The verb probably means "will really live forever". In v. 17b, just as in v. 16b, Paul also deals with eschatological salvation. (3) The term ὁ δίκαιος ("the righteous") then indicates the believer who has been justified by faith, though already existing justification is to be distinguished from as yet anticipated salvation.

Conclusion

Because of the repetition of "to reveal" in v. 18 one could be tempted to assume a symmetry between v. 17 and v. 18; moreover, the two verses can easily be taken as antithetical since "God's wrath" is contrasted to "God's righteousness". However, the motivating γάρ at the beginning of v. 18 shows the grammatical and logical subordination of this verse to v. 17. Strictly speaking, verse 18 does not constitute a new beginning in Paul's reasoning.

In verse 17a a shift occurs: from God to human beings, from revelation to faith, from God's power and righteousness to openness and responsiveness on the part of human beings, from divine gift to human surrender. The two poles are connected; a giver requires a receiver.

In the proclamation of the gospel God's power for salvation is not only made known. In addition, through the preaching, that power is really at work as justification. Revelation is realization. On the human side all that is needed is faith, but this initial faith is capable of growth. Through that ever increasing faith human beings, as justified persons, will continue to live and reach their final salvation. We can compare this growth with 2 Cor 3,18: ἀπὸ δόξης εἰς δόξαν ("from one degree of glory to another"), and with 4,16: ἡμέρα καὶ ἡμέρα (a renewal "day by day").

If the above interpretation of the Habbakuk-citation in Rom 1,17b is correct, then, just as for 5,9-10 and 10,9-10 (see chapter 13 in this book), so also for 1,16-17 the distinction between initial justification and final salvation is appropriate. In 1,16-17 Paul speaks of the dynamic, increasing faith that, out of the once given justification, leads us to eschatological life.

Additional Note

a) With reasons that are worth considering, R. M. THORSTEINSSON, "Paul's Missionary Duty Towards Gentiles in Rome: A Note on the Punctuation and Syntax of Rom 1.13-15", in *NTS* 48 (2002) 531-547, takes both dative phrases of v. 14 as appositions to "the rest of the Gentiles" (end of v. 13) and ὀφειλέτης εἰμι (v. 14) as the beginning of the sentence which continues in v. 15: "I am bound, then, to announce the gospel with goodwill to you also who are in Rome" (p. 544). This sentence "constitutes ... a transition from the first part of the letter's 'body' [= Paul's *captatio benevolentiae*] to the second" (p. 545); it expresses his "main concern with the letter" (p. 546).

b) The comment on Rom 1,15 by R. D. ANDERSON, *Ancient Rhetorical Theory and Paul* (Revised Edition; CBET, 18), Leuven, 1998, p. 208, is appropriate: "*Formally* the proposition for the letter as a whole might be considered to be v. 15. It is the statement (that it is Paul's desire to preach the Gospel to the Roman Christians) that forms the basis for Paul's following remarks (indicated by the ensuing of causal conjunctions [γάρ] ... It would seem that the main body of this letter functions as a temporary substitute for Paul's presence and preaching".

c) M. THEOBALD, "Zorn Gottes. Ein nicht zu vernachlässigender Aspekt der Theologie des Römerbriefs", in ID., *Studien zum Römerbrief* (WUNT, 136), Tübingen, 2001, pp. 60-100, argues that in 1,18 the present ἀποκαλύπτεται stands for a future and that, strictly speaking and as elsewhere in Romans, ὀργή refers to God's final judgment. More than other exegetes he distinguishes between this eschatological judgment and the "innergeschichtlichen" punishments of vv. 24, 26 and 28 (see pp. 74-86). God's wrath certainly includes the judgment of the last day. However, the present of v. 18 most probably is a temporal present (cf. the same verb in the same tense in v. 17); the historical punishments seem to belong, by way of anticipation, to the eschatological judgment.

Sinning to the Greater Glory and Honor of God?
(Romans 3,1-9)

In Rom 3,7-8 it is written: "If through my falsehood God's truthfulness abounds to his glory, why am I still being condemned as a sinner? And why not say ... 'Let us do evil so that good may come'?" How did Paul arrive at formulating such a proposal: Let us do evil, let us sin to the greater glory and honor of God? Verses 7-8 belong to the section 3,1-20. In 2,17-29 Paul explicitly addresses the Jew: "But if you call yourself a Jew..." (v. 17). The Jew boasts in the law but dishonors God by breaking the law (cf. 2,23). Paul asserts: a person is not a Jew who is one outwardly; a real Jew is one inwardly; his heart is circumcised (cf. 2,28-29). The question of 3,1 follows on these last statements: "Then what advantage has the Jew?"

The Text

The pericope of 3,1-9 consists of questions and answers. Paul utilizes the well-known diatribe-style, which involves the convention of discussion with a fictitious opponent.

Jews?

From the first part of the letter one gets the impression that Romans is directed to Gentiles who have become believers, Gentile Christians: see 1,5 and 1,13b. Yet it should be assumed that in Rome there must also have been Jewish Christians. Most likely they formed but a minority in the community, given the expulsion of the Jews by Emperor Claudius in AD 49 (though some of them returned after AD 54). True, the Gentile Christians may have been in origin "God-fearing" people, Gentiles who sympathized with the Jews and to a certain extent were familiar with their scriptures and observed their customs. But it remains strange that in this letter, from 1,18 to 4,25, Paul speaks to (non-Christian) Jews. The actual addressees, in the majority Gentile Christians, were required at this point to listen to a lengthy dialogue of Paul with the Jews.

One preliminary remark should be added. It can be supposed that in 3,9a Paul somehow resumes the question of 3,1. Some commentators, therefore, consider verse 9 as the conclusion of 3,1-9. Yet 3,10-20 clearly follows on 3,9 and with 3,19-20 the major part of chapters 1–3 is concluded. For the analysis of this study, however, the text of 3,1-9 suffices. First a working translation.

The Translation of Rom 3,1-9

1a	Then what advantage has the Jew?
b	Or what is the value of circumcision?
2a	Much, in every way.
b	For in the first place the Jews were entrusted with the oracles of God...
3a	What if some were unfaithful?
b	Will their faithlessness nullify the faithfulness of God?
4a	By no means!
b	Let God be true, but everyone a liar,
c	as it is written,
d	"So that you may be justified in your words,
e	and prevail when you are judged".
5a	But if our injustice serves to confirm the justice of God,
b	what should we say?
c	That God is unjust to inflict wrath (on us)?
d	– I speak in a human way –
6a	By no means!
b	For then how could God judge the world?
7a	But if through my falsehood God's truthfulness abounds to his glory,
b	why am I still being condemned as a sinner?
8a	And why not (say)
b	– as some people slander us by saying that we say –
c	"let us do evil
d	so that good may come"?
e	Their condemnation is deserved!
9a	What then?
b	Do we have any advantage?
c	Not altogether,
d	for we have already charged that all, both Jews and Greeks, are under the power of sin.

For the most part this translation follows the NRSV (but see v. 4e and 9bc). Attention must be given to the following points:

(1) Within v. 3, some exegetes distinguish two questions which are structured in a way different from that in the translation above. There

would be a first brief exclamation: "What then?" (cf. v. 9a), and then a lengthy second question, consisting of a conditional period with protasis and apodosis. Most probably, however, the protasis (= if-clause) belongs to a first question.

(2) In vv. 4a and 6a the negative exclamation μὴ γένοιτο is in literal translation "may (it) not be". In v. 4b the same verb occurs, but in the present: γινέσθω, "let (it) be". The version in vv. 4a and 6a is free: "by no means" (= not at all).

(3) The passive translation of κρίνεσθαι in v. 4e is defended further on in the study, as is the meaning "not altogether" of οὐ πάντως in v. 9c.

(4) The Greek grammar of verse 8 is uneven and no longer so evident. The addition of "say" at the end of v. 8a tries to clarify the structure.

(5) The verb προεχόμεθα in v. 9b could be passive or medium. Its passive form means: "are we excelled?" while the medium literally signifies: "do we hold (something) in front of us" (= do we hide ourselves behind our reasoning?). Neither version makes good sense in the context. Therefore, the verb in its medium form is mostly taken as similar in sense to v. 1a: "Do we (Jews) have any advantage (regarding the Gentiles)?" There is, however, no evidence of this meaning in existing biblical or profane Greek literature. Yet preference is given to it.

(6) Finally, the interruption at the end of v. 2 is marked by three dots (the enumeration after "in the first place" is not continued). The interjections of vv. 5d and 8b are indicated by hyphens.

The Comment

In 2,23-34 Paul presumes that the Jews spoken to in 2,17 are also sinners. They boast about having the law, but by breaking the law they bring shame on God. Because of them the Gentiles speak evil of God's name. What follows in 2,25-29 is Paul's interpretation of the person who is a real Jew (the person who is one inwardly) and of what is a true circumcision (that of the heart). At the end of 2,17-29 one expects a return to the main idea of 1,18–3,20: Jews as well as Greeks are sinners. However this does not occur until 3,9b and d. Moreover, the chain of citations from Scripture in 3,10-18 exclusively emphasizes the sins of the Jews and in 3,19 Paul concludes: "Now we know that whatever the law says, it speaks to those who are under the law, so that every mouth may be silenced, and the whole world may be held accountable to God". In 3,20 he adds his view of the negative function of the law. No doubt, in 3,1-20 the focus is on the Jews.

Advantage? (vv. 1-2 and 9)

The passage of 3,1-9a constitutes an interruption, but this interruption is easily explicable. What Paul says about the true Jew in 2,25-29 almost inevitably elicits the objection: what is the advantage of the Jews over the non-Jews and what is the value of being circumcised (3,1)? How will Paul answer these questions? Positively or negatively? He answers twice, first in v. 2 and then, again, in v. 9b; his answer is nuanced.

In 3,2a he asserts, almost by way of exclamation: much, indeed, in every way. After this assertion one expects an elaboration and, as a matter of fact, Paul writes πρῶτον μέν ("in the first place") in v. 2b: God trusted his oracles (= his covenantal promises) to the Jews. However a list which is similar to that of 9,4 – to Israel belong the adoption, the glory, the covenants, the giving of the law, the worship, and the promises – is missing, and no ἔπειτα ("then") follows. To be sure, after what has been said in 2,25-29 about the breaking of the law and the true circumcision, an enumeration of more privileges is hardly still possible. Thus verse 3 provides a new interruption, another objection.

Yet to the question "what advantage has the Jew?" (v. 1a) Paul's answer was very positive. Given the translation of προεχόμεθα which was proposed for v. 9b, a second time this question is asked: "Do we (Jews) have any advantage?" The brief answer in v. 9c is: "not altogether". This is the literal translation of the expression οὐ πάντως which Paul employs in 1 Cor 5,10 in the same sense. There is no reason to render it otherwise, e.g., by "no, not at all" as it is often done (cf. NRSV). In Rom 3,9c Paul slightly modifies the answer of 3,2. The privileges are not denied, but regarding sinfulness the Jews do not differ from the Gentiles. This is clearly stated in 3,9d: all, Jews and Gentiles alike, are under the power of sin. Through sinning they have put themselves under the power of sin.

God's Faithfulness and Justice (vv. 3-8)

In 3,3-8 one now encounters a threefold objection which is the result of an insistent logical reasoning. The style of the dialogue is maintained.

(1) Verses 3-4: God trusted his promises to the Jews, but is God's faithfulness not endangered by the faithlessness of some Jews? The answer is: no, not at all.

(2) Verses 5-6: But if our injustice shows up God's justice more clearly, is God not unjust when he punishes us? Again the answer is: no, not at all.

(3) Verses 7-8: But if my untruth makes God's truth stand out and serves his glory, why should I be condemned as a sinner and why should I not do evil that good may come? Paul here notes that people falsely accuse him of holding the position implied in this last question.

Each time a double question is formulated: see verse 3ab and verse 5ab (and also compare v. 1ab and v. 9ab). The third objection (vv. 7 and 8acd) likely contains two questions, but the inserted remark ("as some people slander us by saying that we say") somewhat obscures the grammatical structure of v. 8. The answer to the first and second objection is equally twofold (see vv. 4a and 5bcde; vv. 6a and 6b). First comes the emotional μὴ γένοιτο, followed then by a longer explanation. In v. 4de the answer is confirmed by means of a citation (Ps 51,4). After the third objection Paul merely asserts: "Their condemnation is deserved" (v. 8e); they will be condemned, as they should be.

The three objections of 3,3-8 are important and serious; the readers of Rom 2,17-29 will easily ask such questions, even today. Yet Paul's answer does not wholly satisfy: in vv. 4 and 6 God's prerogatives are emphasized, without any argumentation, and verse 8e gives no answer at all.

Content and Style

In verse 4 as well as in verse 5 vocabulary with the root δικαι- ("righteous", "just") occurs. What is its exact nuance?

Justice, Righteousness and Justification

First let us consider verse 4 and the quotation. The translation of the cited Hebrew verse of the psalm is: "against you, you alone, have I sinned, and done what is evil in your sight; so that you are justified in your sentence and blameless when you pass judgment", Ps 51,4). The Septuagint has "words" instead of "sentence", and the last clause of the verse becomes: "and prevail when you are judged". In Rom 3,4de Paul takes over the Greek translation according to which God is no longer passing judgment but is himself being judged. God is on trial; he has to defend himself. In the opinion of the Israelites the Gentile nations are passing judgment on God because of the miserable state of his chosen people.

According to Paul God will be vindicated when accused of not remaining faithful to Israel, even if some Jews are faithless. Their infidelity does not destroy God's fidelity (cf. vv. 3-4). God will win his case; God will be found just; God's justice will be recognized.

In the Hebrew verse the justice-terminology refers to a characteristic of a judging God, a God who through the prophet Nathan condemns David because of his sin (cf. 2 Sam 12,1-14). God rightly condemns David; God is just. Probably the same legal nuance must be assumed not only in the passive verb of Rom 3,4e (κρίνεσθαι) but also in that of 3,4d (δικαιοῦμαι): "so that you may be justified in your words". But is this meaning still present in verse 5: "the justice of God" (θεοῦ δικαιοσύνη)? It would seem that here God's salvific justification is intended. There hardly can be any notable difference between "the faithfulness of God" (v. 3b), "the justice of God" (v. 5a) and "the truthfulness of God" (v. 7a). While mortals lie, God is truthful. Notwithstanding the faithlessness of Israel, God remains faithful to the promises. Although we do not deserve it, God is a justifying and sin-forgiving God.

If this justifying righteousness is assumed, one better understands the question of v. 7b (why should sinners be condemned?) as well as the blasphemous proposal of v. 8cd (let us do evil so that good may come!). The more faithlessness in Israel, the more the faithfulness of God is proved; the more mortals lie, the more God's truthfulness shines; the more injustice, the more God can justify and bring salvation!

Thus, after all, sinning to the greater glory and honor of God? Apparently more than once this slanderous conclusion has been drawn from Paul's gospel; people claim that such was his position (cf. v. 8b). Paul, however, is so aghast that he can barely answer. He reacts with a forceful negation and refers to God, the one who through Jesus revealed his fidelity and mercy, but who equally will be the just judge at the end of time.

The Style of the Diatribe

A final consideration concerns the style of 3,1-9 which, as already pointed out, is that of the diatribe. A diatribe is a popular discussion genre with question and answer, a kind of dialogue that was often used by Cynic or Stoic philosophers. A fictitious opponent either asks the questions or provides the answers. The speaker reacts, often briefly and sharply, often by means of an outcry, with a mixture of earnestness and humor, with much mobility of thought and image. The dialogue employs rhetorical pathos and is full of life. Often the mouth of the hypothetical opponent is shut up without argumentation, strictly speaking; often the opponent is ridiculed. Recently it has been stressed that this style was later also employed in school instructions between teacher and pupil.

It is mostly taken for granted that in 3,1-9 an authentic diatribe is present. According to this opinion the fictitious antagonist is the Jew whom Paul addresses in the foregoing section, 2,17-29. But, then, who is asking the questions and who is giving the answers in 3,1-9? Some maintain that the questions come from the opponent, the answers from Paul. Other exegetes defend the opposite opinion: Paul questions, the Jew answers. Yet it can be asked whether 3,1-9 does contain a real diatribe.

Nowhere in 3,1-9 does Paul clearly indicate the opponent who argues. Moreover, in vv. 5-9 Paul seems to refer to himself by means of the grammatical first person. However, in these verses one must make distinctions. (1) In vv. 5a, 5b, 8c and 9b the first person plural points to Paul and the Jews collectively. This use does not offer any difficulty. (2) In vv. 8b and 9d the "we" is epistolary. By it Paul means himself. (3) In vv. 5d, 7a and 7b one meets, strikingly, the first person singular. The second and third series appear to justify the opinion that in 3,1-9 Paul enters into a conversation with himself in which he makes use of the diatribe characteristics but without a fictitious opponent. It is Paul himself who asks the questions and gives the answers. He himself refers to the paradoxical God who, instead of punishing sinners, justifies them, yet remains righteous. He himself points out the danger of being misunderstood. He himself pays attention to the contestable reasoning and slandering accusation. He himself opposes them.

Summary

The diatribe-like passage 3,1-9 is best seen as an interruption within the argument of 1,18–3,20. By means of his emphasis in 3,9d on universal sinfulness, Paul returns to the main line of thought. But in 3,1-2 and 3,9ab he first asks himself what remains of the privileges of the Jews. The answer is nuanced. The election of the Jews, together with their privileges, continues to exist (v. 2), but the Jews, like the Gentiles, are sinners (v. 9d; cf. vv. 10-18).

Verses 3-8 constitute a new break, an interruption within the interruption. The verses consist of three consecutive objections with their answers. Must one not doubt God's fidelity in view of Israel's infidelity? Is God just when he punishes sin since our injustice serves to confirm God's justice? Should we not sin to increase God's glory and should we not do evil so that good may come (people falsely claim that Paul preaches this)? By means of such diatribe-like questions and answers Paul defends his vision of God's mercy; he also defends himself against malicious misunderstandings.

At the beginning of the Easter Vigil the *Exsultet* praises Adam's *felix culpa*: "O happy fault, O necessary sin of Adam, which gained for us so great a Redeemer!" From this evil came good: our undreamed-of redemption and salvation. Yet believers know that forgiveness is not given "thanks to" sin. One should never do evil so that good may come. One cannot sin to the greater glory and honor of God.

Initial Righteousness and Final Salvation
(Romans 10,9-10)

The chiastic character of Rom 10,9-10 appears to be evident: first a reference to mouth and heart in v. 9, then heart and mouth in v. 10[1]. Moreover, in his recent commentary on Romans, Antonio Pitta points out the concentric pattern of these verses: a b c b' a'[2]. The middle element (c) is "you will be saved" at the end of v. 9. We may present the structured Greek text:

(a) ὅτι ἐὰν ὁμολογήσῃς ἐν τῷ στόματί σου κύριον Ἰησοῦν
(b) καὶ πιστεύσῃς ἐν τῇ καρδίᾳ σου ὅτι ὁ θεὸς αὐτὸν ἤγειρεν ἐκ νεκρῶν,
(c) σωθήσῃ·
(b') καρδίᾳ γὰρ πιστεύεται εἰς δικαιοσύνην,
(a') στόματι δὲ ὁμολογεῖται εἰς σωτηρίαν.

One can also point to the parallelism within both v. 9 and v. 10: compare "you confess with your mouth that..." with "you believe with your heart that..." in v. 9, and "one believes with the heart to (righteousness)" with "one confesses with the mouth to (salvation)" in v. 10.

A number of commentators assume that contentwise not much difference should be sought between the two members in both verses. The parallelism, they maintain, is just "rhetorical", nothing more. Salvation here is righteousness, confession is the outer manifestation of faith; salvation is not the final salvation at the last day. We quote the comment by Douglas Moo on v. 9: "Paul's rhetorical purpose at this point should make us cautious about finding great significance in the reference to confession here, as if Paul were making oral confession a second requirement for salvation"[3]; and on v. 10: "This evident rhetorical interest

---

1. Sections of this text constituted a short paper read during the 2002 SNTS Meeting at Durham (UK).
2. A. PITTA, *Lettera ai Romani* (I Libri Biblici. Nuovo Testamento, 6), Milan, 2001, pp. 365-366.
3. D. J. MOO, *The Epistle to the Romans* (NICNT), Grand Rapids, MI – Cambridge, 1996, p. 657.

suggests that Paul would not want us to find any difference in the meanings of 'righteousness' and 'salvation' here. Each expresses in a general way the new relationship with God that is the result of believing 'with the heart' and confessing 'with the mouth'"[4]. Is this understanding of the parallelism in both verses 9 and 10 correct?

This brief note will try to answer this last question. The context is analysed only in so far as the analysis helps to detect Paul's way of arguing in these verses. So, by way of example, no attention will be given to Paul's particular use of the Old Testament in 10,5-13 nor to the question whether credal formulae or pre-Pauline tradition are present in vv. 9-10.

In a first part we will assemble the reasons which are brought forward to assimilate the parallel clauses in v. 9 and v. 10. The second part will critically examine this position. In the third part, by way of conclusion, the line of thought in Romans 10 will be analysed with special attention to the place and function of vv. 9-10.

Is Righteousness Salvation?

A number of reasons are adduced to argue that "if you confess with your lips that Jesus is Lord" does not constitute a second condition (in addition to belief) for attaining final salvation. Similarly, "if you believe with your heart (that God raised him from the dead)" should not, it is asserted, be viewed as a different requirement for justification than confessing with the lips (that Jesus is Lord).

The Quotation of Verse 8

By means of the quotation of Deut 30,14 ("The word is near you, on your lips and in your heart"; NRSV) Paul explains that it is not necessary to ascend into heaven to bring Christ down nor to descend into the abyss to bring Christ up from the dead. No, righteousness comes from faith; the word of faith is near you, in your mouth and in your heart. It suffices to confess with the lips and to believe with the heart. The doubling "on your lips (= mouth)" and "in your heart", which concretizes the "you" of the quotation, has brought Paul to double the conditions in verse 9 and, in a similar way, to distinguish the two statements of

---

4. Moo, *Romans*, pp. 658-659.

verse 10. That duplication disappears after verse 10. Since the twofold specification within the quotation itself was its cause, proponents of the "assimilation" view argue, one should not pay too much attention to it[5].

Confession

In Romans 10, indeed already in 9,30-33, faith and righteousness are focused upon by Paul. So we read in the context that precedes 10,9-10: Israel did not submit to God's righteousness (v. 3); there is righteousness for everyone who believes (v. 4); the righteousness comes from faith (v. 6); the word is the word of faith that Paul proclaims (v. 8). After 10,9-10 "confession" is no longer spoken of; only faith is mentioned further: no one who believes in Christ will be put to shame (v. 11); how can one believe in Christ of whom he has never heard? (v. 14); faith comes from what is heard (v. 17).

Assimilationists contend that according to Paul in Romans 10 there is only one basic condition for gaining righteousness and salvation: faith in Christ. The doubling of faith and confession in verses 9-10 is more rhetorical than real in content. As a matter of fact, for Paul the parallelism does not indicate two neatly separated requirements[6]. Not only is believing explained by confessing in vv. 9-10, believing is also replaced by "calling on (the name of) the Lord" in vv. 12 and 13 and 14. In this

---

5. Cf. C. K. BARRETT, *A Commentary on the Epistle to the Romans* (BNTC), London, 1957, p. 200: "No distinction is to be drawn between the confession and the faith; the confession is believed and the faith is confessed" (but on pp. 201-202 he writes: "Paul means that believers, already justified, will be saved at the last day"); H.-J. ECKSTEIN, "'Nahe ist dir das Wort': Exegetische Erwägungen zu Röm 10,8", in *ZNW* 79 (1988) 200-220: "synonymer Gebrauch der Begriffe δικαιοσύνη und σωτηρία" (p. 217); E. KÄSE-MANN, *An die Römer* (HNT), Tübingen, ⁴1980, p. 282: "ein syntaktischer Parallelismus, in welchem 10a und 10b identische Feststellungen treffen"; J. D. G. DUNN, *Romans II* (WBC, 38B), Dallas, 1988, p. 609: "it is generally recognized that the distinction is determined by the Deut quotation rather than by any theological distinction ... The near equivalence of 'righteousness' and 'salvation' in the context is wholly Jewish ..."; J. A. FITZ-MYER, *Romans* (AB, 33), New York, 1993, p. 592: "The difference between justification and salvation should not be stressed. The verse [10] formulates rhetorically the relation of human uprightness and salvation to faith and the profession of it"; B. BYRNE, *Romans* (SP, 6), Collegeville, MN, 1996, p. 322: the terms "come close to being identified"; PITTA, *Romani*, p. 366: "... tra la giustizia e la salvezza c'è un'assimilazione...".

6. Cf. BARRETT, *Romans*, p. 202 (v. 10 is called a "neat rhetorical summary"); U. WILCKENS, *Der Brief an die Römer III* (EKK), Neukirchen-Vluyn, 1982, p. 227: a "rhetorischer Parallelismus". Although D. ZELLER, *Der Brief an die Römer* (RNT), Regensburg, 1985, p. 187, distinguishes two different times for righteousness and salvation ("die ja zeitlich nicht zusammenfallen"), he, too, speaks of a "rhetorischer Parallelismus".

context one should take the terms believing, confessing and calling on as virtual equivalents.

Salvation

In the same way, it is claimed, "confessing with the mouth" refers to the outward manifestation of believing. Believing "with the heart" points to the inner quality of the confession. The result is righteousness and salvation. The two terms indicate the same relationship with God.

If one objects that the future σωθήσῃ at the end of v. 9 is temporal and must be understood as referring to the eschatological salvation after death or at the last day, it is answered that the future can be logical or relative: "salvation being the result of, and therefore future to, confessing and believing"[7]. If so, the absolute time remains undetermined. C. E. B. Cranfield, however, rather than de-eschatologizing "salvation" emphasizes the end-time quality of "righteousness". Yet, for him, too, both terms point to the same reality[8].

Not only are righteousness and salvation viewed more or less as equivalents, the same applies, in this context, to "being put to shame" (αἰσχύνομαι), the negative counterpart of "salvation". With "not being put to shame", it is not "confessing with the heart" that is mentioned in 9,33 but "believing", and in 10,13 "calling on".

Conclusion

According to this first reading of Rom 10,9-10 its context advises us to neglect the doubling of mouth and heart, confessing and believing, righteousness and salvation. No great significance should be given to it. The doubling is occasioned by the terms mouth and heart of the Deuteronomy quotation in the preceding verse 8. The doubling is highly, maybe purely, rhetorical. The two clauses illustrate the same condition which the context clearly indicates as "believing" or "faith". Salvation here does not signify eschatological deliverance. Salvation in vv. 9-10 is more or less the equivalent of righteousness, that is righteousness for everyone who believes (cf. 10,4).

7. MOO, *Romans*, p. 658, n. 61.
8. C. E. B. CRANFIELD, *The Epistle to the Romans II* (ICC), Edinburgh, 1979, p. 531: "… it is clear that no substantial distinction is intended between δικαιοσύνη and σωτηρία, both referring to eschatological salvation". Cf. BYRNE, *Romans*, 322.

Initial Justification and Final Salvation

NRSV translates ὅτι at the beginning of verse 9 by "because", but in a footnote mentions that it could be explanatory ("that, namely")[9]. The explication which follows in this verse, I think, is grounding and motivating what is said in verse 8. Something similar must be said about verse 10 since at its beginning we find the particle γάρ Its grounding force ("for, since") should not be neglected; it possesses more than a purely explicative function[10]. This last view implies that verse 10 is subordinated to verse 9. That subordination for its part means that the presentation of verses 9-10 as a chiasmus or as a concentric structure is less correct, even misleading. The two verses are not equal; the grounding verse 10 is not an exact repetition of verse 9; it is not its equivalent.

Verse 9

It would seem that "mouth" and "heart" of the quotation in v. 8 are responsible for the two verbs in the conditional clause (the protasis) of v. 9: if you confess, if you believe. "Word" in that quotation (as well as the added explanation "word of faith" in v. 8) may have suggested both "formulae" in v. 9. One confesses with the lips what the word of faith contains: that Jesus is Lord[11]; equally, one believes with the heart what the word of faith contains: that God raised Jesus from the dead.

"To confess" comes first after the mention of the "word of faith". Yet Paul immediately adds "to believe" since one cannot confess without believing. The order, of course, is not strictly logical. Before confessing one has to believe. All this can be found in almost any commentary[12].

9. Cf. BYRNE, *Romans*, p. 316; MOO, *Romans*, p. 657. Otherwise, e.g., T. R. SCHREINER, *Romans* (Baker, 6), Grand Rapids, 1998, p. 559: the ὅτι "should be understood as explicative rather than causal"; PITTA, *Romani*, p. 388: "un *hoti* esplicativo più che causale"; WILCKENS, *Römer III*, p. 227. FITZMYER, *Romans*, p. 591, hesitates. According to DUNN, *Romans*, p. 607, one should avoid here an "'either-or' exegesis". Yet see CRANFIELD, *Romans II*, pp. 526-527: "The statement of v. 8a is true, because all that one has to do, in order to be saved, is to confess ... and to believe ...".

10. E.g. PITTA, *Romani*, p. 326, translates γάρ "infatti", ZELLER, *Römer*, 182 "nämlich". For a correct emphasis on the grounding function of ὅτι in v. 9 and γάρ in vv. 10.11.12 and 13, see ECKSTEIN, "Nahe ist dir das Wort", p. 214. Cf. J. D. DENNISTON, *The Greek Particles*, Oxford ²1950, pp. 60-61.

11. For DUNN, *Romans II*, p. 607, this is "a public confession of a solemn nature", a "slogan of identification"; "so he who says Κύριος Ἰησοῦς identifies himself as belonging to Jesus".

12. Cf., e.g., CRANFIELD, *Romans II*, p. 527, who also quotes the fine saying of Pelagius "Testimonium cordis est oris confessio"; DUNN, *Romans II*, p. 609: "Paul sees inward

One may wonder, however, whether the fronting of the idea of confession, contrary to the expected logical order and thus striking the reader immediately, does not rhetorically add emphasis to Paul's concern that mere belief is not sufficient.

The second person singular is taken from the quotation in v. 8; in v. 9 it marks the application and renders the style more lively. The protasis with ἐάν points to two future eventualities: "in case you will confess that… and in case you will believe that…". The aorist tense of the subjunctives (ὁμολογήσῃς and πιστεύσῃς) is rather strange[13] but one should probably not understand the meaning to be that one action in the future is referred to twice[14]. The conditional sentence above all stresses the link between the if-clause and the then-clause. The aorist of the protasis may be "constative" and closest to its basic "summary" meaning: it views the action in its entirety[15]. In the next sentence Paul uses the indicative present of the same verbs, that is, without special regard for beginning or end.

The apodosis consists of just one verb: σωθήσῃ ("you will be saved"); therefore, that verb is not without emphasis. Almost certainly, I think, the future is temporal and refers to eschatological salvation[16]. In verse 9 Paul has in mind a person who by believing is justified. But as a believer one has also to bear witness, to confess with the lips. Only then will that believer be saved. Initial faith is not enough for final salvation; the requirement of confessing is added (although here it is placed before that of believing).

---

belief and outward expression in word as inextricably linked, the two sides of the one coin"; FITZMYER, *Romans*, p. 592: "In addition to the verbal confession, an inward faith is demanded, which will guide the whole person in dedication to God in Christ".

13. DUNN, *Romans II*, p. 608, comments on πιστεύσῃς: "here, somewhat surprisingly, Paul uses it in the aorist tense of the act of Christian commitment for the first time".

14. In J. H. MOULTON – N. TURNER, *A Grammar of New Testament Greek. III Syntax*, Edinburgh, 1963, Turner writes: In conditional clauses with ἐάν … the aorist portrays "a definite event as occurring only once in the future, and conceived as taking place before the time of the action of the main verb" (p. 114). Cf. the admittedly free comment in W. SANDAY – A. C. HEADLAM, *A Critical and Exegetical Commentary on the Epistle to the Romans* (ICC), Edinburgh, 1895, p. 290: "The beginning of Christian life has two sides: internally it is the change of heart which faith implies; this leads to righteousness, the position of acceptance before God; externally it implies the 'confession of Christ crucified' which is made in baptism, and this puts a man into the path by which in the end he attains salvation; he becomes σωζόμενος".

15. B. M. FANNING, *Verbal Aspect in New Testament Greek*, Oxford, 1990, p. 395. Fanning claims that Turner's general rule cited in the previous note does not always apply (p. 403, n. 18).

16. Cf. DUNN, *Romans II*, p. 609: a genuine future, "the end product of a process". On the same page he comments: "Note the three tenses involved here – *present* belief and confession, of the epochal *past* event of Christ's resurrection, resulting in *future* salvation".

Verse 10

Paul clarifies and grounds further by means of a γὰρ ... δέ-construction. He now formulates a general thesis. No less than six modifications should be noted[17]. (1) The verbs "to believe" and "to confess" are in the passive form. (2) These two verbs are in the indicative present. (3) The construction is impersonal (no longer "you"). (4) The logical order is introduced: first believing, then confessing. (5) The idea of righteousness is inserted: to believe εἰς δικαιοσύνην[18] is paralleled with to confess εἰς σωτηρίαν. (6) Instead of the "and" linking the two verbs in the protasis of v. 9, a δέ creates an antithetic parallelism: initial faith over against final salvation. Verse 10 with its opposing δέ seems to confirm our understanding of verse 9. In translations and commentaries this δέ is mostly neglected or its oppositional character rejected. One often finds a connecting "and"[19].

Furthermore, as is well known, in a (μὲν) γὰρ ... δέ-construction sometimes the causal force of γάρ may not apply to the first clause but does apply to the second with δέ. The content of the first clause is as it were merely conceded[20]. If one assumes that this grammatical nuance is present in verse 10, the sense can be elucidated by means of the following paraphrase: "for it is true that one believes to gain righteousness (cf. 10,4), but one confesses in order to reach salvation". According to this interpretation Paul highlights the second requirement very much.

"Not being put to shame"

Final salvation is also indicated in 10,13: "everyone who calls on the name of the Lord shall be saved" (cf. 10,1: Paul's prayer for the Israelites is "that they may be saved"; see also 1,16: the gospel "is the power of God for salvation for everyone who has faith").

---

17. Compare the meager sentence which K. HAACKER, *Der Brief des Paulus an die Römer* (THNT, 6), Leipzig, 1999, p. 213, recently devoted to v. 10: "Der Vers illustriert durch seinen Parallelismus die Verwendung von δικαιοσύνη als Heilsbegriff neben σωτηρία (vgl. 1,16f)".

18. Cf. the last part of 10,4: εἰς δικαιοσύνην παντὶ τῷ πιστεύοντι.

19. So, e.g., NRSV; M.-J. LAGRANGE, *Saint Paul: Épître aux Romains*, Paris, 1931, p. 258; KÄSEMANN, *Römer*, p. 274; BYRNE, *Romans*, pp. 316 and 322; MOO, *Romans*, p. 658; HAACKER, *Römer*, p. 201; PITTA, *Romani*, p. 326. FITZMYER, *Romans*, p. 587, translates v. 10 without "but" or "and": "Such faith of the heart leads to uprightness; such profession of the lips to salvation"; *idem* in O. MICHEL, *Der Brief an die Römer* (Meyer, 4), Göttingen, [14]1978, p. 324.

20. See, e.g., M. ZERWICK, *Biblical Greek*, Rome, 1963, nos. 474-477.

The same idea of future and final deliverance is twice expressed negatively through the passive "not being put to shame" in quoted texts. In 10,11 Paul cites Isa 28,16: "No one who believes in him will be put to shame". This idea has already occurred in 9,33: "and whoever believes in him will not be put to shame". "Being put to shame" is eschatologically a highly significant concept.

There can hardly be any doubt that in all these verses Paul points to a future which encompasses more than initial justification[21].

A Parallel Passage

Admittedly, absolute certainty about Paul's distinction between right-eousness and salvation in 10,10 is hardly obtainable. Yet a passage in Romans 5 renders the acceptance of that distinction in 10,10 almost inevitable. After having stated in 5,8 that "while we still were sinners Christ died for us", Paul adds in verse 9: "much more surely then, now that we have been justified by his blood (δικαιωθέντες νῦν ἐν τῷ αἵματι αὐτοῦ, cf. v. 1 and v. 11), we will be saved through him (σωθησόμεθα δι' αὐτοῦ) from the wrath of God". The difference between initial right-eousness and final salvation can scarcely be more evident: past tense over against future tense; life as justified believers already now (νῦν) over against eschatological deliverance from God's wrath.

Rom 5,10 continues: "For if while we were enemies, we were recon-ciled to God through the death of his Son, much more surely, having been reconciled, will we be saved by his life". The justification vocabulary changes (κατηλλάγημεν), but the same distinction is repeated. We have again a past tense over against a future tense, and the life as reconciled believers already now (νῦν, v. 11) over against the salvation which the eschatological life of Jesus is going to bring about.

Of course, in Rom 5,6-11 there are two steps in Paul's argument: from sinful life to justification by the death of Christ, and from justification to salvation by the life of Christ. Faith is mentioned at the beginning of the chapter (δικαιωθέντες ... ἐκ πίστεως, v. 1[22]). In Romans 10, however, Paul reflects upon faith in Christ as the basic condition for justification. However, in 10,9-10 he distinguishes between believing and confessing

---

21. Cf. Moo, *Romans*, p. 659: "... 'not being put to shame' refers to deliverance at the time of judgment" (with reference to Isa 50,7b-8a).
22. Cf. the variant reading in Rom 5,2.

and, moreover, in 10,10 between believing so as to be justified and confessing so as to be saved. To be sure, the two contexts are different. Yet in Rom 5,9 as well as in 10,10 the two concepts of justification and salvation are mentioned and, almost certainly, distinguished (and opposed) in a similar way: already justified, not yet saved.

Conclusion

Both grammar and immediate context strongly suggest that in 10,9-10 Paul distinguishes not only between mouth and heart but also between believing and confessing, and in v. 10 equally between righteousness and salvation. From 5,9 we know that Paul in fact makes that last distinction. Most probably it is also present in 10,10[23]. But how does Paul argue in 10,5-13? Can we follow his way of reasoning and the train of thought of this chapter?

Paul's Reasoning in Romans 10

The line of thought in Rom 10 is not so straightforward as one might wish. In 9,30-33 Paul already emphasizes that Israel, although it made great efforts to achieve righteousness under the law, did not attain it. In chapter 10 he will further explain how and why this happened, but the development of the argument is somewhat tortuous.

Israel's Failure (vv. 1-4 and 14-21)

Paul's prayer to God is for the salvation of Israel (10,1). No doubt, the Israelites had zeal for God, but it was an ill-informed zeal; they sought their own righteousness based on the law, but they did not submit themselves to God's righteousness (vv. 2-3). Already in 9,33 it was said that they stumbled over the stumbling stone which the reader could not but identify with Jesus Christ. Now it is stated in all clarity: Christ is the end (or: the goal) of the law εἰς δικαιοσύνην παντὶ τῷ πιστεύοντι (10,4).

Yet only at the end of the same chapter is Israel's failure emphasized again. In verse 16 Paul states: "Not all have believed the good news"; and

---

23. Cf., e.g., LAGRANGE, *Romains*, p. 258: The 'salvation' of 10,10 "n'est pas identique à la justification et revêt une nuance eschatologique".

with the words of Isaiah he complains: "Who has believed in our message?" Although Israel heard the message, Israel did not understand it (vv. 18-19). Finally, God himself says of Israel through the prophet Isaiah: "All day long I have held out my hands to a disobedient and contrary people" (v. 21).

Of course, what is stated in vv. 14-21 is not without a connection with what is present in vv. 5-13.

Righteousness for Everyone Who Believes (vv. 5-13)[24]

The Israelites tried to establish their own righteousness, that which comes from the law (v. 5). But now the righteousness that comes from faith is not far away. Christ is not (only) in heaven or in the abyss. The word is near you. This word is identified with τὸ ῥῆμα τῆς πίστεως, i.e., the gospel that Paul proclaims (vv. 6-8). That word has to be met with faith[25].

The scripture says: "No one who believes in him will be put to shame" (v. 11). In v. 12 then Paul repeats what he has said many times before and thus motivates the above statement: for there is no distinction between Jew and Greek; the same Lord Jesus is generous to all who call on him, i.e., to all who believe in him and invoke him. Invoking Jesus implies faith in him. One more explanatory and, again, grounding sentence follows: "for everyone who calls on the name of the Lord shall be saved" (v. 13). In v. 11 Paul has said: The believer will not be put to shame; here, in v. 13, he adds: the believer who invokes the Lord shall be saved.

After this lengthy reflection on the righteousness which comes from God Paul in vv. 14-16 further shows that faith depends on hearing, and hearing on proclaiming. Israel has heard the message but did not understand it (v. 18-19); Israel became a disobedient people (v. 21).

---

24. For Paul's reasoning in this section, cf. M. J. SUGGS, "'The Word Is Near You': Romans 10:6-10 Within the Purpose of the Letter", in W. FARMER et al. (eds.), *Christian History and Interpretation. FS J. Knox*, Cambridge, 1967, 289-312, esp. pp. 308-312; ECKSTEIN, "Nahe ist dir das Wort"; J. S. VOS, "Die hermeneutische Antinomie bei Paulus (Galater 3.11-12; Römer 10.5-10)", in *NTS* 38 (1992) 254-270, esp. pp. 258-260 and 267-269; J. P. HEIL, "Christ, the Termination of the Law (Romans 9:30–10:8)", in *CBQ* 63 (2001) 484-498.

25. See ECKSTEIN, "Nahe ist dir das Wort", pp. 219-220, who as many others considers "faith" in the expression "the word of faith" as *fides qua creditur* and renders it by "das Glauben weckende Wort". He maintains that the term ἔγγυς in v. 8 ("nahe") is not so much "leicht erreichbar" or "leicht zu erfüllen", but "im eschatologischen Sinne epiphan und gegenwärtig" (218). Yet cf., among others, MOO, *Romans*, p. 658: "The gospel, then, is 'near' to us because it requires only what our own hearts and mouths can do…".

The Double Requirement (vv. 9-10)

In verses 9-10 "believing" is evidently very much present; it is the condition for righteousness and salvation. But somewhat strangely another requirement appears preceding that of believing: "if you confess with your lips" (v. 9a). Both are needed for salvation. As already stated, the doubling of the requirement flows from the quotation in v. 8 with its diversification of mouth and heart. One may be tempted to consider that new requirement in v. 9 to be a rather disturbing detour or at least an intervening idea, but it reappears in v. 10. Now "confessing with the mouth" is second; it follows "believing with the heart". And εἰς δικαιο-σύνην here corresponds with εἰς σωτηρίαν. While believing leads to righteousness, confession will bring one to salvation. The two ideas are duly opposed by the particle δέ: inward conviction over against outward testimony, private faith over against public confession, initial justification over against future and final salvation. What is confessed ("Jesus is Lord"), of course, supposes what is believed ("God raised Jesus from the dead"). The remarkable and surprising content of verses 9-10 should in no way be explained away.

Although the idea of salvation (or "not being put to shame") was previously mentioned in 10,1 (cf. already 9,33) and will be mentioned again in v. 13 (cf. v. 11), the reference to "confessing" disappears. Paul continues with "believing" alone. Faith appears to function as an all-inclusive term. In vv. 12 and 13 (cf. v. 14), probably under the influence of Joel 2,32, he introduces the phrase and concept of "calling on (the name of) the Lord" which, however, seems different from "confessing"[26].

Conclusion

Within the whole of Romans 10 the explicit mention of "confessing with the lips" as a condition for salvation cannot but surprise the readers. They should, however, not deny its presence. Nor must they exaggerate its importance in this context since, occasioned by the quotation from Deuteronomy in v. 8, it makes its appearance in v. 9 but disappears

---

26. MICHEL, *Römer*, p. 331, considers "to call on the name" the equivalent of "to confess", but this is hardly correct. Cf. H. CONZELMANN, "Was glaubt die frühe Christenheit?", in ID., *Theologie als Schriftauslegung. Aufsätze zum Neuen Testament* (BEvTh, 65), München, 1974, pp. 106-119, esp. pp. 109 and 112-114, who discusses the differences between "Credo" and "Homologie": "Homologie" is "Akklamation" ("Anruf"), but also "Proklamation", its second constitutive element (p. 112).

after v. 10. Nonetheless the distinction between believing and confessing, as well as that between righteousness and salvation, must be taken into account.

Verses 9-10 are part of the reflection on "righteousness for everyone who believes" in vv. 5-13. This reflection itself interrupts 10,1-4 and 14-21 where Paul points out Israel's failure. The reasoning in Romans 10 as a whole is somewhat rough and uneven. In v. 9 one has the impression that Paul writes and expands under the influence of the quotation in v. 8; moreover, the aorists in the protasis are rather strange. In v. 10 Paul reflects and explains further. Now he opposes (δέ) inner faith and public confession. Moreover, the second clause, that of confession, appears to be emphasized. In all probability it refers not so much to a once confessed baptismal formula or the repetition in creeds as to the existential testimony (cf. Mt 10,32, same verb), even in the midst of opposition and persecution[27]. To attain final salvation after justification, such public confession, which supposes inner faith, must consist of much more than just saying "Lord, Lord" (Mt 7,21).

---

27. Cf. CONZELMANN, "Was glaubt die frühe Christenheit?", p. 112: "Daher ist es der Kirche versagt, verborgen zu existieren und in Verfolgung dem Bekenntnis auszuweichen; sie hat nicht die Möglichkeit, sich in 'statu confessionis' in innerliche Übung von Religiosität zurückzuziehen".

14

The Confirmation of the Promises
(Romans 15,8)

In his recent and interesting *New Testament Studies* article "Verheissung und Erfüllung im Lichte paulinischer Theologie" Thomas Söding deals with promise and fulfillment in Paul, mainly by analyzing passages from Galatians and Romans[1]. A brief paragraph entitled "The Service of Jesus Christ to the Circumcision as Confirmation of the Promise for all Peoples (Rom 15,8)" concludes the section on Romans[2]. This note will first present Söding's understanding of Rom 15,8 of that paragraph. Then the major part will be devoted to a critical reaction. A conclusion and a brief reflection on Pauline theology will close the note.

The Exegesis of Rom 15,8 by Thomas Söding

The fulfillment of the promise is to be found in the communion of Jews and Gentiles who with one voice glorify God. Paul elaborates this theme in Rom 15,1-13 which constitutes, according to Söding, the conclusion not only of Paul's exhortation but also of the whole letter. Söding calls verse 8 the *Kernsatz*. His own translation is as follows: "Christ has become the servant of the circumcision, on behalf of the truth of God, in order to confirm the promises to the fathers"[3]. Each of the three elements of this sentence receives a succinct explanation:

(1) Jesus is "the servant of circumcision" as the one who in his death on the cross took on himself the curse of the law (Gal 3,13-14) and brought about reconciliation (Rom 3,21-26).

---

1. T. SÖDING, "Verheissung und Erfüllung im Lichte paulinischer Theologie", in *NTS* 48 (2001) 146-170, esp. pp. 152-161 and 161-168.
2. *Ibid.*, pp. 167-168: "Der Dienst Jesu Christi an der Beschneidung als Bekräftigung für all Völker (Röm 15.8)".
3. *Ibid.*, p. 167: "Christus ist Diener der Beschneidung geworden, für die Wahrheit Gottes, um die Verheissungen der Väter zu bekräftigen".

(2) He suffered this death "on behalf of the truth of God" because, in giving his life, his saving "pro-existence" proved the truth that God does not regret his grace.

(3) Jesus died this death "in order to confirm the promises to the fathers" because he bent "under the law" (Gal 4,4) in such a radical way that he also brought the Gentiles into the sphere of grace. He *confirms* the promises through the fact that he not only reveals the validity of these promises but also fulfills them beyond measure ("über die Massen")[4].

The final sentence of Söding is rather dense: "Rom 15,8 once again discloses where the christological heart of Paul's theology of fulfillment beats and displays that the Pauline christology obtains its biblical-theological format not least within the horizon of his theology of fulfillment"[5].

Critical Reaction

For convenience's sake the critical remarks may be ordered under four headings: vocabulary and expressions, the entire sentence, the context, and some related texts.

Vocabulary and Expressions

"On behalf of 'the truth' of God" does not render the exact meaning of ἀλήθεια. The meaning of this term in v. 8 is "faithfulness" (cf. Rom 3,4: γινέσθω δὲ ὁ θεὸς ἀληθής, and 3,7: ἡ ἀλήθεια τοῦ θεοῦ). In his comment Söding also utilizes the verb "bewahrheiten"[6]; this explanation, again, does not respect the correct nuance of ὑπὲρ ἀληθείας θεοῦ. The expression as such refers to God's faithfulness to his promises. A further analysis of the entire sentence and its context will demonstrate this.

Mention must also be made of "promises" of v. 8b. Söding is of the opinion that Paul here concretely includes a reference to the salvation of the Gentiles (cf. the apostle's reasoning in 4,13-25 and Gal 3,6-9). Yet as

---

4. SÖDING, "Verheissung und Erfüllung", p. 167.

5. *Ibid.*, pp. 167-168: "Röm 15.8 zeigt noch einmal, wo das christologische Herz der paulinischen Verheissungstheologie schlägt und dass die paulinische Christologie ihr biblisch-theologisches Format nicht zuletzt im Horizont seiner Theologie der Verheissung gewinnt".

6. *Ibid.*, p. 167: "... weil die rettende Proexistenz seiner Lebenshingabe bewahrheitet, dass Gott seine Gnade nicht reut".

soon as Rom 15,9a is considered, such a reference becomes improbable. The verb βεβαιῶσαι in v. 8b ("in order 'to confirm' the promises given to the patriarchs") does not appear to indicate the inclusion of the Gentiles nor does it point to a fulfillment of the promises "beyond measure".

The Entire Sentence

Strictly speaking the citations of verses 9b-12 belong to the lengthy sentence which begins at v. 8. However, an analysis of verses 8-9a will suffice for the moment. Grammatically speaking Rom 15,8-9a is notably difficult. Several points must be taken into account[7].

(1) The subject of the infinitive in v. 9a, the Gentiles, is not the same as the implied subject "Christ" of the infinitive in v. 8b. This, together with the absence of εἰς in v. 9a, results in a lack of perfect parallelism between the two clauses.

(2) One should not neglect the oppositional δέ in v. 9a. The contrast, of course, is strengthened by the similar but, in terms of content, divergent expressions ὑπὲρ ἀληθείας θεοῦ in v. 8a and ὑπὲρ ἐλέους in v. 9a.

(3) Note must also be taken of the fact that the first expression qualifies "Christ became a servant to the circumcision (= the circumcised) 'on behalf of God's truth (= faithfulness)'" (v. 8a), while the second expression is part of v. 9a and appears to indicate the reason why the Gentiles should glorify God: they must glorify God "on behalf of [his] mercy", a statement which is almost identical with: they should glorify his mercy.

(4) It now becomes evident that verse 8b further explains the expression "on behalf of God's faithfulness". Faithfulness consists in confirming and fulfilling the promises given to the fathers (= the patriarchs). In the whole of the sentence consisting of vv. 8-12, verse 8b more or less interrupts the flow of thought.

(5) Nonetheless, after reading εἰς τὸ βεβαιῶσαι in v. 8b one spontaneously supposes that the infinitive δοξάσαι in v. 9a participates in the purpose character of that εἰς τό-construction. The logic, however, hardly allows us to assume that "Christ became a servant to the circumcised ... in order that the Gentiles might glorify God for his mercy" (RSV translation). There probably is an ellipsis between v. 8 and v. 9.

7. For this section see the more extensive analysis in my "Syntactical and Logical Remarks on Rom 15,8-9a", in *NT* 42 (2000) 257-261, reprinted in *Collected Studies on Pauline Literature and on The Book of Revelation* (AnBib, 147), Rome, 2001, pp. 29-33.

(6) It would seem that the interruption of v. 8b has caused the elliptical character of v. 9a. One is as it were forced to supply an assertion parallel to that of v. 8a. Can it be taken from v. 7b: "just as Christ has received (or welcomed) you" (cf. 14,3: God has received the weak)? If so, a probable reconstruction of Paul's thought would result in "Christ received the Gentiles on behalf of God's mercy so that they may glorify God".

(7) A final grammatical note concerns the γὰρ ... δέ-construction of vv. 8a and 9a. There could be a hidden μέν present in v. 8a. In such a construction the first clause is often somewhat concessive (= "everybody knows that..."). The real reason (γάρ) and the emphasis on it are to be found in the δέ-clause.

Bringing together all these remarks, the following paraphrase of Paul's ideas in v. 7 and vv. 8a and 9a seems to be justified: "Receive and welcome one another, as Christ has received you, for the glory of God. For, I tell you, everyone knows that Christ became a servant of the Jews on behalf of God's truthfulness, but he received the Gentiles so that they may glorify God for his mercy".

The conclusion of this brief analysis becomes evident. Verse 9a cannot be separated from v. 8. Together they constitute one lengthy sentence. Moreover, v. 8 is presumably not the *Kernsatz*. Within this sentence the emphasis lies on v. 9a. Between v. 8 and v. 9a there appears to be an opposition which is indicated by δέ at the beginning of v. 9a, but also by "circumcision" in v. 8 and Gentiles in v. 9a as well as the expressions "on behalf of God's truth" and "on behalf of [his] mercy". "Truth" in v. 8a means God's fidelity and faithfulness; the term says that God will confirm the promises given to the fathers (v. 8b). Considering the whole of vv. 8-9a, it is unlikely that the plural "the promises" contains a specific reference to the single promise to Abraham that in him the Gentiles will be blessed (Gen 12,3; cf. Gal 3,6-9). In v. 8 Paul's attention appears to be limited to the circumcised and their particular privileges (the promises to the patriarchs)[8].

The Context

In 15,7 Paul exhorts both "strong" and "weak": "Welcome one another just as Christ has welcomed you". Already in 15,2 he has written in an

---

8. Most recently A. PITTA, *Lettera ai Romani* (I Libri Biblici, 6), Milan, 2001, pp. 487-489, disagrees and connects v. 8 and v. 9; he finds parallels in Gal 3,13-14 and 4,4-5. The particle δέ of v. 9a is rendered by "and". Cf., e.g., J. A. FITZMYER, *Romans* (AB, 33), New York, 1993, p. 706 (also "and"): "As Paul understands these promises, both Jews and Gentiles share in them (recall 11:13-24)".

inclusive way: "Each of us must please our neighbor" (NRSV) and in
v. 3, just as in v. 7, the grounding refers to Christ's example: "For Christ
did not please himself". In the wish-prayer of vv. 5-6 the entire community is equally included: "May the God of steadfastness and encouragement grant you to live in harmony with one another". A reference to
Christ follows and then the harmony is stressed again: "so that together
you may with one voice glorify the God and Father of our Lord Jesus
Christ".

Yet in v. 1 Paul has addressed "the strong": "We who are strong ought
to put up with the failings of the weak, and not to please ourselves".
Who are "the strong" and who are "the weak"? An explicit answer is not
given. However, immediately after the inclusive verse 7 Paul distinguishes
between Jews and Gentiles in vv. 8-12. So Paul seems to suggest that "the
strong" are (mainly) Gentile Christians while "the weak" probably consist of Jewish Christians (and Gentiles who want to live like Jews).

What is the focus of Paul's argument? There should be harmony in the
Roman community. The majority of his addressees are Gentile Christians. They must put up with the failings of "the weak". Of course, they
know that God could not but be faithful to the promises given to the
Jewish patriarchs (cf. ὑπὲρ ἀληθείας θεοῦ), but they should, above all,
realize that God has been "merciful" to them, Gentiles (cf. ὑπὲρ ἐλέους).
God's mercy towards the Gentiles constitutes a main point of 15,1-13.
It is the real ground of his exhortation to "the strong". Because of that
(almost unexpected) divine mercy they, "the strong", must be merciful
to "the weak"; they must carry their burdens; they should not please
themselves.

Therefore, what is stated in 15,8 should not be over-emphasized. Within
this context Paul does not specifically refer to the promise given to Abraham, namely that the Gentiles will be blessed in him. In this verse he
does not reflect on Israel's role in the salvation of the Gentiles. In v. 8
he just mentions God's self-evident faithfulness to the promises given to
the fathers before highlighting, in 15,9-12, God's mercy to the Gentiles
by means of many scriptural quotations.

Some Related Texts

In the letter to the Romans Paul more than once emphasizes God's
truthfulness in his dealing with Israel: see 3,2-8 (with the "truth"-ter-
minology in vv. 4 and 8); 9,4-6 (the word of God has not failed); 11,1-2
(God has not rejected his people); 11,28-29 (the gifts and the calling of

God are irrevocable). Twice he underlines that God's mercy has reached the Gentiles: see 9,23-24 ("in order to make known the riches of his glory for the objects of mercy...") and 11,30 (the Gentiles have now received mercy).

One could argue against our explanation of 15,8-9 by referring to 4,16 where Paul uses the same terminology and certainly means the "firm" promise regarding the Gentiles: διὰ τοῦτο ἐκ πίστεως, ἵνα κατὰ χάριν, εἰς τὸ εἶναι βεβαίαν τὴν ἐπαγγελίαν παντὶ τῷ σπέρματι. The "promise" to Abraham depends on faith and rests on grace. It is "guaranteed" for all his descendants, all believers. The promise says that Abraham will be the father of many nations. It should be noted that in Rom 4,13-25 "promise" is used in the singular. Paul clearly means that specific promise. Yet both plural and singular are employed in a similar universalistic context in Galatians 3.

Although in the second part of Romans 9 Paul focuses on the vocation of the Gentiles and in 9,4 the plural is certainly inclusive, in 9,6-18 the singular "promise" appears to be meant for Israel alone, her election by God. Most probably the plural of 15,8, though by itself inclusive, also limits its attention to Israel's privileges and in this verse does not pay attention to her universalist vocation.

We may point out the difference between Rom 9–11 and 15,8-12, that is, the presence or absence of a connection between Israel and the nations. In Romans Paul emphasizes God's faithfulness to the promises but he also reflects on the faithlessness of Israel. Yet Israel's refusal and hardening do function in God's salvific plan. Through the Jews' disobedience to God the Gentiles receive mercy, and by the mercy shown to the Gentiles the Jews will become jealous. Finally Israel too will receive mercy (see Rom 11,28-32). This dialectical junction, however, does not seem to be present in 15,8-12.

Conclusion

The pericope 15,1-13 is not a *recapitulatio* of the entire letter. It is the final section of the exhortation which begins in 14,1: Paul insists on mutual acceptance, especially on the duty of "the strong" to welcome "the weak in faith". Verses 8-12 function as the grounding for the final repetition "welcome one another" in v. 7. In these motivating verses the greatest amount of consideration by far is given to God's mercy shown to the Gentiles, i.e., the Gentile Christians who seem to represent "the strong" (vv. 9-12). As an integral part of this motivation verse 8 points to God's faithfulness to the promises given to the fathers. Because of its probable concessive nuance this verse should not be called the *Kernsatz*. In v. 8 Paul's attention seems to be focused on the promises to Israel, not on its role in the salvation of the Gentiles.

A close reading of 15,8-9a warns us to be cautious with regard to Pauline theology. Typical ideas of Paul cannot always be found in every Pauline text, even if at first sight the phraseology may tempt the reader. The danger of *eisegesis* is never far away.

Knowledge and Love
(1 Corinthians 8,1-13)

The fourth major section of 1 Corinthians, 8,1–11,1, deals with meat sacrificed to idols. Paul's basic position in this section is that Christians, because they know that idols do not really exist, are entitled (cf. 8:9: ἡ ἐξουσία ὑμῶν αὕτη) and free (10,29: ἡ ἐλευθερία μου) to eat sacrificed meat. Yet no matter how much knowledge and freedom are justly valued, love of the weak fellow believers and avoidance of scandal may require a renunciation of that right and liberty (see 8,7-13 and 10,23-30).

In 8,1-13 Paul's reasoning passes through three steps. First he contrasts knowledge and love (vv. 1-3). Then he emphasizes the non-existence of idols as well as the existence of only one God and one Lord (vv. 4-6). Each of these first two subdivisions is introduced by a similar clause with "concerning", "(the eating of) food offered to idols", and "we know". The longer third division (vv. 7-13) deals with the avoidance of scandal. The weak believers who do not possess sufficient knowledge can be brought to fall by those who do possess knowledge and sit at table in an idol's temple (v. 10).

In 1994 the forty-third session of the Colloquium Biblicum Lovaniense was devoted to the study of the Corinthian Correspondence. The congress volume, edited by its president R. Bieringer, appeared in 1996[1]. In this major publication of 41 contributions three of them deal with 1 Corinthians 8: "Coherence and Relevance of 1 Cor 8–10" by J. Delobel, "1 Cor 8,1-6: A Rhetorical *Partitio*" by J. F. M. Smit, and "Theology and Christology in 1 Cor 8,4-6" by A. Denaux[2]. In 2000 Smit republished his study in *About the Idol Offerings*[3]. This book consists of eleven chapters,

---

1. R. BIERINGER (ed.), *The Corinthian Correspondence* (BETL, 125), Leuven, 1996.
2. J. DELOBEL, "Coherence and Relevance of 1 Cor 8–10", 177-190; J. F. M. SMIT, "1 Cor 8,1-6: A Rhetorical *Partitio*. A Contribution to the Coherence of 1 Cor 8,1–11,1", 577-591; A. DENAUX, "Theology and Christology in 1 Cor 8,4-6. A Contextual Redactional Reading", 593-606. Cf., in the same volume, V. KOPERSKI, "Knowledge of Christ and Knowledge of God in the Corinthian Correspondence", 377-396, esp. pp. 389-391.
3. J. F. M. SMIT, *"About the Idol Offerings". Rhetoric, Social Context and Theology of Paul's Discourse in First Corinthians 8:1–11:1* (CBET, 27), Leuven – Paris – Sterling, VA,

five of which have been published previously in the period 1996-2000. The overall vision of Smit, on the one hand, and Delobel (and Denaux) on the other differs greatly. Smit sees idolatry as the main problem in 1 Cor 8–10[4], while for Delobel the core discussion treats the distinction between knowledge and love, between what is allowed in principle and what should be done in practice. This difference of understanding is already visible in the interpretation of chapter 8.

The present contribution is limited to this chapter; it contains three parts: an analysis of verses 4-6 (cf. Denaux), an investigation of the line of thought in chapter 8 (cf. Smit and Delobel) and a brief christological reflection on verse 6.

Analysis of 1 Corinthians 8,4-6

4a Therefore, concerning the eating of food offered to idols, we know
 b that (there is) no idol in the world
 c and that (there is) no God save one,
5a for, if in fact there are so-called gods whether in heaven or on earth
 b – as (indeed) there are many gods and many lords –
6a for us, however, (there is only) one God the Father
 b from whom (are) all things and we (are) for him,
 c and (there is only) one Lord Jesus Christ
 d through whom (are) all things and we (are) through him.

In this literal version the words within parentheses are not in the original Greek. Verses 4-6 constitute one lengthy sentence (see the motivating γὰρ … ἀλλά-clauses of vv. 5a and 6). The parallelism between God and Christ within the last verse may be striking, yet the grammar of the whole sentence is somewhat cumbersome, not only because of the interruption of verse 5b but also because of the change of construction in

2000. See chapter IV: "The Function of First Corinthians 8:1-6: A Rhetorical *Partitio*" (pp. 67-81).

4. Cf. also G. D. FEE, "Εἰδωλόθυτα Once Again: An Interpretation of 1 Corinthians 8–10", in *Bib* 61 (1980) 172-197; republished in ID., *To What End Exegesis? Essays Textual, Exegetical, and Theological*, Grand Rapids – Vancouver, 2001, pp. 105-128; H. MERKLEIN, "Die Einheitlichkeit des ersten Korintherbriefes", in *ZNW* 75 (1984) 153-183. For a brief summary of these two authors, see SMIT, *Offerings*, pp. 8-9; D.-A. KOCH, "'Seid unanstössig für Juden und für Griechen und für die Gemeinde Gottes' (1 Kor 10,32). Christliche Identität im μάκελλον in Korinth und bei Privateinladungen", in M. TROWITZ (ed.), *Paulus. Apostel Jesu Christi. FS G. Klein*, Tübingen, 1998, 35-54; ID., "'Alles, was ἐν μακέλλῳ verkauft wird, esst…'. Die *macella* von Pompeji, Gerasa und Korinth und ihre Bedeutung für die Auslegung von 1 Kor 10,25", in *ZNW* 90 (1999) 194-219.

both verses 6b and 6d. Furthermore, how does Paul reason? What is the difference between the non-existing "idols" (v. 4b) and the existing "so-called gods" (v. 5a) or the "many gods and many lords" (v. 5b)? Some exegetical notes may prove helpful[5].

Verses 4-5

4a περὶ τῆς βρώσεως οὖν τῶν εἰδωλοθύτων οἴδαμεν
 b ὅτι οὐδὲν εἴδωλον ἐν κόσμῳ
 c καὶ ὅτι οὐδεὶς θεὸς εἰ μὴ εἷς.
5a καὶ γὰρ εἴπερ εἰσὶν λεγόμενοι θεοὶ εἴτε ἐν οὐρανῷ εἴτε ἐπὶ γῆς,
 b ὥσπερ εἰσὶν θεοὶ πολλοὶ καὶ κύριοι πολλοί

By means of verse 4a Paul returns to the subject matter announced in verse 1: food offered to idols; yet by adding "the eating" Paul specifies the problem[6]. The readers of verses 4b-6 cannot but note the stylistic rhythm in this text unit which is mainly brought about by the parallelism in verse 4bc: "that (there is) no idol…, that (there is) no God…", as well as in verse 6: "for whom (are) all things and we (are) for him" (v. 6b) and "through whom (are) all things and we (are) through him" (v. 6d). True, in verse 6 one may have expected the repetition of the relative pronoun, "for whom" at the end of 6b and "through whom" at the end of 6d. Twice, the relative clause is replaced by an independent clause, twice also τὰ πάντα by ἡμεῖς: "we are for him" and "we are through him". The grammatical change causes a new beginning and, together with the mention of "we", it is not without emphasis. Yet even more details must be pointed out.

In the "that"-clauses of verse 4bc the verb is lacking. The translation must remain somewhat uncertain: what are the predicates and what kind of verb should be supplied? Because of the parallelism between 4b and 4c and the probable construction "there is no God…" in 4c, the same construction is most likely present in 4b as well: "there is no idol…". Without that symmetry one could easily take verse 4b to mean "an idol

---

5. Cf. C. H. GIBLIN, "Three Monotheistic Texts in Paul", in *CBQ* 37 (1975) 527-547, esp. pp. 529-537; DENAUX, "Theology and Christology" (with ample bibliographical notes); SMIT, *Offerings*, pp. 73-79; W. SCHRAGE, *Der erste Brief an die Korinther (1Kor 6,12–11,16)* (EKK VII/2), Solothurn – Düsseldorf – Neukirchen-Vluyn, 1995, pp. 215-251; R. F. COLLINS, *First Corinthians* (SP, 7), Collegeville, MN, 1999, pp. 313-321; A. C. THISEL-TON, *The First Epistle to the Corinthians* (NIGTC), Grand Rapids, MI, 2001, pp. 628-638 (with bibliography on 8,1-13 on pp. 613-616).

6. A further specification is provided in verse 13 ("meat"). Cf. DENAUX, "Theology and Christology", p. 595.

is nothing"[7]. The parallelism between verse 4b and 4c is not strictly anti-thetical but complementary[8].

In verse 4b one must think of non-existence of the idols insofar as they are powerless and incapable of protecting and saving those who bow to them. Reference can be made to the sarcastic language in Isa 46,1-2 and 6-7 (NRSV):

> Bel bows down, Nebo stoops, their idols are on beasts and cattle; these things you carry are loaded as burdens on weary animals. They stoop, they bow down together; they cannot save the burden, but themselves go into captivity... Those who lavish gold from the purse, and weigh out silver in the scales – they hire a goldsmith, who makes it into a god; then they fall down and worship! They lift it to their shoulders, they carry it, they set it in its place, and it stands there; it cannot move from its place. If one cries out to it, it does not answer or save anyone from trouble[9].

In verse 4c Paul employs the typical Jewish monotheistic formula. In the same chapter of Isaiah just cited one reads: "for I am God, and there is no other; I am God, and there is no one like me" (Isa 46,9). The added "is" in 4c means "really exists". One should probably not suppose that in 4bc Paul is quoting Corinthian slogans[10]. What is stated here is what Paul fully admits. It is already part of his epistolary reaction to what he knows about the situation in Corinth: idols – all those "dumb" lifeless images – have no real existence; there is but one God. Of course, nothing in the content of verse 4 is really new to the Christians in Corinth.

In verse 5a καὶ γάρ ("and for"; cf. the Latin et-enim) points to an explanation. The εἴπερ-clause is mostly taken as a concession: "although"[11]. Does verse 5 cause tension in Paul's logic? In 4b the existence of idols is negated. Yet Paul is going to qualify this statement in 5a: "for, if in fact there are so-called gods". The term λεγόμενοι ("so-called") reminds the readers of non-existence in verse 4b but clashes with what is stated in the protasis: "if in fact there are...".

---

7. COLLINS, *First Corinthians*, pp. 313 and 318, e.g., does not retain the parallelism by rendering v. 4b "in the world an idol is nothing". Cf. also DENAUX, "Theology and Christology", p. 595 and 599.

8. See J. S. VOS, "Das Rätsel von I Kor 12:1-3", in *NT* 35 (1993) 251-269, n. 29 on p. 257.

9. Cf., e.g., Wis 13,10-19.

10. See, e.g., the quotation marks in the NRSV: "no idols in the world exist" and "there is no God but one". See discussion of this hypothesis in THISELTON, *First Corinthians*, pp. 628-630.

11. It would be better to assume that the whole of verse 5 logically functions as a concession.

In verse 5b then the existence of many gods and many lords is plainly asserted[12]. The comparative ὥσπερ ("as") here possesses more or less the value of a motivating "since". Paul, of course, cannot deny the existence of demons represented by gods and lords (see 10,20-21)[13]. One must thus assume the presence of a distinction between idols (with no real existence) and really existing demons[14]. In verse 5b "many" is twice emphasized, and "lords" are mentioned alongside "gods": "as indeed there are many gods and many lords". "Many" will be contrasted by "one" in both 6a and 6c; the addition of "lords" prepares for the naming of the "Lord Jesus Christ" in 6c. The comparative clause of verse 5b constitutes a grammatical interruption.

Verse 6

6a   ἀλλ' ἡμῖν εἷς θεὸς ὁ πατὴρ
 b   ἐξ οὗ τὰ πάντα καὶ ἡμεῖς εἰς αὐτόν,
 c   καὶ εἷς κύριος Ἰησοῦς Χριστὸς
 d   δι' οὗ τὰ πάντα καὶ ἡμεῖς δι' αὐτοῦ.

Verse 6 contains the main affirmation: "but for us...". The clash within verse 5a, as well as the interruption of verse 5b, causes the connection of verse 6 with verse 5a to be somewhat disturbed. However, grammatically verse 5 is not an anacolouthon. The "but for us" at the beginning of verse 6 logically refers to verse 5a; "for us" supposes the hidden presence in verse 5 of "for the Gentiles"[15].

---

12. D. ZELLER, "New Testament Christology in its Hellenistic Reception", in *NTS* 48 (2001) 312-333, refers to the distinction of J. Weiss: "the old popular gods and the innumerable new ones [= the lords] invading Greece from the Orient and called *kyrioi*" (p. 319). See also D. ZELLER, "Der eine Gott und der eine Herr Jesus Christus", in T. SÖDING (ed.), *Der lebendige Gott. Studien zur Theologie des Neuen Testaments. FS. W. Thüsing* (NTA, 31), Münster, 1996, 34-49, esp. pp. 34-35.

13. Paul is not solely pointing to the subjective (real) conviction of the "weak" Christians in Corinth. So G. D. FEE, "Wisdom Christology in Paul: A Dissenting View", in ID., *To What End Exegesis?*, pp. 351-378, esp. p. 356. For a discussion of diverging opinions, see THISELTON, *First Corinthians*, pp. 632-634. Cf. also O. HOFIUS, "'Einer is Gott – Einer ist Herr'. Erwägungen zu Struktur und Aussage des Bekenntnisses 1. Kor 8,6", in M. EVANG, H. MERKLEIN, M. WOLTER (eds.), *Eschatologie und Schöpfung. FS E. Grässer* (BZNW, 89), Berlin – New York, 1997, 95-108, esp. pp. 101-102, and SCHRAGE, *Der erste Brief an die Korinther*, p. 241: "Am ehesten liegt ... wohl eine Identifizierung mit den Dämonen von 10,20 nahe ...".

14. In chapter 8 the term δαιμόνιον is not employed. It occurs four times in 10,20-21, never elsewhere in the undisputed letters of Paul.

15. Cf. COLLINS, *First Corinthians*, p. 315: "There is a contrast between the anonymous persons to whom allusion is made in Paul's 'so-called' of v. 5 and the 'us' of v. 6". For HOFIUS, "Einer ist Gott – Einer ist Herr", pp. 102-103, "for us" is a *dativus iudicantis*: "nach

One can compare the καὶ γὰρ εἴπερ ... ἀλλά-construction of verses 5a and 6 with a μὲν γὰρ ... δέ-construction: the first clause is mostly concessive; the motivation is to be found in the second clause. A free rendering of verses 5a.6 could be as follows: "although (for the Gentiles) there are so-called gods whether in heaven or on earth, for us, however, there is but one God, the Father...". The grammatical analysis shows that verse 6 explains (and develops) verse 4c. What is stated in verse 5a (and 5b) is simply conceded[16]. No doubt the emphasis lies on verse 6.

The major point in verse 6 is Paul's rewriting and expansion of the *Shema* that a Jew recites twice each day: "Hear, O Israel: The Lord is our God, the Lord alone" (Deut 6,4)[17]. Most exegetes assume that in verse 6 Paul quotes a credal formula or a traditional acclamation[18], but perhaps Paul himself composed this text.

Because of the attribute "many" in 5b it would seem that "one" in both 6a and 6c is an attribute: "one God" and "one Lord"[19]. In verse 6ab Paul writes "God the Father" and adds "from whom are (or: come) all things and we are (or: go) to him". At the end of verse 6b the Greek has καὶ ἡμεῖς εἰς αὐτόν ("and we to him") instead of καὶ εἰς ὃν τὰ πάντα ("and to whom all things"). Not only is the expected relative pronoun replaced by the personal pronoun αὐτόν and does καὶ ἡμεῖς begin, as it were, a new independent clause[20], but "all things" gives way to "we", i.e., we Corinthians, we Christians. Thus the idea of an all-encompassing creation is not complemented by a universal destiny, not even by the future of all human beings. Apparently Paul only points to believers, those redeemed by Christ. God is the origin and source of all things; God equally is the final goal for Christians. Both creation and redemption, protology and

---

unserem Urteil". MURPHY-O'CONNOR, "1 Cor VIII.6: Cosmology or Soteriology?" in *RB* 85 (1978) 253-265, speaks of "a comparative value judgment" (p. 258; cf. J. Weiss).

16. SMIT, *Offerings*, p. 75, wrongly, I think, considers 5b as the apodosis: "If indeed there are so-called gods either in heaven or on earth, then in that sense there are many gods and many lords".

17. See the discussion in HOFIUS, "Einer ist Gott – Einer ist Herr", pp. 106-108 (yet somewhat forced); R. BAUCKHAM, *God Crucified. Monotheism and Christology in the New Testament*, Grand Rapids, 1998, pp. 37-39.

18. On the presumed *Traditionsgeschichte* cf., e.g., C. WOLFF, *Der erste Brief des Paulus an die Korinther. Zweiter Teil: Auslegung der Kapitel 8–16* (THNT), Berlin, 1982, pp. 7-10; SCHRAGE, *Der erste Brief an die Korinther*, pp. 221-222.

19. Otherwise HOFIUS, "Einer ist Gott – Einer ist Herr", p. 103: "one" is subject; "God" and "Lord" are predicates.

20. In a note added to number 342 M. ZERWICK, *Biblical Greek*, Rome, 1963, remarks that it is "in accordance with the general Semitic preference for coordination rather than subordination" that "the dependence on the relative is readily abandoned" (with reference to 1 Cor 8,6).

(believers') eschatology, are included. The qualification of God as "the Father" may refer to God as origin and beginning; it certainly also suggests that Jesus Christ is his Son, although this title is not mentioned here in 6c[21].

In the *Shema* God himself is Lord. Paul distinguishes between God the Father and the Lord Jesus Christ. For us believers, he adds in verse 6cd, there is also but one Lord "through whom are all things and we are through him". While in verse 6b ἐκ ("from") was contrasted with εἰς ("to"), in verse 6d only one preposition is used, the instrumental διά ("through"). At the end of v. 6d the Greek text has καὶ ἡμεῖς δι' αὐτοῦ ("and we through him") which presents the same grammatical change as in v. 6b, as well as the same narrowing from "all things" to "we (believers)". Reading verse 6cd immediately after verse 6ab one cannot but realize that Christ is presented as the mediator of all things in creation, as well as the mediator for Christians in redemption: through Christ all things[22] are created; through Christ we believers are redeemed.

The "food offered to idols" (v. 4a) belongs to the realm of created things; they come from God the Father and through the Lord Jesus Christ and therefore can be eaten (cf. the psalm citation in 10,26: "The earth and its fullness are the Lord's"). G. D. Fee comments on verse 6: "This is clearly a Christian restatement of the Shema ..., with *God* now referring to the Father and *Lord* referring to the Son"[23]. The first person plural καὶ ἡμεῖς, "(and) we (are)", at the end of both verse 6b and verse 6d is emphasized; one remembers the equally emphatic "but for us" at the beginning of verse 6a.

The Line of Thought in Chapter Eight

Verses 4-6 deal with knowledge and faith-certainty[24]. In verse 1 Paul asserts: "Now concerning food sacrificed to idols: we know that πάντες

---

21. Cf. FEE, "Wisdom", p. 357 (esp. n. 15).

22. The expression "all things" in 6d must have, it would seem, the same cosmological meaning as in 6b. For MURPHY-O'CONNOR, "1 Cor VIII.6", however, the meaning is twice soteriological: "From God come all things which enable us to return to him. All these things are given through Christ and in him we go to the Father" (p. 265).

23. FEE, "Wisdom", p. 357; cf. also p. 358. The Corinthians' "understanding of the 'one God' needs to be broadened to include Christ as well" (p. 356).

24. In this second part use is made of my brief commentary in W. R. FARMER (ed.), *The International Bible Commentary*, Collegeville, 1998, pp. 1615-20; see also "Universalism in 1 Corinthians 8,1–11,1", in J. LAMBRECHT, *Collected Studies on Pauline Literature and on The Book of Revelation* (AnBib, 147), Rome, 2001, pp. 63-70.

γνῶσιν ἔχομεν". In verse 7a, however, Paul writes: ἀλλ' οὐκ ἐν πᾶσιν ἡ γνῶσις. Does Paul here utter a contradictory statement? It would seem that in verse 7b he clarifies that absence or lack of knowledge. Some Christians, accustomed as they are until now to idols, "eat food as food offered to idols", i.e., they fail to apply the distinction between idols that do not exist and existing demons as is indicated in verses 4-5, and thus their eating constitutes idolatry[25].

The Priority of Love

In verse 1a the fact that all "know" is admitted, but in verse 1b Paul immediately adds a qualification: "knowledge puffs up, but love builds up". Moreover, in verse 2 a further restriction is joined: Anyone who claims to know something[26] does not yet have the necessary knowledge. Such partial knowledge is not as it should be. Over against this rather severe language Paul, in verse 3, sets a reassuring statement: if Christians really love God, they can be sure that they are known by God. The logic surprises the reader. Why does Paul not say: "if one loves God, he knows as he ought to know", or: "if one loves God, he really knows God", or: "if one loves God, he is loved by God"? No doubt, Paul's style is calculated for effect[27].

In verses 4-6, however, not love but knowledge is spoken of again. The verses deal with the problem in Corinth, the eating of food offered to idols, as is explicitly said in verse 4a. Paul's radical solution is already implied, it would seem, in v. 4b: since there really is no idol in the world, a Christian is free to eat that food. Verse 4c, "and there is no God save one", is added in a parallel clause; Paul, as it were, spontaneously complements verse 4b. In the reasoning of verses 5-6 a double shift over against verse 4 should be noted: (1) no longer two parallel statements but first a concession (although for the Gentiles there are so-called gods) and then the main affirmation about God; (2) no longer the well-known expression "no God save one" but the innovative pairing "one God, the Father" and "one Lord, Jesus Christ". Of course, both the concession and the enlargement do not abolish Christian freedom, for God is the universal creator and Christ the universal mediator; moreover, "we

25. Cf. KOPERSKI, "Knowedge of Christ", pp. 390-391.

26. B. M. METZGER, *A Textual Commentary on the Greek New Testament*, London – New York, 1971, p. 556, defends the original τὶ ("something") in the verse.

27. On the presence of "God" and "by him", see METZGER, *A Textual Commentary*, 556-557: "The surprising turn of expression, however, is characteristically Pauline (Ga 4.9; cf. also 1 Cor 13.12)" (p. 557). But for this and the preceding note, see SMIT, *Offerings*, p. 70, who prefers P46 in which all these terms are absent.

Christians" go to God through Jesus Christ. Verse 6 consolidates the liberating conviction of the Christians who possess knowledge.

The line of thought in verses 7-13 is somewhat contorted. Moreover, there is an unevenness in the use of persons: from the third person plural in verse 7 to the first plural in verse 8; then from the second plural in verse 9 over the second singular in verses 10-11 back to the second plural in verse 12. In verse 13 Paul concludes with the first singular and in this way prepares the I-language of the example in chapter 9.

In verse 7 Paul mentions the absence of knowledge in some Christians and explains in what it consists: they eat sacrificed food while considering it as consecrated and contaminated, so that by eating it their weak conscience is defiled. Verse 8 reminds himself and his readers that food as such has neither moral nor religious relevance. In verse 9, then, the warning is given: take care that you, knowing believers, do not become a stumbling block to the weak believers. Paul explains in verse 10 how this could occur; a case is brought forward: on the one hand your behavior (sitting at table in a temple hall) and on the other hand the sin of the weak believer who follows your example against his own conscience. In verse 11 Paul points out the saddening consequence: the loss of the weak brother "by your knowledge"; he adds not without emphasis "the brother for whom Christ died". Then, in verse 12 the implication is drawn: you sin not only against your brother but also against Christ. Verse 13 is a personal and somewhat generalizing conclusion which, however, reminds us of verse 9. Paul formulates a resolution: if food is a cause of falling, I will never eat meat "lest I cause my brother to fall".

In the whole of verses 7-13 the term "love" (of neighbor) is not mentioned. Yet abandoning one's right and adapting to the situation of another is certainly proof of authentic love. Of course, to have insight and knowledge is important. No idols really exist insofar as they are powerless (v. 4b). Although there are so-called gods (v. 5a) and, as demons, many gods and many lords do exist (v. 5b), there is but one God and one Lord. To have this faith-certainty creates liberty; it makes Christians free persons. But love of the weak Christians without a perfect knowledge, love of those who still think of the food they eat as food sacrificed to an idol, is more important than enjoying that liberty. Priority belongs to love.

The Interpretation by Joop Smit

According to J. Smit in 1 Cor 8,1–10,22 only one main issue is dealt with. Paul rejects the Christians' participation in public sacrificial meals, their eating of "idol offerings". The discussion occurs in a double round. In 8,7–9,27 Paul points to the negative effects on the "weak" Christians which such a partaking would produce. The first round can be qualified as a social consideration of the mutual relationships, an argumentation on the human level. It is an oblique approach but one should understand Paul's recommendation not to eat as a negative stand with regard to partaking in sacrificial meals. The second round of the argumentation then treats the same issue in its relationship with God. In 10,1-22 Paul indicates the theological implications of taking part in sacrificial meals. Idolatry means partnership with demons. Here in this second discussion the forbidding language is explicit. The two rounds provide a two-stage argument, first not acting with love, then fellowship in the demonic. One admires Paul's prudent rhetorical strategy: from indirect to direct language, from dissuasion to prohibition[28].

These two rounds of discussion are prepared by the introduction of 8,1-6 which Smit refers to as the *partitio* of chapters 8–10. Verses 1-3 briefly summarize the first argumentation; they speak of knowledge and love; they pay attention to the social side of the argument. Verses 4-6 introduce the theological discussion of chapter 10 by citing credal formulae and commenting on them. Strictly speaking the reasoning in chapter 8 is not straightforward, since verses 4-6 interrupt the first round of discussion[29].

Although Smit claims that he "reluctantly arrived at what looked like the standard pattern of a speech" and that he is "very well aware of the need of caution in this matter and of the danger of forcing texts" into a pattern, the results of his analysis agree with "the grammar of persuasive communication found in the classical handbooks of Greco-Roman rhetoric"[30]. After the *partitio* of verses 1-3 (and 4-6), the first round consists of a brief *narratio* (v. 7), the *propositio* (the two theses of v. 8), and the *argumentatio* which contains first a *reprehensio* (vv. 9-12) and then a *confirmatio* (8,13–9,27)[31].

Four specific exegetical notes should be mentioned. (1) For Smit already in verse 1 the announcement "about the idol offerings" is negative. The term εἰδωλόθυτον "has to be understood as a synecdoche (*pars pro toto*), bringing up for discussion participation in the sacrifices in its entirety"[32]. Therefore, in no way can Paul permit a taking part in such

---

28. Cf. SMIT, *Offerings*, pp. 149-165 (summary of the results).
29. Cf. *ibid.*, pp. 67-81.
30. *Ibid.*, p. 85; cf. also pp. 39-46.
31. Cf. *ibid.*, pp. 83-98.
32. *Ibid.*, pp. 71-72.

idolatrous ceremonies and meals. (2) The two theses of verse 8, both implying that the believers may renounce food without any damage, set the tone for the ensuing argumentation. In verse 9 the expression ἡ ἐξουσία ὑμῶν αὕτη possesses a sarcastic tenor and expresses contempt: "that [presumed] power of yours"[33]. "Paul takes a very reserved and disapproving stand"[34] on that power. Verse 9 should not be interpreted as if Paul acknowledges in principle the Corinthians' freedom and right to eat[35]. Verse 13 clearly shows Paul's personal negative attitude. (3) In 10,20-22 incompatibility between demons and God is emphatically stressed: pagans sacrifice to demons and not to God; believers should not be partners with demons; they cannot partake of the table of the Lord and the table of demons. (4) The absence of a similar explicit injunction in chapter 8 is to be seen as part of Paul's two-step rhetorical strategy which first consists of dissuasion and recommendation (human, social perspective). It would have been unwise to confront the Corinthians straightaway with an unequivocal prohibition (theological perspective). The issue was too sensitive in Corinth. Yet Paul's warning not to cause the weak to stumble actually implies the rejection of eating idol offerings[36].

Paul's Reasoning in Chapter Eight

Not much needs to be said in favor of or against Smit's rhetorical analysis and his finding of a detailed *dispositio*. However, aspects of his four remarks should be questioned. (1) The term "food offered to idols" by itself is not positive, but it would seem that precisely in 1 Cor 8–10 Paul points to the neutral character of this food[37]. Most probably the term is not used as a synecdoche. (2) It is by no means evident that in verses 8-12 Paul thinks of a cultic idolatrous action or a pagan religious rite as far as the strong believers are concerned. The sin that they risk committing is not that of idolatry but that of lack of love. Even if the expression "that [presumed] power of yours" denotes contempt, the "power" (right, freedom[38]) of the strong believers is fully recognized; only

---

33. SMIT, *Offerings*, p. 89.
34. *Ibid.*, p. 98.
35. Cf. *ibid.*, pp. 88-89.
36. Cf. *ibid.*, pp. 58 and 74, chapter V (pp. 83-98) and chapter VII (pp. 121-134).
37. Cf. DELOBEL, "Coherence and Relevance", pp. 182-184.
38. DELOBEL (*ibid.*, p. 184) writes: "The use of ἐξουσία in 8,9 and 9,4.5.6.12.18 in the sense of personal right and liberty is specific to 1 Cor, and differs from its meaning elsewhere in Paul".

its misuse is condemned. Idolatry will be present in the action of the weak believers, if they follow, against their conscience, the example of the strong. (3) The situation in chapter 10 differs from that in chapter 8. In 10,20-22 cultic actions and pagan worship are spoken of. (4) One should hesitate to assume the proposed specious two-step Pauline strategy in 1 Cor 8–10.

But how does Paul's reasoning proceed in chapter 8? There appears to be more unity of content in this chapter than one would assume at first sight. The theme of "knowledge" assures a thought unity between verses 4-6 and 1-3, as well as between verses 7-13 and 1-6. In verse 1 the knowledge concerns food sacrificed to idols, but no details of that knowledge are given in verses 1-3. This occurs in verses 4-6 which are introduced by "hence, as to the eating of food offered to idols". Christians know that no idols exist, only one God (v. 4), or better, that although demons exist, i.e., in the eyes of the Gentiles many gods and many lords (v. 5b), for Christians there is but one God creator and one Lord mediator. By means of the article in ἡ γνῶσις in verse 7 Paul refers back to what precedes. "This" knowledge, however, is not in every believer since some still see the idols as really existing and consider idol food as contaminated by demons. Such people defile their conscience by eating that food. Over against this lack of knowledge Paul fears misuse of knowledge. In verses 8-13 he very much insists on the priority of love of neighbor. This is the main point in the whole chapter[39].

The explanation of verse 10 must remain uncertain. Is eating in the temple of an idol permitted on the condition that scandal is avoided or is that eating always prohibited because of a possible scandal? Whatever answer one prefers, the "knowledge" provided in verses 4-6 remains: food offered to non-existing idols is not contaminated and can on principle be eaten. This is stated in so many words in 10,19 (food sacrificed to idols is nothing special), in 10,26 ("the earth and its fullness are the Lord's") and also in Rom 14,14 (Paul knows and is persuaded that nothing is unclean in itself).

The Mediator

The christological expansion in 8,6 does not function as such in the reasoning of chapter 8. Yet Paul must have composed this verse with

---

39. An analogous type of reasoning is present in chapter 9 (Paul forsakes his right of living by the gospel), in 10,28-29 (avoidance of scandal is required) and in Rom 14,1–15,13 (love respects the lack of knowledge in other Christians).

utmost care. Already in verse 5b the elaboration of "so-called gods whether in heaven or on earth" (v. 5a) by means of "many gods" and "many lords" no doubt prepares the two expressions "one God the Father" and "one Lord Jesus Christ" of verse 6. Moreover, the two expansions of 6b and 6d confirm Paul's attentiveness. Verse 6 provides the reader with a blueprint of Paul's theology and christology, as well as his protology, soteriology and eschatology.

Rom 11,36 is the end of 11,33-36, the solemn conclusion of Romans 9–11. Paul praises God: "From him and through him and to him are all things. To him the glory forever. Amen". Here the three prepositions "for", "through", and "to" point to God alone. 1 Cor 8,6 is different. Just as "God the Father" is separated from "the Lord Jesus Christ", so also the prepositions "from" and "to" are applied to the Father while "through" is now employed for Christ[40].

That in 1 Cor 8,4-6 the one Lord Jesus Christ is opposed to the many lords of the pagan environment is in itself not surprising, but Paul's radical adaptation of the Jewish *Shema* is simply astonishing. For Jews JHWH alone is God; he is the unique Lord of Israel. Christians see alongside God the Father his Son, the Lord Jesus Christ. The *Shema* is christianized. A distinction is made between God and Lord; yet both are brought together as closely as possible. Can we go as far as Richard Bauckham recently writes: "Thus, in Paul's quite unprecedented reformulation of the *Shema*, the unique identity of the one God *consists of* the one God, the Father, *and* the one Lord, his Messiah"?[41] As far as Paul is concerned probably not[42]. Christ is both the preexistent mediator in creation and the eschatological mediator in redemption.

Just as in the "hymn" of Philippians, a nuance of "subordination" should not be missed. The use of different prepositions in verse 6 shows this: "from" and "to" for God the Father, "through" for the Lord Jesus Christ. Some exegetes here refer to Jewish wisdom speculation. What contemporary Judaism proclaimed of God's personified wisdom and personified logos – their assistance in creation – is in 1 Cor 8,6 transferred to the Lord Jesus Christ, a person and no longer just a personification. He is the divine mediator, yet not the absolute origin nor the final goal[43].

---

40. In his investigation of tradition and redaction in 1 Cor 8,4-6 DENAUX, "Theology and Christology", pp. 603-606, deals with 1 Thess 1,9-10 (pp. 605-606).

41. BAUCKHAM, *God Crucified*, p. 38.

42. In German a distinction is made between *Gleichsetzung* and *Identifizierung*, hence between equality and identity. Cf. DENAUX, "Theology and Christology", p. 601 (with reference to J. A. Fitzmyer in n. 16).

43. Cf., e.g., L. W. HURTADO, *One God, One Lord. Early Christian Devotion and Ancient Jewish Monotheism*, London, 1988, pp. 98-99. Hurtado sees Jewish speculations on divine

However, the preexistent relationship between God and Christ is not further spelled out[44]. (See the contribution number 21 in this volume.)

What Paul proposes and explains in 1 Cor 8,4-6 does not seem to be meant as a new doctrine for the Corinthians, not even the content of verse 6. In his adaptation of the *Shema* he most probably is also employing and integrating already existing credal formulae[45]. Most strikingly, for Paul and his Christians alike, this pairing of God and Lord, of Father and Son, has in no way damaged their monotheistic faith. Therefore, together with others, Bauckham speaks of a "christological monotheism"[46].

A few witnesses expand verse 6 by adding "and one Holy Spirit in whom (are) all things and we (are) in him". In his discussion of this late variant reading Bruce M. Metzger notes: "The trinitarian form was current as early as the close of the fourth century"[47].

agents as the background. However, Paul's dependence on the Jewish wisdom tradition is vigorously denied in the recent study of FEE, "Wisdom", pp. 350-378: "there is nothing inherent in this passage nor in its surrounding context that would suggest that Jewish Wisdom lies behind Paul's formulation" (p. 359).

44. Cf., e.g., ZELLER, "Der eine Gott", pp. 47-49. By means of verse 6 JEROME (*PL* 30, col. 741) defends the equality of Father and Son against the Arians: "Si ideo non est Filius Deus, quia unus est Deus Pater: ergo et Pater non erit Dominus, quia unus est Dominus Christus. Si autem Pater non excluditur a dominatione: nec Filius a deitate: sed utrumque utrique commune est". This text became famous and has been re-employed against later heretics. Cf. SCHRAGE, *Der erste Brief an die Korinther*, p. 246.

45. FEE, "Wisdom", p. 359, points to "the *presuppositional* nature in these passages of *the historical person*, Jesus Christ, as pre-existent and as the personal agent of creation itself".

46. BAUCKHAM, *God Crucified*, e.g., p. 40 (already K. Barth). There Bauckham again emphasizes: Paul "maintains monotheism, not by adding Jesus to but by including Jesus in his Jewish understanding of the divine uniqueness". For the expression "christological monotheism" cf. also, e.g., N. T. WRIGHT, *The Climax of the Covenant. Christ and the Law in Paul's Theology*, Edinburgh, 1991, p. 129.

47. METZGER, *A Textual Commentary*, p. 557: known to Gregory Nazianzus. Cf., e.g., COLLINS, *First Corinthians*, p. 320; SCHRAGE, *Der erste Brief an die Korinther*, p. 246, esp. n. 206.

The Woman's Veil
(1 Corinthians 11,2-16)

Recently a journalist visited the "modern" monastic community of Boz in North Italy and wrote a lengthy report on these men and women living together a new form of religious life. In that report the journalist also mentions: "In the chapel they (= the members of that community) have a white cowl and, according to a time-honored tradition, during the religious offices the women ('nuns') put a cap on their head".

The Publication of G. Biguzzi

In 2001 the Italian exegete Giancarlo Biguzzi published a major monograph *Veil and Silence. Paul and Woman in 1 Cor 11,2-26 and 14,33b-36*[1]. He examines these two passages from the First Letter to the Corinthians in which Paul deals with women: during prophecy and prayer a woman must have a veil over her head and during the religious meetings she must keep silent. The monograph is composed in an exemplary way: clear exposition, step by step analysis, strict logic in the reasoning, and, moreover, a captivating style. However the results of the study's first part are surprising.

Biguzzi is not the only commentator who maintains that in 1 Cor 11,2-16 Paul does not deal with the veil of women but with their hairdress. Paul, he asserts, opposes a concrete misbehavior. Through a particular hairdress some Corinthian women intend to deprecate their femininity, to hide their womanhood. They do not respect what is given by creation: to the woman long hair, to the man short hair. In their conduct these women do not entirely accept their own identity. Another point. Biguzzi explains verse 3a in a strange way. Christ is the head of each man;

---

1. G. BIGUZZI, *Velo e silenzio. Paolo e la donna in 1Cor 11,2-16 e 14,33b-36* (SupplRivBib, 37), Bologna, 2001.

yet, in his opinion, "man" (ἀνήρ) here means all human beings, thus man and woman together. In verse 3b (and further on in the passage) "man" refers to men only. In verse 3 the term κεφαλή ("head") occurs three times. According to Biguzzi its metaphorical sense differs in each case and has nothing to do with "authority", only with "origin".

There are more peculiar data in this monograph, but this summary presentation may suffice as an introduction to the brief discussion that follows. This reflection is not meant as a complete exegesis of the pericope, but special attention will be devoted to Paul's way of reasoning. A few linguistic and exegetical notes are presented which should be reckoned with, I think, in each broader comment. But first the text.

Analysis

The Translation of 1 Cor 11,2-16 (mainly NRSV[2])

2 I commend you because you remember me in everything and maintain the traditions just as I handed them on to you.

3 But I want you to understand that Christ is the head of every man, and the husband is the head of his wife, and God is the head of Christ.

4 Any man who prays or prophesies with something on his head disgraces his head,

5 but any woman who prays or prophesies with her head unveiled disgraces her head – it is one and the same thing as having her head shaved.

6 For if a woman will not veil herself, then she should cut off her hair; but if it is disgraceful for a woman to have her hair cut off or to be shaved, she should wear a veil.

7 For a man ought not to have his head veiled, since he is the image and glory of God; but a woman is the glory of man.

8 Indeed, man was not made out of woman, but woman out of man.

9 Neither was man created because of woman, but woman because of man.

10 For this reason a woman ought to have (a sign of) authority on her head, because of the angels.

11 Nevertheless, in the Lord woman is not without man, or man without woman.

12 For just as woman (came) out of man, so man (comes) through woman; but all things (come) out of God.

13 Judge for yourselves: is it proper for a woman to pray to God with her head unveiled?

14 Does not nature itself teach you that if a man wears long hair, it is a dishonor for him,

2. In some verses the rendering is more literal because of the parallelism present in the original Greek text.

15 but if a woman wears long hair, it is a glory for her? For her hair is given
   to her for a covering.
16 But if anyone is disposed to be contentious – we have no such custom,
   nor do the churches of God.

The Asymmetric Verse 3

The four Greek clauses in verse 3 are as follows:

3a θέλω δὲ ὑμᾶς εἰδέναι ὅτι
 b παντὸς ἀνδρὸς ἡ κεφαλὴ ὁ Χριστός ἐστιν,
 c κεφαλὴ δὲ γυναικὸς ὁ ἀνήρ,
 d κεφαλὴ δὲ τοῦ Χριστοῦ ὁ θεός.

The term "head" is employed three times in a metaphorical way; it signifies "authority, power". Christ has authority and might over every man,
man has authority over woman, God over Christ. Of course, the basis
of that authority is different regarding God, Christ and man, but in this
verse Paul does not pay attention to this diversity. Verses 7-8 and 12 confirm the basic meaning present in v. 3. Paul employs the term "head" as
metaphor of authority – which in Greek is rather uncommon – because
further in the passage he will speak of "head" in its physical sense (see
vv. 4-5, 7 and 10).

It would seem that the grammatical construction of v. 3b on the one
hand and v. 3cd on the other is not exactly the same. The over-literal
translation of v. 3bcd is:

3b of every man the head is Christ,
 c but [the] head of woman [is] the man,
 d but [the] head of Christ [is] God.

In v. 3b "Christ" most likely is the predicate and "the head" (with article) the subject: the head of every man is Christ. In v. 3c, as well as v. 3d,
"head" (without article) seems to be the predicate while "the man" and
"God" function as subject: the man is above woman, God above Christ.
NRSV translates verse 3c: "the husband is the head of his wife".

It would seem that in verse 3bc Paul opposes man and woman and
wants to indicate a different authority ("head") for each of them. Yet in
verse 3 the emphasis lies on v. 3c, more than on v. 3b which possibly even
possesses a concessive nuance. In v. 3b Paul repeats what every Christian
already knows. In v. 3c Paul wants to stress the subordination of woman;
therefore the predicate "head" is in the front. Verse 3d is also important,
but it is mentioned at the end, one would almost say a little late, as a

necessary afterthought. The proper order would have been: God, Christ, man, woman. Paul will return to God as creator further in his argument.

Veil and Verses 4-6

The term κάλυμμα does not occur in the pericope. By means of the adjective ἀκατακάλυπτος ("not covered", v. 5 and v. 13) and the verb κατακαλύπτομαι ("to cover", v. 6, twice; cf. v. 7) Paul refers to a head covering or veil. This seems to be the most obvious sense. Men pray and prophesy with bared heads (cf. vv. 4 and 7); during these activities women have to cover their heads by means of a veil. By the term "uncovered" Paul can hardly indicate a provocative hairdress of a woman, that is her wild, tousled or loose hair. A woman who refuses to wear a head covering or veil should have her hair cut or her head shaved. In v. 6 Paul says in a sarcastic way: "bareheaded" and "hairless" are equally disgraceful for a woman, a shameful thing.

Because one finds in v. 4 the expression κατὰ κεφαλῆς ἔχων (literally: "having [something] which hangs down the head"), some commentators think of a man's long hair which falls down his head (cf. v. 14 which refers to men). However a woman's veil or covering easily hangs down as well. The term περιβόλαιον, which occurs in v. 15, literally means "cloak" (which "surrounds" the body), hence also "covering", "veil".

Line of Thought in Verses 7-10

Grammatically speaking the emphasis in verses 7, 8 and 9 each time lies on the second part of the sentence, thus on what is said about woman and her status of subordination.

In verse 7a the expression "the image and glory of God" certainly contains an allusion to the first creation narrative, Gen 1,27 ("So God created humankind in his image, in the image of God he created them"). Paul, however, applies Gen 1,27 to man alone, although in the same verse of Genesis it is stated: "male and female he created them". Moreover, Paul changes the text: instead of "in his image", man simply "is" the image (εἰκών) and glory (δόξα) of God; "in" disappears and "glory" is added. Woman is but the glory (not the image), and only the glory of man (not of God). What's more, while praying and prophesying she must cover this glory. It also strikes the reader that, in contrast to verse 3, Christ is absent in verse 7. The sequence is: God, man, woman. According to Paul this sequence is simultaneously the order of precedence.

In verse 8 Paul grounds his thesis by referring to the origin of woman according to the second creation narrative, Gen 2,21-24: woman is taken ἐκ ("out of") man. In verse 9 he still has in mind this Genesis passage: woman is created διά ("because of") man, man not "because of" woman. Biguzzi translates διά plus accusative here twice by "by means of", but the meaning of this preposition + acc. is not instrumental but causal and purposive: "for the sake of" (cf. NRSV; the weaker Italian *attraverso*, I think, also misses the exact sense). According to the narrative of Gen 2 man needs woman, "a helper as his partner" (2,18); a man clings to his wife (cf. 2,24).

By διὰ τοῦτο ("because of this"; "for this reason") verse 10 logically follows on verse 9, more specifically on v. 9b: woman is "because of" man. In v. 10 Paul now adds: "for this reason" woman must have an ἐξουσία ("authority") on her head. This statement probably does not mean that woman has dominion and might over her own head or body. No, Paul seems here to employ ἐξουσία with reference to the head covering, the veil. Since "head" means authority (cf. v. 3), "authority on the woman's head" in v. 10 probably points to the veil as a sign or a symbol of man's authority over woman.

The expression "because of the angels" at the end of verse 10 surprises the reader and remains obscure. Must woman cover her head because of the angels who are watching over creation? or of angels who are present in the liturgy of the Christians? Or does Paul allude to angels who, like those of Genesis 6, can be tempted by women? This last suggestion may be the most likely one, although the sense remains uncertain.

A New Consideration in Verses 11-12

By means of πλήν ("nevertheless") in verse 11 Paul introduces a new nuancing thought. One gets the impression that he is now providing a Christian consideration, since at the end of the verse the expression "in the Lord" is present. Biguzzi claims that this expression means "in the Lord 'God'", but it is much more likely that Paul, as he almost always does in such expressions, refers to Christ. The following paraphrase, it would seem, is justified: from a Christian viewpoint woman and man cannot exist without one another. In verses 7-10 Paul underlines the subordination of woman: she is taken out of man; she is created for the sake of man. In verse 11, however, the emphasis lies on the fact that man is nothing without woman, just as woman is nothing without man; the reciprocity is very much stressed.

Although Paul has added "in the Lord" at the end of verse 11, in the motivating comparison of verse 12 he returns to the order of creation. The comparison does not deal with redemption but with the origin of both male and female: "for just as woman (came) from man (ἐκ τοῦ ἀνδρός), so man (comes) through woman (διὰ τῆς γυναικός)". In v. 12, as in v. 11, the second part of the verse is emphasized. The reader already knows that woman came from man (v. 12a). Man's dependence on woman is now underlined (v. 12b). Yet by "through woman" Paul no longer refers to Genesis 2; he has in mind the birth of every man. At the end of verse 12 he adds: "but all things (come) from God (ἐκ τοῦ θεοῦ)". Again a kind of needed afterthought: God is the ultimate origin of all things, all mortals included, man as well as woman. God is the creator of all.

So verses 11-12 offer a new, surprising reasoning: man, too, cannot exist without woman; the two are thrown together. They need mutual help; they are equivalent. In the final analysis they have God as a common origin. Perhaps, by "in the Lord" of v. 11 Paul intends to say that his startling consideration stems from a reflection as Christian or, even better, that man and woman have equal value thanks to their relation to the Lord: "There is no longer Jew or Greek, there is no longer slave or free, there is no longer male and female; for all of you are one in Jesus Christ" (Gal 3,28).

Hair as Illustration in Verses 13-15

By the appeal "judge for yourselves if it is proper for a woman to pray in public with nothing on her head" (v. 13) Paul returns to the reasoning of verses 4-6. The same term ἀκατακάλυπτος occurs again. In v. 6 Paul has asserted that it is a shameful thing for a woman to shave her head or cut her hair. Now he says to the Corinthians that they must use their common sense: Which are the universally admitted norms?

According to verses 14-15 nature teaches that long hair is a disgraceful thing for a man, but it is a woman's glory, since it has been given her to serve as a covering: ἀντὶ περιβολαίου. The meaning of ἀντί ("instead of") is probably weakened to "as". In Paul's argumentation this reference to hair functions as a kind of illustration, of confirmation. The long hair that has been given to woman by nature and covers her in a fitting way teaches us that the veil is equally fitting. To be sure, this reasoning is somewhat surprising: a woman who prays or prophesies thus has two coverings, the hair and the veil! However, otherwise than Biguzzi (and others), we maintain that the hair itself is not the veil which is meant by

Paul. The natural hair shows the correctness of the woman's veil. Her long hair suggests and advises the use of a veil.

Conclusion and Beginning: Verses 16 and 2

Verse 16 breaks off the argument. From this verse ("but if anyone is disposed to be contentious") we learn that probably Paul did not expect all the Corinthians to agree with his reasoning. Some seem to have defended the women's behavior. Moreover, this verse gives the impression that Paul himself realizes that his argumentation will hardly convince everybody. In a somewhat nervous way – and at his wit's end? – he refers to "custom", his own custom and that of the other churches. Already from verse 13 on ("judge for 'yourselves'") he directly addresses the Corinthians (cf. v. 14: "does not nature itself teach 'you'?"). He goes on to do this in v. 16.

In verse 2 Paul had also addressed the Corinthians by means of 'you'. However, this verse must be taken as a *captatio benevolentiae*, an effort to please his addressees: I do praise you because you always remember me and follow the teachings that I have handed on to you. This sentence probably introduces more than the passage on the veil. Yet the beginning of this passage, verse 2, with its praise, corresponds to the closing verse 16 with its rebuke: both refer to tradition or custom. In this way the verses "frame" Paul's entire plea.

Critical Reflection

1 Cor 11,2-16 is a difficult passage. To today's readers the background is no longer evident; moreover, the Greek text is not everywhere equally transparent. In no way is the pericope pleasing to modern sensibility. There is a real danger that the exegete, almost unconsciously, will try to adapt the text to the reigning mentality, but that is the wrong method. First Paul must be allowed to speak for himself, to explain what he means; one must listen to him attentively, even if there is disagreement with what he says. Only then there may be room, if need be, for criticism. R. Bultmann coined the term *Sachkritik*, content criticism. Perhaps one can not always agree with the content of Scripture, but the first task of both commentator and reader remains to know and correctly understand what Scripture says.

Today one will no longer agree that woman is not God's image in an equally direct way as man. Further, the wearing of a head covering or veil is without any doubt a custom conditioned by time or culture. Moreover, Paul lives in a patriarchal society that he could not radically criticize. In support of man's authority he also employs arguments from Genesis which hardly carry conviction. Yet, it must be admitted, the content of verses 11-12 strikes the reader positively. Almost casually and without much emphasis, Paul here speaks of the equal value of man and woman in a beautiful Christian way.

We no longer know exactly what constituted the problematic behavior of some women in Corinth. Perhaps it was (only) somewhat provocative; one must not too easily assume that they imitated men and completely rejected their femininity or identity. Yet Paul does stress the difference between woman and man. Also today most of us may want to preserve the diverging male and female identities; they constitute an enriching complementarity, but to what extent should this difference be manifested by hairdress and clothing, by gender specific roles and functions (church ministries)? Today this problem will certainly not be solved in the same way as before. The discussion continues relentlessly.

It should be noted: otherwise than in 1 Cor 14,33-36, the fact that in 11,2-16 both men and women publicly pray and prophesy is not under debate.

The Spirit and Jesus
(1 Corinthians 12,3)

In 1993 the Dutch exegete Johan Vos devoted an interesting article to the difficult verse from the First Letter to the Corinthians entitled "The Riddle of 1 Cor 12,3"[1]. Against the opinion of many commentators he claims that in this verse Paul does not deal with the discernment of spirits. Vos carefully analyses the text, especially the way Paul reasons and argues. He also pays much attention to 12,2 and to the logical connection with the context, the whole of chapter 12. The aim of this brief study is more limited: the logic of verse 3 itself will be the focus of our critical investigation.

First the three clauses of the Greek text and its literal translation:

3a διὸ γνωρίζω ὑμῖν ὅτι
 b οὐδεὶς ἐν πνεύματι θεοῦ λαλῶν λέγει· Ἀνάθεμα Ἰησοῦς,
 c καὶ οὐδεὶς δύναται εἰπεῖν· Κύριος Ἰησοῦς, εἰ μὴ ἐν πνεύματι ἁγίῳ.

3a Therefore I want you to understand that
 b no one speaking by the Spirit of God [ever] says "Jesus [is] cursed!"
 c and no one [can] say "Jesus [is] Lord" except by the Holy Spirit.
    (RSV, without the square brackets)

A First Analysis

In verse 3a διό ("that is why") is certainly important since this adverb brings about the logical link with verse 2. Also the verb γνωρίζω ("to make known"), after ἀγνοεῖν ("to be ignorant") in verse 1 and οἴδατε ("you know") in verse 2, must be duly considered. But above all clauses 3b and 3c are striking because of their symmetry and antithesis.

---

1. J. S. Vos, "Das Rätsel von I Kor 12:3", in *NT* 35 (1993) 251-269. On p. 251 Vos mentions that W. C. VAN UNNIK, "Jesus: Anathema or Kyrios (I Cor. 12:3)", in B. LINDARS and S. S. SMALLEY (eds.), *Christ and the Spirit in the New Testament, FS C. F. D. Moule*, Cambridge, 1973, 113-126, called the verse a *crux interpretum* (p. 113), and J. SMIT, "De rangorde in de kerk", in *TvT* 29 (1989) 325-343, "een berucht raadsel" (a notorious riddle) (p. 327).

(1) The parallelism is evident: twice the negative οὐδείς ("no one"), twice τὸ πνεῦμα ("the Spirit of God" in v. 3b and "the Holy Spirit" in v. 3c), twice Ἰησοῦς, twice a nominal clause which, moreover, is introduced by "to say" (λέγει in verse 3b and δύναται εἰπεῖν in verse 3c).

(2) The antithesis between ἀνάθεμα ("cursed") in verse 3b and Κύριος ("Lord") in verse 3c cannot but be eye-catching. One could be tempted to take "cursed Jesus" as the imploring of a curse ("cursed be Jesus", so RSV; NRSV: "let Jesus be cursed"); few will take "Lord Jesus" as an invocation or a vocative. It would seem that the two antithetical expressions are symmetrical. Verse 3c is almost certainly an affirmative nominal clause ("Christ 'is' Lord") and verse 3b is probably also nominal in the same affirmative sense ("Jesus 'is' cursed"). If so, both clauses are not wishes but assertions: "cursed is Jesus" and "Lord is Jesus".

(3) The partial chiasmus should also be mentioned: "no one speaking by the Spirit of God" stands almost in front of verse 3b and "except by the Holy Spirit" is at the end of verse 3c.

(4) Of course, there also are small divergences: the exceptive εἰ μή ("if not") of verse 3c does not find its corresponding expression in the participle λαλῶν ("speaking") of verse 3b. Nor is the modal δύναται λέγειν ("can say") of verse 3c identical with the simple λέγει ("says") of verse 3b.

The question cannot be avoided: Does Paul, in verse 3c, repeat the same idea by means of a partially different vocabulary and partially diverging grammatical construction, or is there between verse 3b and verse 3c a real opposition? Or is the parallelism perhaps complementary and, therefore, does verse 3c say something different from (or something more than) verse 3b? In order to retrieve Paul's train of thought it may seem be advisable to simplify the two clauses, to convert the negations into positive constructions and to propose equivalent paraphrases. In this way the comparison of the two clauses might become easier.

Johan Vos

Attention must now be given to the warnings of Johan Vos and to his own proposal of simplification.

a) Vos cautions the reader against four incorrect assumptions[2].

(1) Verse 3bc should not be employed as a criterion for the so-called

---

2. VOS, "Rätsel", pp. 252-259.

discernment of spirits. In verse 3b Paul does not write: "No one saying 'Jesus is [or: be] cursed' speaks through the Spirit of God". In this case Paul would reason from the result or effect to the cause, i.e., from cursing Jesus to the action of the Spirit. No, Paul argues in the opposite way.

A similar remark also applies to v. 3c. Paul does not regard the confession "Jesus is Lord" as the sign for real speaking by the Spirit. On the contrary, the possession of the Holy Spirit is the cause of the confession of Jesus as Lord.

(2) Verse 3b and 3c do not present a perfect parallelism. In order to make verse 3b and 3c perfectly symmetrical, verse 3b must be altered as follows: "no one can say 'cursed is Jesus' except by the evil spirit". But Paul does not write this.

(3) Neither do the two clauses form an antithesis. Of course, there are the antithetical elements "cursed" and "Lord", but the two clauses are linked by the connective καί ("and"). It would be mistaken to take this καί as having the oppositional nuance of "but". Moreover, the fact that the whole of verse 3 constitutes the opposite of verse 2 suggests that the existence of an opposition within verse 3 is not very probable. With regard to verse 3b and verse 3c Vos notes: "Der Parallelismus ist also synthetisch oder komplementär"[3]. He asserts that in verse 3 there is "eine zweigliederige These"[4].

(4) Perhaps one would like to propose a way of reasoning similar to that of, e.g., Sirach 3,30: "Water extinguishes a blazing fire, and almsgiving atones for sin". The first clause functions as a comparison: "Just as water extinguishes a blazing fire, so also almsgiving atones for sin". Yet the clause of 1 Cor 12,3b does not have a comparative function regarding 3c.

b) Which is then the simplification proposed by Johan Vos? The first step is the removal of the negations in verse 3b and verse 3c: "Jeder Pneumatiker bekennt sich zu demselben Herrn" ("Every *pneumatikos* 'clings' to the same Lord") (v. 3b), and: "Jeder, der Jesus als den Hernn bekennt, hat Anteil an demselben Geist" ("every person who confesses Jesus as Lord participates in the same Spirit") (v. 3c)[5]. Paul emphasizes the connection of the Christians with the same Lord and the same Spirit, and at the same time claims that the spheres of influence of the Lord and the Spirit are co-extensive:

---

3. Vos, "Rätsel", p. 257.
4. *Ibid.*, p. 259.
5. *Ibid.*

Jeder Pneumatiker hat Anteil an demselben Herrn und jeder Gläubige hat Anteil an demselben Geist. Beide Sätze besagen, dass der Wirkungsbereich des Geistes mit dem Herrschaftbereich des Herrn zusammenfällt[6].

This analysis, I think, invites three critical questions. First, where does one find, in verse 3, "the same" Lord and "the same" Spirit or, in other words, does verse 3 already deal with the one Spirit and the one Lord, the theme that will be treated in verses 4-11? Second, can it be held that a "Pneumatiker" is meant in verse 3b while in verse 3c Paul speaks of a normal believer? Third, in verse 3 can a distinction be made between the action or influence of the Spirit and the lordship of Jesus, between the *Wirkungsbereich* of the Spirit and the *Herrschaftsbereich* of the Lord? It would seem that the answer to the first two of these three questions is not a simple yes.

A New Proposal

Is it possible to clarify the negative clauses of verse 3b and verse 3c? It would seem that one can correctly substitute "whoever ... not" for "no one": "Whoever speaks by the Spirit of God, does not say 'cursed is Jesus' (v. 3b)". In other words, a person who really is animated by the Spirit can in no way curse Jesus. The reasoning goes from the presence of the Spirit to the impossibility of cursing Jesus, that is, as Vos emphasizes, from cause to effect.

Verse 3c must be clarified in a similar manner: "Whoever can say 'Jesus is Lord' is only able to do this under the influence of the Spirit". In other words, a person who can honestly say "Jesus is Lord" is enabled to do this by the Spirit. Although the grammatical construction in verse 3c differs from that in verse 3b, the argumentation in verse 3c also goes from cause to effect, i.e., from the possession of the Spirit to the confession of Jesus.

Yet verse 3c says more than verse 3b. According to verse 3b the presence of the Spirit does not permit a cursing of Jesus; according to verse 3c the presence of the Spirit enables one to bless Jesus, i.e., to confess that Jesus is Lord. Just as "not black" is not synonymous with "white", so also "not cursing" is not the same as "blessing"[7]. The imperfect parallelism can

---

6. Vos, "Rätsel", pp. 259-260. Vos distinguishes between *Wirkungsbereich* ("region [or sphere] of action") and *Herrschaftsbereich* ("region [or sphere] of lordship").

7. Cf. the distinction between "contradictory" and "contrary" concepts, between "black – not black" and "black – white".

better be expressed as follows: "The one who possesses the Spirit cannot curse Jesus" (v. 3b) and: "Only the one who possesses the Spirit can bless Jesus" (i.e., confess him as the Lord) (v. 3c). The second clause does not exactly repeat the first one; the second clause is complementary.

Perhaps some may insist: at least in Paul's mind, does "not cursing Jesus" in fact not equal "blessing Jesus"? Although logically speaking this is less correct, it is possible that Paul had in mind such equalization. Then, in verse 3b ("the one who has the Spirit cannot curse Jesus") Paul already intends to say "such a person cannot do otherwise than bless Jesus". In this case verse 3b has the same content as verse 3c.

Does the Context Support the New Proposal?

The question must be asked how verse 3 functions within Paul's train of thought in 12,1-11. A few details merit special attention.

In 12,1 Paul begins a new topic: περὶ δὲ τῶν πνευματικῶν, ἀδελφοί ("now concerning spiritual gifts, brothers"). In verse 2 he reminds his readers of the time that they were still Gentiles and were led astray to (worship) idols. Two verbs are in the passive form, ἤγεσθε ("you were led") and ἀπαγόμενοι ("being led away"). One must most probably mentally supply the agent: "(led and led astray) by the evil spirits"[8]. One thinks here of Paul's distinction in chapters 8-10 between "idols" who have no real existence (see 8,4; 10,19) and really existing spirits, "demons" (see 10,20-21). In 12,2 Paul points to the influence which the evil spirits had on the Gentile Christians before their conversion. Now, however, as Christians they are influenced and led by the Spirit of God, "the Holy Spirit" (v. 3). The conversion itself is not narrated and Johan Vos, rightly, calls verse 2 a "fragmentarisch erzählte Geschichte"[9].

The adverb διό ("therefore") of verse 3 underlines the logical consequence of this conversion. If in verse 3b Paul has in mind a particular spiritual gift (or a number of such gifts), then in verse 2 he must also refer to similar (ecstatic?) phenomena. Yet in verse 3c this "speaking by the

---

8. No consensus exists as to whether verse 2 is an assertion or a question. Its grammatical construction, moreover, is highly uncertain. With regard to ὡς ἄν: do these particles repeat ὅτι and is ἀπαγόμενοι then reinforcing ἤγεσθε: "how you were irresistibly drawn"? Or should we suppose that ἀπαγόμενοι is part of a periphrastic construction: "you know that when still pagans you used to be led astray to dumb idols as you (ὡς ἄν) were ever being led"? This intricate philological discussion, however, is less important for the present study.

9. See VOS, "Rätsel", pp. 263-268.

Spirit" yields to a saying which is "confessing": whoever confesses under the influence of the Holy Spirit that Jesus is Lord. Can one suppose that Paul in v. 3c suddenly means every Christian? If so, not much attention appears to be given to this shift.

In verses 2-3 Paul opposes the activity of the spirits; therefore, "idols" and "Jesus" are also contrasted. In verse 3 he emphasizes the solidarity of the Spirit and Jesus: they are inseparably connected. The Spirit makes it impossible to curse Jesus and the Spirit enables the possibility of confessing Jesus as Lord. Here, however, no emphasis lies on the unicity of the Spirit nor on that of the Lord; it is the connection between the Spirit and Jesus that Paul underlines[10].

A new thought is brought in by verses 4-6 (cf. δέ at the beginning of v. 4: "but"): diversity in unity. There is a great variety of gifts but only one and the same Spirit, there is a great variety of services but only one and the same Lord, there is a great variety of activities but the one and the same God activates all of them. Johan Vos correctly stresses that the three verses are parallels contentwise[11]. The terms χαρίσματα, διακονίαι and ἐνεργήματα refer to the same "activities"[12]; Spirit, Lord and God refer to the same common origin.

Then in verse 7 it is stated that to each the manifestation of the Spirit is given for the benefit of the whole community, for the common good. This is worked out by an enumeration in verses 8-10: the utterance of wisdom and of knowledge are mentioned first, then three miraculous gifts – wonder-working, healings, and mighty works – finally prophecy and its discernment, as well as tongues and their interpretation (or translation into intelligible language). It is not by accident that the gift of tongues – so highly desired in Corinth – stands, together with the interpretation of them, in the last position. Verse 11 summarizes the whole development: The same Spirit activates all gifts (cf. v. 6: God); this Spirit "varies" or "allots" at will (cf. "varieties", the very term that is used three times at the beginning of verses 4, 5 and 6); each receives the appropriate gift (cf. v. 7 and vv. 8-10).

Paul's reasoning in 12,1-11 can easily be traced. Verse 1 begins the theme. In verses 2-3 the opposition between past and present follows, together with the emphasis that for believers Spirit and Jesus belong together. In

10. Cf. VOS, "Rätsel", p. 259.

11. *Ibid.*, p. 260: "Am besten liest man diese Sätze als einen synonymen Parallelismus. Paulus sagt dreimal mit anderen Worten das Gleiche".

12. Yet, as said above, according to VOS, "Rätsel", p. 259, Paul would distinguish between the "*Wirkungsbereich des Geistes*" and the "*Herrschaftsbereich des Herrn*" already in verse 3. However, this seems less probable.

verses 4-6 Paul stresses the diversity in unity and in verses 7-11 he concretizes that diversity and similarly emphasizes that the one who activates all gifts is the one and the same Spirit.

Parallel Texts

Over against the many gods and lords of the Gentiles Paul in 1 Cor 8,6 states: "for us, however, there is only one God the Father from whom are all things and we are for him, and one Lord Jesus Christ through whom are all things and we are through him". As stated above, idols have no real existence; demons really exist. Here too, Christian faith is contrasted to pagan idolatry. But 8,6 differs from 12,3 by its context (eating food sacrificed to idols), by its stress on Jesus as mediator in creation as well as in redemption, by the position of Jesus vis-à-vis the Father who is the absolute origin of all things and their ultimate aim, and, lastly, by the fact that the Spirit is not mentioned. In 8,4-6 Paul is not only engaged in a polemic with pagan polytheism, he also profoundly reflects upon monotheism and in verse 6 rewrites the *Shema* (cf., e.g., Deut 4,35)[13].

In Phil 2,11 Paul closes the so-called christological "hymn": "and (so that) every tongue should confess that Jesus Christ is Lord, to the glory of God the Father". Through the confession "Jesus Christ is Lord" this verse is very much like 1 Cor 12,3. But Phil 2,11, too, is different from 1 Cor 12,3: through its introductory verb ὁμολογέω ("to confess"), through the mention of God's glory as the ultimate aim and through the fact that in Phil 2,11 the future and universal recognition of Jesus as Lord at the end of times is focused upon[14].

In Rom 10,9-10 Paul distinguishes between "believing with the heart" and "confessing with the mouth". One believes that God raised Jesus from the dead; one confesses that Jesus is Lord. One believes with the heart and so is justified; one confesses with the mouth and so will be saved. Just as in 1 Cor 12,3, so also in Rom 10,9 the confession of Jesus as Lord is explicit. Yet the contexts differ greatly; furthermore, in contrast to 1 Cor 12,3, Paul distinguishes in Rom 10,9-10 between believing and confessing, between initial righteousness and final salvation[15].

---

13. See pp. 174-187 in this volume, no. 15: "Knowledge and Love (1 Corinthians 8,1-13)".

14. See pp. 245-262 in this volume, no. 21: "The Identity of Christ Jesus (Philippians 2,6-11)".

15. See pp. 155-166 in this volume, no. 13: "Initial Righteousness and Final Salvation (Romans 3,1-9)". In his discussion of 1 Cor 12,3, A. C. THISELTON, *The First Epistle to the*

Finally, one must not lose sight of the absence in the three parallel texts of the utterly strange expression "cursed is Jesus" (1 Cor 12,3b).

By Way of Conclusion

Paul's reasoning can be pursued. Out of "the person who speaks by the Spirit of God, does not say 'Jesus is cursed'" (v. 3b) logically follows "thus the person who curses Jesus does not have the Spirit" (from effect to cause). And out of "the person who says 'Jesus is Lord' cannot speak this confession except under the influence of the Spirit" (v. 3c) follows "the person who honestly says 'Jesus is Lord' has the Spirit (again from effect to cause)". To be sure, Paul himself does not draw these conclusions, but the rules of logic justify the development of his thoughts. Such conclusions express what is traditionally called "the discernment of spirits". So, be it indirectly, 1 Cor 12,3 deals with that discernment.

In 12,3 Paul emphasizes the unity of the Spirit and Jesus. All who possess the Spirit of God and speak by that Spirit can in no way curse Jesus. And only through the possession of the Holy Spirit is one able to confess the risen Jesus as Lord. However, through the centuries Christians have also reasoned from Jesus to Spirit: the person who recognizes Jesus as the risen Lord and publicly confesses him – which implies, of course, the observation of his commandments – only that person is certain of having Jesus' Spirit. This criterion is infallible, much safer than the manifestation of extraordinary gifts. Yet, otherwise than in Paul's statement of 1 Cor 12,3, the reasoning goes from effect to cause, more or less as in Mt 7,20: one knows the tree by its fruits.

Corinthians (NIGTC), Grand Rapids, 2000, pp. 924-925, emphasizes the "performative, self-involving, illocutionary, commissive" character of a confession. "Confessing" presupposes the "stance of the heart", the "doing", the "lifestyle and disposition". Though it seems unlikely that Paul would ever dissociate the idea of commitment from that of confession, that commitment does not seem to be his primary focus in chs. 12–14.

The Future Immortal Life of the Christians
(1 Corinthians 15,22)

Chapter 15 of 1 Corinthians is commonly divided into three parts. The first part (vv. 1-11) deals with the resurrection and appearances of Christ, while the second and third parts (vv. 12-34 and 35-58) treat the future bodily resurrection of the believers. Verses 20-28 constitute the middle section of the second part. In vv. 12-19 and 29-34 Paul expands on the implications which the loss of the belief in Christ's resurrection would have. After v. 19 he writes:

20 Νυνὶ δὲ Χριστὸς ἐγήγερται ἐκ νεκρῶν ἀπαρχὴ τῶν κεκοιμημένων.
21 ἐπειδὴ γὰρ δι' ἀνθρώπου θάνατος,
    καὶ δι' ἀνθρώπου ἀνάστασις νεκρῶν.
22 ὥσπερ γὰρ ἐν τῷ Ἀδὰμ πάντες ἀποθνῄσκουσιν,
    οὕτως καὶ ἐν τῷ Χριστῷ πάντες ζῳοποιηθήσονται.

The idea of order (v. 20: "the first fruits"; cf. v. 23) returns in verses 23-28. The already risen Christ arrives as the first; at his parousia those who belong to him will be raised; then comes the end (vv. 23-24). What precedes the end and what will occur at the end itself is further expounded: Christ must reign as king until all his enemies, death included, are cast under his feet. Eventually, the Son will subject himself to God (vv. 25-28).

In this paper our attention will mainly be devoted to verse 22. Do the two occurrences of πάντες in this verse have the same extension: the whole of humanity, all humans? Does Paul speak in v. 22b of the general resurrection, indeed, or should we assume that in the middle of v. 22 there is a shift, and that "all" of v. 22b designates only all Christians? If the second alternative is correct, Paul points to the future resurrection only of those who belong to Christ.

Before analyzing in detail verse 22 and its context, we first present the opinion of those who argue that the "all" of v. 22b indicates a general resurrection: all will be raised, all dead will come back to life on the last day. In the final section another question will be asked regarding vv. 21-22: is an eschatological resurrection really in view?

The General Resurrection

A minority of exegetes claim that in v. 22b Paul has in mind the resurrection of all human beings. This opinion is still defended today with great conviction. The views of three representatives are presented below.

Andreas Lindemann

In the Festschrift *Eschatologie und Schöpfung*, offered to Professor Grässer, the contribution by A. Lindemann is entitled "Die Auferstehung der Toten. Adam und Christus nach 1. Kor 15"[1]. Lindemann emphasizes the correspondence of Christ with Adam. He points out that verse 21 consists of two symmetrical clauses without a verb. They are, as it were, *sententiae*, and provide a kind of thesis or heading for what comes next. Verse 21 is "eine Aussage der Logik": "Weil das eine der Fall ist, gilt auch das andere"[2]. From the first clause, "death (came) through a human being", logically follows the second: "the resurrection of the dead (comes) through a human being". Of course, the added verb "comes" of v. 21b refers to a future event. Furthermore, the concept which corresponds to "death" of v. 21a, i.e., "life" (or "eternal life"), is replaced by "resurrection". This is caused by the fact that Paul is thinking not only of the taking away of death, a consequence of Adam's death, but also of a qualitatively new life. The whole context of this chapter is devoted to the idea of resurrection. In 1 Cor 15, otherwise than in Romans 5, Paul is not dealing with death as punishment for sin. Death is just the end of human life. "So gewiss der Tod, so gewiss auch die Auferstehung der Toten"[3]. For Lindemann this cannot but mean the resurrection of all dead, all deceased people.

Verse 22 further explains and concretizes the two clauses of verse 21. In v. 22b the verb is in the future, but, instead of the expected "will rise", one reads a divine passive: "all will be made alive" by God. "In Christ" should not be taken as determining "all" (all who are in Christ). No, the expression has the same function as "in Adam" of v. 22a. The appropriate conclusion must be drawn. Just as Christ (the new Adam) corresponds with (the old) Adam, so also the two "all"s correspond mutually. In each

1. A. LINDEMANN, "Die Auferstehung der Toten. Adam und Christus nach 1. Kor 15", in M. EVANG, H. MERKLEIN, M. WOLTER (eds.), *Eschatologie und Schöpfung. FS E. Grässer* (BZNW, 89), Berlin – New York, 1997, 155-167; for 1 Cor 15,21-22, see pp. 157-162.
2. *Ibid.*, p. 158.
3. *Ibid.*, p. 159.

clause the whole of humanity is meant. The *Heilsgeschehen* matches the *Schöpfungsgeschehen*[4].

Moreover, according to Lindemann, the context confirms his universalistic explanation. In v. 12 it is stated that some Corinthians deny the resurrection of the dead. Neither these Corinthians nor Paul have in mind a limited number of dead, that is, of deceased Christians alone.

In v. 22 Paul argues with the same logic as in v. 21. From the indisputable experience that all humans die in Adam (v. 22a), he concludes that all humans will be made alive in Christ by God. Since Christ's resurrection already has taken place, the future eschatological resurrection of all those who died and will die is secure[5].

Sven Hillert

The doctoral dissertation of S. Hillert was published in 1999 under the title *Limited and Universal Salvation*[6]. The author examines whether Paul supports or denies the modern belief in universal salvation. An investigation of 1 Corinthians could not be omitted in such a project.

Somewhat strangely, Hillert is of the opinion that in 15,20-28 Paul's hidden concern is that the deceased are not subordinated to the living. In v. 22b the term "all" cannot contain a more limited number than the "all" in v. 22a. According to Hillert there is no linguistic reason to weaken the strict parallelism in v. 22.

According to v. 23, Christ arrives as the "first fruits" of the harvest. Those who belong to Christ come later; they constitute the complete harvest. One should not feel justified in limiting the "all" of v. 22b in view of the expression οἱ τοῦ Χριστοῦ in v. 23. All human beings must be present in the harvest of all. From v. 20 onwards it is impossible to separate Christians and non-Christians. Paul has in mind the whole of humanity[7].

4. LINDEMANN, "Die Auferstehung der Toten", p. 160: "Wenn gilt, dass 'in Adam', also dem Schöpfungsgeschehen entsprechend, *alle Menschen* sterben, dann – so folgert Paulus – gilt auch, dass 'in Christus', also dem Heilsgeschehen entsprechend, *alle Menschen* lebendiggemacht werden".

5. Cf. W. VERBURG, *Endzeit und Entschlafene. Syntaktisch-sigmatische und pragmatische Analyse von 1 Kor 15* (FzB, 78), Würzburg, 1996, pp. 141-142: "Allgemeinheit von Auferstehung". R. F. COLLINS, *First Corinthians* (SP, 7), Collegeville, MN, 1999, pp. 548 and 551, does not clarify his choice of the meaning of "all".

6. S. HILLERT, *Limited and Universal Salvation. A Text-Oriented and Hermeneutical Study of Two Perspectives in Paul* (ConBNT, 31), Stockholm, 1999, esp. pp. 214-217.

7. "When counteracting division and arguing for equality Paul ... seems to pass all limits and refers to the Christians as if there were no others, or rather expresses himself

According to v. 26 the last enemy, death, is destroyed. It is a death which is the destiny of all human beings. Once again we see how Paul cannot limit the resurrection; all those who die will rise[8]. In this verse, too, there is no evidence of a distinction between believers and non-believers.

Hillert does not generalize his conclusions. He carefully analyses also Pauline passages which speak of a separation between those who are being saved and those who are perishing, and equally texts in which Israel's election occupies a central position. Yet Hillert is convinced that the idea of universal salvation not only can be found in Paul but that, in the final analysis, this idea prevails[9].

Wolfgang Schrage

In 2001 the fourth part of the major commentary on 1 Corinthians by W. Schrage appeared[10]. This work excels through utmost care and balance in judgment as well as through its wealth of bibliographical references to previous discussions. On pp. 161-166 Schrage deals with "all" in 1 Cor 15,22. He repeatedly emphasizes the universal meaning of "all" in v. 22b. Just as in v. 22a so also in v. 22b the whole of humanity is included, although he fully recognizes that elsewhere in the chapter and in other writings Paul speaks only of the future resurrection of believers, never of that of non-believers. In v. 21b "through a man" corresponds to the same expression in v. 21a; so also in v. 22b "in Christ" corresponds to "in Adam" in v. 22a. All clauses in vv. 21-22 postulate the same extension. One should not qualify "all" of v. 22b by referring to v. 23 ("those who belong to Christ"), nor limit its expansion, nor soften this striking universalistic assertion. Paul appears to retain the meaning of "all" which the pre-Pauline Adam-Christ typology requires[11].

---

in a way that makes it impossible to separate the category of Christians from the category of human beings" (*ibid.*, 216).

8. Cf. M. C. DE BOER, *The Defeat of Death. Apocalyptic Eschatology in 1 Corinthians 15 and Romans 5* (JSNT SS, 2), Sheffield, 1988, esp. pp. 160, 170 and 187: "so he [= Paul] finally obliterates the distinction between believers and non-believers"; death is a "cosmic power"; "the destruction must be of cosmic scope as well".

9. Although R. H. BELL, "Rom 5.18-19 and Universal Salvation", in *NTS* 48 (2002) 417-432, maintains that "all" in 1 Cor 15,22 refers to those who belong to Christ (p. 428), he nevertheless defends the "most natural reading" of Rom 5,18-19: "just as all have participated in the sin of Adam, so all have participtated in the 'righteous act' of Christ, i.e., his sacrificial death" (p. 432).

10. W. SCHRAGE, *Der erste Brief an die Korinther. 4. Teilband: 1Kor 15,1-16,24* (EKK VII/4), Düsseldorf – Neukirchen-Vluyn, 2001.

11. *Ibid.*, p. 161: "So wie Adam in kosmischer Weite den Tod in die Welt gebracht hat, so hat auch Christi Auferweckung vom Tod eine universale, die Menschheit einschliessende

This typology – the first time Paul uses it – causes a tension in the passage (resurrection of all humans vs. resurrection of believers)[12]. A close reading makes clear the "un-Pauline" character of verses 21-22: Paul takes over "all" in v. 22b (without qualification); resurrection is brought about "by a man" (v. 21b), not by God as usually elsewhere; in vv. 21-22, otherwise than in Rom 5,12-21, no reference is given to human sin as the cause of universal death (5,12-14); in the comparison between Adam and Christ, the action of Christ is not especially stressed (contrary to the "much more" and "all the more" on the side of Christ in Rom 5,15-21); resurrection is not presented as a free gift of God (compare justification in Rom 5,15-21); in 1 Cor 15,21-22 Paul does not indicate human acceptance as is the case in Rom 5,17 ("those who receive")[13].

Schrage defends this interpretation although he clearly states that in vv. 21-22 Paul's editing is not completely absent: in v. 21b, instead of "life" which one could expect as the oppositional term to death, Paul uses the expression "resurrection of the dead", and in v. 22b, instead of the neutral verb "live" which would match "die", he employs the future of the verb "will be made alive" which has an evidently theological semantic connotation and applies to Christians only[14]. Yet, because of logic in the parallelism between Adam and Christ, both uses of "all" in v. 22 must point to all humans.

It cannot but strike the reader that at the end of his discussion Schrage seems less outspoken. By way of conclusion he speaks of an alternative: either one assumes that through writing vv. 21-22 Paul, consciously or unconsciously, creates that tension or one postulates that by an "appended" specification in v. 23 ("those who belong to Christ") Paul qualifies the difficult "all" of v. 22b and means by it "all believers". According to Schrage, however, the second alternative is "less probable"[15].

Those Who Belong to Christ

A majority of commentators prefer the view that "all" in 1 Cor 15,22b refers to "all Christians" and not to "all humans" as in v. 22a. What are

Wirkung zur Lebendigmachung..."; p. 163: "Offenbar geraten die vorstellungsimmanenten Dimensionen der universal konzipierten Adam-Christus-Typologie hier mit sonstigen Aussagen des Paulus in Spannung".

12. Paul here introduces "einen vorgeprägten, vermutlich auch den Korinthern schon bekannten ... Gedanken" (SCHRAGE, *1 Korinther IV*, p. 162).

13. *Ibid.*, p. 162.

14. *Ibid.*, p. 164: an "eindeutig positiv-soteriologisches Gebrauch" of this verb.

15. *Ibid.*, pp. 165-166.

the arguments which plead for a remarkable shift within v. 22? We first examine verses 20-22 and their immediate context; then attention will be given to verses 45b-49 and 51-52; the analysis will be rounded off by a brief comparison with 1 Thess 4,13-18 and Rom 5,11-21.

Verses 20-22

First a literal translation:

20a   But now Christ has been raised from the dead,
  b   the first fruits of those who have fallen asleep,
21a   for since through a man (there is) death,
  b   through a man (there) also (is) resurrection of the dead,
22a   for just as in Adam all die,
  b   so also in Christ all will be made alive.

"To fall asleep" is, of course, a metaphor for "to die" (cf. vv. 6, 18, 19 and 7,39 and 11,30). Verse 20 functions as a thesis which is explained first by the two symmetrical nominal clauses of v. 21 (ἐπειδὴ γάρ), and, after that, by the equally symmetrical clauses of v. 22 (γάρ). In v. 21 the reasoning uses a grounding "since ... (therefore)"-construction; in v. 22, within the second motivating sentence (γάρ), a comparing "just as ... so also"-construction appears. The parallelism in v. 21 between "death" and "resurrection of the dead" is imperfect; yet because of the symmetry a verb in the present tense ("is") has to be supplied in v. 21a as well as in v. 21b. The verbs "die" and "will be made alive" (divine passive) in v. 22 do not match completely: in v. 22b one expects "live" in the present tense. In v. 21b and v. 22b Paul appears to employ specifically theological (or even christological) terms.

Both "in Adam" (v. 22a) and "in Christ" (v. 22b) qualify the verb; the prepositional expressions most probably possess an instrumental nuance; "through (διά) a man" of v. 21 may still influence the expressions. Yet some local nuance is perhaps not absent: since all are "in" Adam or "in" Christ, all are affected by Adam or Christ.

The risen Christ is "the first fruits of those who have fallen asleep" (v. 20b). Just as Adam constitutes a beginning in time but also a cause, so also Christ. So we are brought to assume that the Christians' future "resurrection" in v. 21b and their "being made alive" in v. 22b must be similar contentwise to the resurrection of Christ. More is meant here than a simple coming to life again. Christ's soteriological "life-giving" is further mentioned in v. 45 (cf. Gal 3,21 and Rom 8,11).

In v. 18 Paul speaks of "those who have fallen asleep in Christ" (aorist tense). Quite spontaneously one supplements "those who have fallen asleep" in v. 20 (perfect tense) with "in Christ". After Christ as the first fruits in v. 23, the enumeration continues in v. 23b with "those who belong to Christ" (literally: "those who are of Christ"). Then it stops; in v. 24a the end is mentioned immediately and explicitly. Paul does not add a third group of non-believers. So, both verse 18 and verse 23, two verses which frame, as it were, verses 20-22, confirm our guess that the central verses as well are dealing with the deceased believers.

Given the fact that in both verses 21 ("the resurrection of the dead" vs. "death") and 22 ("will be made alive" vs. "die") the parallelism of the opposing terms is imperfect, it can perhaps more easily be admitted that the logical consistency in the use of "all" is imperfect as well: all humans over against all Christians. Paul breaks the strictures of a probably pre-Pauline thought. Moreover, one can hardly conceive what Paul could mean in this context by asserting the resurrection of all humanity. Neither in 1 Corinthians 15 nor anywhere else in his writings does he speak of a universal "being made alive", one affecting believers and unbelievers alike[16].

Verses 44b-49

"But someone will ask: 'How are the dead raised? With what kind of body do they come?'" (1 Cor 15,35). Can the possibility of change and transformation of the body be shown? In verses 36-44a three steps are taken. Paul first relates an analogy from nature (vv. 36-38), then he comments on the different types of bodies (vv. 39-41), and finally he applies this to the resurrection of the dead (vv. 42-44a). Verse 44a constitutes the climax of the argumentation: "It is sown a physical body, it is raised a spiritual body". In vv. 44b-49 Paul's argument takes a turn. He now appeals to the authority of Scripture. The conditional period of v. 44b draws the conclusion from vv. 42-44a and clearly expresses Paul's conviction. On the basis of Gen 2,7 the Adam-Christ typology is brought back (cf. vv. 21-22). It is developed in vv. 45-47 and then applied to believers in vv. 48-49.

16. Cf., e.g., J. HOLLEMAN, *Resurrection and Parousia. A Traditio-Historical Study of Paul's Eschatology in 1 Corinthians 15* (SupplNT, 84), Leiden – New York – Köln, 1966, pp. 49-57; H. RÄISÄNEN, "Did Paul Expect an Earthly Kingdom?", in A. CHRISTOPHERSEN, C. CLAUSSEN, J. FREY, B. LONGENECKER (eds.), *Paul, Luke and the Graeco-Roman World. FS A. J. W. Wedderburn* (JSNT SS, 217), Sheffield, 2002, 2-20, esp. pp. 10-13.

In vv. 44b-49 little or no explicit attention is devoted to the inclusive character of both figures. Their universalistic dimension is not even mentioned. Verses 48-49, however, are of interest to this study. In v. 48 Paul writes: "As was the man of dust, so are those who are of dust; and as the man of heaven, so are those who are of heaven". The two groups, both referred to by the same term τοιοῦτοι ("those who"), are by no means co-extensive. To the first Adam the whole of mankind belongs; to the last Adam will belong only those who are raised by "the life-giving spirit" (v. 45b). The term ἐπουράνιος ("of heaven") indicates the risen Christians who are also pointed to by Paul in v. 49: "Just as we have borne the image of the man of dust, we will also bear the image of the man of heaven". Through this metaphorical language Paul refers to the future resurrection of Christians.

The conclusion is evident: again, just as in vv. 21-22, the extension of the first Adam and the last Adam is not identical. With regard to Christ, only believers will be included.

Verses 51-52

Verses 50-58 constitute the final subdivision of the third part of chapter 15 (vv. 35-58). Within this unit verses 51-52 are important for our purposes:

51a	Look, I tell you a mystery.
b	We will not all die,
c	but we will all be changed,
52a	in a moment, in the twinkling of an eye, at the last trumpet;
b	for the trumpet will sound,
c	and the dead will rise imperishable,
d	and we will be changed.

In vv. 50-55 Paul first focuses on a principle: there is an opposition between on the one hand human beings, living or dead, called "flesh and blood" and also "perishable", and on the other the kingdom of God which is characterized by imperishability (v. 50). Flesh and blood cannot inherit the kingdom.

In verse 51 a mental leap takes place; a mystery is announced. "Mystery" refers to a hidden truth which will be fully manifest in the eschaton. Paul can announce it; he pays special attention to the events at the parousia. He himself expects to belong to those who will still be alive at the coming of the Lord. Yet all, living and dead, must be changed.

The textual witnesses of v. 51bc provide a number of variant readings. The most probable reading is itself not without irregularity:

51b   πάντες οὐ κοιμηθησόμεθα (literally: "all of us will not sleep"),
51c   πάντες δὲ ἀλλαγησόμεθα ("but we all will be changed").

It would seem that the striking sequence of πάντες οὐ in v. 51b is intended to oppose πάντες δὲ in v. 51c. The line of thought in this passage renders the meaning "we all will 'not sleep' (= all remain alive)" impossible. Almost certainly it should be taken as "not all" (οὐ πάντες) and, therefore, verse 51b as "we will not all sleep" (= some will remain alive)[17].

This statement contradicts that of v. 22a ("all die in Adam"). The difference is twofold. First, in v. 51b Paul claims that some people will be alive at the moment of the parousia; they will not die. Second, the context, as well as the first person plural, excludes any doubt that with "all" in v. 51b Paul means believers (not "human beings" as in v. 22a): not all believers will be dead before the parousia.

In v. 52ab Paul adds a few details taken from apocalyptic imagery: the change will occur in a moment. The parousia remains present in v. 52cd. Paul distinguishes the resurrection of the dead in incorruptibility (literally: "they will be raised imperishable") and the transformation of those who are still alive ("we"; the verb "change" of v. 51c, is used again, be it restricted here to the living).

After the reading of v. 53 the identity of those spoken of becomes evident. Paul deals with the eschatological transformation of all Christians at the parousia: all will be imperishable and immortal. This is confirmed by passages from Scripture in vv. 54-55.

The brief analysis of vv. 50-55 supports our interpretation of v. 22b. In verses 51-52, as in v. 22b, Paul employs the term "all" and deals with the "resurrection" or "being made alive". Here he speaks of the resurrection of deceased Christians which equals the change or transformation into incorruptibility of those Christians who will still be alive.

1 Thess 4,13-18

First Thessalonians is about five years older than First Corinthians. In 1 Thess 4,13-18 Paul discusses the situation of the dead and living believers at the return of Jesus Christ. He emphasizes that those who are left until the coming of the Lord will not precede those who have died. Verses 14 and 16-17 may prove to be a help for our investigation.

---

17. For a recent overview of the variant readings, see SCHRAGE, *1 Korinther IV*, p. 370.

In vv. 16-17 it is stated that the dead in Christ (οἱ νεκροί ἐν Χριστῷ) will rise first. Then, "we who are alive, who are left, will be caught up together with him" to meet the Lord. Here, and already in v. 15, the distinction is made between deceased Christians and those still alive at the parousia.

The parallelism in v. 14 is imperfect and, moreover, the Greek unclear:

14a   εἰ γὰρ πιστεύομεν ὅτι Ἰησοῦς ἀπέθανεν καὶ ἀνέστη
  b   οὕτως καὶ ὁ θεὸς τοὺς κοιμηθέντας διὰ τοῦ Ἰησοῦ ἄξει σὺν αὐτῷ.

The comparative "even so" which introduces the main clause does not match the "if" of the protasis. In the main clause a "we believe that" is missing, and instead of "will rise" it is stated that "God will bring with him (= Jesus)". Not a few exegetes take "through Christ" in v. 14b as qualifying "those who are asleep" (the deceased in Christ, the Christians who died), but presumably the preposition διά ("through") is instrumental and goes with the verb ἄξει[18]. 1 Cor 15,22b comes back to mind; what is stated there is probably the same as in 1 Thess 4,14b: that God will make all alive in (= through) Christ.

Between 1 Cor 15,50-55 and 1 Thess 4,13-18, however, a difference must be noted. In 1 Cor 15 the parousia indicates the resurrection and the change taking place, as it were, at the same time, while in 1 Thess 4 the resurrection of deceased Christians comes first – but is this already a final resurrection? – and only then comes "the rapture" of those who are raised as well as of those who are left[19]. Yet it can be asked whether one should interpret this sequence in a "historical" way. In any case, both in 1 Thess 4 and 1 Cor 15 the non-believers are not spoken of by Paul. They remain outside his horizon. Attention is given solely to the Christians.

Rom 5,12-21

For the purpose of this paper the passage from Romans 5 needs to be examined because of its Adam-Christ typology. "One man", Adam or Christ, conditions "all". In 5,12 Paul writes: "... sin came into the world

---

18. Cf. the NRSV: "even so, through Jesus, God will bring with him those who have died". It remains, however, somewhat strange that Jesus is spoken of twice: "through Jesus" and "with him".

19. Cf. J. PLEVNIK, *Paul and the Parousia: An Exegetical and Theological Investigation*, Peabody, MA, 1997, pp. 168-169: (on 1 Thess 4,13-18) the "'resurrection' provides the starting point, the terminus a quo, of the translation to the Lord"; (on 1 Cor 15,50-55) "there is no translation. ... Paul talks of instantaneous transformation ... The resurrection here entails a transformation of the dead directly" (p. 169).

through one man, and death came through sin, and so death spread to all because all have sinned", and in 5,18: "... just as one man's trespass led to condemnation for all (cf. v. 19), so one man's act of righteousness leads to justification and life for all". In verses 12-21 Christ is compared with Adam; Christ is also opposed to Adam; and from Adam to Christ there is an *a minore ad maius* reasoning (see "much more" in vv. 15, 17 and "all the more" in v. 20).

A first reading tends to conclude that the extension of "the many" in both clauses of v. 15 and in both clauses of v. 19 must be the same. So also "condemnation for all" in v. 18a and "justification and life for all" in v. 18b refers, one would think, to the same universal humanity. Yet a second reading leaves no doubt: "the many" and "all" on the side of Christ include only those who are justified, those who receive "the abundance of grace and the free gift of righteousness" (v. 17), the believers. The parallelism between Adam and Christ is all but perfect: the whole of humanity on the one hand, all Christians on the other. The wording as well as the line of thought of this passage show this clearly.

Rom 5,12-21 proves that in no way is Paul bound by a formal parallelism. Although in the much shorter text, 1 Cor 15,21-22, the evidence is not so overwhelming, yet the analysis has indicated that both in text and context a similar shift in the meaning of "all" is most probably also present here.

A Rising of Dead (Persons)?[20]

One more problem must be raised. In 1 Cor 15,21b Paul utilizes the expression ἀνάστασις νεκρῶν. Before the two nouns, nominative and genitive, the article is missing. Should one not translate "a resurrection of dead (persons)" and claim that Paul in no way refers to the general resurrection on the last day nor to that of the deceased Christians? If the answer to this question is positive, how can verse 21 be connected with both verse 20a and verse 22b? More questions should be asked.

Some Dead Are Raised

According to the recent brief contribution by Michael Bachmann the expression ἀνάστασις νεκρῶν means "ein Heraustreten aus dem Kreis der

---

20. In the following section the expression "dead (persons)" is used for the anarthrous νεκροί.

Toten" since the definite articles are missing, not only in v. 21b, but also already in v. 12b and v. 13 (in v. 42a we find ἡ ἀνάστασις τῶν νεκρῶν: "the resurrection of the dead"). Nor does one find the Greek article before νεκροί in v. 15c ("if it is true that dead [persons] are not raised"), v. 16a ("if dead [persons] are not raised"), v. 29b ("if dead [persons] are not raised at all"), and 42c ("if dead [persons] are not raised"). The article, however, is present in vv. 29a, 35a and 52c[21].

According to this author (and a few others), in 15,12-19 Paul does not refer to the resurrection of the dead on the last day (nor to that of deceased Christians), but to a "resurrection of dead (persons)". Some Corinthians are said to deny the possibility of such a resurrection (cf. v. 12b). Paul defends that resurrection by pointing to Christ's resurrection. He shows that those who say that "resurrection of dead (persons)" does not exist should also deny the resurrection of Christ (v. 13 and v. 16) and he explains in great detail the negative consequences for the Christians if Christ is not risen.

Bachmann asserts: What according to the Corinthians and Paul the category "resurrection of dead (persons)" concretely could mean is clearly indicated by Jesus himself in Mt 11,5: "(the) dead rise" or "(the) dead are raised" (cf. Lk 7,22). Of course, in the gospel the earthly Jesus refers to his miracles. Some of the dead have been brought back to life. Yet the eschatological characteristics of glory, immortality, incorruptibility and bodily transformation are lacking in such resurrections.

Bachmann emphasizes that in vv. 12-19 Paul points only to the "possibility" of dead (persons) rising (through the risen Christ) on earth, not to the certainty of the future, eschatological resurrection of believers. Where the Greek definite article is employed – and only there – Paul speaks of the resurrection of all dead or all deceased Christians, e.g., in vv. 22b, 35a, 42a and 52c.

---

21. M. BACHMANN, "1 Kor 15,12f.: Resurrection of the Dead (= Christians)", in ZNW 92 (2001) 295-299. This study is a vigorous reaction to my note "Just a Possibility? A Reply to Johan S. Vos on 1 Cor 15,12-20", in ZNW 91 (2000) 143-145. Bachmann writes: "Bei ἀνάστασις νεκρῶν dürfte ... nicht eine oder die Auferstehung der Toten, sondern ein Heraustreten aus dem Kreis der Toten gemeint sein, man könnte wohl auch formulieren: so etwas wie die Auferstehung Toter" (p. 298). In footnote 16, he refers to J. JEREMIAS, "'Flesh and blood cannot inherit the Kingdom of God' (1 Cor. xv.50)", in NTS 2 (1955-56) 151-159; repr. in Abba. Studien zur neutestamentlichen Theologie und Zeitgeschichte, Göttingen, 1966, pp. 298-307: "in the whole chapter the Apostle is carefully distinguishing between nekroi and hoi nekroi ..., hoi nekroi denoting the deceased Christians" (p. 303). Cf. also VERBURG, Endzeit und Entschlafene, pp. 120-126; and also already M. BACHMANN, "Zum Gedankenführung in 1. Kor. 15,12ff.", in TZ 14 (1978) 265-276.

The Grammatical Argument

The use or omission of the article cannot constitute a decisive factor, certainly not in Biblical Greek. With regard to the expression with a genitive ("resurrection of dead [persons]" in vv. 12b, 13a and 21b), it may suffice to refer to what according to M. Zerwick is almost a grammatical rule. When the noun preceding the genitive lacks the article, that genitive usually, through a sort of assimilation, is without the article as well. This rule above all applies, it would seem, to expressions such as "Spirit of God", "word of God", "day of (the) Lord" and "resurrection of (the) dead"[22]. The use of an article in translations depends, of course, on the stylistic requirements of the proper language.

Moreover, the omission of the article before νεκροί in vv. 15c, 16a, 29b and 32c first of all shows that the author regards the dead not so much as "these" dead, but that he rather considers their state and situation of being dead[23]. Again, whether or not the article is used in translations depends on the specific language and the passage's context.

It appears, therefore, that the grammatical argument is of little or no help in this discussion.

Not Just Coming Back to Life

In vv. 12-19 Paul does not reason according to the logical thesis: one exception (i.e., in fact Christ is risen) destroys the validity of a universal rule (i.e., no resurrection of the dead). This is, however, almost generally assumed.

According to Paul the resurrection of Christ is causally connected to the future resurrection of others. It is extremely unlikely that Paul would consider the resurrection of Christ as a glorious transformation of his body while he would consider that of the others (mentioned mostly in the same verse) in a weaker sense, as just coming back to earthly life. Whatever the Corinthians may have meant by their denial, for Paul their denial negates the future resurrection of Christians, the glorious transformation of their bodies into imperishability and immortality.

The emotional exclamatory question of v. 12 can be simplified to a conditional period: "if Christ has been raised from the dead, then the dead (= the deceased Christians) will be raised as well". Similarly, the

---

22. M. ZERWICK, *Biblical Greek*, Rome, 1963, no. 183. There may be Semitic influence (the Hebrew *status constructus*). Cf., e.g., SCHRAGE, *1 Korinther IV*, p. 128, n. 574.
23. *Ibid.*, n. 571.

double negation in verses 13 and 16 can rightly be converted into the positive counterpart: "if Christ is risen, the dead (= the deceased Christians) will rise as well". With these statements and in the whole of vv. 12-19 Paul does not refer to just a possibility. He expresses his faith certainty regarding the future resurrection of those who belong to Christ[24].

It can be safely claimed that nowhere in 1 Cor 15 does Paul speak of "a resurrection of dead (persons)" as a coming back of some to earthly life. Nor does he speak in this chapter of a neutral general "resurrection", the pre-condition for all to be present at the judgment on the last day. For Paul the verb "to be raised" is a term that is positively filled: to be raised imperishable (cf. v. 52). For Paul "change" in vv. 51-52 means a glorious transformation of all Christians, after or without resurrection. For Paul the verb ζῳοποιηθήσεται ("will be made alive") in v. 22b means "will be brought to resurrection life". In this chapter no information is given with regard to the eschatological future of non-believers. While arguing Paul is, as it were, completely taken up by Christ's resurrection and the future resurrection of those who belong to Christ. This has caused, it would seem, the rather harsh shift in the meaning of πάντες from v. 22a to v. 22b.

---

24. Cf. LAMBRECHT, "Just a Possibility?". Cf. SCHRAGE, *1 Korinther IV*, pp. 125-128 and 139-142.

Brief Anthropological Reflections
(2 Corinthians 4,6–5,10)

In her discussion of the phrases the "outward self" and the "inward self" in 2 Cor 4,16 Professor Margaret E. Thrall distinguishes two lines of approach, one reflecting a dualistic way of thinking, the other holding that each phrase refers to the human person as a whole[1]. As elsewhere in her commentary, the discussion is nuanced in an exemplary way. In the process Thrall manifests her preference: "At least it seems probable that Paul at times made more of a distinction between body and spirit than is sometimes allowed"[2]. On page 351 she remarks: "The first alternative is not as un-Pauline as it is said to be, and it is without doubt the simpler. Furthermore it fits the context". A few lines further on the same page she then concludes: "At the deepest level, in his inmost self, he [Paul] is subject not to decay but to renewal. Whether or not this is 'dualism', it makes good sense, and it is the preferable interpretation".

Hans Dieter Betz's presidential lecture at the 54th General Meeting of the Studiorum Novi Testamenti Societas at Pretoria, South Africa (1999), entitled "The Concept of the 'Inner Human Being' ('Ο ἔσω ἄνθρωπος) in the Anthropology of Paul", is now published[3]. In his comment on 2 Cor 4,16 Betz assumes that "Paul accepts the concepts of 'outer' and 'inner' human being" from the Middle-Platonic dualism present in

---

1. M. E. Thrall, *The Second Epistle to the Corinthians. I* (ICC), Edinburgh, 1994, pp. 347-351.

2. *Ibid.*, p. 349. Just before the quotation Thrall comments: "There are, in fact, several occasions where the more natural interpretation might well be 'dualistic' in a general sense: Rom 7.22-25; 1 Cor 5.5; 7.34; 2 Cor 7.1". Cf. A. J. Malherbe, *The Letters to the Thessalonians* (AB, 32B), New York, 2000, p. 338: "Paul's use of anthropological terms is neither original, systematic, nor consistent".

3. H. D. Betz, "The Concept of the 'Inner Human Being' ('Ο ἔσω ἄνθρωπος) in the Anthropology of Paul", in *NTS* 46 (2000) 315-341. See ID., "Der Mensch in seinen Antagonismen aus der Sicht des Paulus", in J. Beutler (ed.), *Der neue Mensch in Christus. Hellenistische Anthropologie und Ethik im Neuen Testament* (QD, 109), Freiburg – Basel – Wien, 2001, 39-56.

Corinth. "Accordingly, the human being is a composite entity"[4]. However "the apostle interprets the concepts in ways characteristically different from the Platonic tradition". The outer human being and the inner human being must not be distinguished as body and soul; they "are the two aspects of the same ἄνθρωπος"[5]. In his exegesis of 1 Cor 15 Betz had already emphasized that "the identity of the Christian as ἄνθρωπος is associated with the σῶμα, rather than with the σάρξ. While the σάρξ is regarded as mere perishability, the σῶμα is a 'spiritual' entity destined for imperishability"[6].

The question may be asked: does 2 Cor 4,7–5,10 justify the view of the body as a "spiritual" entity? How does Paul, in this passage, see the connection between the outer self and the body? What are the differing nuances between Thrall and Betz? The second part of this brief contribution will deal with "outer" and "inner" in 4,7-18, the third with death and life in 5,1-10. However, because of the broader context and the interpretations of Thrall and Betz, a first reflection precedes; it brings together the reasons for a "missionary" interpretation of 4,6.

Illumination

In the phrase πρὸς φωτισμόν of 4,6 Thrall is not inclined to see a reference to Paul's evangelistic work ("that he might bring to others the enlightenment") since "the subject of this activity is more naturally the same as the subject of the verb ἔλαμψεν", i.e., God[7]. Yet literal translation of the whole verse could read as follows: "For (it is) the (same) God who said, 'Let light shine out of darkness', who has caused his light to shine in our hearts to spread the light of the knowledge of God's glory in the face of Jesus Christ"[8]. Verse 6 grounds (cf. "for") verse 5. Paul is not proclaiming himself but Jesus Christ as Lord; he himself is but a servant, a

---

4. BETZ, "The Inner Human Being", p. 334.
5. Ibid.
6. Ibid., p. 328. In his interesting study Betz does not refer to the monograph by R. H. GUNDRY, Sôma in Biblical Theology with Emphasis on Pauline Anthropology (SNTSMS, 29), Cambridge, 1976. Probably as a consequence, Gundry's distinctive use of the term 'duality' is also absent. The book of Gundry is likewise omitted in the bibliography of D. B. MARTIN, The Corinthian Body, New Haven – London, 1995 (moreover, one misses a reference to 2 Cor 4,6–5,10, the discussion of which certainly would qualify Martin's views of Paul's anthropology).
7. 2 Corinthians, p. 318.
8. Cf. THRALL, 2 Corinthians, pp. 297-298: "… [God] is the one who shone in our hearts, to effect the enlightenment of the knowledge…"; BETZ, "Inner Human Being",

servant for Jesus' sake. To prove verse 5 Paul reminds his readers of the
event of his conversion and call to apostleship, the christophany given
him by God Creator. The second λάμπω in v. 6 could have a causative
meaning ("has caused his light to shine"). The term φωτισμός retains its
original active sense of "enlightenment, illumination"[9] which points to
Paul's missionary task.

The reasons which favor the missionary understanding of πρὸς φωτισμόν are numerous, at least five. (1) It is probable that a grounding of the
missionary verse 5 equally refers to Paul's evangelistic task. (2) Through
the mention of God verse 6 contrasts with verse 4 which speaks of "the
god of the present age". The two verses, however, are very similar in wording and structure. Verse 4 deals with unbelief and refusal to see the light
of the gospel. This suggests, it would seem, a positive, missionary sense
for verse 6. (3) The same applies to the whole of 4,1-6, a passage which
itself corresponds with 2,14–3,6, especially 2,14-17: Paul presents himself
as a minister of the new covenant, sent by God and made competent by
God. (4) In 4,7-15, the passage which immediately follows 4,6, Paul
demonstrates the antithetical character of his apostolic existence. (5) The
fifth and last reason depends on the most probable answer to the alternative questions: does the last part of verse 6 only repeat and explain the
inner result of the Damascus event (the conversion)[10] or, rather, does it
not point to the missionary task which flows from that event: "in order
that Paul may make the knowledge of God's glory in the face of Jesus
Christ illuminate the others", i.e., that he may spread the gospel?[11]

The missionary interpretation presumes that Paul is the implied subject of the action of enlightening[12] and that the direct object itself (the

---

p. 331: "… [God] who has caused a light to shine in our hearts, to provide the enlightenment which comes from the knowledge …"; NRSV: "… [God] who has shone in our
hearts to give the light of the knowledge …".

9. In 4,4 the term could mean "light", the equivalent of φῶς which is present in v. 6a:
"let light shine…". Cf. LXX Ps 26,1 and, perhaps, Ps 138,11; see also LIDDELL-SCOTT, *sub
voce*.

10. Cf. BETZ, "The Inner Human Being", pp. 331-331, who limits the content of 4,6
to an occurrence of enlightening of the human heart which results in the renewal of the
inner self.

11. Cf. R. BULTMANN, *The Second Letter to the Corinthians*, Minneapolis, 1985, pp. 108-
109: "… so that (through our preaching) we bring to light" the very knowledge… (108);
M. WINTER, φωτισμός, in *EDNT*, III, col. 450: "Paul is not referring here to his own
enlightenment …, but rather to the purpose of his proclamation …"; S. KIM, *Paul and the
New Perspective* (WUNT, 140), Tübingen, 2002, pp. 101-102 and 112, n. 38: Paul interprets
his own commission to the Gentiles in terms of the role of the *Ebed* in Isa 42,6 and 49,6.

12. Note that "knowledge" probably is not an objective genitive (so Bultmann) but a
subjective genitive or one of origin.

others, the Gentiles), not expressed, can be mentally supplied. These two
hypotheses within the same clause of verse 6 are perhaps too much for
a sound exegesis. A clear-cut decision, i.e., a palatable choice between the
purely autobiographical and the missionary explanations, does not appear
possible. With regard to the difficult verse 6 we may, at the end of our
first reflection, quote Betz and agree with his statement: "Untying this
verbal package is not easily done"[13].

Outer and Inner

Although 2 Cor 4,7–5,10 can be divided into two passages, 4,7-15 and
4,16–5,10[14], for this analysis we must take 4,16-18 together with what precedes. In verse 16 one encounters the seemingly anthropological opposition of "outer" and "inner" in the phrases ὁ ἔξω ἡμῶν ἄνθρωπος and ὁ
ἔσω ἡμῶν (ἄνθρωπος).

Notwithstanding the various shifts within 4,7-18, that same opposition is focused upon in the entire text unit. One can take the first person plural as pointing primarily to Paul. By means of "in our hearts" in
verse 6 the inner center of Paul himself is indicated. In verse 7 the "treasure", contrasted with "clay jars", probably refers both to the enlightenment of his heart and the ensuing ministry; at the end of the same verse,
the opposition between Paul and God appears. Verses 8-9 depict the
antitheses of, on the one hand, outer hardships, nearness to death and,
on the other, through God's power, perseverance and salvation. In verses
10 and 11 Paul explains that opposition in the minister's existence christologically: the presence of Jesus' death and simultaneously the manifestation of Jesus' life. The shift in verse 12 is remarkable: in the apostle
(only) death is at work, in the Corinthians, life. Verse 13 adds a comparison with Israel's past (the same faith in the apostle as that of the
psalmist) and in verse 14 Paul connects his future resurrection with the
past resurrection of the Lord Jesus. God is the one who raises. Then in
the summarizing verse 15 Paul states that his entire apostolic existence is
meant for the sake of the Corinthians in order that the thanksgiving may
increase and "abound to the glory of God". The beginning of verse 16 is
an anacolouthon; in the rest of the verse one meets the contrast between

---

13. "The Inner Human Being", p. 331.
14. Cf. my *Second Corinthians* (SP, 8), Collegeville, 1998, p. 76.

the outward self (ὁ ἔξω ἄνθρωπος) who is wasting away and the inward self (ὁ ἔσω ἄνθρωπος) who is renewed day by day. This contrast is extended, in verse 17, by a temporal one ("momentary" and "eternal") and by one of weight ("light" and exceedingly "heavy"), and furthermore in verse 18 by the opposition between "what is seen" and "what is unseen", as well as by that between "transitory" and "eternal".

We can say that in the whole of this passage Paul, by means of a variety of concepts and terms, clearly distinguishes between two "men" in himself, his outer ἄνθρωπος and his inner ἄνθρωπος (v. 16). But is this distinction purely anthropological and completely balanced? Almost certainly not.

True, the outer self is the clay jar (v. 7), the suffering body (v. 10), the mortal flesh (v. 11). It is visible, wasting away, transitory. In this context the term "flesh" is employed in a neutral anthropological sense, not "hamartiologically", thus without a reference to its proneness to sin (so typical of Paul). Therefore, the outer self (v. 16) is not ὁ παλαιὸς ἄνθρωπος of Rom 6,6; it is the body (cf. v. 10) but not τὸ σῶμα τῆς ἁμαρτίας of that same verse from Romans[15].

However the opposite concept, the inner self in verse 16, is not merely anthropological[16]. The center of Paul, his heart, is indwelled by God's power. It is regenerate; it is being renewed day by day (cf. 3,18). It is able to endure the hardships and carry Jesus' death and thus to manifest the life of Jesus. Paul himself realizes in his inner self that his tribulation is producing eternal glory, already now, though it remains invisible. Thus the inner self is not the inner side as such, only human. No, it is the inner self of a regenerate human being, a Christian, rescued by God, redeemed by Jesus Christ, living in the Spirit[17].

---

15. Cf. GUNDRY, Sôma, p. 136: "The outer man is not the old man of sin, then, but the physical body subject to hardship, decay, and death".

16. Otherwise GUNDRY, Sôma, pp. 136-137: "The inner man is the human spirit, the center of psychological feelings. We cannot evade anthropological duality in 2 Cor 4:16" (p. 137).

17. In Rom 7,22-23, on the contrary, the distinction within the unregenerate "I" appears to be solely anthropological. Cf. C. MARKSCHIES, "Innerer Mensch", in RAC 18 (1998) 266-312, esp. pp. 280-282: the human being as intended by God, but in fact sold under sin; J. LAMBRECHT, The Wretched "I" and Its Liberation. Paul in Romans 7 and 8 (LTPM, 14), Leuven, 1992. In the "I" Paul appears to distinguish the ἔσω ἄνθρωπος (and the "mind") from the "body" (and the "members"). The "I" is sold into slavery under sin; so the "I" is "of the flesh" (cf. v. 14). Through the inner self the "I" delights in the law of God; however, the law of sin is at war with the law of the mind and dwells in the members of the "I". Its body is destined to death (cf. vv. 22-24).

Death and Life

Is it correct to state that for Paul in 2 Corinthians the outer and inner are aspects of the human person[18], that the outer self as well as the inner self are the whole person – be it considered differently – and that therefore a human being does not "have" a body but "is" a body? A careful reading of 5,1-10 does not justify a positive answer to these questions.

Paul can look to what is unseen and eternal since he knows that the destruction of the earthly house or tent, concretely speaking his death, is not fatal. Another body is ready in heaven: a building from God, an eternal house not made with hands (v. 1)[19]. While still alive in this suffering and mortal body Paul groans; as a matter of fact, he desires to put on his heavenly body as an over-garment over his earthly body (v. 2). A new idea is expressed here: future possession of the eternal body after death (resurrection) becomes "putting on over", i.e., transformation of the body before death. From verse 3 we learn indirectly that Paul does not want to be found "naked"; he apparently fears a disembodied state. In verse 4 he seems to indicate two reasons for his sighing and groaning: first, he is weighed down by the burdensome body which suffers pain and hardship; second, he wishes not to die but to be transformed, not to take off but to put on over. From verse 4c ("in order that what is mortal may be swallowed up by life") arises the impression that the very thing which immortal and glorious "life" accomplishes is not the destruction of Paul's body (v. 1) but the radical transformation of his body still alive at the parousia. For this future event God has prepared Paul through the gift of the Spirit (v. 5).

A surprising shift then occurs in verses 6-10. Paul knows that being in the earthly body means being away from the Lord (v. 6). Faith is not yet sight, not yet face to face vision (v. 7). Therefore, Paul now says, he would rather go away from the body, that is, die before the parousia, and get home to the Lord immediately (v. 8). Fear of death seems to have disappeared. What remains, however, is his profound aspiration to please the Lord since he realizes that he will be "manifested" before the tribunal of Christ and judged according to what he has done through his earthly body (vv. 9-10).

18. Cf. BETZ, "Inner Human Being", p. 334.
19. Most probably Paul envisions that this body will be given at the parousia, not at the moment of death. Otherwise, as far as 2 Cor 5,1-10 is concerned, THRALL, *Second Corinthians*, pp. 370, 373, 392 and 399.

In 5,1-10 Paul speaks of the earthly body in an objective way, as if it were a substance, an entity of its own. It is a house to dwell in; it is a garment to put on; it is the opposite of the heavenly body. Paul even refers to the possibility of a "naked", disembodied state. Paul is at home in the body, now, but he would prefer to go away from this body. He fully realizes, however, that what he has done he did through his body. Moreover, he is convinced that in the eschaton eternal life supposes a risen and transformed body. Finally, though what is mortal will be annihilated, both resurrection and transformation point to a continuity between the two bodies: body is more than flesh and corruption.

The reality of the "outer self" of 4,16 is taken up in 5,1-10 by several terms and concepts: the nouns house, tent and garment; the adjectives earthly and mortal; the verbs to be destroyed, to take off and to be at home in; but above all, the term "body" in verses 6, 8 and 10. Given this vocabulary and given the fact that in verse 1 regarding the heavenly body the verb ἔχομεν is used, one can hardly deny that Paul as it were claims "to have and possess" a body. It must strike the reader that within 5,1-10 the "inner self" of 4,16 is no longer explicitly distinguished. Paul employs the first person plural and thus points to himself, whether "in the body" or "out of the body". However this "we" seems to be the incorporeal self[20]. That in verses 6-10 the fear of death and a disembodied state has disappeared may probably be explained by Paul's increasing conviction that his union with Christ in the life of faith, already on earth, cannot be destroyed by death. He must have thought that leaving the earthly body at death would bring him "closer to the full, immediate presence and the face to face vision"[21].

The way Paul speaks both of himself and his earthly body in 5,1-10 does not indicate a dualistic view of the human person according to which the body is inherently evil. Yet, assuming in 4,7–5,10 only an external influence of hellenistic terms and categories of thought does not go far enough[22]. The term "duality" seems appropriate, although we saw that in 2 Corinthians the duality of "outer self" and "inner self" or that of "we" (Paul) and "body" is not completely balanced. Paul is in Christ; but the Christian Paul is still in the mortal flesh and the earthly body. His reflection is not purely anthropological.

---

20. Cf. GUNDRY, *Sôma*, p. 149: "Paul writes quite dichotomously here".
21. LAMBRECHT, *Second Corinthians*, p. 89.
22. Cf., e.g., THRALL, *Second Corinthians*, p. 347: Paul "uses, though in modified form, hellenistic categories of thought which might appeal to some of his readers"; and, of course, the publications by Betz.

To round off our three reflections: it would seem that for Paul "body" is not just an aspect of the person. In 5,1-10, as in 4,7-18, there is no radically holistic use of the term σῶμα[23]. Because the human being constitutes a living unity, the "body" (as, e.g., the "heart") is representative of the whole. Of course, in order to stress the unity of this dually composed human being, one can say that Paul is his body; but he is more than his body. Therefore, one can also say that Paul has an earthly body. Moreover, in the eschaton Paul and all Christians expect a glorified, "spiritual" body, which implies a somatic existence.

23. Cf. GUNDRY, *Sôma*, passim.

20

The Fool's Speech and Its Context
(2 Corinthians 10–13)[1]

It would seem that in 2 Cor 10–13 the Fool's Speech begins in 11,22 and ends in 12,10. What is the connection between the foolish discourse and its broad context? Chapters 10–13 constitute a substantial, very emotional part of Paul's second letter to the Corinthians of which 13,12-13 brings the final epistolary greetings and blessing. Therefore, one should probably not expect too much of a rigid, balanced structure, i.e., not a rhetorical *dispositio* nor another type of strict organisation of the various items. Yet, both recurring vocabulary and ideas surprisingly, strikingly suggest that a somewhat cyclic, "enveloping" train of thought is present. Can it be depicted objectively, without forcing the spontaneous character of Paul's way of writing here? Can the theological relevance of such an arrangement be indicated?

We will begin by reflecting upon some characteristics of the Fool's Speech and the introduction to this text. The second section will be devoted to the context, especially to the different "rings" which can be detected in the surrounding passages. The final section then will attempt to formulate theological insights and conclusions which appear to be validated by the analysis[2].

---

1. On May 22, 2001 the substance of this text was given in Italian as a farewell address at the Pontifical Biblical Institute of Rome.

2. This study of structure and line of thought in 2 Cor 10–13 employs, and sometimes cites, the following of my previous publications: *Second Corinthians* (SP, 8), Collegeville, MN, 1998; "Dangerous Boasting. Paul's Self-Commendation in 2 Corinthians 10–13", in R. BIERINGER (ed.), *The Corinthian Correspondence* (BETL, 126), Leuven, 1996, 325-346; "Paul's Appeal and the Obedience to Christ: The Line of Thought in 2 Corinthians 10,1-6", in *Bib* 77 (1996) 398-416; "Strength in Weakness. A Reply to Scott B. Andrew's Exegesis of 2 Cor 11.23b-33", in *NTS* 43 (1997) 285-290. The last three articles are reprinted as nos. 11, 12 and 13 in my *Collected Studies on Pauline Literature and on The Book of Revelation* (AnBib, 147), Rome, 2001, pp. 107-129, 131-148, and 149-156.

The Fool's Speech

Paul's foolish discourse is often interrupted and, moreover, its focus in boasting changes more than once. A lengthy introduction to it and a retrospection inform the reader of the basic characteristics of Paul's particular manner of arguing. A schematic preview of the data may be useful:

a) The Fool's Speech (11,22–12,10):
   Reflexive interruptions in 11,23b.30-31; 12,1a.5-6.9de-10
   Shifts in boasting at 11,23b.27.28.30; 12,1b.7.
b) Announcements in 11,1-21:
   Tolerate me in a little foolishness (vv. 1-4)
   I too will boast in folly (vv. 16-18)
   Since you tolerate others, I too dare to boast (vv. 19-21)
c) Retrospections (12,11a and 19a)

Interruptions in 11,22–12,10

Paul's foolish discourse of 11,22–12,10[3] is not of one piece. It is several times obstructed by what can be called "reflexive interruptions". This hardly surprises the readers after the breaks and hesitations present in 11,16-21, the preceding passage. Already in 11,23b Paul interrupts himself and repeats an introductory idea: "I am talking as if out of my mind" (cf. his last reference to it in 11,21). At the end of the catalogue of hardships (11,23b-29), before continuing his discourse, Paul again pauses in 11,30-31 and inserts several ideas:

> If boasting there must be, I will boast of the things (that manifest) my weakness. The God and Father of the Lord Jesus – he who is blessed for ever! – knows that I am not lying.

A third interjection comes in 12,1, immediately after the brief report of the flight from Damascus (11,32-33); it announces more boasting: "There must be further boasting. Although it is no use, yet I will come to the visions and revelations of the Lord". In 12,5-6 a fourth, lengthy interruption appears:

> About this (person) I will boast, but about myself I will not boast, except about my weaknesses. But if I want to boast I will not be foolish, since I

---

3. Some exegetes propose 11,21b as the beginning, but in that verse Paul is still describing what he is going to do. U. HECKEL, *Kraft in Schwachheit. Untersuchungen zu 2. Kor 10–13* (WUNT II, 56), Tübingen, 1993, pp. 22-23, e.g., distinguishes between the Fool's Speech in a broader sense (11,1–12,13) and its "Kernteil", i.e., the Fool's Speech proper (11,21b–12,10).

will be speaking the truth; but I refrain in order that no one esteems me above what he or she sees of me or hears from me.

In 12,7-9abc Paul then continues his discourse and speaks of the thorn given in his flesh, the beating of Satan's messenger, and of his prayer for deliverance and Jesus' answer. He adds in verses 9de-10 a fifth and conclusive reflection:

> Most gladly, therefore, I rather will boast of my weaknesses in order that the power of Christ may come to rest upon me. That is why I am well pleased with weaknesses, insults, hardships, persecutions, and constraints (endured) for Christ. For whenever I am weak, then I am strong.

It would seem that boasting of weaknesses is still foolish boasting (cf. 12,11: "I have become foolish; you forced me [to it]").

Shifts in 11,22–12,10

With regard to Paul's boasting one should pay due attention to the shifts within 11,22-33, at verses 23b, 27, 28, and 30. These shifts provide us, it would seem, with five types of boasting defined by the object Paul boasts about. (1) In verses 22-23a, while comparing himself with his opponents and enumerating his Jewish and Christian titles, he visibly boasts as a fool, according to the flesh, not according to the Lord (cf. vv. 17-18). (2) Within the catalogue of hardships itself, Paul proves his superiority over the opponents by listing in verses 23b-26 a great number of adverse circumstances, external difficulties. Yet after the twofold "more often" in verse 23b the opponents are no longer referred to explicitly. (3) Within that same catalogue, in verse 27, he points to his own toils and labors, to hardships which are more directly connected to his daily life as God's servant, and then, (4) in verses 28-29, to his personal active – one would say: "most active" – endeavor. (5) Finally, in verses 32-33 a situation is depicted where Paul's utter weakness, i.e., the absence of his own power, is emphasized: his escape from Damascus with the help of others. In verse 30 he had announced: "If boasting there must be, I will boast of the things (which manifest) my weakness (τὰ τῆς ἀσθενείας μου)". Yet in this particular event, just as in all other hardships, he has also experienced God's effective help[4]. Thus Paul successively boasts of titles, of adverse circumstances and persecutions, of toils and hardships in his way of life, of his apostolic care and of his, as it were, miraculous liberation. One can

---

4. Cf. *Second Corinthians*, p. 198; "Strength in Weakness", pp. 288-290.

rightly ask the question whether the expression τὰ τῆς ἀσθενείας μου (11,30) adequately covers all that is listed in verses 23b-33[5].

In 12,1-10 Paul speaks of his personal life, no longer of his apostolic endeavors[6]. A shift is also present here. After having resumed his boasting, now about visions and revelations (v. 1), he breaks off the report of one such vision (vv. 2-4) abruptly and instead goes on: in order that I might not be unduly elated through those revelations, a thorn was given me in the flesh; notwithstanding my prayer that messenger of Satan did not go away from me. Paul receives the Lord's answer: "My grace is sufficient for you, for power is made perfect in weakness" (vv. 7-9). One thus notices the contrast between abundant privileges and a lasting personal suffering. At the end of the discourse Paul even dares to say: I will boast all the more gladly of my weaknesses; finally, by way of summary: I am content with weaknesses and hardships and persecutions for the sake of Christ. The power of Christ dwells in him; whenever he is weak, then he is strong (cf. vv. 9-10)[7]. We see that there is, again, a shift with regard to the object of boasting: boasting of revelations and of weaknesses.

Paul's foolish discourse contains a whole range of objects for boasting, indeed.

Announcements in 11,1-21

In 11,1-21 Paul hesitatingly and repetitively announces what he is going to do in his speech. Two passages merit our special attention: verses 1-4 and verses 16-21 (cf. πάλιν λέγω in v. 16).

In verses 16-18 and 21b five elements can be distinguished: (1) Paul makes an explicit appeal: "accept me..." (v. 16); (2) he manifests his decision to boast; (3) he considers boasting a foolish action and, therefore, excuses himself by admitting it; (4) however, he is convinced that properly speaking he is not a fool; and (5) Paul refers to other people, his opponents: "Since many boast according to the flesh, I too will boast"

---

5. It seem almost impossible that, after ὑπὲρ ἐγώ (11,23), Paul in vv. 23-29 only refers to human weakness and not simultaneously, if not primarily, to his God-given human endurance and strength.

6. HECKEL, *Kraft in Schwachheit*, p. 307: "Nach seinen Berufserfahrungen in Kapitel 11 geht er [= Paul] in 12,1 zur privaten Seite seiner Existenz und zu seinem persönlichen Verhältnis zu Christus über".

7. Cf. *Second Corinthians*, pp. 204-205.

(v. 18; cf. v. 21b). The logical connection between those five elements can be paraphrased in the following way: "Although I am not really a fool, if you think I am, accept me then as a fool, for I want to boast; I admit that boasting is not appropriate, but since others glory I am going to do it as well"[8]. As far as terminology is concerned two items which characterize Paul's discourse should be mentioned: the vocabulary of foolishness (ἀφροσύνη, ἄφρων; cf. παραφρονῶν in v. 23) and that of boasting (καυχάομαι, καύχησις).

In 11,1-4 Paul has already been pleading: "If only you would tolerate me in a little foolishness; yes, do tolerate me" (v. 1). The Corinthians should tolerate him since he is jealous for them with God's jealousy; he is afraid that the opponents may lead them astray from the sincerity and the purity which Christians, as a chaste virgin, must have toward Christ (vv. 2-3). His fear is well grounded since the Corinthians readily tolerate newcomers who preach another Jesus, a different spirit and gospel (v. 4).

A similar reproach of "toleration" comes up anew in verses 19-21a: "After all, you gladly tolerate fools since you are so wise. For you tolerate it when some enslave you … To my shame I admit that we have been too weak for that". The verb ἀνέχομαι ("to tolerate") is repeated in verses 19 and 20 (cf. v. 1, twice, and v. 4). The Corinthians tolerate the opponents who are fools and dare to boast; therefore, Paul will speak as in folly and dare to boast as well. The Corinthians must "tolerate" Paul's foolish boasting.

Retrospection in 12,11a and 19a

Paul writes in 12,11a: "I have become foolish; you forced me (to it). In fact, I ought to be commended by you…". Apparently the discourse proper is finished. Paul looks back at what he has been doing. "I have been a fool!" (NRSV-translation): his speaking was foolish. The reason why he has done it was the behavior of the Corinthians. They tolerated the opponents and, so, they as it were forced Paul to boast of himself, just as the opponents are boasting. Paul adds that, as a matter of fact, the Corinthians should have been the ones who commend him.

Yet in 12,11b-18 Paul goes on defending himself. Therefore, in verse 19a he cannot but ask: "Are you thinking again that we defend ourselves before you?" Through this question he indirectly qualifies not only verses 11-18 but his whole foolish discourse as an apology, and an apology it really is. But at the same time he can say: "in God's sight we speak in

8. Cf. *Second Corinthians*, p. 194.

Christ; beloved, all (is done) for your upbuilding" (v. 19b; cf. the qualification in v. 6: "I will not be foolish, since I will be speaking the truth").

There can be no doubt: 12,11a and 12,19a are retrospective.

Three Rings in the Context

Within the larger context the introductory verses 1-4 and 16-21 of chapter 11 as well as the retrospective clauses of 12,11a and 19a are obviously
connected with the Fool's Speech. But what about the rest of that
context? Is the whole of what surrounds the discourse related to it and,
if so, how? Our impression is that a kind of ring composition exists, a
concentric way of arranging verses and passages. An anticipative diagram
of the rings may help the reader:

```
10,1 (exhortation)
    10,2-18 (authority)
        11,5-12 (denial of inferiority)
            The Fool's Speech (11,22–12,10)
        12,11b-18 (denial of inferiority)
    13,1-10 (authority)
13,11 (exhortation)
```

The analysis will proceed in three steps, from the outer verses in chapters 10 and 13 towards the text-units which are closer to the center, i.e.,
to the Fool's Speech.

A First Ring: Exhortation in 10,1 and 13,11[9]

a) *An anacolouthon.* There appears to be a change in the train of
thought between 10,1 and 10,2. In verse 1a Paul writes: "I myself, Paul,
appeal to you by the meekness and gentleness of Christ". The reference
to Christ's meekness and gentleness suggests that Christ is in one way or
another an example for Paul's attitude and, even more, that the apostle
is going to request from the Corinthians a moral conduct similar to that
same example. Above all, the meekness of Christ and his gentleness furnish an authoritative grounding for Paul's exhortation. Verse 1b, grammatically a relative clause which qualifies the subject "I", alludes to a
reproach at the address of Paul: "I who admittedly (am) humble when
face to face among you, but when absent bold toward you". Yet the verb

---

9. For the whole of this section see my article "Paul's Appeal".

"I beg" of verse 2 does not seem to continue or concretize the appeal of verse 1a. It is rather linked with the content of verse 1b: "Yet I ask (you) that when present I do not need to be bold (towards you)…". Moreover, in the whole of verses 2-6a Paul defends himself against those who think that he is walking according to the flesh, and he produces threats. Although he is walking *in* the flesh, the war that he is going to wage will not be *according* to the flesh[10].

A conclusion can already be drawn. In 10,1-6 there is a substantial change with regard to more than one aspect. In verse 1a Paul appears to announce a moral exhortation. But from verse 1b onwards he speaks of an accusation brought forward against him and he defends himself. Opponents and critics of his person have entered the scene. At the beginning of the chapter one expects that the Corinthians would be exhorted to a better Christian life. But, certainly from verse 2 onwards, Paul seems to be very much occupied with himself and his enemies; he indicates how he himself acts and will act as an authoritative apostle. Paul wants to show that he does not lack boldness. He will oppose his enemies and demolish their arguments and pretension; his weapons will prove powerful. Only at the very end, in verse 6b, do the addressees come back to the forefront; their obedience must have reached completion before Paul can effectively deal with the opposition. Then, Paul will be ready to punish every disobedience.

b) Παρακαλῶ *in 10,1a.* The beginning of 10,1 is very solemn: αὐτὸς δὲ ἐγὼ Παῦλος παρακαλῶ ὑμᾶς… Paul employs the verb παρακαλῶ frequently. As is well known the range of meanings of this verb is wide: from exhorting and appealing to comforting and consoling. Besides 2 Cor 10,1, Paul employs παρακαλῶ three more times with the preposition διά followed by a genitive: Rom 12,1; 15,30 and 1 Cor 1,10[11]. The last three verses are very similar (see, e.g., the vocative address and the infinitive construction or ἵνα-clause)[12]. Of course, the content of the appeal differs: in

---

10. One cannot exclude the possibility that, through his use of the first person plural in vv. 2b-6a, Paul intends to refer also to Timothy (cf. 1,1). Yet the radical refusal of an "epistolary we" here by M. MÜLLER, "Der sogenannte 'schriftstellerische Plural' – neu betrachtet. Zur Frage der Mitarbeiter als Mitverfasser der Paulusbriefe", in *BZ* 42 (1998) 181-201, esp. pp. 196-197, is hardly justified.

11. 2 Cor 5,20 ("God appealing through us") is different from the other texts regarding grammar and content.

12. Seven items can be listed: (1) a connective particle (δέ or οὖν), (2) the subject of appeal (Paul), (3) the addressees (Christians), (4) the vocative address ("brothers"), (5) the διά plus genitive phrase which through this reference to God or Christ grounds the appeal, (6) an infinitive construction (or its *koinè* substitute with ἵνα), and (7) the "moral" content of the appeal.

1 Cor 1,10 Paul exhorts the Christians to be united; in Rom 12,1-2 he urges them to conduct a Christian ethical life; and in Rom 15,30-32 he makes the more specific appeal to strive together with him in prayer for the good outcome of his plans for the future. Now, as far as 2 Cor 10,1 is concerned, the parallelism is obvious, but only to a certain extent. The absence of "brothers" or the presence of the emphasis αὐτὸς ... ἐγὼ Παῦλος should not disturb us but at the end of verse 1a there is the brusque interruption: no infinitive construction, no indication of the content of the appeal. It would seem, therefore, that at the beginning of 2 Cor 10,1 Paul intends to do what he does in the three other passages, namely to formulate an exhortation to moral Christian life. But while writing "by the meekness and gentleness of Christ" his attention seems to be diverted; he remembers the slanders against his person which his opponents and critics are spreading. The "humble" Paul of verse 1b, as well as the Paul "walking according to the flesh" of verse 2b, was their misrepresentation of him. He must have realized that their way of portraying him was, perhaps against their own intention but as matter of fact, a caricature of Christ being meek and gentle.

What Paul asks of his Christians in Corinth in verse 2 is certainly a change of attitude and behavior. They should conduct themselves in such a way that he is not forced to show against them the same boldness which he counts on showing against the intruders. But is this the content of the appeal which he had in mind when he wrote verse 1a? Hardly! One cannot but assume that what is actually requested from the Corinthians in verse 2 has a narrower scope; it becomes focused on the struggle between Paul and the opponents, and, of course, also on the sides which some Corinthians are taking. The specific aim is the removal of all disobedience and the completion of the Corinthians' obedience to Christ. It is no longer the exhortation to an authentic life as Christians he originally intended to give when he composed verse 1a.

c) *Παρακαλῶ in 13,11*. At the end of the letter, in 13,11, Paul employs the verb in the passive: παρακαλεῖσθε[13]. It must be translated by a paraphrase such as "heed my appeal", "listen to my appeal", "take my appeal to heart". The verb itself does not indicate the content of that appeal, but the other imperatives in the same verse provide very clearly what is requested from the Corinthians: "rejoice, mend your ways ... be of the

---

13. The meaning of the same verb in 12,8 and 12,18 is clearly different: "About this one I begged (παρεκάλεσα) the Lord three times that..." and "I urged (παρεκάλεσα) Titus and, together with him, I sent the brother".

same mind, live in peace". Is this not the kind of moral exhortation which we were entitled to expect at 10,1a? More indications are present in the verses which precede 13,11.

d) *Moral references in 12,19–13,10*. Paul's return to exhortation in 13,11 is not unprepared. At the end of 12,19, after the solemn declaration "In God's sight we speak in Christ", he adds: "beloved, all (is done) for your upbuilding" (cf. 13,10). Then, in a rather unexpected way, in 12,20-21, Paul gives a list of numerous sins still existing in Corinth (cf. 13,2). He announces his intention "not to refrain" from severe action when he will come to them for the third time (cf. 13,1-4 and 13,10). The injunction of 13,5 is most probably not without a note of moral insistence: "examine yourselves to see whether you are in the faith; test yourselves". An ethical urgency is evident in Paul's prayer of 13,7: "We pray God that you may do no wrong ..., that you may do what is good", and also in the statement at the end 13,9: "What we pray for is this, your improvement". God gave him authority "for building up and not for destroying" (13,10).

e) *Content*. The first elements which point to a ring composition are small to the extreme: 10,1a and 13,11. Yet both verses certainly contain moral exhortation; they as it were "frame" the whole of chapters 10–13 (and thus also the Fool's Speech). As ethical admonition verses such as 10,1a and 13,11 are typical of a Pauline letter. The explicit exhortation of 13,11 is being prepared in 12,19–13,10. Since Paul's self-defense is not without a call to obedience, a more or less hidden warning and hortatory tone is present in the whole of chapters 10–13[14]. Yet one should distinguish between this specific appeal and a more general parenesis[15].

A Second Ring: Paul's Authority in 10,1b-18 and 13,1-10

Chapter 13 refers back to chapter 10 in many respects. We may mention the following headings: motifs, vocabulary and time reference. The

---

14. On the hortatory character of 2 Cor 10–13, cf. V. FURNISH, *II Corinthians* (AB, 32A), Garden City, N.Y., 1984, pp. 48 and 580.

15. HECKEL, *Kraft in Schwachheit*, pp. 9-10, considers 10,1-6 and 12,19–13,10 primarily as the parenetical framework, while 10,7–12,18 can be characterized as an apologetic comparison with the opponents (cf. p. 43: in 12,19 a "Gattungswechsel" occurs from apology back to parenesis). It would seem, however, that in 10,1-6 as well as 12,19–13,10 the distinction mentioned in our text between general and specific is needed. Of course, both types of exhortation cooperate in the "upbuilding" of the Corinthians.

two chapters can be considered, to some degree, as framing and including the middle chapters 11 and 12.

a) *Motifs*. A number of motifs are present in both chapter 10 and chapter 13[16]:

(1) Paul speaks of his absence and presence at Corinth (10,1.2.11 and 13,2.10) and of his future (third) coming (10,2.4-6.11 and 13,1.2.10).

(2) In both chapters he threatens to show boldness, to be severe and not to spare anyone at his coming (10,2.11 and 13,2.10)[17].

(3) The motif of obedience-disobedience on the part of the Corinthians which is explicitly spoken of in 10,6 also seems to be present in 13,1-2.5.9-10.

(4) In 10,9-11 but also in 13,10 Paul mentions his earlier letters and/or his actual writing.

(5) In both chapters Paul contrasts the themes of humility and boldness, of weakness and power: see 10,1-6.10 and 13,3-4.8-9.

(6) Moreover, utilizing an almost identical wording, in 10,8 and 13,10 he points to the authority[18] which the Lord has given him for building up and not for tearing down (cf. 12,19c: "all [is done] for your upbuilding". The reference to Jeremiah can hardly be missed.

(7) In 10,18 one meets the motif of test and approval, which is dominant in chapter 13 (see 13,3.5-7)[19].

(8) "To belong to Christ" in 10,7 recurs in the slightly different expressions of 13,5: to be living in the faith; Jesus Christ is in you (cf. 13,3: "Christ is speaking through [ἐν] me").

b) *Vocabulary*. In view of the presence in both chapters of all these motifs, it should not surprise us that there is a similarity in their respective vocabularies as well: e.g., present and absent, power and powerful, authority and building up, "not for destruction", letters or writing, faith and test[20]. Given these parallels, É.-B. Allo can justly affirm:

16. Cf. *Second Corinthians*, pp. 158-159.

17. It should, however, be noted that in chapter 13 Paul has in mind not only those Corinthians who favor his opponents, but also those who have gravely sinned previously and do not repent (13,2, cf. 12,20-21).

18. According to K. PRÜMM, *Diakonia Pneumatos. Der zweite Korintherbrief als Zugang zur apostolischen Botschaft. Auslegung und Theologie.* Vol I: *Theologische Auslegung des zweiten Korintherbriefes*, Rome – Freiburg – Wien, 1967, p. 577, ἐξουσία points to Paul's powerful and "strafendes Einschreiten" both in 10,8 and 13,10.

19. Cf., e.g., HECKEL, *Kraft in Schwachheit*, p. 193.

20. We may enumerate the following terms. Compare

ch. 10	with	13,1-10
1 ταπεινός		(cf. 12,21: ταπεινώσει)
ἀπών (11 ἀπόντες)		2.10 ἀπών

"L'apologie' des 4 chapitres font un tout très harmonique, où la fin rejoint le commencement"[21].

c) *Time dimension.* Finally, in contrast to chapters 11–12, which contain Paul's "foolish" boasting only about what he was (and is) and all that he did and suffered in the past, chapter 10 as well as chapter 13 mainly look to the future[22]. Paul announces his third visit to Corinth. He states how he is going to act there and what his attitude will be. In an entreating yet warning style, he also writes to the Corinthians about what he expects from them: obedience, self-examination and improvement. All this primarily concerns the future.

d) *Content.* The similarities between 10,1b-18 and 13,1-10 are too numerous and too specific to be explained by purely accidental repetition. In composing these clearly corresponding chapters Paul brings about a second ring which further includes the Fool's Speech. However, a conscious and deliberate composition by Paul does not mean that he intended a strict concentric structure.

What is the main theme of this second ring? In view of the attacks and reproaches against his person, Paul is ready to manifest his authority (cf. 10,8.11 and 13,10; see also 12,19); he will not refrain from using it (13,2). This authority is given him by the Lord, not for destroying or tearing down the Corinthians but for building them up (10,8 and 13,10). But, if needed, Paul will punish every disobedience (10,6), he will deal with the Corinthians by the power of God (13,4). In fact, that is why he writes this

2 παρών (11 παρόντες)	2.10 παρών
4 δυνατός	3 δυνατέω, 4 δύναμις, 9 δυνατός
6 ἐν ἑτοίμῳ ἔχοντες	(cf. 12,14: ἑτοίμως ἔχω)
7 Χριστοῦ εἶναι	5 Χριστὸς Ἰησοῦς ἐν ὑμῖν
8 περὶ τῆς ἐξουσίας	10 κατὰ τὴν ἐξουσίαν
ἧς ἔδωκεν ὁ κύριος	ἣν ὁ κύριος ἔδωκέν μοι
εἰς οἰκοδομήν	εἰς οἰκοδομήν (cf. 12,19: ... ὑπὲρ τῆς ὑμῶν οἰκοδομῆς)
καὶ οὐκ εἰς καθαίρεσιν	καὶ οὐκ εἰς καθαίρεσιν
9-11 ἐπιστολαί	10 γράφων
15 πίστις	5 πίστις
18 δόκιμος	7 δόκιμος, 3 δοκιμή, 5 δοκιμάζω, 5.6.7 ἀδόκιμος

See LAMBRECHT, "Dangerous Boasting", pp. 330-331, esp. footnote 10.

21. É.-B. ALLO, *Seconde épître aux Corinthiens* (ÉB), Paris, ²1956, p. 240. Cf. also M.-A. CHEVALLIER, "L'argumentation de Paul dans II Corinthiens 10 à 13", in *RHPR* 70 (1990) 3-15, esp. pp. 13-14; P. ROLLAND, in *Bib* 71 (1990) 73-84; J. D. HARVEY, *Listening to the Text: Oral Patterning in Paul's Letters*, Grand Rapids, 1998, pp. 215-216.

22. True, in 10,7-8 and 10,12-18 there are references to the past. Note, however, how in 10,15b-16 the future is envisaged. Furthermore, it would seem that at the end of 10,11 the future tense ("we will be") must mentally be supplied.

letter while absent so that, when present, he may not have to act severely (13,10).

In chapters 10 and 13 Paul defends himself against the charge of weakness. In 10,12-18 he compares himself with the intruders polemically: in contrast to them he is not boasting beyond measure. Because of the work done in Corinth the Lord recommends him. In chapters 10 and 13 Paul is not boasting about his weakness nor is he speaking paradoxically of strength in weakness, that is, not yet in chapter 10, no longer in chapter 13. The tone in these chapters is that of severe admonition. Paul refers to his authority and announces his future decisively bold intentions. He mentions his anticipative resurrection power; it will be a proof that Christ is speaking through him (cf. 13,3-4).

A Third Ring: Denial of Inferiority in 11,5-12 and 12,11b-18

Just as for the second ring we will first deal with the common motifs in the two passages and then point to their identical or similar vocabularies. A third noteworthy feature here will be the consideration of the sequence of the motifs.

a) *Motifs.* No less than nine recurring motifs can be listed.

(1) Both in 11,5 and 12,11b Paul emphasizes that he is in no way inferior to the super-apostles[23].

(2) Twice, be it rather differently, he also admits that something was lacking in his appearance during his stay at Corinth: "Even if I am unskilled in speech" (11,6a; cf. 10,10); "even though I was nothing" (end of 12,11; probably in a more fundamental sense).

(3) His reference to "knowledge" and the fact that he has "made that clear" to the Corinthians "in every way and in all things" (11,6) can be compared, it would seem, with the reference to "the signs of the apostle" which were done among the Corinthians (12,12): in both cases Paul wants thus to deny his so-called inferiority.

(4) It strikes the reader that immediately after this emphasis on not being inferior Paul speaks of his refusal of support (11,7-12 and 12,13-18).

(5) Within that context of preaching the gospel free of charge the mention of "sin" (ἁμαρτία) and "wrong" (ἀδικία) appear unexpectedly in

---

23. Cf. HECKEL, *Kraft in Schwachheit*, p. 23: "Wie durch eine Klammer zusammengehalten wird die Narrenrede von der *Leitthese* in 11,5 und deren Wiederaufnahme in 12,11" (cf. also, e.g., p. 305).

the two passages: "Did I commit a sin...?" (11,7), and: "Forgive me this wrong" (12,13).

(6) In both passages, too, Paul emphasizes that he did not burden the Corinthians: see 11,7.9 and 12,13.

(7) He admits, however, to have received support from elsewhere: see 11,8-9 (Macedonia) and 12,13 (other churches).

(8) In both contexts Paul also stresses his firm intention not to burden Corinth in the future, i.e., not to change his way of acting in this matter: see 11,9-10.12 and, in a less pronounced but still clear way, 12,14 ("I will not burden you").

(9) Twice he explains his specific behavior of refusing support as a sign of genuine love of the Corinthians: see 11,11 and 12,15.

b) *Vocabulary*. One should not only look for the identical grammatical forms nor, necessarily, for the same nuances of meaning. The fact that the same or similar – or oppositional – wording appears is in itself significant: to be inferior; the super-apostles; sin and wrong; to humble oneself and to spend (or be spent); to be exalted; churches; not to burden; brother(s); to love[24].

Again, in view of all these correspondences, both in theme and wording, it would seem that in Paul's composing procedure pure coincidence must be excluded.

---

24. We compare 11,5-12 with 12,11b-18:

11,5:   μηδὲν ὑστερηκέναι (cf. v. 9: ὑστερηθείς, ὑστέρημα)
        12,11b: οὐδὲν ... ὑστέρησα
11,5:   τῶν ὑπερλίαν ἀποστόλων (cf. v. 13: ψευδαπόστολοι)
        12:11b: τῶν ὑπερλίαν ἀποστόλων
11,7:   ἁμαρτίαν (cf. v. 8: ἐσύλησα)
        12,13:   ἀδικίαν (cf. v. 16: πανοῦργος, δόλῳ, and vv. 17-18: πλεονεκτέω)
11,7:   ἐμαυτὸν ταπείνων
        12,15:   δαπανήσω καὶ ἐκδαπανηθήσομαι
11,7:   ὑψωθῆτε
        12,13:   ἡσσώθητε
11,8:   ἄλλας ἐκκλησίας
        12,13:   ὑπὲρ τὰς λοιπὰς ἐκκλησίας
11,9:   οὐ κατενάρκησα οὐθενός
        12,13:   οὐ κατενάρκησα ὑμῶν (cf. 14: οὐ καταναρκήσω)
11,9:   οἱ ἀδελφοὶ ἐλθόντες ἀπὸ Μακεδονίας
        12,18:   συναπέστειλα τὸν ἀδελφόν
11,9:   ἀβαρῆ
        12,16:   οὐ κατεβάρησα
11,11:   οὐκ ἀγαπῶ ὑμᾶς;
        12,15:   εἰ περισσοτέρως ὑμᾶς ἀγαπῶν, ἧσσον ἀγαπῶμαι;

c) *Sequence*. In this third ring there is even more than motifs and vocabulary. A remarkable identical order, a parallel sequence of data is present in 11,5-15 and 12,11-18. We mention five consecutive elements: First, notwithstanding apparent weaknesses (although unskilled in speech, 11,5; even though being nothing, 12,11) Paul is not inferior to the super-apostles; second, Paul has proved his "equality" by wisdom (11,6) or signs (12,12); third, refusing support is extensively dealt with immediately after this; fourth, Paul makes known his intention not to burden the Corinthians in the future; fifth, not burdening them should be interpreted as loving them.

Of course, differences in length and wording must be allowed in such compositions. Moreover, the parallelism is not carried through until the end. Each of the two passages has its own surplus. In 11,9 Paul explains how Macedonia has helped him while in 11,12-15 he expansively and bitterly deals with the opponents, those deceitful workers who apparently receive support and want Paul to do the same. On the other hand, in 12,16-18 Paul defends himself against the Corinthians' suspicion that he may have defrauded them through Titus and the brother he sent, visibly with regard to the collection; such a reference is not present in the first passage.

d) *Content*. The data gathered in the preceding paragraphs are so abundant as well as so significant that one is led to postulate, for this third step too, a somewhat concentric composition, whether or not this is intended as such by Paul.

The most strange yet remarkable feature is the double and presumably not accidental link between the idea of denial of inferiority and his preaching free of charge. In the opinion of the Corinthians the apostle Paul must have been considered as inferior to his opponents. Lack of boldness and rhetorical capacities when present certainly constitutes one of their reasons (11,6a; cf. 10,1b.10). Paul twice immediately reacts. In 11,6 he replies: I am not inferior in knowledge; we have made that clear to you; in 12,12 he protests: the signs of the apostle were done among you. One can follow such an argument.

But how does refusal of support enter the scene? Paul must have offended the Corinthians, probably because in accepting help from other churches he humiliated that of Corinth, probably also because by his refusal of gifts he denied the sympathy and friendship of the richer people of the community, and further maybe also because through his manual work he socially abased himself. In its own way our analysis has established – and confirmed – that Paul's refusal of support happened to be in Corinth an extremely sensitive issue (cf. also 1 Cor 9). Obviously, notwithstanding Paul's protest, it was not taken as a token of love[25].

It must strike the readers of chapters 10–13 that in the "denial-of-inferiority" sections Paul is not boasting foolishly nor boasting of his weaknesses, i.e., not yet in 11,5-12 and no longer in 12,11-18. He openly defends himself; he wants to prove that in no way is he inferior. Therefore, he points to his wisdom which, he says, is manifest, to his wonders and miracles, and to his preaching free of charge in order not to burden the Corinthians and to show his real love of them.

Structural and Thematic Considerations

Three insights which result from this lengthy analysis may be formulated. We shall consider first Paul's composition of chapters 10–13 (discourse and context), then the main themes which "frame" the Fool's Speech, and finally two specific passages which, it would seem, more explicitly relate to this discourse.

Results Regarding Structure

It has been put forward that the Fool's Speech properly begins in 11,22 and ends at 12,10. In 11,1-21 the Speech possesses its extended introduction. It may be claimed now that, roughly speaking, three circles of texts frame the discourse by way of a ring composition: an inner ring (11,5-12 and 12,11b-18), a middle ring (10,2-18 and 13,1-10) and a very small exhortative outer ring (10,1 and 13,11; 13,12-13 forming the epistolary closing).

However, a warning is needed at once. One should not exaggerate the structural qualities of these chapters. In his second letter to the Corinthians Paul is writing very emotionally in the last four chapters. The Fool's Speech itself is not a tight unit. This discourse is often interrupted, and "foolish boasting" as such does not possess a sustained unique object (cf. the shifts). Again, as we saw, the introduction to the Fool's Speech in 11,1-21 is all but smooth: hesitation and breaks – hence a new start in 11,16 – and repetitions.

---

25. On the passages on "manual labor" and "working" in 1 and 2 Thessalonians, see now A. J. MALHERBE, *The Letters to the Thessalonians* (AB, 32B), New York, 2000, esp. pp. 160-163 and 454-457.

Although the context certainly presents concentric features, one must in no way present chapters 10–13 as an enveloping composition of which, so to say, the central *d*-core (the Speech) is surrounded by neatly delineated *a b c* and *c' b' a'*-sections (the three rings). There is no evidence that Paul wanted a rigid, formal ring composition. To be sure, after the discourse Paul most probably consciously repeated themes and language taken from the context before the discourse, and he does this in an inverse order. However, his manner of composing is too loose and probably too spontaneous to postulate on the part of Paul an explicitly intended cyclic arrangement.

The Main Themes in the So-called Rings

The thin outer ring (10,2 and 13,11) is one of exhortation, that is, an appeal to moral Christian life. Paul mentions Christ's mercy and gentleness. Exhortation constitutes a normal ingredient of the Pauline letter. In 2 Corinthians, however, this is not developed. The appeal to a worthy Christian conduct is interrupted before it could really begin. One could claim that moral exhortation is replaced by self-defense, pleas to obedience and also threats. Only at the very end of the letter does Paul, explicitly by the verb in 13,11 but no doubt already in 12,19b–13,10, return to the ethical problems of the Corinthian community. The outer ring is meant for the Corinthians. This hortatory inclusion is, one should say, almost unconnected with the Fool's Speech itself.

In 10,2-18 and 13,1-10 we meet a Paul who is in an argumentative mood. Twice he rewrites a text from Jeremiah with regard to his ἐξουσία (10,8 and 13,10). He points to his apostolic authority that the Lord has given him for building up and not for tearing down. He intends to boast of that authority (10,8). He thinks of the Corinthians, those who accuse him of lack of boldness and of contemptible speech. These Christians are influenced by false apostles. Paul defends himself: he will fight back and announces severe action (10,2-6); he, too, belongs to Christ (10,7); through comparing himself with his opponents, he points out the legitimacy of his authority in Corinth (see 10,12-18). Notwithstanding visible human weakness Paul is sure of possessing the power of God. He will not fail to meet the test (see 13,1-6). He announces his future visit; he will act in full authority and, if needed, severely (13,10). Angry mood, comparison with the opponents, mention of future boasting: all this is not "foolish" boasting and certainly not boasting of his weakness. These utterances, however, reveal Paul's conviction of being the legitimate, duly authorized apostle.

The inner ring consists of 11,5-12 and 12,11b-18. We noted that the introduction to the discourse is to be found in 11,1-4.16-21, the brief retrospections in 12,11a and 12,19a. In the inner ring itself Paul deals with the Corinthians' false opinion that he is inferior to the super-apostles (11,5 and 12,11b). In both sections, before and after the discourse, he emphasizes that he is not of lower rank and less importance. He tries to prove this: he is at least as good as his opponents; he points to his wisdom which was made manifest (11,6) and to the "signs" done in Corinth (12,12). Twice also, immediately after that explicit claim, he suddenly defends his apostolic preaching without cost (11,7-12 and 12,13-18). The Corinthians have visibly misinterpreted it, he argues; in fact, refusing support is a manifestation of his authentic love. One may ask why Paul does not mention this generous attitude in his foolish discourse; he could have boasted about this "weakness". Yet he seemingly is of the opinion that this serious matter which interrupts the very introduction to the foolish discourse and will appear again, surprisingly, soon after the discourse, does not lend itself for boasting in a foolish way.

So three main items – moral exhortation, personal authority, and denial of inferiority – are the concerns which enclose the Fool's Speech. By themselves they do not lead to foolish boasting. Yet in an essential way they complete the portrait of a Paul who in his Speech boasts foolishly and boasts paradoxically of weaknesses.

Boasting, Comparing, and Attacking

Within the broad context two passages appear to stand in closer connection with the foolish discourse. In 10,8.12-18, verses rather far off from the Fool's Speech, and in 11,3-4.12-15.18-20, verses close by, Paul appears to be preparing his boasting and speaking as a fool.

In 10,8 he tells the reader that he is going to boast "rather much"[26] about his authority and, then, in 10,12-18, while protesting that he "does not dare compare himself with others nor recommend himself" and while accusing those people of being "not wise" and boasting "beyond measure" (10,12-13), Paul in fact compares his apostolic competence with that of his opponents and is already boasting, be it not, he claims, "beyond

---

26. It is possible that the expression περισσότερόν τι is not used "idiomatically" but "comparatively" and means "somewhat more", i.e., more than Paul ordinarily does. See P. BARNETT, *The Second Epistle to the Corinthians* (NICNT), Grand Rapids – Cambridge 1997, 473, n. 33 (with reference to P. E. Hughes). Luke 12,4 has the negation: they cannot do "anything more" than kill the body.

measure in the labor of others" (10,13-16). The reader understands that in the final analysis Paul himself is the one who boasts of the Lord and who is approved and recommended by the Lord (10,17-18). Vocabulary as well as content are not so different from what he later promises to do in boasting foolishly.

According to Paul his opponents disguise themselves as "apostles of Christ" (11,13). The characterization is very much like that in the discourse itself. At the beginning of the Fool's Speech, after three brief initial questions about origin, he asks by way of climax: "are they servants of Christ?" (11,23a). Paul reacts to the implicit positive answer by saying – talking as if out of his mind – "I am more" (11,23c). The whole speech which continues unto 12,10 functions as a proof not of his equality but of his superiority in comparison with these opponents. The extremely negative picture of them in 11,3-4 ("just as the serpent deceived Eve by his cunning"), in 11,12-15 (boasting people, "false apostles, deceitful workers", "servants" of Satan) and in 11,18-20 (tyrannical intruders) constitutes Paul's proximate psychological preparation for his foolish discourse of boasting, itself an indirect but fierce attack.

It should be noted that major characteristics of Paul's apostolic behavior remain outside the Fool's Speech: his belonging to Christ (10,7), the foundation of the Corinthian community (10,12-18), his wisdom (11,6), the refusal of support (11,7-12 and 12,13-18), the signs of the apostle (12,12), his power of God (13,4). All this could have been part of his "foolish" boasting just as that of origin, circumstances and revelations. It appears that the shift toward weakness has prevented that.

Conclusions

Five conclusions can be drawn from this study, the first three already well-known. First, chapters 10–13, rightly considered as a united major and self-contained part of Paul's second letter to the Corinthians, are far from monolithic, certainly streamlined in sections but not as a whole. Second, the Fool's Speech itself (11,22–12,10) is not of one piece; it is characterized by many shifts in the content and it is often interrupted by reflexive remarks and new starts. Third, notwithstanding pleas, hesitations and interruptions, 11,1-21 can be called the introduction to the Fool's Speech.

Fourth, the wider context contains a very small hortatory frame (10,1 and 13,11), a double defense of Paul's apostolic authority (10,2-18 and 13,1-10), and also a double clarification of his conviction that, notwithstanding outer appearance and refusal of support, he is not inferior to the other missionaries (11,5-12 and 12,11b-18). One can speak, therefore, of three unequal rings which loosely surround the discourse, each with its own thematic emphasis: parenesis, authority, denial of inferiority.

Fifth, in 10,8.12-18 and 11,3-4.12-15.18-20, Paul compares himself with opponents, blames and denigrates them; it would seem that in these small sections Paul prepares himself, through comparison and invective, to proceed to something he does not like to do, that is, to boast in a foolish way[27]. However, the boasting of titles gives way, almost at once, to boasting of hardships and weakness.

Lack of perfect organization does not prove lack of unity and absence of inner connections. Therefore, one must not deny the prevailing coherence of 2 Cor 10–13. In 12,19 Paul claims: "In God's sight we speak in Christ; beloved, all (is done) for your upbuilding". This basic intention applies, of course, to the emphasis present in the three rings: moral exhortation, personal authority and denial of inferiority (vilification of the opponents included), but equally to what he expounds in his Fool's Speech, boasting foolishly, and then paradoxically boasting of his weaknesses. In a lengthy discourse, surrounded by an equally extensive context, Paul shows how the power of Christ is made perfect in his human weakness. Paul depicts his so-called weaknesses but also, in them, his God-given human strength: whenever Paul is weak, then he is strong (cf. 12,9-10).

27. It goes without saying that a loose and only partly concentric arrangement of the context, as well as the shifts and interruptions both in the discourse and the introduction to it, render an intended rhetorical *dispositio* very unlikely. For a rhetorical proposal regarding 11,1–12,13, see HECKEL, *Kraft in Schwachheit*, pp. 27-29; C. STRÜDER, *Apostolische Schwäche in kräftiger Sprache. Die Rhetorik der Narrenrede* (Unpublished Seminararbeit, Pontifical Biblical Institute, Rome, 2000).

The Identity of Christ Jesus
(Philippians 2,6-11)

The aim of this study is a careful reading of the "hymn" Phil 2,6-11 as well as a reflection upon Paul's early christology, i.e., his view of Jesus' identity. An appropriate entrance into the subject matter may be a look at the continuing discussion of the "hymn" in the last ten years. Then the passage Phil 2,6-11 itself will be analyzed. Some christological considerations will conclude this paper.

Philippians 2,6-11 in Recent Research

First attention may given to Ralph P. Martin as author and editor, as well as to James D. G. Dunn and N. T. Wright. Then a number of other recent studies will be mentioned.

An Ongoing Discussion

a) *A Hymn of Christ (Martin)*. In 1997 Ralph P. Martin provided a third edition of his well-known *Carmen Christi* (1967), under the new title *A Hymn of Christ*[1]. The book deals with Philippians 2,5-11 and the history of interpretation of this passage. Extensive prefaces to the second (1983) and the third editions are included (pp. vii-xxxix and xl-lxxiv). In the last preface Martin restates and somewhat clarifies his interpretation of the hymn. First of all he emphasizes that verses 6-11 are more than exalted prose; they constitute a pre-Pauline Christ hymn used in early Christian liturgy. The four possible Pauline additions are: "taking the form of a slave" (v. 7b), "even death on a cross" (v. 8c), "in heaven and

---

1. R. P. MARTIN, *A Hymn of Christ: Philippians 2:5-11 in Recent Interpretation and in the Setting of Early Christian Worship*, Downers Grove, IL, 1997. This is the third revised edition of *Carmen Christi* (1967) with a supplemented state of the question and an updated bibliography.

on earth and under the earth" (v. 10b), and "to the glory of God the Father" (v. 11c). Paul thus emphasizes his personal understanding.

Secondly, Martin explains the hymn as christological. The preexistent Christ was in the form of God. He refused to grasp at equality with God but became incarnate. Because of this deliberate choice, i.e., his κένωσις and further humiliation, God super-exalted him and gave him that refused equality: divine name, lordship over the world, universal veneration by spirits and humans. Martin understands v. 6a in a concessive sense: "although he was…". In his view ἁρπαγμός is a thing not yet possessed (*res rapienda*); equality with God is more than what Christ possessed in his preexistent state. Christ received that equality after his death, at his exaltation. In this hymn Christ is implicitly contrasted with Adam.

b) *Where Christology Began (Dunn)*. The publication *Where Christology Began: Essays on Philippians 2*, edited by Ralph P. Martin, together with Brian J. Dodd, is the result of a symposion on the Christ hymn[2]. In this book ten studies are published. Authors and titles sufficiently indicate the importance of this at first sight rather modest volume.

After "*Carmen Christi* Revisited" by Martin himself (pp. 1-5), the still influential studies of E. Lohmeyer and E. Käsemann are discussed: "Ernst Lohmeyer's *Kyrios Jesus*" by Colin Brown (pp. 6-42) and "Incarnation, Myth, and Theology: Ernst Käsemann's Interpretation of Philippians 2,5-11" by Robert Morgan (pp. 42-73). The contribution by L. D. Hurst, "Christ, Adam and Preexistence" (pp. 84-95), is a revised and expanded version of an earlier article (1986); Hurst critically evaluates the position of J. D. G. Dunn. The brief article "Christ, Adam, and Preexistence" by Dunn himself in this volume (pp. 74-83) is already a reaction to that of Hurst. But what is the position of Dunn?

In his latest publications James D. G. Dunn is less outspoken and radical, yet he still defends the presence of an Adam christology in the hymn. Of course, Adam christology is evidently present in 1 Cor 15,20-28 and Rom 5,12-21. Dunn emphasizes that one should be tuned to "an awareness of how allusions function" and avoid a narrow either-or exegesis; one should listen to resonances and intertextual echoes, recognize the broad semantic fields and the interplay of images. In so doing, one will easily admit the probability of references to Adam in the hymn. A reader of v. 6 is reminded of Gen 1,27 ("in the image of God") and 3,5 ("you will

---

2. R. P. MARTIN and B. J. DODD (eds.), *Where Christology Began: Essays on Philippians 2*, Louisville, KY, 1998.

be like God"). The obedience unto death of v. 8 probably contains an allusion to Gen 2,17 ("you shall die"). The exaltation of v. 9 may refer to Ps 8,5-6 ("adam"; cf. 1 Cor 15,27 and 45). To the question what "emptied himself and took the form of a slave" of v. 7ab means, Dunn answers that, given the addition of "became in the very likeness of humankind" (v. 7cd), one more naturally thinks of birth. Yet a transition from the pre-historic (mythic) *adam* ("humankind") to *adam* (concrete first human being) could also be possible. Or, after all, is the earthly Jesus alone as counterpart of Adam meant in Phil 2,6-8? If so, Adam's grasping and disobedience is contrasted with Jesus' refusal and obedience. His free acceptance of death, the consequence of Adam's sin, resulted for Jesus in exaltation which was originally intended for Adam and humankind (cf. Ps 8,6). Dunn himself prefers not to assume in Paul's text a reference to Christ's preexistence[3].

In the volume *Where Christology Began* attention is also devoted to particular verses: by Gerald F. Hawthorne in "In the Form of God and Equal with God (Philippians 2,6)" (pp. 96-110)[4], by Larry J. Kreitzer in "'When He at Last Is First!': Philippians 2,9-11 and the Exaltation of the Lord" (pp. 111-127), and by Richard J. Bauckham in "The Worship of Jesus in Philippians 2,9-11" (pp. 128-139). The final two articles of the volume deal with the christological and ethical interpretations of the hymn in its context: "Christology and Ethics in Philippians 2,5-11" by Stephen Fowl (pp. 140-153) and "The Story of Christ and the Imitation of Paul in Philippians 2–3" by Brian J. Dodd (pp. 154-161).

Where Christology Began is, it would seem, interesting for the careful presentations of Lohmeyer and Käsemann and the critical reactions to Dunn, more than for the proposals of some of the other contributors. We should notice that most authors in the volume assume in verse 6 a reference by Paul to Christ's preexistence.

---

3. Cf. DUNN's brief article in *Where Christology Began* (n. 2) and, above all, *Christology in the Making*, London, 1980; see the Foreword to the second edition, 1989, reprinted in ID., *The Christ and the Spirit. 1: Christology*, Edinburgh, 1998, pp. 287-314. See the critique by, among others, C. E. B. CRANFIELD, "Some Comments on Professor J. D. G. Dunn's *Christology in the Making*", in ID., *On Romans and Other New Testament Essays*, Edinburgh, 1998, pp. 51-68. It would seem that C. M. TUCKETT, *Christology and the New Testament: Jesus and His Earliest Followers*, Edinburgh, 2001, pp. 54-56, supports Dunn.

4. Hawthorne is the author of a commentary on Philippians in the WBC series (Waco, TX, 1983). In his contribution in this volume he compares the results of recent publications on v. 6 with his own former ideas.

c) *The Contribution of Wright*. The well-known study by N. T. Wright
(1986), not present in this volume but referred to by more than one
author, is now available in an expanded version in his *The Climax of the
Covenant* (ch. 4: "Jesus Christ is Lord. Philippians 2,5-11") (1992)[5]. In the
first part of this study Wright discusses Lightfoot's approach but also, and
quite thoroughly, that of R. P. Martin. Wright criticizes a great number
of points[6].

Not the least value of Wright's extensive study is the critical survey of
the interpretations of ἁρπαγμός. Wright himself follows the conclusions
of R.W. Hoover[7]. The term ἁρπαγμός has lost its original meaning of
"robbery" and, together with the verb, it functions here in a Greek idiom
meaning "to regard something as ἁργαμόν". Idiomatically the expression
signifies "to consider something to be taken advantage of". Christ did not
regard his equality with God in this way; he refused to take advantage
of his position and thus was different from oriental despots who understood their position as something to be used for their own advantage.
In Wright's opinion the preexistent Christ, being in the form of God,
possesses divine equality (the definite article before "being equal" in v. 6b
is anaphorical and takes up the content of v. 6a). However, Christ interprets this equality as giving, thus not getting, and therefore empties himself and becomes obedient unto death. The exaltation of the crucified one
is God's endorsement of that interpretation. Is Christ then returning to
the same state of glory as he had in his preexistence? Wright claims that
exaltation does not include a higher state; only one possible difference
could be admitted in that now Christ is also exalted as a human being.
For Wright there is a cryptic reference to Adam, but more than christological, the hymn is theological. The song explains God as self-giving
love[8].

---

5. N. T. WRIGHT, "*harpagmos* and the Meaning of Philippians 2:5-11", in *JTS* 37 (1986)
321-352; reprinted in ID., *The Climax of the Covenant: Christ and the Law in Paul*, Edinburgh, 1992, pp. 56-98.

6. In the preface to the third edition of *Carmen Christ* (see n. 1: *A Hymn of Christ*,
pp. lxv-lxxix), Martin presents a lengthy but, it would seem, not always convincing reaction.

7. R. W. HOOVER, "The Harpagmos Enigma: A Philological Solution", in *HTR* 56
(1971) 95-119. This idiomatic meaning (passive; cf. ἁρπαγμα) supposes expressions with
a double accusative. Hoover adds on p. 118: "a status which belonged to the pre-existent
Christ"; the expression points to "something already present and at one's disposal". Yet
Tuckett, *Christology and the New Testament*, writes: "The debate about the precise nuance
of the Greek word is very fierce, but the issue may not be resolvable on strictly semantic or lexical grounds" (p. 55).

8. For the study of WRIGHT, cf. n. 5.

Jesus Christ and Jewish Monotheism

An exhaustive listing of studies on Phil 2,6-11 is by no means intended. Yet it may prove helpful to present some other recent publications under three headings.

a) *Preexistent, Incarnate, Exalted.* In his own vigorous way Martin Hengel goes on asserting that the Jewish-Christian faith in the preexistent Son is very old: it may already have existed in 34-36 AD in Syria-Cilicia[9]. At any rate the first two decades of Christianity are more revolutionary regarding christology than the following seven centuries. For Hengel, in Philippians 2 "equality with God" is contentwise the same as "being in the form of God" (a divine *Seinsweise*). Subordination of the Son to the Father is self-evident and should not disturb us. It appears that Christ's exaltation to becoming the universal Lord implies a higher state than that of the preexistent, but this is, according to this author, difficult to clarify further. Hengel does not find an Adam christology in the hymn. He does think that the Christ-psalm may have been composed by Paul himself. He asks how such a faith came into existence, and suggests that to answer this question one has to reckon with the impact of the earthly Jesus as well as the resurrection experiences. Hengel also refers to Jewish Wisdom and Torah speculations. He emphasizes the Christian meditative reflection on Scripture, especially Ps 110.

C. A. Wanamaker does not accept references to Adam[10]. Christ bore the outward μορφή, the visible glory of his Father. He emptied himself of it and he did not grasp at divine equality (something different from "being in the form of God"). The qualifications present in v. 7cd indicate that the incarnate Christ is different from other human beings because of his sinlessness. In vv. 7-8 two steps are clearly distinguished: the emptying (incarnation) and the humbling to death on a cross. Christ is exalted to the equality with God which he did not possess before the incarnation. Yet, even after his exaltation the subordination remains. Christ is the Son of the Father, his agent and vice-regent.

In his commentary Ulrich B. Müller refers to Phil 2,6-11 as a Christ hymn, a pre-Pauline hymn to which Paul has added the end of v. 8 and

9. M. HENGEL, "Präexistenz bei Paulus?", in C. LANDMESSER, H.-J. ECKSTEIN, H. LICHTENBERGER (eds.), *Jesus Christus als die Mitte der Schrift. Studien zur Hermeneutik des Evangeliums. FS O. Hofius* (BZNW, 86), Berlin – New York, 1997, 479-518.
10. C. A. WANAMAKER, "Philippians 2.6-11: Son of God or Adamic Christology", in *NTS* 33 (1987) 179-193.

the end of v. 11[11]. The caesura in v. 7 lies between 7ab and 7cd. Christ was preexistent: "die göttliche Person hielt nicht gierig daran fest, 'Gott gleich zu sein'" (p. 94). The divine equality is "eine schon vorhandene Realität" (p. 95). Christ did not regard it "als einen Gewinn, der aus-zunützen ist" (p. 94). The κένωσις is understood in a radical way; incarnation means a free and complete forsaking of divine equality. Müller does not explain how one can understand this. In vv. 9-10 he distinguishes between the giving of the name, i.e., the enthronement which has already occurred, and the eschatological, still future προσκύνησις and acclamation. The background of preexistence is the Jewish speculation on wisdom.

In 1992 Gordon D. Fee published "Philippians 2,5-11: Hymn or Exalted Pauline Prose?"; in 1995 his commentary on Philippians followed[12]. In Fee's opinion this "narrative about Christ that is at once one of the most exalted, most belied, and most discussed and debated passages in the Pauline corpus" (commentary, p. 192) is decidedly not a hymn; the passage is composed by Paul himself. The style is solemn. While verses 6-8, with the numerous participles, possess a poetic narrative character, verses 9-11 contain argumentative prose. Fee vigorously rejects an allusion to Adam, above all because in the text there is no linguistic parallel to the Adam story in Genesis (μορφή in Phil 2,6-7 is not the equivalent of εἰκών, "image", in Gen 1,26-27). There can be no doubt that according to v. 6 Jesus Christ is preexistent. In vv. 7-8 two discrete steps are pointed out: "as God he emptied himself"; "as man he humbled himself". In these verses "is the closest thing to Christology that one finds in Paul. ... For in 'pouring himself out' and 'humbling himself to death on the cross,' Christ Jesus has revealed the character of God himself. Here is the epitome of God-likeness" (p. 197).

A few notes on one more recent commentary, that by Markus Bock-muehl, may be presented here[13]. Christ did not think he needed to take advantage of his equality with God; he refused to act selfishly with regard to his pre-incarnate state. The opening "and" of v. 7d suggests that a new

---

11. U. B. MÜLLER, *Der Brief des Paulus and die Philipper* (THNT), Berlin, 1993; see also ID., *Die Menschwerdung des Gottessohnes. Frühchristliche Inkarnationsvorstellungen und die Anfänge des Doketismus* (SBS, 140), Stuttgart, 1990.

12. G. D. FEE, "Philippians 2:5-11: Hymn or Exalted Prose?", in *Bulletin for Biblical Research* 2 (1992) 29-46; reprinted in ID., *To What End Exegesis? Essays Textual, Exegetical, and Theological*, Grand Rapids – Vancouver, 2001, pp. 173-191; *Paul's Letter to the Philippians* (NICNT), Grand Rapids, 1995.

13. M. BOCKMUEHL, *The Epistle to the Philippians* (BNTC), London – New York, 1998.

sentence begins. However, it would seem that this second sentence explains "taking the form of a slave" (v. 7b); properly speaking it is not a second step. The expression "even death on a cross" (v. 8c) "is not extraneous to the passage but is singled out as the deliberate climax at least of verses 6-8" (p. 139). Jesus has received the name of God himself, i.e., "Lord". Does the assignment "imply that Christ is more highly exalted after the crucifixion than before the incarnation?" (p. 144). Bockmuehl answers this question: "It is certainly true that there seems to be a difference between 'before' and 'after': there is no reason to think that the end is just a restoration to the beginning. ... The humiliation and triumph of the incarnation ... make an identifiable difference even within the God-head" (*ibid.*). The author concludes his discussion of the "theological and christological centrepiece" of Philippians by stressing Christ's relation to the Father: "all this 'high' christology emphatically enhances rather than diminishes the glory of God, firmly securing the unequivocally monotheistic orientation of Paul's thought" (p. 148).

b) *Inspired by Wisdom Speculations?* Recently it has been claimed that ancient Jewish monotheism, although decidedly exclusivist and therefore radically opposed to the surrounding polytheisms even in their more structured and hierarchal forms, was nevertheless prepared and, as it were, open to viewing Christ as divine. So, e.g. Larry W. Hurtado[14] refers to personifications, quasi-personal entities in some biblical books and in the intertestamental literature (especially wisdom and word), to exalted angels (e.g., Michael) and exalted patriarchs (e.g., Henoch and Moses). Jews could see, alongside God, a divine agency and even a principal, chief agent. Of course, in order to consider Christ as divine and to worship him, a distinctive mutation is still needed. The conviction of Christ's transcendent and unique connection with God could not come into existence without specific prepaschal and postpaschal experiences nor without the active presence of the Spirit in the liturgical meetings of the early communities. Yet in that admittedly early phase, foundational for Christianity, Judaism with its divine agency tradition prepared the way and provided the basic conceptual categories (cf. the "New *Religions-geschichtliche Schule*")[15].

---

14. L. W. HURTADO, *One God, One Lord. Early Christian Devotion and Ancient Jewish Monotheism*, London, 1988.
15. Cf. J. E. FOSSUM, *The Name of God and the Angel of the Lord* (WUNT, 36), Tübingen, 1985.

Yet quite recently Richard Bauckham[16], while not denying such influences, is of the opinion that the Christian movement properly included Jesus in the unique divine identity, protologically and eschatologically. The preexistent and exalted Christ belongs inherently to what God is. Christ and the Father together constitute the unique identity of the one God. From the very beginning the New Testament presents a christological monotheism. This is not without some foundation in Judaism. "Precisely Deutero-Isaianic monotheism is fulfilled in the revelation of Jesus' participation in the divine identity" (p. 53). Early Christian worship of Christ is the recognition of his divine identity. Therefore, one should better not speak of a functional christology in early Christianity and even less of an ontic or ontological christology. The conceptual context is too different. One finds in the New Testament the highest christology from the beginning. Not only is the exalted Christ included in the divine identity, but the earthly Jesus himself and his story are intrinsic to God. Within that divine identity one has to postulate an interpersonal relationship from all eternity[17].

c) *Also Greco-Roman Influence?* Samuel Vollenweider[18] emphasizes the importance of biblical and Greco-Roman narratives which depict how pagan rulers on earth (e.g., Antiochus IV, Alexander, Caligula) desire to become gods. This motif was well known. Vollenweider asserts that in Phil 2,6 the nuance of robbery ("Raub") is still present in ἁρπαγμός. He prefers the meaning of "erstrebtes Gut", a divine equality not yet possessed. "Being in the form of God" does not indicate "die volle Göttlichkeit" (pp. 431 and 433). According to the hypothesis of Vollenweider the hymn found its origin in Greek speaking Jewish Christianity. Christians try to find out how their veneration of Christ can go together with their Jewish monotheism. This author points to "Prozesse der Identitätsfindung unter den frühen Judenchristen" (p. 432). As a preexistent being Christ rejects usurpation; he refuses to contend for equality with God. This equality God gives him after his death by way of lordship over the world. In vv. 6-8 Christ is depicted "als Gegenbild zum Typ des sich selbst erhöhenden Herrschers" (p. 431). For vv. 9-11 the hymn employed Isa 45,23.

16. R. BAUCKHAM, *God Crucified. Monotheism and Christology in the New Testament*, Grand Rapids, MI – Cambridge, 1998. Cf. also his article in *Where Christology Began* (n. 2).
17. On Hurtado and Bauckham, see already in no. 15: "Knowledge and Love (1 Corinthians 8,1-13", pp. 186-187.
18. S. VOLLENWEIDER, "Der 'Raub' der Gottgleichheit: Ein religionsgeschichtlicher Vorschlag zu Phil 2.6(-11)", in *NTS* 45 (1999) 413-433.

According to Dieter Zeller[19] more attention should be paid to the Hellenistic reception by the readers of Philippians 2. Greek-speaking Christians must have been reminded by verses 6-7 of a celestial being appearing on earth, a metamorphosis which ends in an apotheosis (the exaltation). Of course, the model is thoroughly adapted, radically transposed to what Jesus meant to them. But the well-known category is there, however much modified by Paul. Zeller suggests that in Syria this "etiology" may have been created to point to Christ's unique relation to God[20].

Summary

What are the more recent tendencies in the research? It would seem that in these days some scholars, more than before – yet not the majority – prefer to see Phil 2,6-11 as a Pauline text, not a pre-Pauline hymn[21]. Its twofold division is mostly accepted with the caesura after v. 8. There is no clear consensus regarding v. 6b: does it repeat the idea of v. 6a or does it indicate Christ's decision which leads to the execution in v. 7? Furthermore, no unanimity is reached regarding the point at which a minor caesura exists within v. 7.

By far the majority of exegetes see in v. 6b a reference to the pre-existent Christ. James Dunn and some others become, it would seem, more and more the exception. The amount of references to Adam is judged quite differently: from a quasi-negation of any allusion to the acceptance of multiple rather hidden references. Although the use of Isa 45,23 in

19. D. ZELLER, "New Testament Christology in its Hellenistic Reception", in *NTS* 46 (2001) 312-333.

20. On the "epiphany" cf. also S. VOLLENWEIDER, "Die Metamorphose des Gottessohnes. Zum epiphanialen Motivfeld in Phil 2,6-8", in *Das Urchristentum in seiner literarischen Geschichte. FS J. Becker* (BZNW, 100), Berlin – New York, 1999, 107-131. For even more emphasis on the socio-political context of this passage, see M. TELLBE, *Paul between Synagogue and State. Christians, Jews, and Civic Authorities in 1 Thessalonians, Romans and Philippians* (ConBNT, 34), Stockholm, 2001, pp. 253-259.

21. Cf., e.g., R. BRUCKER, *"Christushymnen" oder "epideiktische Passagen"? Studien zum Stilwechsel im Neuen Testament und seiner Umwelt* (FRLNT, 161), Göttingen, 1997, pp. 30-319: this Pauline "epideictic" passage is better called an ἔπαινος ("Christus-Epainos"), not a hymn nor a *carmen Christi* but a *laus Christi* ("Christuslob"). Most recently J. B. EDART, *L'Épître aux Philippiens, rhétorique et composition stilistique* (ÉB, 45), Paris, 2002, pp. 138-149, defends the existence of the (perhaps Pauline) liturgical hymn prior to the letter. Inserting this hymn into his letter Paul adds v. 8c and διὸ καί of v. 9a. Edart does not assume a "succession temporelle" between ἐκένωσεν and ἐταπείνωσεν (cf. pp. 154-155). The whole hymn, also vv. 6-7b, deals with the comportment of the earthly Jesus.

verse 10 is evident, not many commentators defend the position that the text in v. 7 (and elsewhere) refers to the suffering Servant.

Christological reflection must have been intense, if not explosive, within the first twenty years of Christianity. This appears to be a fairly common assumption nowadays. The so-called hymn or Paul's text found its origin among Greek-speaking Jewish Christians. Does that hymn continue a development of Jewish monotheism with its Wisdom speculations and its exaltation of divine agents? Or does Christ's divinity have to be placed differently and in even more revolutionary fashion within that Jewish monotheism (cf. Bauckham)? Finally, mention should also be made of a discrete but decisive return of the assumption of possible pagan hellenistic influences (metamorphosis and apotheosis), at least as far as the reception by the readers is concerned[22].

Analysis of Philippians 2,6-11

The Text: Literal Translation and Structure

I
6a   (Christ Jesus) who, although he was in the form of God,
 b   did not regard equality with God as something to be exploited,
7a   but emptied himself,
 b   taking the form of a slave[23].

---

22. The discussion on Pauline christology has grown increasingly interesting in recent years. One is also reminded of the animated debate in Great Britain with regard to J. HICK (ed.), *The Myth of God Incarnate*, London, 1977, and equally to the christological revisions proposed by theologians such as H. Küng, E. Schillebeeckx and P. Schoonenberg. Many of the publications mentioned above treat more Pauline texts than the Philippian hymn alone and sometimes also passages elsewhere in the New Testament. Two major recent books from Germany should be mentioned; both appeared in 1990: K.-J. KUSCHEL, *Geboren vor aller Zeit? Der Streit um Christi Ursprung*, Munich (ET: *Born before All Time? The Dispute over Christ' Origin*, London, 1992) and J. HABERMANN, *Die Präexistenzaussagen im Neuen Testament* (Europäische Hochschulschriften, 23/362), Frankfurt. In R. LAUFEN (ed.), *Gottes ewiger Sohn: die Präexistenz Christi*, Paderborn, 1997, the discussion is even more broadened. In this volume exegetes (e.g., Thomas Söding) as well as patristic and systematic theologians critically evaluate the minimalistic position of Kuschel, investigate biblical passages and ask questions about the enduring value of the christological and trinitarian dogmas of the first four ecumenical councils.

23. It would seem that the first sentence ends with v. 7b. Cf. MÜLLER, *Philipper*, p. 96, and *Menschwerdung*, p. 20; BRUCKER, "*Christushymnen*", pp. 308-309; EDART, *Philippiens*, pp. 129-133. "The form of a slave" (v. 7b) corresponds with "the form of God" (v. 6a). V. 7d repeats v. 7c and together they constitute a new beginning. On the paratactic καί in v. 7d, see FEE, *Philippians*, n. 3 on p. 214 and ID., "Hymn or Exalted Prose?", p. 185.

c Having become in the likeness of human beings
d and having been found as to fashion like a human being,
8a he humbled himself
b becoming[24] obedient unto death,
c even death on a cross.

II
9a Therefore also God highly exalted him
b and gave him the name that is above every name,

10a in order that at the name of Jesus every knee should bend,
b in heaven and on earth and under the earth,
11a and every tongue should confess
b that Jesus Christ is Lord,
c to the glory of God the Father.

It would seem that the analysis of Gordon D. Fee is convincing: Phil 2,6-11 is not a hymn or psalm song in early Christian liturgy in praise of Christ; this text is most probably composed by Paul himself. He wrote the lengthy relative clause of vv. 6-8, as well as the independent sentence of vv. 9-11. Of course, in this he uses already traditional credal motifs[25]. The passage consists of two parts with Christ Jesus as grammatical subject in the first part (vv. 6-8), and God in the second (vv. 9-11)[26]. The caesura evidently lies before διὸ καί ("therefore also") of verse 9. In the first part the descending line consists of two steps (strophes): (1) The pre-existent Christ Jesus emptied himself, i.e., he became a human being (vv. 6-7b), and (2) having become a human being Christ Jesus humbled

---

24. NRSV translates the participle γενόμενος in v. 8b by means of a personal verb: "'and he became' obedient...". We translate the aorist participles λαβών (v. 7b) and γενόμενος (v. 8b) by a present: "taking" and "becoming"; the action is contemporaneous with the personal verbs respectively in v. 7a ("emptied") and v. 8a ("humbled"). In v. 7cd γενόμενος and εὑρεθείς precede the verb "humbled" (v. 8a) and the nuance to the past is retained: "having become" and "having been found". Cf. EDART, *Philippiens*, pp. 353-354.

25. For FEE see p. 250 above and especially the article referred to in n. 12.

26. In his remarkable analysis R. G. GUNDRY, "Style and Substance in 'The Myth of God Incarnate' According to Philippians 2:6-11", in S. E. PORTER, P. JOYCE, D. E. ORTON (eds.), *Crossing the Boundaries. FS M. Goulder* (BibIntSer, 8), Leiden – New York – Köln, Brill, 1994, 271-293, proposes a "concentric structure of meaning, which meaning receives additional emphasis from a number of chiasms ..., as well as from other parallels" (pp. 271-272):

A 6 Preexistent divine being
B 7a Slave-like death
C 7bc Incarnation as a human being
B' 8 Slave-like death
A' 9-11 Postexistent acknowledgment as divine

Nonetheless, both the improbable interpretation of v. 7a ("slave-like death") and the extraordinary length of A' (vv. 9-11) over against A (v. 6) argue against this proposal.

himself by obedience unto death, the death on a cross (v. 7c-8). In the second part the two main verbs and expressions in v. 9 (God "highly exalted him" and "gave him the name that is above every name") are juxtaposed and point to the same enthronement which results in the post-paschal exalted status of Jesus Christ. Verses 10 and 11 contain the lengthy double final clause (ἵνα, "in order that", "so that") which indicates the future universal recognition of that status: προσκύνησις and acclamation.

Verses 6-8

5	Τοῦτο φρονεῖτε ἐν ὑμῖν ὃ καὶ ἐν Χριστῷ Ἰησοῦ,
6a	ὃς ἐν μορφῇ θεοῦ ὑπάρχων
b	οὐχ ἁρπαγμὸν ἡγήσατο τὸ εἶναι ἴσα θεῷ
7a	ἀλλὰ ἑαυτὸν ἐκένωσεν
b	μορφὴν δούλου λαβών.
c	ἐν ὁμοιώματι ἀνθρώπων γενόμενος
d	καὶ σχήματι εὑρεθεὶς ὡς ἄνθρωπος
8a	ἐταπείνωσεν ἑαυτὸν
b	γενόμενος ὑπήκοος μέχρι θανάτου,
c	θανάτου δὲ σταυροῦ [27].

In v. 7 Christ's action "he emptied himself" is the implementation of his decision that is included in the clause "(he) did not regard..." of v. 6b. The participle ὑπάρχων ("being") of v. 6a is rendered in the NRSV by a concessive clause: "though he was in the form of God"; this is probably correct[28]. It means that, theoretically, Christ could have regarded equality with God as "something to be exploited", namely, by enjoying the concomitant glory of that equality[29]. In the first step "the form of God" at the beginning of the sentence (v. 6a) is contrasted with "the form of

27. The punctuation is that proposed by EDART, *Philippiens*, p. 131.

28. Cf., GUNDRY, "Style and Substance", p. 283. Otherwise, e.g., T. WONG, "The Problem of Pre-existence in Philippians 2,6-11", in *ETL* 62 (1986) 267-282. Wong interprets v. 6a as a grounding clause ("because") and sees v. 6b as a confirmation of Christ's divinity: "As the eternal Son of God, he did not consider this privilege as a usurpation, i.e., it belonged to him by right" (p. 274). According to Wong ἁρπαγμός retains its original abstract sense; it is the act of grasping: "usurpation". BOCKMUEHL, *Philippians*, pp. 133-134, sees "Christ's self-humbling as an expression of his divinity" (p. 133). The nuance of ὑπάρχων is not "although" but almost "since".

29. "Exploiting" includes the notion of "grasping" in the sense of holding on to. "Grasping", however, may also mean reaching for something one does not have (*res rapienda*), while one can only exploit something if one already has it. "Exploiting" includes the notion of enjoying, but "grasping" does not. Cf. MÜLLER, *Menschwerdung*, p. 123: the hymn claims "dass der Gottessohn trotz seines gottgleichen Wesens nicht auf der ihm zukommenden Würde beharrt".

a slave" at the end (v. 7b). The term μορφή ("form") twice points to the visible structure and status[30], first God's glory, then the miserable human condition. Since "the form of a slave" (v. 7b) is clarified by "the likeness of human beings" and "as to fashion like a human being" (v. 7cd), the opposition which lies between the two forms is that of divine glory and human incarnation, not immediately between God and the extreme slavish condition of a human being[31]. "Equality with God" does not imply a complete identification with God the Father. Yet Christ possesses divine equality; he participates in divinity.

In this hymn the sense of ἁρπαγμός (literally "robbery") probably is "something to be (fully) exploited"[32]. Christ did not regard his equality with God as something to be used for his own advantage; Christ "refused to take advantage of his position"[33]. R. Bauckham appropriately comments: "the issue is not whether Christ gains equality or whether he retains it ... He has equality with God and there is no question of losing it; the issue is his attitude to it"[34].

It would seem that by the two expressions "in the likeness of human beings" (v. 7c; cf. Rom 8,3) and "as to fashion like a human being" (v. 7d) Paul wants to suggest that Christ is not just human, i.e., that notwithstanding his human condition he remains equal to God[35]. The second step (vv. 7c-8) takes place after the incarnation and consists in utter abasement. As a human being Christ Jesus humbles himself. This is specified as an obedience that does not avoid death, even death on a cross.

---

30. Cf. M. BOCKMUEHL, "'The Form of God' (Phil 2:6). Variations on a Theme of Jewish Mysticism", in *JTS* 48 (1997) 1-23: μορφή indicates the "visible identifying features of a person or object" (p. 11). The "form of God" refers to "visible divine beauty and appearance" (p. 23). Yet see also his commentary, p. 124: "Although it originally denoted the visible outward appearance of a person or object, the word 'form'... could also come to mean the distinguishing characteristics that correspond to this appearance" (cf. pp. 126-127).

31. By supposing in v. 7a (and v. 8c) an allusion to Isa 53,12, GUNDRY, "Style and Substance", esp. pp. 290-293, interprets "emptied himself" as referring to Jesus' slave-like death on a cross; so other commentators as well. Yet in view of the clarification of v. 7b by v. 7c and given the second step in vv. 7c-8 (humbling) such an allusion is unlikely.

32. Cf. MÜLLER, *Philipper*, p. 94: "Die göttliche Person hielt nicht gierig daran fest 'Gott gleich zu sein'". See also WRIGHT, "Harpagmos", p. 340.

33. WRIGHT, "Harpagmos", p. 345. For this meaning reference is mostly made to HOOVER, "The Harpagmos Enigma".

34. *God Crucified*, 57. Bauckham refers here to the classical distinction between *res rapienda* (to gain) and *res retinenda* (to retain). The other current expression is *res rapta* ("something stolen", "booty"). Cf. the lengthy survey in WRIGHT, "Harpagmos", pp. 328-344.

35. Yet BOCKMUEHL, *Philippians*, e.g., does not see in v. 7c "a deliberate suggestion that in some aspects Christ was *unlike* human beings" (p. 137).

Verses 9-11

9a   διὸ καὶ ὁ θεὸς αὐτὸν ὑπερύψωσεν
 b   καὶ ἐχαρίσατο αὐτῷ τὸ ὄνομα τὸ ὑπὲρ πᾶν ὄνομα,

10a   ἵνα ἐν τῷ ὀνόματι Ἰησοῦ πᾶν γόνυ κάμψῃ
 b   ἐπουρανίων καὶ ἐπιγείων καὶ καταχθονίων
11a   καὶ πᾶσα γλῶσσα ἐξομολογήσηται
 b   ὅτι κύριος Ἰησοῦς Χριστὸς
 c   εἰς δόξαν θεοῦ πατρός.

Resurrection is not mentioned but certainly supposed. God "highly exalted" (ὑπερύψωσεν) Christ (v. 9a). This in the first place refers to Christ's exalted position over against all created beings. Yet the compound verb also seems to assert that Christ's new status is not exactly the same as that before his incarnation[36]. One may refer here to the distinction in Romans 1,3-4 between the preexistent "Son" and the "Son of God with power" after his resurrection[37]. Some confusion arises regarding "the name that is above every name" in v. 9b. That name can hardly be "Jesus" of v. 10a, although at the name of Jesus[38] every knee bends. Is it, then, God's name itself, YHWH, as some emphatically assert[39]? Probably not. The name is given subsequently, it would seem, in the title "Lord", which is the predicate in the confession of v. 11b. Universal recognition, acclamation and worship are given to this "Lord". The new name is that of "Lord". For Jews "Lord" in Greek has become the name of God[40] since YHWH cannot be pronounced.

---

36. Cf. GUNDRY, "Style and Substance", p. 283: "… *dio* makes the incarnation and especially death on a cross the reason for an exaltation matching the preexistent equality with God which made that incarnation and death so lovingly irregular … as to deserve such a compensation". Is "matching" the exact term?

37. Cf. the prudent remark of WRIGHT, "Harpagmos", p. 346, n. 92: "a possible sense of further exaltation". "In his exaltation Christ does not merely return to a state of glory corresponding to that of his pre-existence, but is now exalted as *man*, God's intended ruler of the world". BOCKMUEHL, "The Form of God", p. 22, points to three differences between Christ's preincarnate and eschatological states: name, worship, sonship with power.

38. FEE, *Philippians*, p. 223, n. 31, explains "the name of Jesus" as "the name Lord that belongs to Jesus": "Most likely this genitive means 'the name [= Lord] which has been bestowed on Jesus,' not the name Jesus itself". Cf. BOCKMUEHL, *Philippians*, pp. 142-144 (with a discussion of Moule's position that Jesus is that name).

39. Cf., e.g., HURTADO, *One God, One Lord*, pp. 96-97; BAUCKHAM, *God Crucified*, pp. 37-38.

40. Cf. FEE, *Philippians*, p. 222: "… what Paul has in mind is none other than *the* name, Yahweh itself, but in its Greek form of 'the Lord'"; see also p. 225, and BOCKMUEHL, *Philippians*, p. 142.

There is no doubt that in vv. 10-11 a text from Isaiah is being adapted. In Isa 45,22 one reads: "Turn to me and be saved, all the ends of the earth! For I am God, there is no other"; then further in v. 23: "To me every knee shall bow, every tongue shall swear". The threefold specification given in v. 10b, heaven, earth and under the earth, points to heavenly being (angels and demons) and human beings[41].

In vv. 9-11 no attention is devoted to the time between exaltation and parousia as is done in 1 Corinthians 15,23-28. There, during that period, the risen Christ is actively reigning; he is destroying the enemies, death the last enemy included (vv. 24-26). In both passages, however, a sort of "subordination" to God is pointed out. The closing expression "to the glory of God the Father" (v. 11c) can be compared with 1 Cor 15,28, the Son himself will be subjected to God (who is called "the Father" in 15,24). The term "Son" does not occur in Philippians but "God the Father" at the end of the hymn (v. 11c) makes clear that Christ is his Son.

The exaltation and name-giving of verse 9 are already realized eschatology. What is indicated in verse 10 (universal worship) and verse 11 (universal acclamation) remains in the future and will occur at the end of days[42]. It would seem that the ἵνα which commands the two clauses of vv. 10-11 retains its final force: "in order that…".

Special Remarks

Two remarks must be added. First, the majority of scholarly opinion considers this christological text as pre-Pauline. Second, not a few exegetes detect in the text allusions to Adam and/or to the Isaian Servant figure.

a) In Phil 2,6-11 a number of terms appear which are absent elsewhere in Paul's letters. Moreover, one cannot avoid the impression that the content of the second strophe (vv. 9-11) is not needed for the illustration that verse 5 demands: the attitude of Christ which should be imitated. If it is assumed that the passage is pre-Pauline, the second strophe could have been quoted because it constitutes an integral part of the already existing "hymn". Finally, many regard v. 8c ("even death on a cross") as a Pauline addition which is meant as an intensifying comment[43]. All this

---

41. In Greek the terms are adjectives, most probably masculine. Not everybody sees in "under the earth" a reference to demons.

42. Cf. GUNDRY, "Style and Substance", p. 287; MÜLLER, *Philipper*, p. 107.

43. Yet O. HOFIUS, *Der Christushymnus Philipper 2,1-11. Untersuchungen zu Gestalt und Aussage eines urchristlichen Psalms* (WUNT, 17), Tübingen, 1976, defends the presence of

data together appear strongly to suggest the pre-Pauline character of the passage.

Although the majority view favors the hypothesis of such an origin, certainty can hardly be reached. However, even if the text is (probably!) created by Paul himself[44], its content does not seem to have offered new information to the Philippians or deal with a point of discussion. Paul appears to suppose that his addressees are familiar with the ideas contained in the passage[45]. As to the second strophe, one easily understands that after the mention of the death on a cross Paul wants to continue with appropriate words about Christ's exaltation.

The Greek text of the introduction in 2,5 is not altogether clear. How must one understand "what (or which) also in Christ Jesus"? Is it: what you also possess in Christ Jesus, or: which is also present in Christ Jesus? The New English Bible renders: "Let your bearing towards one another arise out of your life in Christ Jesus"[46]. Yet most probably preference should be given to the more traditional and less forced understanding: "Have this frame of mind in you (or among you) which was also in Christ Jesus", or with the NRSV: "Let the same mind be in you that was in Christ Jesus"[47].

Finally, if the explanation of vv. 6-7b, the first step, is correct, it cannot be maintained that Paul considers only the attitude of Christ Jesus on earth as a guideline for Christian conduct. No, the "kenosis" itself refers to what the preexistent Christ chose and did in an exemplary way. He refused to use his equality with God for his own advantage and took the form of a slave, being born in human likeness. Then the second step (vv. 7c-8), describes Christ's obedience on earth: to the point of a death on the cross.

b) Even if in v. 6 Paul most probably does not speak of Christ's "snatching at equality with God"[48], a tacit allusion to Adam who tried

this expression in the original text. Cf. FEE, *Philippians*, p. 217 and "Hymn or Exalted Pauline Prose?", 185: "a simple, but powerful, appositional coda".

44. So, e.g., BAUCKHAM, *God Crucified*, p. 57; GUNDRY, "Style and Substance", p. 288: "Paul's own exalted prose. But what a text!"; FEE, *Philippians* and "Hymn or Exalted Pauline Prose?".

45. Fee more than once uses the term "presuppositional".

46. See the change in the REB: "what you find in Christ Jesus".

47. Cf. the discussion of this verse by V. KOPERSKI, "Philippians", in *The IVP Women's Bible Commentary*, Downers Grove, IL, 2002, 706-713, esp. pp. 709-710, and by EDART, *Philippiens*, pp. 177-184.

48. According to such a theory Christ did not possess equality with God; he was not preexistent.

to grasp equality still remains possible. Yet a sustained parallelism of Christ and Adam in the whole passage should not be assumed.

The adaptation of Isa 45,22-23 in vv. 10-11 hardly provides a sufficient reason for claiming that in vv. 7-9 conscious allusions are present to the Suffering Servant of Isa 52,13–53,12[49].

God's Own Son

In the opinion of Paul (and the early Church) Christ is equal with God. "Existence *in* God's form" does not mean "less than *being* God's form"[50]. However, no univocal identification with God is affirmed. Christ is not a second God; he is not God the Father. As Son he remains "subordinated" to God Father. It is God who exalted him highly and gave him the name that is above every name. All will confess that Jesus Christ is Lord, but that will take place "to the glory of God the Father" (v. 11c). Although in the whole of Philippians the term "son" is not mentioned, Jesus Christ is the Son of God the Father. He is his own Son.

This Christ was preexistent, i.e., prior to his becoming human he was a fully divine being alongside God in heaven. He "belongs to an order of being other than the created temporal one"[51]. In that order, as it were still outside time, he considered the possible options. Taking the form of a slave was his decision. Thus, in Paul's understanding, being equal with God did not preclude Christ from being himself and, out of his protological identity, "a person" before and in that decision. All this is an unexpressed implication present in this text.

In the passage "redemption" is not explicitly dealt with, but the whole first part – Christ being born in human likeness and humbling himself by becoming obedient and dying on a cross – certainly refers to what Paul believes: "the Son of God who loved me and gave himself for me" (Gal 2,20). In order to enhance his exhortation that the Corinthians complete their collection for Jerusalem, Paul in 2 Corinthians, just as in Philippians, points to the example of Christ: "For you know the grace

---

49. This is defended by, e.g., L. CERFAUX, "Hymne au Christ – Serviteur de Dieu (*Phil.*, II,6-11 = *Is.*, LII,13–LIII,12)" in ID., *Recueil Lucien Cerfaux*, vol. 2 (BETL, 7), Gembloux, 1954, pp. 425-437; GUNDRY, "Style and Substance"; BAUCKHAM, *God Crucified*, pp. 56-61.

50. GUNDRY, "Style and Substance", p. 283.

51. B. BYRNE, "Christ's Pre-Existence in Pauline Soteriology", in *TS* 58 (1997) 308-330, esp. p. 311.

of our Lord Jesus Christ: though he was rich he became poor for your sake, so that you might become rich by his poverty" (2 Cor 8,9). One meets here the nucleus of the first part of the hymn; but the salvational aim of Christ's "generous act" is added[52].

The high exaltation of Christ and his receiving the name that is above every name indicate his eschatological enthronement, Christ's definitive status which according to Paul even in some sense surpasses, it would seem, his protological position. Certainly, at the end of time universal confession will recognize Jesus' participation in the divine identity.

---

52. Cf. J. LAMBRECHT, *Second Corinthians* (SP, 8), Collegeville, 1999, p. 143. NRSV translates "grace" by "generous act".

Exhortation in the Apocalypse
(Revelation 13,9-10)

In 1980 Professor Joël Delobel published a study entitled "Le texte de l'Apocalypse: Problèmes de méthode"[1]. On the last five pages he discusses the singular reading of the Codex Alexandrinus in Revelation 13,10cd (εἴ τις ἐν μαχαίρῃ ἀποκτανθῆναι αὐτὸν ἐν μαχαίρῃ ἀποκτανθῆναι), a reading which is grammatically most difficult if not impossible, yet accepted by the GNT³-N²⁶ and commented upon by Bruce M. Metzger[2]. In a note Delobel himself suggests that δεῖ in 10d, although not present in manuscript A, may be original[3]. The aim of the present study, however, is not text-critical. I intend to investigate the function of 13,9-10 in the line of thought in chapter 13 and evaluate the importance of these and similar exhortative verses in the Book of Revelation as a whole.

In his 1986 study "The Apocalypse of John and the Problem of Genre" David E. Aune mentions three complementary functions of apocalyptic literature. The first function is to legitimate "the transcendent authorization of the message"; the second is to mediate "a new actualization of the original revelatory experience through literary devices, structures and imagery"; and the third is to encourage "cognitive and

---

1. J. DELOBEL, "Le texte de l'Apocalypse: Problèmes de méthode", in J. LAMBRECHT (ed.), *L'Apocalypse johannique et l'Apocalyptique dans le Nouveau Testament* (BETL, 53), Gembloux – Leuven, 1980, 151-166.

2. B. M. METZGER, *A Textual Commentary on the Greek New Testament*, London – New York, 1971, pp. 749-750. The comment is kept unchanged in the second edition (Stuttgart, 1994, pp. 674-675); a clarification, however, is added regarding the idea of retribution brought in by many copyists, "an idea that is contrary to the reading of Alexandrinus, where the subject throughout the verse remains the Christians themselves" (with a reference in note to J. Schmid and also to the study by Delobel). N²⁷ adopts the same reading as in the previous edition.

3. DELOBEL, "Le texte", p. 165, n. 61: "Pour 10d, il nous paraît finalement plus simple d'accepter le caractère primitif de δεῖ qui a pu être omis accidentellement par le scribe de A ou par un prédécesseur. Notons que δεῖ figure probablement déjà dans notre plus ancien document (P⁴⁷)". Cf. D. A. AUNE, *Revelation 6–16* (WBC, 52B), Dallas, TX, 1998, pp. 719 and 750.

behavioral modification based on the message communicated from the transcendent world". With regard to the last function he adds: "In this sense apocalypses are basically ideological, and are basically paraenetic even though the specifically paraenetic features appear at first sight to be in short supply"[4]. One can observe an apparent paucity of hortatory materials in the main part of Revelation (chs. 4–22), in contrast to its first part (chs. 1–3). Yet is this surface impression correct? A careful reading of 13,9-10 within its context (chapter 13) warns us against a straightforward judgment.

Chapter 13

With Rev 12–13, a so-called interruption which prepares for the final judgments of chapters 15–20[5], the readers come to know three apocalyptic figures of evil: the dragon in chapter 12, the first and second beasts in chapter 13 (cf. 16,13 where the three are mentioned together: dragon, beast and false prophet). The great dragon, "with seven heads and ten horns, and seven diadems on his heads" (12,3), that ancient serpent, is called "the Devil and Satan, the deceiver of the whole world" (12,9). He pursues the woman who has given birth to the male child (see 12,13; the woman stands for the church). He makes war on "the rest of her children, those who keep the commandments of God and hold the testimony of Jesus" (12,17).

The First Beast (13, 1-10)

Verses 1-4 present the first beast which symbolizes the Roman empire. It arises out of the sea (v. 1a). In verses 1b-2a its description is given: just as the dragon, it has seven heads and ten horns with ten diadems upon the horns, not on the heads; it is like a leopard, its feet are like those of a bear and it has a mouth like that of a lion. One of its heads has received a mortal wound, but the wound has been healed (v. 3a). Power and great authority are given to the beast by the dragon (v. 2b and v. 4a). The whole earth follows and worships the beast (vv. 3b-4).

---

4. D. A. AUNE, "The Apocalypse of John and the Problem of Genre", in *Semeia* 36 (1986) 65-96, esp. pp. 88-91; cf. ID., *Revelation 1–5* (WBC, 52A), Dallas, TX, 1997, p. LXXXII.
5. Cf. J. LAMBRECHT, "A Structuration of Revelation 4,11–22,5", in LAMBRECHT (ed.), *L'Apocalypse*, 77-104, esp. pp. 97-99.

Verses 5-8 focus on the blasphemy of the first beast and, again, empha-size its authority and success. The mouth, which utters blasphemy against God and those who dwell in heaven, is given to the beast; that blasphe-mous authority ultimately comes from the dragon (vv. 5a and 6). A limited time period, however, is indicated: forty-two months (v. 5b). The beast is also allowed to make war on the saints still alive and conquer them (v. 7a). All inhabitants of the earth are under its authority and worship it (vv. 7b-8a), with the exception of those whose names are written "in the book of life of the Lamb that was slaughtered" (v. 8b). Further details of the first beast are mentioned in 17,7-14.

13,9-10 interrupts the depiction of the beast[6]. This is the Greek text:

9   εἴ τις ἔχει οὖς ἀκουσάτω.
10a   εἴ τις εἰς αἰχμαλωσίαν,
10b   εἰς αἰχμαλωσίαν ὑπάγει·
10c   εἴ τις ἐν μαχαίρῃ ἀποκτανθῆναι
10d   αὐτὸν ἐν μαχαίρῃ ἀποκτανθῆναι.
10e   Ὧδέ ἐστιν ἡ ὑπομονὴ καὶ ἡ πίστις τῶν ἁγίων.

In verse 9 there is an explicit summons to attention: "Let anyone who has an ear listen"[7]. The last clause of verse 10 contains a scarcely hidden injunction to endurance and faithfulness. Verses 9 and 10e, therefore, constitute an inclusion; they frame the parallel clauses in verse 10abcd[8]. Just as verse 9, so also clauses 10a and 10c begin with a conditional εἰ. Yet in 10b and 10d no command or invitation appears to be present[9]. In an attempt to utilize inclusive language, the NRSV translates the third person, introduced by εἴ τις in 10a and c, by means of the second per-son ("if you") and, consequently, retains the second person in 10b and d.

---

6. Cf. M. V. LEE, "A Call to Martyrdom: Function as Method and Message in Reve-lation", in *NT* 40 (1998) 164-194: "The sentences are even more striking since John steps out of his normal mode of narrating the visions to exhort the hearers directly..." (p. 191 on 13,10 and 14,12).

7. But does this fomula call "attention to Jer 15:2 that follows"? So AUNE, *Revelation 6–16*, p. 749.

8. Cf. *ibid.*, pp. 749 and 751.

9. The grammatical construction of 13,10cd is of the utmost irregularity. M. ZERWICK and M. GROSVENOR, *An Analysis of the Greek New Testament*, Rome, 1981, p. 762, take the aorist infinitive passive ἀποκτανθῆναι (twice) as imperatival: "(is) to be killed"; cf. the reading with δεῖ in v. 10d. METZGER, *Textual Commentary*, p. 675, notes, with refer-ence to R. H. Charles, that the construction "seems to be a literal rendering of a dis-tinctively Hebrew idiom". See the four similar clauses in 22,11: "Let the evildoer still do evil, and the filthy still be filthy, and the righteous still do right, and the holy still be holy". Variants in 13,10cd may be influenced by Mt 26,52: "... for all who take the sword will perish by the sword".

Moreover, this version has chosen another reading for verse 10c: εἴ τις ἐν μαχαίρῃ ἀποκτενεῖ. The verb is in the active form, literally: "if anyone will slay with the sword", which becomes in the NRSV: "if you kill with the sword". Verse 10d then follows: "with the sword you must be killed". In this rendering the idea is retribution. It has been pointed out, however, that, "as in the first two lines of the verse, the third and fourth lines teach fulfillment of the will of God"[10]. Or should one assume a nuance of unavoidability and inescapability instead of that of fulfillment of the will of God[11]?

Yet neither fulfillment nor inescapability render, it would seem, the exact sense. Three points must be noted. (1) Probable influence from LXX Jer 15,2[12], where in similar statements the verbs are equally missing, strongly suggests that the short and more difficult text in v. 10abcd is original. (2) G. K. Beale calls such language "decretal". The verbs can mentally be supplied: "If anyone (is destined) for captivity, to captivity he (must) go. If anyone (is) to be killed by the sword, by the sword he (must) be killed"[13]. (3) Strictly speaking verse 10abcd contains an exhortation, a command to do what is decreed. John encourages the saints to endure faithfully their destiny of prison ("captivity") or even death by the sword.

So at the end of the description of the first beast the whole of verses 9-10 is warning and exhortation. Verse 10abcd again highlights what necessarily will take place and thus brings the reader back to the dark prophecies of verses 1-8. Moreover, 10abcd may concretize the injunctions of verses 9 and 10e.

The Second Beast (13, 11-18)

Another beast now rises out of the earth (v. 11a). The second beast is later called the false prophet: see 16,13; 19,20; 20,10. This beast represents

---

10. METZGER, *Textual Commentary*, p. 675.

11. Cf. DELOBEL, "Le texte", p. 163: "l'accomplissement inéluctable".

12. Jer 15,2: ὅσοι εἰς θάνατον, εἰς θάνατον· καὶ ὅσοι εἰς μάχαιραν, εἰς μάχαιραν· καὶ ὅσοι εἰς λιμόν, εἰς λιμόν· καὶ ὅσοι εἰς αἰχμαλωσίαν, εἰς αἰχμαλωσίαν. AUNE, *Revelation 6-16*, p. 750, notes: "In Jeremiah, such punishments are the consequences of the sins of the people, whereas in Revelation the fates of captivity and the sword (i.e., death) are the fated consequence of those who practice the qualities of faith and endurance". Cf. the same construction in LXX Jer 50,11: οὓς εἰς θάνατον, εἰς θάνατον· καὶ οὓς εἰς ἀποικισμόν, εἰς ἀποικισμόν· καὶ οὓς εἰς ῥομφαίαν, εἰς ῥομφαίαν.

13. Cf. G. K. BEALE, *The Book of Revelation* (NIGTC), Grand Rapids, MI – Cambridge, 1999, pp. 704-707.

the propaganda for the imperial cult (and the local deities?) within the Roman Empire[14]. It has two horns like a lamb and it speaks like a dragon (13,11b). The false prophet exercises the authority of the first beast; he makes "the earth and its inhabitants"[15] worship the first beast (v. 12). On behalf of the first beast the false prophet deceives by signs, tells the inhabitants of the earth to make an image for the beast, and gives that image life and speech (vv. 13-15a). The prophet is allowed to kill those who do not worship the image (v. 15b). All people must be marked by the number of the beast; otherwise they cannot participate in the economic life (vv. 16-17; cf. also 19,20).

Verse 18 at the end of this second passage can be compared with verses 9-10. This is the Greek text of verse 18:

18a Ὧδε ἡ σοφία ἐστίν.
18b ὁ ἔχων νοῦν ψηφισάτω τὸν ἀριθμὸν τοῦ θηρίου,
18c ἀριθμὸς γὰρ ἀνθρώπου ἐστίν,
18d καὶ ὁ ἀριθμὸς αὐτοῦ ἑξακόσιοι ἑξήκοντα ἕξ.

Again, the author abandons his depictive narrative and directly addresses his readers. Moreover, like verse 10e, verse 18a is a ὧδε-logion, and the clause of verse 18b recalls verse 9. There is, again, a call to attention; one must use one's intelligence and calculate the number of the beast, possibly the sum of the separate letters. In Hebrew, translated from the Greek, "Neron Caesar" has the numerical value of 666; the Latin of the variant reading 616 equally points to that emperor: "Nero Caesar"[16]. It could be, however, that a literal calculation and identification with an individual is not intended. As so many other numbers in Revelation, 666

---

14. See, e.g., G. BIGUZZI, "Ephesus, Its Artemision, Its Temple to the Flavian Emperors, and Idolatry in Revelation", in *NT* 40 (1998) 276-290. According to Biguzzi, John accurately distinguishes two idolatries, that of idols and that of the Beast. "The idolatry of the Beast polarizes John's interest and consequent condemnation much more than the traditional idolatry" (p. 289).

15. With good arguments G. BIGUZZI, "'La terra' da cui sale la Bestia di Ap 13,11", in L. PADOVESE (ed.), *Atti del VI simposio de Efeso su S. Giovanni Apostolo*, Roma, 1996, 111-126, defends that in ch. 13 the term "sea" points to the Mediterranean Sea and the regions surrounding it, thus to the Roman Empire, while the term "earth" concretely only refers to Asia Minor. This distinction is important regarding the two beasts. The whole world adores the first beast, i.e., the Emperor of Rome; as a pseudo-prophet in the service of the first beast the second beast is active in Asia Minor, the region of Revelation's addressees. See Biguzzi's conclusion: the text analysis confirms the hypothesis "secondo cui la prima Bestia che sale dal mare è l'imperatore, signore del *mare nostrum* e dell'ecumene, e la Bestia che sale dalla terra è l'organismo promotore del culto del sovrano in Asia minore" (p. 126).

16. Cf., e.g., AUNE, *Revelation 6–16*, pp. 770-773.

might be symbolic and "six" over against "seven" might signify imperfection: "six repeated three times indicates the completeness of sinful incompletedness in the beast"[17].

Conclusion

To a certain extent, 13,1-10 and 13,11-18 appear to be parallel in composition: first a detailed and lengthy presentation of the first and second beasts[18], then, in conclusion, an exhortation; by means of that exhortation the narrative is interrupted. It should be kept in mind that the second beast, the false prophet, receives his authority from the first beast and exercises his deceiving and miraculous power completely in the service and on behalf of the first. The name and number mentioned in verses 16-18 are those of the first beast. Idolatry through worship of the beast's image, together with economic boycott and even the killing of Christians, is very much emphasized.

Structurally speaking, verses 9-10 and 18 are similar: in his pastoral care the author addresses his readers and admonishes them. Yet at first sight these verses also differ. In vv. 9-10 the call is to be attentive and morally, religiously faithful, while in v. 18 the call is for wisdom, and the readers are exhorted to use their mind and intellect in calculating the number of the beast. Or does v. 18b not command a literal calculation? In that case the whole of v. 18 becomes warning and is even more parallel to vv. 9-10. What is the function of these and comparable verses in the whole of the Apocalypse?

The Christians in the Book of Revelation

The main outline of the Apocalypse can easily be agreed upon. The epilogue of 22,6-21 corresponds with the prologue of 1,1-3. The author begins the letter proper in 1,4 with the address ("John to the seven churches that are in Asia") and concludes it at 22,5. The opening of the letter contains the salutation, a praise of Jesus Christ and Christ's announcement of his return (1,5-7). This opening ends with the Lord

---

17. BEALE, *Revelation*, pp. 718-728 (citation on p. 722).
18. In both presentations one can distinguish the following pattern: (1) an agent steps forward; (2) power is given to him; (3) the effect of this authorization is indicated. For this structure reference is made to Dan 7. Cf. BEALE, *Revelation*, pp. 728-730.

God speaking: "I am the Alpha and the Omega … who is and who was and who is to come, the Almighty" (1,8). The letter body consists of two parts, the relatively brief first vision with above all the warning messages to the seven churches (1,9–3,22) and the much longer and prophetic section (4,1–22,5).

In the vision of the first part (1,9–3,22) John sees "one like the Son of Man" (1,13; cf. 14,14), the risen Christ, whom he depicts in 1,12-16 with rich colors. Jesus speaks from 1,17b to 3,22. He was dead but now he is the living one, alive for evermore (1,18). He recalls his redemptive work; he is gloriously exalted (cf. the many titles); he walks among the seven golden lampstands which represent the seven churches (2,1). In the seven messages which follow in 2,2–3,22, Christ praises and blames the Christians; he admonishes and warns them.

The Structure of 4,1–22,5

There is no consensus at all concerning the structure of the second part of Revelation (4,1–22,5)[19]. In chapters 4–5 John narrates his very impressive vision of what is occurring in heaven: God on his throne with the twenty-four elders and four living creatures who give him honor, and the Lamb who takes the scroll from God in order to open its seals.

How do the three septets of seals, trumpets and bowls in chapters 6–16 relate to each other? If the plagues of the trumpets are being compared with those of the bowls, one may be inclined to assume repetition, but from seals to trumpets and from trumpets to bowls there is certainly also progression and an intensification of the punishments. There are, however, also interruptions; from the Apocalypse itself it is not immediately clear why such breaks are brought in. Furthermore, the seventh seal is opened (see 8,1), but the expected punishment does not follow. One has the impression that this seventh seal encompasses the seven trumpets (chs. 8–9). Something similar applies to the seventh trumpet. The angel blows that trumpet (see 11,15), but what this involves is not narrated within the immediate context. Again, one is inclined to suppose that the

---

19. See, e.g., U. VANNI, *La struttura letteraria dell'Apocalisse* (Aloisiana, 8), Brescia, 1980 (with added chapter); LAMBRECHT, "Structuration"; F. D. MAZZAFERRI, *The Genre of the Book of Revelation from a Source-Critical Perspective* (BZNW, 54), Berlin – New York, 1989; G. BIGUZZI, *I settinari nella struttura dell'Apocalisse* (SupplRivBib, 31), Bologna, 1996; J. LAMBRECHT, "The Opening of the Seals (Rev 6,1–8,6)", in *Bib* 79 (1998) 198-220 (on Biguzzi); BEALE, *Revelation*, pp. 108-151.

seven bowls, which follows later (see chs. 15–16), constitute the very content of the seventh trumpet. At any rate, the seventh element of the series of the seals as well as that of the trumpets remains open.

Therefore, it would seem that in 4,1–22,5 a somewhat strange progressing structure is to be assumed: intensification along with advancement on the line of the prophetic narrative. After the first six seals (ch. 6), according to this proposal, in 8,1, as well as in what follows, we have the seventh seal; and after the first six trumpets (chs. 8–9), in 11,15, as well as in what follows in chs. 15–16, we have the seventh trumpet. Then, with the seventh bowl in 16,17-21 the end events begin for good. The last stages of the judgment are described in 19,11–20,15. It should be clear, however, that the very negative judgment itself prepares for a positive outcome: the new creation and the New Jerusalem (see 21,1-8). One more remark should be added. The lengthy Babylon section of 17,1–19,10 and the equally elaborate Jerusalem section of 21,9–22,5 comply with each other; each of these paired revelations contains the explanation by "one of the seven angels who had the seven bowls" (17,1 and 21,9) and provides further visionary or auditory descriptions[20].

Within the progressive narrative three large insertions can be pointed out. The first is to be found after the sixth seal in chapter 7 and the second, hardly by accident, after the sixth trumpet in chapter 10 and 11,1-13. It is, moreover, striking that the second "woe" contains the sixth trumpet as well as this second insertion: see 9,13–11,14a (cf. the first "woe" which consists only of the fifth trumpet, 9,1-11). The last and largest insertion, chapters 12–13 and 14, belongs to the seventh trumpet (and the third "woe"; see 11,14b) and sets the conditions for the seven bowls. With regard to the composition of the second part of the Apocalypse, the three intercalations have, no doubt, a retarding function. Moreover, in opposition to the septets with almost exclusively punishments of the unbelievers, these intercalations direct the attention to the oppressed and endangered believers and encourage them. They also emphasize the demonic opposition and so justify God's punishing wrath.

As to the dispersed hymnic materials in Revelation: these liturgies comment upon and complement the visions and auditions of the book and function somewhat in the same manner as the choruses in the Greek

---

20. Compare also 17,1: "Come, I will show you the judgment of the great whore…" with 21,9: "Come, I will show you the bride…", and 19,10 with 22,8-9. Cf. C. H. GIBLIN, "Structural and Thematic Correlations in the Theology of Revelation", in *Bib* 55 (1974) 487-505; C. R. SMITH, "The Structure of the Book of Revelation in Light of Apocalyptic Literary Conventions", in *NT* 34 (1994) 373-393, esp. pp. 384-393; AUNE, *Revelation 1–5*, pp. XCV-XCVII.

drama. They often anticipate the eschaton; they may possess, moreover, a somewhat hidden parenetical intent.

A Twofold Image of the Christians

Obviously, between the first and the second parts of the Book of Revelation great differences exist, not only regarding their extension[21]. True, according to 1,10 and also to 4,2 John is "in the spirit"; twice John is granted a most solemn vision. Yet in the first part John remains on earth. Apparently only the risen Christ, not God, is seen by him. Christ holds seven stars in his right hand (1,16.20 and 2,1) and walks among the seven golden lampstands (2,1). "The seven stars are the angels of the seven churches, and the seven lampstands are the seven churches" (1,20). From Christ's mouth comes "a sharp, two-edged sword" (1,16). John is told to write a message to each of the seven churches. Nothing else takes place.

In the second part of Revelation, however, John goes up to heaven where a door stands open (cf. 4,1). He sees God on a throne, surrounded by the four living creatures and the twenty-four elders and countless angels; they praise God and give glory to him. Then, between God's throne and the four living creatures, and among the elders, John sees a "Lamb standing as slaughtered" (5,6). The Lamb-Christ takes the scroll with the seals. "What must take place after this" (4,1) is written on this scroll. God and the Lamb will condemn and punish the devil, the beasts and the sinful inhabitants of the earth with almost endless, ever increasing cosmic catastrophes and plagues (chs. 6–20). After all this, a new heaven and new earth, the new Jerusalem, will come down out of heaven from God (chs. 21–22). So, in this second part the whole of future history, together with its final outcome, is prophesied in great detail. Many, many things are going to happen[22]. As already stated, the overburdened apocalyptic-prophetical announcement is more than once interrupted by intercalations and liturgies.

In distinction to the first part, the addressees in 4,1–22,5 are not explicitly named but, of course, the second part is also intended for the Christians of the Roman province of Asia (in southwest Asia Minor). However, John now deals with the whole creation, no longer with matters

21. For this section see BIGUZZI, *I settinari*, pp. 281-294.
22. For the last two visions, see J. LAMBRECHT, "Final Judgements and Ultimate Blessings: The Climactic Visions of Revelations 20,11–21,8", in *Bib* 81 (2000) 362-385, also in ID., *Collected Studies on Pauline Literature and The Book of Revelation* (AnBib, 147), Rome, 2001, pp. 395-417.

in the individual churches. In the world (and in heaven) two camps can be distinguished: on the one hand the sinful earth-dwellers, the perverse Babylon, the dragon and the two beasts; on the other hand the martyrs in heaven (6,9-11), the 144,000 who are sealed on earth (7,4-8) and in heaven, by way of anticipation, the "great multitude that no one can count" (7,9; cf. 14,1-5), furthermore the two witnesses (ch. 11), the woman, her child and the rest of her children (ch. 12). For those on earth a change from one camp to the other does not appear to occur. To be sure in 11,13 it is stated that "the rest" of the people who survive the earthquake are terrified and give glory to the God of heaven. But does this remark indicate a conversion to faith in Christ? Probably not. Perhaps 14,6-7 contains such a call to conversion, an invitation to the nations to worship God, but this, too, is not certain[23]. What about the Christians? Admittedly, in the second part of Revelation one comes across implicit and even some explicit warnings. Yet John does not seem to consider the possibility of apostasy (but see 14,9-13 and the discussion on pp. 277-278). The church is presented idealistically, just as a worsening, a demonization takes place regarding God's enemies. There can be no doubt that in the second part of Revelation a dualistic description of the two camps is provided.

The realistic image of the Christians in the first section is completely different. The messages to the churches hardly allude to the political or social situation of the outside world. John addresses local communities which differ among themselves: from laudable endurance to lack of faith. Within the same church there are evildoers and good people (cf. 2,2). In Pergamum Antipas has become a martyr ("my faithful witness", 2,13), but in the same church some people listen to the pernicious teaching of

---

23. "Fear God and give him glory, for the hour of judgment has come; and worship him who made heaven and earth, the sea and the springs of water" (14,7). R. BAUCKHAM, *The Climax of Prophecy. Studies on the Book of Revelation*, Edinburgh, 1993, tries to show that for the author of the Apocalypse the conversion of all peoples is a central theme (see pp. 238-337, a lengthy chapter: "The Conversion of the Nations"). For 11,13, see pp. 273-283; for 14,6-7, see pp. 286-290 and 307-337. His argument, however, fails to convince; see the criticisms by BEALE, *Revelation*. H. GIESEN, *Die Offenbarung des Johannes* (RNT), Regensburg, 1997, pp. 326-328, holds, against the majority opinion, that in 14,6-7 John addresses his fellow Christians and proclaims to them the eternal gospel "concerning" (ἐπί + accusative) the nations. Believers must give glory to God; for them "ist der Sieg Gottes im Gericht über die gottfeindliche Welt eine gute, frohmachende Botschaft" (p. 328). See also A. P. VAN SCHAIK, " Ἄλλος ἄγγελος in Apk 14", in LAMBRECHT (ed.), *Apocalypse*, 217-228; U. B. MÜLLER, *Die Offenbarung des Johannes* (ÖkTKNT), Gütersloh, 1984, pp. 266-267 (the call is addressed to the whole world but does not contain an invitation to conversion).

Balaam and the Nicolaitans (2,14-15; cf. 2,5: in Ephesus). In Thyatira the prophetess Jezebel is tolerated and has her followers (2,20-23). In Laodicea there is great complacency and laxity (3,17-18). John fears that persecution might bring about apostasy. In Ephesus some have abandoned the love they had at first (2,4) and in Laodicea the Christians are "neither cold nor hot" (3,15). John praises steadfastness; one must be "faithful until death" (2,10). Many Christians need a conversion to a better life (2,5.16; 2,21; 3,3.19). Apparently, eating food sacrificed to idols and immorality (2,14.20-22)[24], together with the temptations of riches (3,17), are all but real in some churches. Each letter ends with the same summons: "Let anyone who has an ear listen to what the Spirit is saying". From these messages one gets an idea of the concrete situation of those Christian communities. Some attitudes in them are worthy of praise, but lax and sinful behavior is severely censored.

A Converging Message?

How can these two seemingly opposing images of the church be explained? According the second part of the Apocalypse the Christians are sealed and without blame, martyrs and "holy". According to the first part the actual Christians of the churches of Asia Minor are realistically depicted, some good and some less good, still others bad. Are there, for that matter, any connections between the two parts of the Apocalypse?

Complementarity and Corrections

With its seven letters the first part of Revelation focuses on Christ and the spiritual life of the Christians. One can guess that (pagan) oppression is present in these churches (cf. 2,10); moreover, inimical Jews are mentioned twice (2,9 and 3,9)[25]. But no further details are provided concerning the religious and political circumstances in the Roman empire or

---

24. It would seem that this terminology of eating food sacrificed to idols and whoredom has to be taken also literally and not only metaphorically as merely pointing to idolatry. See BIGUZZI, *I settinari*, pp. 317-327; after a brief discussion of 9,20-21; 21,8 and 22,15, he writes: "Pare dunque che anche in 2,14.20 πορνεία non abbia *sic et simpliciter* il valore di idolatria, ma perlomeno implichi anche un'accusa di libertinismo sessuale" (p. 317).

25. Cf. J. LAMBRECHT, "Synagogues of Satan (cf. Rev 2,9 and 3,9). Anti-Judaism in the Apocalypse", in R. BIERINGER, D. POLLEFEYT, F. VANNEUVILLE (eds.), *Anti-Judaism and the Fourth Gospel* (Jewish and Christian Heritage, 1), Assen, 2001, 512-528, also in LAMBRECHT, *Collected Studies*, pp. 341-356.

its province of "Asia". Christ, through the prophet, exhorts the Christians to faithfulness, endurance and conversion. The information we get from the letters is one-sided and incomplete.

The second part fulfils a complementary function. The horizon is wide; the setting is universally broad: God and his heavenly court and the Lamb that was slaughtered; the evil powers (Satan and the two beasts); the inhabitants of the earth and Babylon-Rome. A dramatic survey of the future events is worked out: punishments by means of cosmic catastrophes and plagues, wars of the enemies and their final judgment, God's victory and the salvation of the saints. Even if one reckons with the genre of apocalyptic style and imagery, corrections are still needed. The author of the Apocalypse exaggerates and generalizes aspects of the situation. Babylon-Rome is totally corrupt; devil, beast and false prophet are dangerously active. The Christians are persecuted. Both camps are fixed, both their people sealed or marked. Most probably, at the end of the first century A.D. there was not an empire-wide, official persecution of Christians. Yet this does not mean that local oppression was nowhere present[26].

Some exegetes are of the opinion that the first part of Revelation was written last[27]. By means of this part John would have "domesticated" the wild visions of the second part and made them subservient to his pastoral care for the churches. It could equally be put forward that by means of the exhortations in the first part John wanted to prepare the inner life of his Christians for the eschatological struggle in which, according to the second part, the enemies from outside will rage[28].

One more point must be made. The number "seven" is not accidental. As a symbol of completeness it probably also has a representative function: all churches in the province of "Asia" are warned, and perhaps

---

26. Cf., e.g., E. SCHÜSSLER FIORENZA, "The Followers of the Lamb: Visionary Rhetoric and Social-Political Situation", in *Semeia* 36 (1986) 123-146, esp. pp. 134-140; H. GIESEN, "Ermütigung zur Glaubenstreue in schwerer Zeit. Zum Zweck der Johannesoffenbarung", in *TrTZ* 105 (1996) 61-76, esp. pp. 61-67; T. B. SLATER, "On the Social Setting of the Revelation to John", in *NTS* 44 (1998) 232-256: "I propose a socio-religious setting for the Revelation to John in which Asian Christians experienced local harassment, ridicule, discrimination and oppression in the early 90s for their religious beliefs and customs" (p. 254); there is sufficient evidence "of the continuing regional tensions between some non-Christians and Christians in the eastern region of the Roman Empire" (p. 255).

27. Cf., e.g., AUNE, *Revelation 1-5*, pp. CXX-CXXII.

28. Cf. SLATER, "Social Setting", p. 239: "The general function of the letters was to describe the internal religious life of each church so that each church might become spiritually strong enough to endure and withstand the coming apocalyptic trials and subsequently 'enter the new Jerusalem'".

the other communities in the Roman Empire as well[29]. All who have an ear must listen to what the Spirit says to the seven churches. It appears that the horizon of the first part is more universal than the reader at first sight might be inclined to assume.

Implicit Exhortation

In 4,1–22,5 the "saints" and their enemies are radically opposed. John speaks of the souls of the martyrs under the altar in heaven; each is given a "white robe" (6,9-11). In an anticipatory way John already contemplates the great multitude without number, "from every nation, from all tribes and peoples and languages", standing before the throne and the Lamb (7,9-13); he sees a hundred and forty-four thousand who have God's name on their foreheads and sing the New Song (14,1-3); they are blameless; they have not defiled themselves with women; they are virgins (14,4-5)[30].

On the other hand the inhabitants of the earth will be punished; Babylon will fall; the first beast as well as the false prophet, and the Satan, too: the three will be conquered and thrown in the lake of fire (chs. 17–20). Anyone whose name is not found written in the book of life is thrown into the lake of fire: the cowardly, the faithless, the polluted, the murderers, the fornicators, the sorcerers, the idolaters, and all liars; that lake is the second death (20,15 and 21,8). Nothing unclean will enter the city of God, only those who are written in the Lamb's book of life (21,27), for they are the peoples of God (21,3).

Notwithstanding this deterministic and dualistic language, the Christian readers of the first part cannot but hear a hidden hortative tone in the second part[31]. Not all is decided yet. The power of evil is ominous;

---

29. Cf. BAUCKHAM, *Climax*, p. 30.

30. On those male virgins, see SCHÜSSLER FIORENZA, "Followers of the Lamb", pp. 133-134, and now also the study of D. C. OLSON, "'Those Who Have Not Defiled Themselves with Women': Revelation 14:4 and the Book of Enoch", in *CBQ* 59 (1997) 492-510. According to this last author John most probably alludes to 1 Henoch 6–19 (the Book of Watchers), which tells the story of the "sons of God" (angels) who defile themselves with the "daughters of humans" (cf. Gen 6,1-4). John probably wants to present the 144,000 as angels, the counterpart (and replacement?) of those fallen angels. The Christians are a kingdom of undefiled priests serving God (cf. Rev 1,6). Cf. BEALE, *Revelation*, p. 739, who prefers to understand the term 'virgins' "as a metaphor of *all* true saints who have not compromised in various ways with the world *because* they have remained loyal as a virgin bride to her betrothed (as in 19:7-9; 21:2; 2 Cor. 11:2)".

31. Cf. BIGUZZI, *I settinari*, p. 336: "Ap 13 dimostra che il dualismo di Ap 4–22, inteso come impossibilità di passare da un campo all'altro, non è un dualismo di fondo, ma è artificiale e strumentale".

until the very end evil is dangerously busy in the world. Christians are suffering; some are put to death. One can hardly assume that in his prophecies John is only announcing the vengeance of the martyrs' blood, i.e., the judgment of the enemies and God's final victory. He is also warning his fellow-Christians in an implicit way[32]. G. K. Beale goes as far as to contend that the focus of the book of Revelation "is exhortation to the church community to witness to Christ in the midst of a compromising, idolatrous church and world"[33].

The Beatitudes

The number of beatitudes in Revelation is seven; this is hardly accidental. We find one of them in the prologue (1,3) and two in the epilogue (22,7 and 14). The other four are spread over the second part of the Apocalypse: 14,13; 16,15; 19,9 and 20,6[34].

As is well known, a beatitude often contains a condition; through that condition the speaker of the beatitude also exhorts. "Blessed is the one who reads aloud the words of the prophecy, and blessed are those who hear and who keep what is written in it, for the time is near" (1,3; cf. 22,7)[35]. In order to be blessed from now on and forever, one must not only hear the prophecy but also keep what is written in it. "Blessed are those who wash their robes, that they may have the right to the tree of life and that they may enter the city by the gates" (22,14): the washing, i.e., the cleansing from sins, is the necessary condition to be allowed to the tree of life and to enter the city of God. Thus only those who keep the words of the prophecy and only those who wash their robes are blessed. The hearer of the beatitudes is invited to reflect upon these conditions and to take the right decision.

In 19,9 ("blessed are those who are invited to the marriage supper of the Lamb") and 20,6 ("blessed and holy are those who share in the first

---

32. For the entire preceding section, see GIESEN, "Ermutigung"; SCHÜSSLER FIORENZA, "Followers of the Lamb", pp. 129-134 ("The Rhetorical Strategy of Revelation"): "By juxtaposing visions and auditions of salvation with those of the anti-divine powers the seer seeks to persuade and motivate his audience to make their decision for salvation" (p. 132).

33. *Revelation*, p. 33.

34. Cf. GIESEN, *Offenbarung*, pp. 64-72; ID., "Kirche in der Endzeit. Ekklesiologie und Eschatologie in der Johannesapokalypse", in *SNTU* 19 (1994) 5-43, esp. pp. 20-27.

35. The Greek of 1,3 has only one "blessed", in the singular at the beginning of the verse.

resurrection") the moral conditions are not expressed; nevertheless, one cannot but be asking why they are blessed.

The beatitude of 16,15 interrupts the sixth bowl which announces the battle of Harmagedon (16,12-16): "See, I am coming like a thief! Blessed is the one who stays awake and is clothed, not going about naked and exposed to shame". In the letter to Sardis (3,1-6), the motif of the sudden "coming like a thief" adds a reason why the Christians must "wake up" and repent (3,2-3). Here in 16,15, very close to the climax of the punishments of the second part of Revelation, John[36] addresses his Christians and by means of this beatitude requires the same alertness of "being awake"; he urges them to the proper religious-moral behavior. Only then will they be blessed[37].

The last beatitude to be dealt with, that of 14,13, is the most impressive. John appends it to his vision of the third "other" angel within the lengthy and composite intercalation of chapter 14: see vv. 9-11[38]. In 14,9a we read: "Then another angel, a third, followed them [= the first two angels], crying with a loud voice". It would seem that in 14,9b-11 the angel envisages the possibility of a Christian worshiping the beast and its image and receiving a mark on his forehead or his hand (v. 9bc). If such an apostasy should happen, God's wrath will come upon that person and torment him with fire and sulfur (v. 10). Just as for the others "who worship the beast and its image", so also for him the torment will go on for ever and ever; there will be no rest day or night (v. 11)[39]. Then, in 14,12-13, the author appears to pause[40]:

36. In 16,14 the "knowledgeable" narrator John is giving the explanation with regard to the three foul spirits. Although there is no evidence of change, it would appear that in 16,15 Jesus is the speaker. For a discussion, see J. R. RAMSEY, "Revelation 1.19 and the Narrative Voices of the Apocalypse", in *NTS* 37 (1991) 604-620, esp. p. 613 ("an abrupt insertion of a prophetic word of Christ").

37. Cf. M. KARRER, *Die Johannesoffenbarung als Brief. Studien zu ihrem literarischen, historischen und theologischen Ort* (FRLANT, 140), Göttingen, 1986, pp. 276-277: "So bringt Apk 16,15 zur Geltung, dass das Gericht in den Plagen für die widergöttlichen Mächte und deren Anhänger keine Heilsgarantie für die Christen bedeutet, die ihnen ein unzureichendes Handeln erlaubte" (p. 277).

38. In 14,6-13 three "other" angels speak, one after the other: vv. 6-7, 8, and 9-11. Giesen correctly emphasizes that these verses constitute a tight text unit and that all three angels, also the first, address the Christians (see note 23 above).

39. This reading of the text appears to be justified (1) by the twofold εἴ τις-construction in v. 9 and v. 11 which probably points to an exception in the Christian ranks, (2) by the distinction between "those who worship" in v. 11b (non-Christians?) and (literally) "if anyone takes the mark of its name" in v. 11c (an apostate Christian?), and (3) by the subsequent call for faithfulness in vv. 12-13.

40. For AUNE, *Revelation 1–5*, p. CXXVII, "it is probable that both v 12 and v 13, which interrupt a series of angelic revelations, are later interpolations or expansions by the author-editor".

12a   ᵉὯδε ἡ ὑπομονὴ τῶν ἁγίων ἐστίν,
  b   οἱ τηροῦντες τὰς ἐντολὰς τοῦ θεοῦ καὶ τὴν πίστιν Ἰησοῦ.
13a   Καὶ ἤκουσα φωνῆς ἐκ τοῦ οὐρανοῦ λεγούσης γράψον·
  b   μακάριοι οἱ νεκροὶ οἱ ἐν κυρίῳ ἀποθνῄσκοντες ἀπ᾽ ἄρτι.
  c   ναί, λέγει τὸ πνεῦμα, ἵνα ἀναπαήσονται ἐκ τῶν κόπων αὐτῶν,
  d   τὰ γὰρ ἔργα αὐτῶν ἀκολουθεῖ μετ᾽ αὐτῶν.

The third angel no longer speaks. John himself first addresses his readers: "Here is the call for endurance of the saints, those who keep the commandments of God and hold fast to the faith of Jesus" (v. 12). But immediately after this announcement, in 14,13 he again hears a voice from heaven which says: "Write this: Blessed are the dead who from now on die in the Lord"[41]. "Yes", says the Spirit, "they will rest from their labors, for their deeds follow them". These deeds must be seen as positive, i.e., worthy of a blessing for the Christians at the moment of their death. Therefore, one should in no way miss the implicit exhortation[42]. The beatitude of verse 13b, moreover, is extremely solemn: the voice from heaven speaks it (v. 13a); the Spirit explains and confirms it (v. 13cd); it is introduced by the ὧδε-saying of verse 12. More can be said about ὧδε in the book of Revelation.

The ὧδε-sayings

In the second part of the Apocalypse one comes across four ὧδε-sayings – rhetorical markers! – which also contain a scarcely hidden call to attention: 13,10 and 18; 14,12; 17,9[43]. Next to 14,12, which was quoted in the preceding paragraph, two have already been mentioned in the analysis of chapter 13 (see pp. 264-268): verses 10 and 18 conclude the two parts of that chapter. Three of these sayings have to do with the first beast: 13,10 (a conclusion drawn from its tyranny), 13,18 (the calculation of its – symbolic? – number), and 17,9 (the knowledge of its identity and that of its seven heads). In both 13,18 (ὧδε ἡ σοφία ἐστίν) and 17,9

41. On "write this", see RAMSEY, "Revelation 1.19", pp. 617-618: "Even though everything John saw and heard is to be written down in 'the words of the prophecy of this book' (22.7, 9, 10), γράψον is one way of calling attention to matters of decisive import" (p. 618).

42. Cf. T. HOLTZ, "Die 'Werke' in der Johannesapokalypse", in ID., *Geschichte und Theologie des Urchristentums. Gesammelte Aufsätze* (WUNT, 57), Tübingen, 1991, pp. 347-361: "Solange der Mensch in seiner Geschichte lebt, ist ihm ein Verhalten abgefordert" (p. 347).

43. According to the lexicon of Bauer-Aland the adverb ὧδε here has an "erweichte örtliche Bedeutung" and means "hierbei, bei dieser Gelegenheit". In three of the four sayings in Revelation (13,10.18 and 14,12) an ἐστίν follows. For a treatment of these sayings, see BIGUZZI, *I settinari*, pp. 339-342.

(ὧδε ὁ νοῦς ὁ ἔχων σοφίαν), the call could be to a correct understanding – an activity of the human intellect. Yet, just as in 13,18 the number in 17,9b may be figurative and "seven" may in the first place refer to "the fullness of oppressive power"[44]. The wisdom is more than a sharp intellect. "The understanding having wisdom" is the grace needed to avoid deception.

Within the context of 14,9-13, the exhortation of 14,12 is decidedly both religious and moral: the saints must persevere; they must keep God's commandments and the faith in Jesus[45]. They must avoid apostasy at all costs. Their good deeds will follow them. "Blessed are the dead who from now on die in the Lord" (14,13). As has been seen above, in 13,9-10 John brings in an appeal after the "objective" description of the first beast. He begins that appeal with a summons to attention: "If anyone (εἴ τις) has an ear, let him hear" (v. 9). Then, with two more εἴ τις-constructions, each one with an apodosis like a decree (v. 10abcd), he points to the beast's activity and its results which the believers must suffer. These clauses indicate why one should pay attention (v. 9) and equally why there is a call for the endurance and faith of the saints: ὧδέ ἐστιν ἡ ὑπομονὴ καὶ ἡ πίστις τῶν ἁγίων (v. 10e). So one sees how the ὧδε-saying of 13,10e anticipates that of 14,12. Notwithstanding the "dualistic" presentation of the beast's persecution and the Christians' destiny, John does not omit forceful exhortations. The Christians are in danger; they must remain faithful.

General Conclusion

It cannot be denied that within the "deterministic" second part of Revelation a number of data justifies the reader in taking the "realistic"

---

44. BEALE, *Revelation*, p. 869; see also the whole discussion of 17,9 on pp. 867-870 and cf. p. 725: the saying "serves to exhort Christians not to be taken in by the beast's deceptions like the rest of 'the earth-dwellers' (17:8). It also functions to exhort them to perceive the symbolic meaning of the beast's 'seven heads,' which continues the idea from 17:7-8 about the state's deception".

45. Cf. HOLTZ, "Die 'Werke'", p. 360: the first phrase ("God's commandments") points to the Torah: "für die Apk macht freilich die Zufügung des zweiten Gliedes deutlich, dass die Gebote erst im Bekenntnis zu Jesus auf ihren Sinn gebracht werden". The genitive Ἰησοῦ is an objective genitive: faith in Jesus (cf. 12,17). On the term ὑπομονή, see SCHÜSSLER FIORENZA, "Followers of the Lamb", p. 134: "the constant resistance or staying power of the saints". On 14,12 and the relation with 13,10 and 13,18, see BEALE, *Revelation*, pp. 765-767.

first part as a hermeneutical key for its correct interpretation. In turn, the second part, with its amplified cosmic visions, contextualizes the first part. The author intends thus to emphasize the seriousness of the situation, at least as he sees it. By no means are the two parts contradictory nor are they irreconcilable. They must be read together. Believers who listen to the message of the so-called letters and, moreover, pay careful attention to the appeals which more than once interrupt the visionary sections, will be prepared to withstand the attacks of the demonic enemy and to avoid compromises with the pagan culture. They will be able to endure trials and oppression and remain "faithful until death" (2,10). Bringing together the threefold function, which was indicated at the beginning of this study, Aune defines the Book of Revelation as follows: "a literary replication of the original and unique revelatory experience of John the Seer which ... communicates the author's paraenetic message with divine authority"[46].

In 21,7a the seven "Überwindungssprüche" of the messages[47] are, as it were, summarized a final time: (literally) "He who conquers will inherit these things". By "these things" (ταῦτα) a reference is presumably made to the new creation and the new Jerusalem which has just been depicted in 21,1-4 (cf. v. 5). At any rate, an explanation follows in 21,7b by means of the adoption formula: "and I will be his God and he shall be my son". In 21,5-8 God himself is speaking (cf. 1,8). "To conquer" is no doubt the condition for inheriting; verse 7a possesses a parenetical nuance. Verse 8 surprises in this context, but it is not without an indirect stern warning: the second death is awaiting the faithless and the sinners (cf. 21,27 and 22,15). To be sure, more important than the avenging of the martyrs' blood (6,10) is the covenant promise that God will dwell with his peoples (21,3) and, even more, that of the filial adoption (21,7b)[48]. But one has to conquer (21,7a).

---

46. AUNE, "The Problem of Genre", p. 91. Cf. BEALE, *Revelation*, pp. 1119-20: "John's final goal and purpose in writing" is "to exhort God's people to remain faithful".
47. Rev 2,7.11.17.26; 3,5.12.21.
48. Cf. LAMBRECHT, "Final Judgments and Ultimate Blessings" (see n. 22).

Scripture Index

Author Index